Women in the Acts of the Apostles

A Feminist Liberation Perspective

IVONI RICHTER REIMER

translated by
LINDA M. MALONEY

FORTRESS PRESS   MINNEAPOLIS

WOMEN IN THE ACTS OF THE APOSTLES
A Feminist Liberation Perspective

First published by Fortress Press, 1995

English translation copyright © 1995 Augsburg Fortress

Translated from *Frauen in der Apostelgeschichte des Lukas: eine feministisch-theologische Exegese,* published 1992 by Gütersloher Verlagshaus Gerd Mohn, Gütersloh.

Cover design: Cheryl Watson
Interior design: Lois Torvik

Library of Congress Cataloging-in-Publication Data
Reimer, Ivoni Richter, 1959–
    [Frauen in der Apostelgeschichte des Lukas. English]
    Women in the Acts of Apostles : a feminist liberation perspective
  / by Ivoni Richter Reimer : foreword by Luise Schottroff :
translation by Linda M. Maloney.
       p.   cm.
    Includes bibliographical references (p.   ).
    ISBN 0-8006-2840-3 (alk. paper)
    1. Bible. N.T. Acts—Feminist interpretation. 2. Women in the
Bible. 3. Feminist theology—Latin America. I. Title.
BS2625.2.R4512   1995
226.6809228082—dc20   95-23363
                                                        CIP

The paper used in this publication meets the minimum requirements of American National Standard for Information Sciences—Permanence of Paper for Printed Library Materials, ANSI Z329.48-1984.

Manufactured in the U.S.A.   AF 1-2840
00   99   98   97   96   95   1   2   3   4   5   6   7   8   9   10

Therefore, since we are surrounded by so great a cloud of witnesses, let us also lay aside every weight and the sin that clings so closely, and let us run with perseverance the race that is set before us, looking to Jesus the pioneer and perfecter of our faith.

—Hebrews 12:1-2

. . . a woman writing
thinks back through her mothers.

—Virginia Woolf,
A Room of One's Own

Contents

Foreword

This book on the women in Acts came into existence during my residence of almost five years in West Germany, in connection with my husband's doctoral studies. He had received official authorization and support from the Lutheran Church in Brazil to study for the doctorate, but it took a lot of effort on my part to gain support for my own studies as well. In this respect too, the present book represents a break with patriarchal structures of thought and behavior, which surface more strongly for women when a whole family goes abroad for study and are experienced more vividly at such times.

I am grateful to P. Ernesto Schlieper and Peter Lettow, who worked hard within the External Affairs Office of the Evangelische Kirche in Deutschland to obtain support for my project. I also owe thanks to the Faculdade de Teologia in São Leopoldo, Brazil, for having opened the initial avenues of theological study for me. My special gratitude and remembrance belong to the impoverished children, women, and men who live and shape liberation theology in their daily praxis. They were my first "hermeneutical" teachers.

During my studies, in this process of seeking, self-assertion, and struggle against resignation and falling back into patriarchal family relations, all the while this book was being written, I not only came into contact with many women and men, but I remain united with them in gratitude. During the formal preparations and the writing of this book, Luise Schottroff was not only a good teacher, but also a dear friend. I am most deeply grateful for her manifold and empowering commitment. I have special memories of our circle of doctoral candidates in Kassel, because of our hermeneutical and exegetical discussions and mutual encouragement. In the final editing of the work, corrections of the language were indispensable, and for her encouraging and helpful suggestions I am grateful especially to Marlene Crüsemann. My thanks also go to Ulf Schlien. In the last days of intensive work and the final reading of the text, Karin Volkwein and Andreas Ruwe were especially supportive. All these have helped in making possible this contribution to a reconstruction of part of the history of women in the Acts of the Apostles.

I owe special thanks to my husband, Haroldo. Both before and after the birth of our son, Daniel, we were able to lead our lives in such a way that our marriage was not an obstacle, but a new, mutual, and empowering bond. I thank him for his challenging support on the way toward liberation.

For my whole life, I remain united in gratitude with my mother, Frida, a small farmer in southern Brazil. She has always been for me a gentle but important support.

—IVONI RICHTER REIMER

Introduction

Ivoni Richter Reimer's book was prepared under my guidance. During the time that we were working together, I received many important ideas from her. This was the cooperative work of a teaching student and a learning teacher. By way of introducing the book, let me give a brief overview of its method and results.

Method

This book presents itself as a scholarly work from the perspective of a *feminist theology of liberation*. This means that the history of women must be reconstructed, even though the sources, because of their *androcentrism*, reflect this history only partially and reveal only some aspects of it. The androcentrism of the historical sources, in this case the book of Acts, has a linguistic aspect (e.g., the practice of addressing men and women both as "brothers"), but is also expressed in the choice of materials (e.g., orientation to the historical works of important men) and in the depiction of events. This androcentrism in the sources is based on a social order that is generally referred to in this field of research as *patriarchy*. Patriarchy refers not merely to a subordination of women to men, but to an entire social organization with patriarchal marriage as its core and structured by a series of hierarchies encompassing all aspects of life. Political, social, religious, and racial aspects are interconnected. (We can also speak of "racism" in the societies of the first century of our era, because both the dominant view of slaves and the common opinion of people from the eastern parts of the Roman empire were characterized by the same elements that make up modern racism.)

Part of the concern of a feminist theology of liberation is to keep alive a memory of the history of oppression and of the work of liberation. The present book serves this purpose by recalling the history of the liberation of women and men in early Christian communities as it can be discerned in the Acts of the Apostles. The story of oppression that is revealed in the Acts is primarily that of the subordinated peoples within the orbit of the *pax Romana*. The history of liberation is that of the early Christian communities in continuity with Jewish traditions.

The *historical method* of this dissertation (as of feminist theology of liberation in general) makes use of the customary methods of traditional theology, including textual, source, and form criticism, extensive word analyses, etc. The *social historical* analysis, likewise, is not fundamentally different from what is customary within the framework of traditional historical criticism or historical theology. We may mention in passing that at the present time there is a deficiency in German theology with respect to social-historical questions, but it should be undisputed that, in fact, a social-historical approach must be part of the historical critical task.

Here, as is generally the case in scholarship today, the Acts of the Apostles is treated as a consistent literary document written near the end of the first century C.E. It makes use of older sources, but the precise content of those sources cannot be reliably determined. Even though the events reported may not have occurred exactly as they are described, the accounts do permit us to draw conclusions about the real lives and world of ideas of the community or communities in the context of which the unknown author (conventionally called "Luke") writes. The disdain for Luke evident in New Testament scholarship since the 1950s ("beat up on Luke" was the motto) has, more recently, been all but universally rejected in traditional research in favor of an appreciation of the theology of this work.

The *difference* between the scholarly method of a feminist theology of liberation and traditional theology consists in the open acknowledgment of the author's own *perspective* and the critical *investigation of unacknowledged perspectives* in existing texts, whether those of the old sources or of their interpreters. Thus, for example, it is evident that the androcentrism of Acts is still being transmitted to the so-called first world at the present time by the androcentrism of the interpretations.

To give a single example: The Nestle-Aland 26th edition of the Greek New Testament (1979) prefers, in Acts 18:3, a reading that by its own rules is clearly the weaker ("and he worked") rather than the reading ("and they worked") that concedes the possibility that Prisca was also an active worker (cf. pp. 197–99 below). This means that, in this t-extual edition central to the work of New Testament scholarship, the activity of women in the world of business and trade is made invisible—a phenomenon that can be repeatedly demonstrated in androcentric texts and patriarchally oriented perceptions.

The Social-Historical Findings

Ivoni Richter Reimer approaches her material with very precise and well-defined questions. The development of the questions can be followed in the text, and this participation in the research process clearly shows how it is possible to arrive at such fundamentally new results. In contrast to the findings of previous research, Richter Reimer presents new views of each text, and her results are grounded in a highly competent application of social-historical methods. Let me point to her analysis of the behavior of Sapphira and the connection of this story (Acts 5:1-11) with Jewish marriage laws. Let me also mention her analysis of Lydia's business activities as a purple merchant, which was previously interpreted in most of the literature as showing that she was a well-to-do dealer in luxury articles. Richter Reimer shows convincingly that this was a type of craft labor that, from the perspective of the upper classes of the time, belonged among the despised trades. Equally important are the results of her analysis of the story of the prophetic slave in Philippi and of the craft of tentmaking. Richter Reimer's social-historical investigations make use of literary and inscriptional material and of the corresponding discussions in the field of classical scholarship.

Theological Content

Richter Reimer understands the early Christian communities as foci of the praxis of solidarity, where liberation from patriarchal oppression in all its aspects, including economic oppression, was a lived reality. They were also places of faith, remembrance, and hope for the reign of God. It is especially important to her to discover how, in the reality of these communities and in the texts that tell of them, people acquired the *power* to live a life of resistance. To me, her conclusion that the story of

Ananias and Sapphira should be read as a story of liberation is a high point of this study. She shows that Sapphira's participation in her husband's action is the way to death, but at the same time it makes clear, indirectly, the way to life. She provides access to this story, so often felt to be alienating, by making it plain that Peter does not utter a death sentence on this couple, something that traditional interpretations have taken for granted, usually without discussion.

Another key theological term that describes the essential content of this book is "integrity." Working for the Gospel and working to earn a living must be seen together, for example, when we consider the stories of Lydia, Prisca, and Paul. In this connection, the integrity of the presentation of "good works" in the Jewish sense (see Acts 9:36) is important. Economic questions cannot be eliminated from Christian faith (see Acts 5:1-11). In this book we see that the loss of integrity has already occurred to some extent in the New Testament texts themselves, but it has become the rule in modern scholarly interpretation. Richter Reimer's theology is connected to the *liberation theology* of her Brazilian homeland, and of Latin America as a whole, both with regard to its eschatology and to its understanding of liberation, christology, and pneumatology.

With this book, Ivoni Richter Reimer has presented an important contribution to the further development of a feminist theology of liberation in my context (Germany), and certainly in her own Brazilian environment. Her book is a scholarly theological work that succeeds in approaching committed lay people as well. Ivoni Richter Reimer teaches us in this book to read biblical texts with new eyes. Her enthusiasm for the biblical tradition and the liberating power of the gospel of God penetrates the androcentrism of the texts and brings to light hidden treasures from the history of liberation in early Christianity. But at all times she presents carefully drawn historical arguments and makes certain that her ideas and paths to knowledge can be followed to the end. It is astonishing what riches of information can be unlocked from even the smaller details of the text when they are investigated with such skill. The lively character of this book will draw its readers into its spell.

—LUISE SCHOTTROFF

Preface

The women liberation theologians in Latin America have begun to recover and appropriate their history in order to initiate changes leading toward just, non-patriarchal relationships. At the Latin American Conference on Liberation Theology from the Perspective of Women, in October–November 1985, women theologians of liberation from the whole continent and the Caribbean met in Buenos Aires. They interpreted their conference as the coin that was lost and found (Luke 15:8-10):

> The drachma symbolizes our self-encounter and self-discovery through our experience of God and through our theological work that we experience in our daily lives. This experience continues to expand until it becomes a celebration. . . . Buenos Aires, the capital of Argentina, has been the site of this celebration in which we have shared different ways of searching for our drachma, our different ways of doing theology.[1]

Those who gathered in Buenos Aires discerned some clear theological tasks for Latin American women theologians of liberation, tasks that called for their cooperation. This theological labor strives to be:

- Communitarian and relational: this emerges from our experiences in base communities;
- Contextual and concrete: our theological work is shaped by the everydayness of life as a site where God is made manifest;

- Militant (*combativa*): the work is situated within and participates in the global movement of liberation of the impoverished;
- Marked by joy and celebration, and by a spirituality of hope: it thereby reveals the assurance of faith that God is with us. At the same time it expresses strength, suffering, and thanksgiving;
- Reconstructive: it aims to refashion the stories both of biblical women and of women today. The rediscovered women are symbols of struggle and resistance, wisdom and leadership, solidarity and fidelity, justice and peace.

Latin American liberation theology from women's perspective continually emphasizes that it is embedded in liberation theology and the movements of liberation. The option for the poor and the commitment to liberation from structures of oppression are preconditions for this theology.[2] We want to walk this road together with our male companions in the struggle. But this walking, this coordination of feminist and popular movements, is not a simple matter, especially since liberation theologians themselves often continue to work within machistic/masculinist thought patterns. The victims of this ideology are "men [and] the many women who are accomplices as well as victims."[3] In this statement, Elsa Tamez expresses something of central importance in a context of oppression: the matter of complicity. A Latin American feminist theology of liberation that attempts to reconstruct the history of women and to take part in the renewal of life today will become increasingly aware that this is not a matter of a poster campaign of women against men. Our perspective and our initiative extend farther than that: "Our struggle . . . is against machistic ideology, the victims of which are not only men but also the many women who are accomplices as well as victims."[4] With these insights, women take their place in the Latin American theology of liberation and radicalize it by their critique of *machismo. Machismo,* or patriarchy, is understood as a socioeconomic and political-ideological system that creates a hierarchy of oppressions and subordinations and continually legitimates them; one of the ways it does this is to attempt to play off the marginalized forces within a society, thus drawing many people into complicity with it.

Latin American women are stubborn in their campaigns for life and justice, struggles that "have been linked together and lived out as expressions of faith, as the presence of God in the struggles of history."[5] Because women today are drawing their power of resistance from faith and from the liberating God whom liberation theology has rediscovered

and reclaimed for us, all of which is expressed in the idea of the com-
munion of saints, they are asking again, and in great numbers, about
the faith experiences of biblical women. In our struggle with colonialist
theology and corresponding church structures, and by our direct access
to the Bible, we are turning to our foresisters who strengthen us in our
critique of the dominant theology. Latin American theology of liberation is and remains the ground on which we move. We women,
especially in the base communities, have contributed to its birth. We
will not surrender it, because it is part of our own history. With this
assertion we also declare that we continue to be united with those in
this liberation movement who have been murdered by the wielders of
power and those behind them. They are the martyrs of our century, and
they too are our mothers and fathers and belong to the "cloud of
witnesses."

The struggle for life in situations of oppression is hard and often
deadly. Therefore it is important to seek the experiences of other children, women, and men that can show us ways to organize. Because the
Bible is "our" book,[6] it is not only a bond between different base
communities, but also a connecting link with our foresisters and
-brothers. From the perspective of the poor, Latin American women
turn their eyes with new intensity to biblical women.[7] We are curious to
learn how our foresisters lived their faith in a just and liberating God in
a patriarchal and hierarchical world. This "biographical" starting point[8]
is important for women who are beginning to deal with their own
history and to struggle both with the mechanisms of their oppression
and, at the same time, with their own complicity inside death-dealing
power structures. This biographical starting point quickly expands and
is combined with reflections on theology, christology, pneumatology,
and ecclesiology.[9]

The advent of liberation theology brought about a shift in social
location: the study of theology is no longer in the service of a social
structure that creates injustice, but instead is on the side of the members
of society who have been deprived of their rights. They are supported
by committed priests and pastors, women and men, in their efforts to
achieve a clear understanding of their situation by attempting, through
direct access to the Bible, to illuminate their own lives in the light of
biblical narratives. Thus we understand the Bible as our own heritage,
from which the power for change can be drawn. There we find people
and situations with which to identify. The Bible reflects a great deal of
our own experience: in many of the situations described there, we find

ourselves. With the poor and those deprived of their rights, "professional theologians" learn to read biblical stories from a different perspective: from below, and from the other face of the history made by victors and masters.

Feminist liberation theologians in the "first" world who identify themselves in solidarity with the oppressed women of the other two-thirds world who are appealing for liberation have taken up these insights and options and carried the hermeneutical discussion farther. Among them I should mention especially Christine Schaumberger,[10] Luise Schottroff,[11] and Elisabeth Schüssler Fiorenza.[12] Biblical exegesis has made a significant contribution through its use of contextual-critical methods and by calling attention to particular problems. The hermeneutical preconditions, as listed by Elisabeth Schüssler Fiorenza, and the social-historical feminist analysis of texts, as practiced by Luise Schottroff, have been both supportive and challenging to us as we go forward. Elisabeth Schüssler Fiorenza concludes that a critical feminist interpretation of the Bible must distinguish between the androcentric language in which the biblical texts are written and patriarchy as a system of power relationships in which this language is embedded.[13] This language conceals a good deal of information about women's experiences of oppression and liberation, and thereby lends ideological support for the retention of these patriarchal systems of power. Elisabeth Schüssler Fiorenza concludes that "the so-called 'passages about women' in the Bible can no longer be made the starting point for a feminist biblical interpretation; instead, their function must be sought within their textual, historical, and social—that is, in their patriarchal—context."[14] She develops a set of complementary hermeneutical steps for such a critical feminist biblical interpretation: the hermeneutics of suspicion is applied to the composition of the text itself, the process of canonization, and interpretation; the hermeneutics of historical remembrance gives expression both to the history of women's liberation and to the history of their oppression and attempts to recover all this as the heritage of women and other oppressed people that can give a liberating impulse for present praxis; a critical-theological hermeneutics of proclamation demands that patriarchal and oppressive texts should no longer be proclaimed as the word of God;[15] a hermeneutics of creative actualization attempts to retell the liberating potential and visions of the Bible in a new way. Luise Schottroff augments and radicalizes these hermeneutical initiatives in her social-historical studies. She intensifies the search for the life situation of the oppressed, especially women in the Roman empire. Her social-historical biblical interpretation "attempts to clarify two social contexts: first, relationships within the Roman empire and the situation of the Jewish people at the time of the beginnings of Christianity, and second, the social conditions under which biblical interpretation is being done at the present time."[16] Through intensive study of ancient sources she acquires information about the real-life situation of women and men at that time. This information can also intensify the utterance of biblical stories and sayings by shedding light on them. The specific question of women's and men's work makes it possible for us to sketch a more precise picture of the Jesus movement and early Christianity.[17] Social-historical exegesis is thus an interdisciplinary effort that draws information from other fields of scholarship with two purposes in view: first, to tell the biblical story more vividly, and second, by means of these vivid and concrete biblical truths to supply people, in their present conditions of life, with strength to apply themselves on behalf of the reign of God.[18] Thus both of these feminist liberation theological initiatives agree in their efforts to contribute to the liberation of the oppressed. Their biblical interpretation is done not for its own sake, but in the service of oppressed women and men.

The present book attempts to reconstruct the various stories of women in the Acts of the Apostles from the perspective of Latin American liberation theology and its clarification through feminist liberation theology. I have chosen the Acts of the Apostles for three reasons: first, because the experiences and stories reported there, especially in the first part, are of particular interest to Latin American liberation theology; second, because up to now there has been no thoroughgoing analysis of the "women" passages in Acts; and third, primarily because women, then as now, have a central position in house churches or base communities and therefore are strongly represented, at least at the local level.

It has been all the more important for me to carry out this task because the stories of the Jerusalem community of the saints have a strong impact on the life of base communities and have been the objects of special interest for women who are seeking change. This shows that the "Jerusalem project" did not end in Jerusalem. This project aiming at a community of solidarity not only continued as an initiative in the "diaspora" of those days, within house churches, but also is alive even today, and in various places in Latin America is creating new hope for a liberated life in solidarity. In this context we should not emphasize only the positive statements about "community of goods" because they support people in their struggle for justice. In the process of liberation itself it is also important to keep clearly in mind the conflicts that existed within the community of the saints in Jerusalem. These are evident in the case of Sapphira and Ananias, and their roots are to be found in the community's dealing with material goods.[19]

Carlos Mesters has suggested an important key to the reading of Acts.[20] He attempts to read Acts on the basis of the conflicts or tense situations depicted there. Of these there are many. But it is striking that in such situations, or at least in their final phases, women often appear: e.g., Sapphira, the Hellenist widows, the women persecuted and pursued by Paul, Lydia, the prophetic slave, Bernice, and Drusilla. In unexpressed or unmentioned conflicts, women also play an important role: e.g., the silence regarding women's work of proclamation, which expresses the conflict, for example, between the authority of Peter and that of Mary Magdalene.[21] The Acts of the Apostles has nothing to say about such conflicts.

My book is a commentary on those passages in the Acts of the Apostles in which women are mentioned. A central concern is to discover what is said about women with reference to community and business life. My concentration on particular passages serves this purpose and can also be explained in terms of Luke's own reporting, in which women are often mentioned only in passing. An important precondition for my attempt to reconstruct part of the history of women is the evaluation of the points of contact in the underlying text. Often these are only minor details, which I have attempted to pursue and to trace in other sources. The "minor details" in the text can help us to find entry into a history that is closed to us. Still more important: many such details, when investigated, can expand our historical horizons and thus bring to light other women besides those mentioned in the text. Hence the investigation or rediscovery of a part of the history of women in early Christianity can add to the history of women in the first century C.E.[22] It may appear, for example, that Christian women were not exceptional in their participation in religious life or in their pursuit of craft and business activities. Lydia, to take one example, has opened a door for me leading to many other women who lived and worked much as she did.

My investigation has repeatedly shown that dominant New Testament exegesis has neglected the question of women's "material" work. One gets the impression that women were constantly shoved into the "sacred" niche in the patriarchal family and were taken care of by their men. This not only ignores the fact that women worked hard then, just as they do today, but it also sharply limits the history of women. I will take issue with such exegesis at the appropriate points in the book.

The method of procedure in this book is as follows: I will begin by listing the passages to be commented on. Then I will investigate in separate chapters the passages that offer additional information or points of departure for a development of women's history. In the chapters on individual women, the starting point is the information furnished by Luke's text. Historical-critical exegesis will be applied in discussing the text-critical and form-critical problems. In reading the text, I will also give attention to certain details that may offer access to the world of women. A remarkable number of hapax legomena in the "women" passages demand investigations of particular words. In the process, extrabiblical, literary, and inscriptional witnesses[23] must be drawn upon to illuminate the stories within their broader context. An especially important question for this reconstruction is whether and to what extent the theological and ecclesiological understanding expressed in the text can be more clearly brought to light. At the end of each chapter I will summarize the results of the investigation in retrospect and prospect. Finally, at the end of the book I will take a look at the passages in which women are mentioned briefly and usually without names. In doing so, I will also sketch some hermeneutical ideas that are important in reading the Lukan stories. It is for this reason that I recall women who are not mentioned in this part of Luke's work. The concluding chapter is not only a summary of the results of the investigation, but an attempt to trace some lines of connection between the individual stories of the women.

Notes

1. "Theology from the Perspective of Women. Final Statement: Latin American Conference, Buenos Aires, Argentina, Oct. 30–Nov. 3, 1985," trans. Philip Berryman, in ed. Elsa Tamez, *Through Her Eyes: Women's Theology from Latin America* (Maryknoll, N.Y.: Orbis, 1989), 150. (For original publication in Spanish, see bibliography.) In the next paragraph I will also refer to the tasks and goals of Latin American feminist liberation theology summarized on p. 151.

2. According to Clodovis Boff, *Befreiung*, 16, liberation theology's primary purpose is not theology per se, but the liberation of oppressed people who are called forth out of structures of injustice created by human beings. Liberation theology is in the service of this deliverance. For theology as critical reflection on a preceding praxis, see the basic work of Gustavo Gutiérrez, *A Theology of Liberation*; for the hermeneutical initiative of a liberation-theological interpreta-

tion of the Bible, see, for example, P. Richard, "Leitura popular," 8ff.; M. Schwantes, "Von unten gesehen," 383ff.; J. Comblin, "Pobres," 36ff.

3. See Elsa Tamez, "Introduction: The Power of the Naked," in *Through Her Eyes*, 8. In her book *Against Machismo*, Tamez published a series of interviews with liberation theologians. The subject of the interviews was the relationship of these famous liberation theologians to women.

4. Elsa Tamez, "Introduction: The Power of the Naked," in *Through Her Eyes*, 8.

5. Ivone Gebara, "Women Doing Theology in Latin America," in *Through Her Eyes*, 47.

6. On reading the Bible, its strengths and difficulties, see esp. Carlos Mesters, *Flor*, 30ff.

7. See, for example, Elsa Tamez, "Mulher," 56ff.; idem, "Mujer," 12ff.; R. M. Rothe, "Mulheres," 21ff.; R. M. Figur Messer, "Tamar," 5ff.; I. Richter Reimer, "Lídia," 36ff.

8. This involves examining stories centered on women. Such work is to be found in collections of pamphlet literature, what we may call "minor theological works." See, for example, R. Lamb, "Aufbruchsversuche," 76ff.; H. Brandt, "Glut," 159ff. This minor literature has been collected in Latin America since 1988 and is listed in the *Bibliografia Bíblica Latinoamericana*. Copies of any essays desired may be ordered from: *Bibliografia Bíblica Latinoamericana*, Avenida São João Batista 40, Caixa Postal 5150, 09731 São Bernardo do Campo—SP.

9. See, for example, in *Through Her Eyes*, ed. Elsa Tamez; Consuelo del Prado, "I Sense God in Another Way," 140–49; Alida Verhoeven, "The Concept of God: A Feminine Perspective," 49–55; Nelly Ritchie, "Women and Christology," 81–95; María Clara Bingemer, "Reflections on the Trinity," 56–80; Aracely de Rocchietti, "Women and the People of God," 96–117.

10. See Schaumberger's essays "Freiheit," 332ff., and "Verschleiern," 126ff., which give impulses for further thought.

11. See, for example, the republication of many of her essays in L. Schottroff, *Befreiungserfahrungen*, 7ff. Some of these essays are collected, in English translation, in *Let the Oppressed Go Free. Feminist Perspectives on the New Testament* (Louisville: Westminster/John Knox, 1993).

12. See especially Elisabeth Schüssler Fiorenza's fundamental work, *In Memory of Her*, esp. 68–95, and *Bread Not Stone*, esp. 43–63.

13. See, for example, Elisabeth Schüssler Fiorenza, "Biblische Grundlegung," 13–27; for a sketch of a theory of (capitalistic) patriarchy, see Maria Mies, "Patriarchat," p. 22 n. 13: Maria Mies. *Patriarchat und Kapital. Frauen in der internationalen Arbeitsteilung*. Zürich: Rotpunkt Verlag, 1988. English: Maria Mies, *Patriarchy and Accumulation on a World Scale*. London: Zed Books, 1986, esp. 53ff.; Christine Schaumberger, "Freiheit," esp. 350ff.; idem, "Verschleiern," 126ff.

14. E. Schüssler Fiorenza, "Biblische Grundlegung," 24. See the fuller discussion in idem, *In Memory of Her,* 41–67, 160–204.

15. E. Schüssler Fiorenza, "Biblische Grundlegung," 26.

16. L. Schottroff's introduction to the volume of her essays, *Befreiungserfahrungen,* 8.

17. For this, see L. Schottroff, "Mächtige," 247ff.; idem, "Volk," esp. 167ff.; idem, "Vergessene," 685ff.

18. For this, see also Luise and Willy Schottroff, *Macht,* 7ff.

19. Leomar Pydd, "Ananias," 3, rightly emphasizes that we resemble Sapphira and Ananias rather than Barnabas in our dealing with material possessions.

20. Carlos Mesters, "Conflitos," 21ff.

21. On this, see pp. 230, 253 nn. 9–10 below.

22. For further details on this process of investigation of sources for reconstructing women's history, see Bernadette J. Brooten, "Frühchristliche Frauen," esp. 75ff.

23. When possible, translations will be cited to afford readers easier access to the sources.

Passages to Be Investigated

To begin with, I will list all the passages in which women are explicitly mentioned. These are:

1:14 which mentions that women, including Mary the mother of Jesus, were part of the Jerusalem church from the beginning;

2:17-18 a quotation from Joel 2:28-32, in which women appear as actors;

5:1-11 the story of Sapphira in the literary and ecclesiological context of the first Jewish Christian community at Jerusalem;

5:14 women are explicitly mentioned in the context of the church's growth;

6:1 the report that Hellenist widows are being neglected in the daily *diakonia;*

8:3 the statement that men and women were persecuted by Saul;

8:12 the statement that men and women were converted;

8:27 the Candace, queen of Ethiopia, is mentioned;

9:2 the report of Paul's plan to imprison Christian men and women in Damascus;

9:36-43 the story of the disciple Tabitha;

12:12-19 the story of the house of Mary, the mother of John Mark, in Jerusalem;

13:50 mentioning noble, godfearing women in Antioch who are stirred up against Paul and Silas by the Jewish authorities;

16:1 the allusion to a believing Jewish woman, the mother of Timothy;

16:13-15, 40 the story of Lydia;

16:16-18 the story of the slave with the Pythian spirit;

17:4 mentioning important women in Thessalonica who were converted to Christ;

17:12 mentioning noble, godfearing women in Beroea who were converted to Christ;

17:34 the report of the philosopher Damaris in Athens, who was converted to Christ;

18:1-3, 18-19, 24-28 the story of Priscilla;

21:5-6 the report that women and children also took leave of Paul in Tyre;

21:9 the story of the women prophets in Caesarea;

22:4 Paul recalls that he persecuted Christian men and women;

23:16 the report that Paul had a sister;

24:24 the mention of Drusilla, the wife of Felix, the governor;

25:13, 23; 26:30 mentioning Bernice, the wife of King Agrippa.

In making such a list we are struck by the fact that the majority of passages concerning women report that they were converted to Christ. It is equally striking that the women mentioned toward the end were not converted. In the report of Paul's last journey, when he comes in contact with the kings and queens of the earth, there are no more conversions (unlike what we would expect from Acts 9:15). Only in 5:1-11; 9:36-43; 16:13-15, 40; and 18:1-3, 18-19, 24-28 do we receive detailed information about women who converted to Christianity. These texts will be investigated first in detail, each in a separate chapter.

Sapphira: A Woman's Story for Mourning, or: The Deadly Guilt of the Co-Conspirator (5:1-11)

Preliminary Observations

This chapter is particularly concerned with the conditions underlying the concealment of part of the proceeds of the sale of a piece of land, and the meaning of this action done by Ananias with the knowledge of Sapphira. The question of Sapphira's guilt within this game of greed must also be posed in this context. Since the story exists within the larger context of the community of goods practiced by the Christians of Jerusalem, I will attempt to understand it in that context.

The narrative in Acts 5:1-11 is strongly realistic, so much so that it still shocks its readers. To put it another way: it continues to express the terrifying power of sin and its consequences. It reminds us that the reign of God is still only a fragmentary and experimental reality. It attests that membership in the community of the saints is by itself no guarantee that we are fully delivered from the power of sin. Christians, too, are daily confronted with the temptations of πλεονεξία, the desire to acquire more and to secure themselves against the future. They are therefore called to constant resistance and solidarity. Thus Acts repeatedly refers to the first Christians as being "of one heart and soul," in order to keep that memory alive and vivid for us. Because the power of sin threatens to destroy not only the individual, but the community, and does indeed destroy them if it is given sufficient scope, the narrative is intended to raise opposition to sin again and again by repeatedly arousing the audience's fear of such a thing happening (vv. 5, 11). This is the fear of the divine, the deepest form of knowledge, a readiness to take

God seriously in the very place where unjust human action causes death—for others and for oneself. This fear is also intended to make people take the dreadful power of sin seriously, because it is capable of anything and takes advantage of the tiniest crack in order to reveal its power. It is a mighty force that stops at nothing, but cannot spread itself without limit if it is resisted. When people work together with God, with their whole hearts and souls—and as a united force—the resistance can be effective. The element of "fear" is meant to encourage us to draw consequences from this story for our dealings with fellow human beings, including matters having to do with property, which exists in order to prevent the suffering of others. Ultimately that means also that we are to question ourselves anew: is it possible that we may, even unconsciously, be cooperating with the death-dealing power of sin? The story of Sapphira and Ananias invites us to a self-critical examination of our daily Christian lives.

Interpretation of the Text

First of all, we must inquire about the status of women with respect to Jewish customs of property rights within marriage, because Sapphira is mentioned, together with her husband, in the context of the sale of a piece of land. We need to know whether the concept of νοσφίζεσθαι, "to conceal," has a negative connotation, and whether deception of the community is intended from the outset. In this connection, we must ask whether lying to the Holy Spirit and concealment are the same thing, or whether these are two different actions, independent of one another. We have to interpret v. 4 against the background of and in connection with Acts 2:42-47 and 4:32-37. For the whole pericope it is important to know whether and to what extent Sapphira's statement in v. 8 is to be regarded as a lie. After clarifying these particular questions, I will attempt an interpretation of the pericope as a whole.

Women's Property Rights in Marriage

To what extent was Sapphira actively involved in the sale of the property? What is the meaning of the assertion, in v. 1, that Ananias sold the field "together with" (σύν) his wife, Sapphira? The fact that Sapphira was not a completely passive participant is stated expressly in v. 8: Peter determines that not only Ananias, but both partners sold the field. The two verses complement one another in determining the participation of the couple in the sale. I will trace this thread in the text by inquiring about women's property rights within marriage under Jewish law.[1] Why does the text emphasize that Sapphira was involved? Could a husband not carry out the business by himself? Did he not have total control over the property, and could he not, as master, act alone?

This question is not addressed by the commentaries. It does not seem very important. We must seek outside the exegetical commentaries for an answer.

I received enormous help and guidance from the work of Elisabeth Koffmahn,[2] commenting on the duplicate documents discovered in Wadi Murabba'at in 1952, which afford us a deep insight into Jewish law as it affected private life. These duplicate documents are papyri on which the same text is written twice, one version beneath the other, so that "a space about two to three centimeters wide is left between the two texts; the upper writing was then rolled up, tied with papyrus threads drawn through a slit or several holes in the middle of the space, and sealed, while the lower text was simply folded together in order that it might be easily read at a later time."[3] This was the fundamental concept of the duplicate document, which was always signed by at least two witnesses in addition to the parties involved. It was common practice in Judaism, not only in the Egyptian diaspora, for example, but also and especially in the Palestinian homeland. This was especially, though not exclusively, the case in the first two centuries C.E. because this form of legal documentation always flourished in periods when "an official location for the attestation and preservation of documents was no longer accessible."[4] Such a situation occurred repeatedly in times of war and persecution, which visited Palestine more sharply than ever in the first two Christian centuries. Thus the duplicate documents constitute a central sign of Jewish resistance to Roman rule, even in the sphere of private life.[5]

We find traces of every kind of business in these duplicate documents: contracts for the purchase and sale of slaves, horses, real property and other things; loan contracts, marriage contracts and agreements, divorce documents, promissory notes, and so on. In short, we find all the forms of business dealings within the sphere of Jewish private life attested by duplicate documents. They afford us complete access to these matters.

Of special interest to us in this connection is the group of documents touching property rights within Jewish marriages, with which I want to deal in detail. At the time of marriage, contractual obligations were established affecting a variety of strata of property. (The marriage contract was called *kethuba,* but the same word also refers to a particular category of property included.) Let me quote Elisabeth Koffmahn's summary:

> . . . in the Jewish law of property rights in marriage the following types of property were distinguished . . . :
>
> 1. *Kethuba* [in the narrow sense]: the share of the husband's property that was to be transferred to the wife if the marriage was dissolved, and for which the husband's whole property was obligated *ex lege;*
>
> 2. *Mohar:* the bride price, that is, the sum that the bridegroom must give to his wife's father or her family when the marriage was consummated; this, however, is attested only in biblical times;
>
> 3. *Dowry:* Hellenistic in origin, this was conveyed by the bride's father to the possession of the husband, but it remained the property of the wife. The dowry corresponded to the φερνή in Greek law: the wife's property was protected and, on the dissolution of the marriage, must be conveyed *in natura* (or according to value?) to the wife; here again, the husband was responsible with his whole property for this sum;
>
> 4. *Outfit:* clothing, jewelry and personal effects that the bride's father was required to give her when she married, corresponding to the παράφερνα in Greek law. The wife was the owner of these goods, and her husband had only the right of use.
>
> 5. *Bridal gifts:* given by the bridegroom to the bride. She had exclusive right to use these and they were her own property.[6]

This author clearly emphasizes that, on the one hand, these five categories of property were not necessarily included in every marriage contract or *kethuba* (in the broader sense of the word), but on the other hand, by Talmudic law, *every wife, whether rich or poor, had to have a kethuba* in which the "marriage total" was stated: the amount that, in case the marriage was dissolved, would guarantee the wife at least the minimum necessary to sustain her existence.[7] We must therefore distinguish among the five categories of property listed by Koffmahn.

Thus, for example, the dowry the wife brought with her into marriage, which was derived from her father's property, must be distinguished from the *kethuba* (in the narrow sense), which was drawn from the husband's property.[8] We can observe from other documents that this law of marital property was actually practiced.[9]

The marriage contract was assurance for the wife that, if the marriage dissolved, her husband was responsible with his whole property for carrying out the terms of the *kethuba.* Hence, with respect to Acts 5:1ff., we must give attention to the question of the sale of real property.

It would appear that, ordinarily, a woman did not bring real estate with her when she married. If she did,[10] her husband only had the right to administer the property, and not to sell it without the consent of his wife.[11]

Contracts for the sale of real property appear to have been made in writing in most cases.[12] I will cite three duplicate documents that seem important in the present context: Mur 26, 29, and 30.[13] These are contracts for the sale of land, all of them also signed by women, i.e., wives, as co-sellers. Mur 26 (first century C.E.) is fragmentary, with only the end of the contract preserved. A woman signs as co-seller. The property was apparently hers. In Mur 29[14] (134 C.E.) we read, alongside the signature of the wife, "Safirah, daughter of Jeshua, on her own account, has call[ed for] the documents." It is also signed by three witnesses. The wife's witnesses are not the same as the husband's. This could be a sign that the wife was probably not compelled by her husband to sign. Mur 30 (135 C.E.) is a very well-preserved document. It contains the names of the buyer and seller, the location of the land, together with house, trees, and plants, the sale price, the declaration of payment, and the signatures of the parties and their witnesses. The situation of the wife is also described in great detail in lines 26ff.: "And I, Salome, the wife of this Dosthes, the daughter of Choni, son of Jehonathan, surrender this (property) sold on condition that I receive 30 (denarii) each year after (your death) . . . (and am allowed to remain) in your house, my husband."[15]

Thus we have documentary evidence that a wife had rights over property held within marriage, in this case a piece of land, and that she surrendered these rights only in return for compensation: here, the husband was obliged to be responsible for housing her and to guarantee her, by bequest, thirty denarii per year in case of his death. Both the transaction and its documentation took place in Jerusalem.

This document offers us the following important insight into the story of Sapphira and Ananias: "The signature of the wife appears to have been necessary, even though she was not a contracting party or seller, for the sale contracts regarding these properties (i.e., Mur 29 and 30); both involved the disposal of a piece of land or a dwelling in which the wife had a material claim at law. Since . . . the husband's whole property was obligated for the payment of the wife's *kethuba* if the marriage was dissolved, the wife's signature was necessary to insure that the object sold was free of obligation. She thus relinquished a security for her *kethuba* to which she was entitled."[16] We may add: supposing that she demanded no conditions of her husband regarding the sale of the property.

Acts 5:1 clearly states that a piece of land was sold by Ananias "with his wife Sapphira." The mention of Sapphira in this connection can only indicate that Ananias required Sapphira's consent to the sale, because the land apparently served as security for her *kethuba*. Thus Sapphira's consent is a precondition for the sale. By this transaction she relinquished the security for her *kethuba*. In surrendering this part of her marital right, Sapphira had abandoned some future financial security, even though it may not have been especially significant. But why did she support her husband in his act of concealment? Did she hope somehow, in this way, to retrieve her *kethuba* from the sum concealed, by helping her husband to retain part of the property? Did she have any opportunity at all to obtain an advantage from this concealment, inasmuch as, after consenting to the sale, she could no longer make any claim to her rights?

The Accusation: Betraying the Community of the Saints Is Lying to the Holy Spirit

The assertion that Ananias, with the knowledge of Sapphira, had concealed part of the proceeds of the land that was sold is, in my opinion, of central importance in light of the community of goods. It illustrates the temptations, dangers, and evasions in the use of common property that must have been very much present at all times, and are so even now, and it gives them a theological interpretation.

First it is "neutrally" asserted in v. 2 that Ananias, Sapphira's husband, kept back (νοσφίζεσθαι) part of the money from the sale of the field. The action is then described and interpreted by Peter in v. 3. The concealment is thus theologized. In this way, monetary dealings and theological confession are placed or kept in close relationship. I think it is important in this context to attempt to explore in more detail the meaning of this concealment, its preconditions, and all the factors that may have entered into it. The concept of νοσφίζεσθαι, "keeping back," is used only three times in the New Testament and twice in the LXX: Acts 5:2, 3 and Titus 2:10 ("pilfer"); Josh. 7:1 ("take"); 2 Macc. 4:32 ("steal"). It also appears a few times outside the biblical text, as described below. I will look first at these instances, and then apply the insights thus gained to clarifying the actions of Ananias and Sapphira.

The word νοσφίζεσθαι is used in the LXX translation of Josh. 7:1 to describe Achan's taking the "devoted things." According to v. 21 these were items of booty taken in war: Achan had taken a beautiful Babylonian mantle, two hundred shekels of silver, and a bar of gold weighing fifty shekels, all of which he buried under his tent. This was understood as "sin" or "transgression" (7:11) because everything (silver, gold, copper and iron utensils) was sacred to the Lord (6:19). Achan was punished with death.[17] According to Lev. 27:28-29, every offense against something dedicated to God is punishable by death.

We find the same significance in 2 Macc. 4:32. Here it is a matter of the theft of golden objects from the Temple treasury by the high priest Menelaus. Some of them he gave to Andronicus, the king's deputy, and others he sold. This passage occurs in the context of a far-reaching power conspiracy in which corruption plays a considerable role. Menelaus first comes to power as a result of this corruption, and he remains high priest for some time afterward (4:50). Only at 13:1-8 do we get an account of his disgraceful death in the wake of the unrest caused by Menelaus since the time when he stole the Temple treasure. Here again there is a clear statement that the theft of objects dedicated to YHWH results in death.

Josephus uses the concept of νοσφίζεσθαι in interpreting Deut. 22:1,[18] as a description of the secret retention of "the property of another" (ἀλλότρια). He applies both concepts to a flock that has gone astray and that someone finds by accident. If the owner of the flock is not found, the one who discovered it is to keep it, but at the same time the finder should call on God to witness that he or she is not keeping the flock as his or her own property, but is only watching over it.

Polybius uses the concept of νοσφίζεσθαι in the following context: the Roman army is making war on Spanish Carthage and captures it. In this connection, Polybius describes Roman procedure on taking possession of a city. Half of the soldiers plunder it, and the other half guard them while they do it. The war tribunal then divides the booty equally among all the soldiers and military officials. An oath sworn by all the soldiers is supposed to prevent them from secretly retaining part of the booty for themselves. The booty is declared to be the common property of the army, belonging equally to all: ". . . that no one is to keep back (νοσφίζεσθαι) any of the booty, but must observe fidelity[19] to the oath that all swear when they first assemble in camp before the battle—of this we have already . . . spoken above."[20]

A similar situation to that described by Polybius is found in Xenophon, who asserts that there is a great deal of χρήματα in the camp, which may not be appropriated (νοσφίζεσθαι) because it is common property (κοινά).[21]

In the fifth chapter of his *History*, Diodorus Siculus also describes the life of the Celtiberians. In speaking of the customs of the Vaccaei, in section 34, he says: "For this people each year divides among its members the land which it tills and making the fruits the property of all they measure out his portion to each . . . , and for any cultivators who have appropriated (νοσφίζεσθαι) some part for themselves they have set the penalty as death."[22]

The decree of Calaurea[23] from the third century C.E. attests to a sacrificial gift for the temple of Poseidon: the interest on a sum of money lent, and a piece of land. Interestingly, it states that the sacrifice was presented as written in the "stelae," or tables. The whole matter was then completed with a contract (σπονδή) solemnly concluded with a drink offering; nothing of the sacrificial gift may be kept back (νοσφίζεσθαι). Supervision is assigned to the (state or temple) officials.

Aristides, in his *Apology*, gives a report to the emperor on the lives of Christians. It says, among other things, that they "do not practice adultery and immorality, give no false witness, keep back (νοσφίζεσθαι) no goods on deposit (χρήματα), and do not covet what is not their own."[24]

After a review of these texts, it appears to me that a conclusion *per negationem* is already appropriate at this point: the concept of νοσφίζεσθαι is not used as synonymous with κλέπτω, "steal," "seize with cunning, unnoticed,"[25] or with ἁρπάζω, "rob," "take something forcefully."[26] Ἁρπάζω is used to describe a violent robbery or kidnapping (cf. Matt. 12:29; 13:19; Acts 23:10; 1 Cor. 6:10; Rev. 12:5, etc.). Κλέπτω also means stealing or breaking in, but it need not be violent (cf. Matt. 6:19-20; 19:18; 24:43; Luke 12:33; John 10:1, 10; 1 Cor. 6:10; Rev. 3:3, etc.). The actions of "stealing" and "robbing" are committed by outsiders who break in, usually with violence. "Keeping back" or "pilfering" is something different: it is done by "insiders," secretly and without violence.

We may here state two connected insights that aid our understanding of νοσφίζεσθαι and are derived from the texts considered above. They also help us to understand Acts 5:1-11. First, the concept of νοσφίζομαι is not applied to describe an action I do to my own property. We find no report that someone has kept back a property (or part of one) that was his or her own. The keeping back occurs only when the property does not belong, or no longer belongs, to oneself. The passage cited from Diodorus Siculus makes clear that even the declaration that something of my own is now common property is a sign that I no longer have control over it. The control passes to those on whose behalf the common property exists. This brings us to the second insight: that the action of keeping back is directed against the common property that exists also for my sake, or that belongs to a community of which I am a member. The keeping back injures the community. Describing an action as "keeping back" or "pilfering" presumes that, before this, community decisions have been made that govern property relationships, and that people within the community have acknowledged a clear set of rights and obligations. Clear, common, for the most part even contractual relationships or those governed by and agreed upon through an oath are the preconditions for an act of keeping back something. Before one entertains the idea of keeping something back, one is already aware of the consequences: this is a punishable act.

This insight into a practice of that period with regard to community property throws light on the text of Acts. The story begins with a report that Ananias and his wife, Sapphira, had sold a field. According to Jewish marital property law, Ananias needed the consent of Sapphira, since a husband was responsible, with all his possessions, for the wife's *kethuba*. After selling the field, he kept back part of the proceeds. His wife knew of his deed. Then he took part (the text does not say whether it was the larger or the smaller portion, and this is no longer important) and laid it at the feet of the apostles. With this action, he ritually surrendered control over the property to the community. Three distinct actions are described: the sale, the concealment of part of the proceeds, and the handing over of the remainder. I have already indicated that holding back is an action that can only be done with respect to community property or the property of another, not with respect to one's own property. Ananias and Sapphira must have known already, when they sold the field, that the proceeds were to be placed at the disposal of the community. It appears that even before the sale common decisions had been made, although the text does not mention them, perhaps because that would be superfluous. It seems to me that it is appropriate, in light of v. 4, to inquire about the "community of goods" in Jerusalem, so as not to read the story of Sapphira and Ananias in isolation. But first we must look at v. 3, which can also help us to interpret this punishable action.

The text attests that a "holding back" can only occur when a person is not wholeheartedly committed to something and does not put her or his whole effort into it. In v. 3, Peter gives a theological interpretation of the concealment: Satan has filled the heart of Ananias. The question of *why* Satan has filled his heart is illuminated by other texts[27] and by

the larger context. The New Testament concept of the "heart" corresponds to that in the Old Testament. The heart is not only "the central
organ of the body, and the seat of physical vitality,"[28] but also "the
center of the inner life of [the human being]," from which feelings and
decisions arise. Thus the heart is also the "seat of understanding, the
source of thought and reflection" and the "seat of the will, the source of
resolves." This concept of the heart is part of biblical anthropology.
Here it is theologized on the one hand, and on the other hand is applied
as an ecclesiological image. Thus the Jerusalem community's self-defini-
tion as being of one heart (4:32) means nothing less than that different
people have decided to follow the way of God together and, in doing
so, to make their decisions in common as well. Being "of one mind,"
"one heart and one soul" was an existential question for the primitive
community. The fact that Satan had found lodging in one of them
signaled that the community was not, after all, one in heart. The existence of the community is in danger. Satan can only fill someone's heart
if there is room for him there. The door that permitted entry to Satan
was the door of money and greed. I agree with Rudolf Pesch at this
point: "The reason why the *Satan* . . . could fill the heart of Ananias
and make it an instrument of an evil plan . . . is obvious: because
Ananias had not surrendered his whole heart to God (and God's people,
the community), but devoted part of it to mammon."[29]

According to the text this business of "being filled by Satan" is the
reason for lying to the Holy Spirit, which is concretely realized in
the carrying out of the concealment. The identification of the two statements—concealment or holding back and lying to the Holy Spirit—is
possible if we understand the καί in v. 3 epexegetically. Its function is
thus explanatory: lying to the Holy Ghost consists, namely, in Ananias's
having kept back part of the proceeds.[30] The concealment is the out-
ward expression of the lie that Ananias had planned in his heart. The
betrayal of the community corresponds to the lie offered to the Holy
Spirit. Luke T. Johnson comes to a similar conclusion, even though he
emphasizes that it is not the community but the Spirit of God who is
threatened by the conspiracy to conceal.[31] In my opinion, as already
shown, the text maintains a close association between both these spheres
of influence.

This interpretation is further strengthened by the use of the word
πρᾶγμα in v. 4b. Ananias has planned and determined this "deed" of
holding back in his heart. Acts 5:4; 2 Cor. 7:11; and Jas. 3:16 attest to
the judgment implied by this word: it refers to deeds or circumstances

that are connected with evil intentions and bad consequences.[32] Ultimately, this action represents lying to God. The ecclesiological interpretation is therefore aligned in the most intimate fashion with the pneumatological and theological understanding. Betrayal of the community corresponds to a lie given to the Holy Spirit, that is, to God. Wounding the integrity of a community presumes a break between the human being and the divine.

In summary: the concept of νοσφίζεσθαι indicates the possibility of corruption within a human grouping in which it is fundamentally impossible that there should be corruption, because no one in the group is to be at a disadvantage. It shows that even in optimally functioning groups, there are always people who are not completely free of πλεονεξία, the desire to have more, and the idea that they should always keep something for themselves in reserve. This thought contemplates the possibility of the collapse of the community and looks to securing a future for itself after that collapse. Holding back is an internal offense from two points of view: economically, and in regard to trust. It is an offense against a necessity of life: the survival of the community. The concealment itself signals a division within the person who does it: she or he has one foot inside and the other outside, and is not wholeheartedly committed. Such people do not have complete confidence in the cause and do not risk everything on the project, the system of solidarity in the community. And those who do not trust will not commit themselves completely to the cause. Their divided hearts will come to terms with a double life. In the course of this attempt, ecclesiological and pneumatological offenses appear; here they manifest themselves on the economic level. The dividedness of one or two persons means that the community is no longer "of one mind." This mutual effect is also expressed by the concealment.

Disregard for a Choice Freely Made

Ananias's action—keeping back a portion of the proceeds of the sale, with the complicity of Sapphira—presumes an obligation toward the community that must have been agreed upon before the sale, since such an act can only be done with respect to community goods or the property of another. It must have been decided in the Jerusalem community, even before the sale of any goods, both that the proceeds would be transferred to the control of the community and what would be done with them.

In the tradition of interpretation of this passage it is repeatedly emphasized that v. 4 contradicts, or at least is in tension with Acts 2:42-47 and 4:32-37.[33] I will attempt to determine whether this interpretation can be maintained in light of v. 4. In fact, Acts 5:4 emphasizes that neither the sale nor the concealment connected with it needed to happen: "While [the field] remained unsold, did it not remain your own? And after it was sold, were not the proceeds at your disposal?" To begin with, Ananias was not compelled to sell the field. In the second place, he need not have divested himself of the proceeds of the sale. Third, if he had done neither, he would not have committed the act of concealment for which punishment is required.

I think that in light of v. 4 we can look back at 2:42-47 and 4:32-37 and obtain a more precise and differentiated picture of the "community of goods" at Jerusalem. The reports continually emphasize the unanimity of the saints: They were of one heart and soul; they were one. This is the precondition for their doing and owning everything in common (2:44; 4:32). No one had to say: "this is mine," because everyone was taken under the protection of the community in which everything belonged to everyone. Therefore no one suffered want, for as it was necessary, some of the things that had been declared to be the property of the community were sold and the proceeds were distributed to all according to need.[34] Our texts from Acts unfortunately do not tell us how this sale process was carried out. They are also silent about the way in which the decision to sell something was made and who made it, and whose turn it was to sell the property that had been assigned to the community. I propose the following scenario:

Everyone who entered the community was aware, in case she or he had any property, that this would be declared the property of the community and, if necessary, would have to be sold. The necessity of the sale was conditioned on what the members needed for survival. No long-term planning was possible. Every new member agreed to be ready at a moment's notice to relinquish the property declared to belong to the community by putting it up for sale, in order that the community, which was a genuine *unity*, might survive. I can also easily imagine that the decision about whose turn it was to sell something in any given situation was made in some kind of general assembly. We cannot completely exclude the possibility of a casting of lots in such a situation, since that system had been used in the community (see 1:26). But it is not so important to know how the decision was made. More important, it seems to me, is that it was probably not an individual decision, but that all the members took part—not least because of the importance of their unanimity.

In this reading we need not make Barnabas (4:36) a hero, nor must we see Ananias as nothing but an approval-seeking imitator of Barnabas. That kind of interpretation focuses on the praise that is supposed to have accrued to individuals in the community for having heroically sold their property. I suppose instead that the possibility of sale was accepted from the beginning, upon entry into the community; such a sale was not a heroic deed, but the consequence of a decision to enter wholeheartedly into this community in order that it might continue to be "one heart and one soul."

From this point of view I also see that Ananias and Sapphira's sale of the field was understood from the beginning within the context of things that might become necessary. The community decided that the time had come for Ananias and Sapphira to relinquish the field that they had declared to be part of the community's property and to lay the whole proceeds at the feet of the apostles, in accordance with community norms (Acts 4:35, 37). They were aware that this could happen; they simply did not know when it might be.

I agree with Rudolf Pesch's interpretation of v. 4: "Peter's *argument* is presented in two rhetorical questions that recall something that is taken for granted. There is a reminder of the norms that are in force. That the sale of property rests entirely on free decision is as clear as that only *those* who are of one heart and soul (and one 'body') with the community of believers can regard nothing as private, but see everything as existing for the common use."[35] Let me simply add, most emphatically, that this free decision had already been made upon entry into the community. And I do not know whether, for those who were one in heart and soul, there could even have been an idea of not selling what had been declared to be communal property, if the survival of the community, as one, depended on it. If any were not wholeheartedly committed in this way, it would seem that their more probable course of action would have been to leave the community.[36] Perhaps Peter's words indicate that Ananias should not have entered the community of the saints in the first place, if he wanted to keep the field or its proceeds for himself. If, de facto, he wanted to hold on to them, the statement in v. 4a appears to contradict, or to represent a development beyond, what is said in 4:32, that "no one claimed private ownership of any possessions, but everything they owned was held in common." It appears to me that, according to this statement, those who entered the community surrendered all claim to their property at that very moment. Property owners declared their goods to be the property of the community, but probably they continued to be legally responsible for them. That would mean that not just anyone within the community would sell something; this was the responsibility of those to whom the property still legally, though no longer factually, belonged. Business dealings must still have been the legal responsibility of private individuals, but they were done for the sake of the community. And v. 4b can be understood in precisely this sense: legally, Ananias may have had the disposition of the money in his own control, but not before God, since he had entered into God's holy community in which all the wealth had been declared to be the property of the community. Therefore the concealment is an offense against the community and at the same time a lie told to the Holy Spirit. Hence we must maintain that Acts 5:4 (in its context) does not contradict the "community of goods," but is instead to be understood precisely as a "proof that there was a community of goods."[37] The freedom of decision referred to in v. 4 thus consists primarily in the decision to belong unambiguously to this community, or not. In any case, it is not desirable to take part with a divided heart and thus to attempt to serve several masters at the same time (Luke 16:13). Ananias and Sapphira, rather than leaving the community or not entering it in the first place, remained members, but only with divided hearts. Hence Satan found room in their hearts, since they were not completely committed. Satan, rather than the Holy Spirit, ultimately filled the heart of Ananias.

Co-Conspirator, One with Her Husband, and Therefore Co-Actor

Sapphira was complicit in the concealment practiced by her husband. Her guilt began with her knowledge of what he was doing. The text speaks of mutual knowledge and agreement when it refers to Sapphira (v. 2) or when she is directly addressed (v. 9). In the view of the New Testament—within a patriarchal society—this shared knowledge is unique to the woman, especially since the verb in this form ($\sigma \upsilon \nu \epsilon \iota \delta \upsilon \iota \eta \varsigma$, "having-knowledge-with," the feminine participle of $\sigma \upsilon \nu o \iota \delta \alpha$) is a hapax legomenon, being used only here. This nuance of meaning already points to a patriarchal social structure. Sapphira is mentioned only in connection with her husband and the pursuit of his perverse plan.

According to the text (vv. 2-4), the keeping back of part of the proceeds was planned and carried out by Ananias. It is said of his heart, not that of Sapphira, that Satan has filled it. But what does it mean that Sapphira has played along with this and supported her husband with her shared knowledge? Does it not mean that she, too, had a divided heart with respect to the community? Was it not ultimately more important to her to support her husband in his unjust and deceitful action by keeping silence? With this action, which arises out of her shared knowledge, she accedes to the violence of a patriarchal marriage that in fact was already overcome, or should have been overcome, within the community of the saints.[38] Such guilty shared knowledge can only exist in the presence of degenerate structures of power; that is, it presupposes, for example, a patriarchal marriage structure. I understand the structure of patriarchal marriage to be the exercise within marriage of power that is not equal, but hierarchical in its form and use. We see it illustrated here in that the man both plans and carries out the actions: his heart, the seat of decision and will, was filled by Satan. But the wife conspires with him in carrying out the planned injustice. They have agreed with one another to test the Spirit of the Lord in this matter. The question is why Sapphira consented and obeyed. One possible answer is that she also had a divided heart, did not wholly trust the community, and could not or would not withdraw from the control of patriarchal power. But she surely would have had nothing to fear in the community of equals if she had resisted her husband in this matter. Her guilt consists in having supported her husband in his decision to conceal part of the proceeds of the sale; in doing so, she withdrew from the system of solidarity within the community, if she had ever been a part of it to begin with. The tragedy of Sapphira's story is clear from the following question: what did she expect to gain from her shared knowledge, which ultimately made her a cooperator in the action as well?[39] What interest did she have in retaining a part of the proceeds of the sale of some of the marital property if, in consenting to the sale (as we saw above in the discussion of women's property rights in marriage), she had already relinquished her marital property rights? This legally sanctioned relinquishment, supported by her consent, would have denied her, as a widow, any share in the money secretly kept back. Thus she is a sharer of knowledge and a co-actor without being able to profit directly from the business. Sapphira, in consenting to her husband's corrupt and greedy plan, played along with and cemented the rules of patriarchy that reduce women to immature beings and make them incapable of resistance to the injustice that is often planned within their houses.

Sapphira is not less guilty in the whole business than Ananias (see pp. 16–23 below) because she did not directly plan and carry out the concealment. As one who shared knowledge of the deed, she is responsible for it. Her knowledge does not excuse her; rather, it makes her guilty. Shared knowledge is an active deed insofar as Sapphira undertook nothing against her husband's plan and its accomplishment. That is her guilt: By failing to take counteraction, she became a partner in the deed. To withdraw from countermeasures, or not even to consider them, means letting evil reign. For that very reason, Peter accuses her in v. 9. In his accusation it is again clear that Ananias and Sapphira had agreed about the concealment. Being in agreement presumes, if not a formal contract or decision, at least a preliminary discussion (see Matt. 20:2, 13).

Sapphira is not playing some harmless game. Complicit knowers always allow themselves to be involved in situations that are very dangerous to themselves as well as to others. They, too, are called to account by history. Acts 5:1-11 does not differentiate between the actual deed of Ananias, and Sapphira's knowledge of the deed. There is no qualitative difference between them. Unresisting knowledge is cooperation in the action itself. It participates, even if only passively, in the commission of the sin. It cooperates in the creation and preservation of injustice. This story of Sapphira teaches us that one cannot simultaneously participate in sinful actions and enjoy membership in the community of the saints without further consequences. According to Luke 16:13 this means that women and men cannot simultaneously serve two realms ruled by different powers, nor can they enjoy membership in both at one and the same time.

The Deadly Power of Sin's Reign of Terror.
Confronting the Traditional Interpretations

In this section I will inquire particularly about the consequences of Ananias and Sapphira's sin, and investigate whether liberating power for women can be derived from this story, or at least from its obverse. But first let me make some remarks about the form-critical discussion that is part of the history of the interpretation of this text.

A number of commentators designate this narrative a "legend of miraculous punishment,"[40] seeing as its possible historical core either an excommunication[41] or the death of a married couple.[42] Others consider it a "cautionary tale,"[43] whose *Sitz im Leben* is to be sought in a catechetical framework. It is difficult to choose one of these interpretations. However, the form-critical question is not what is crucial here. Consequently, I can be satisfied for the moment to offer my opinion that probably a number of experiences are concentrated in this narrative. To pin the story down from a form-critical perspective would risk reducing them all to a single category.[44] Nevertheless, I think it is necessary at this point to cite Gerd Theißen's definition of a "punishment miracle" or "rule miracle of punishment."[45]

Gerd Theißen defines a "punishment miracle" or "rule miracle of punishment" as a set of actions that express the violation of a norm and the punishment of the violation. He lists some miracles of Epidaurus and some Talmudic punishment miracles and asserts: "Whereas in the Epidaurus punishment miracles we found a 'moderate' *ius talionis*, . . . in the Jewish rule miracles the issue is almost always one of life or death. Breaches of the law lead to death; observance of the law preserves from death. . . . This . . . is a sign of great seriousness about the observance of the divine will: in the presence of God the issue is one of life or death."[46] He correctly observes that there are no punishment miracles in the Jesus tradition. Interestingly enough, in listing the "punishment miracles" he does not consider the regulations from Qumran, which we will discuss hereafter. Within the New Testament, he counts only the story in Acts 5:1-11 as a punishment miracle "in which a condemnation is confirmed by a miracle."[47] My opinion on this point differs: I do not think that Peter utters a "condemnation." Instead, his statement uncovers the couple's sin. He does not pass sentence on them. His function is not that of a judge, but rather that of a legal representative of the community of saints. He intends to uncover death-dealing actions; they must be made known. The judge is God alone. Not even the words Peter says to Sapphira in v. 9 need be understood as condemnation. The word ἰδού—"see"—can be a word of judgment, but it is not carried out by Peter: Peter expresses his conviction that, now that Sapphira has tried to cover her sin with a lie, God's dealing with her will surely be similar to the fate of Ananias.[48] As I understand it, Peter's words are anything but joyful; they are surely spoken in sorrow. There is no feeling of smug satisfaction; instead, we find a painful admission that sin continues its reign. The death of the couple can be seen as a confirmation of Peter's successful effort to uncover the fact of sin committed, but not as a punitive action carried out by him. If we read Peter's words as "condemnation," we would have to draw the logical conclusion that, practically speaking, he sentences the couple to death, or at least to punishment. Ernst Haenchen[49] does express this conclusion in all its untheological radicalism: Peter "wants to kill—and succeeds." I can in no way share these or similar ideas.[50] It is not the words of Peter (as a sentence of punishment) that kill, but the sinful deed that is revealed to the community. Its consequence is a total, radical exclusion from the community. The revelation of the sin merely brings to a conclusion the self-destruction that is already inherent within it.

We must mention here, in agreement with G. Schille, that this story of Sapphira and Ananias was necessarily subjected to "the sharpest criticism from liberal exegesis at the turn of the century—a sign of its fundamentally bourgeois character,"[51] precisely because it supposed that Peter had issued a death sentence on the pair. That interpretation found it difficult to consider the horrible, death-dealing power of sin in connection with attitudes toward money and property.

For example, Jürgen Roloff says that in this story there is an echo of a "rigorism . . . that is scarcely compatible with the spirit of Jesus and that, consequently, did not find a following even when church discipline [!] reached a fuller development within early Christianity."[52] He then continues by saying that the church must "go on living with sin and hypocrisy." My interpretation does not exclude the possibility that sin's death-dealing reign of terror continues, or tries to persist, even within the holy community. But that does not mean that we must simply resign ourselves to observing sin and hypocrisy without offering any criticism or resistance. And we can only talk of "rigorism" if we see the cause of death, of radical exclusion from the community, in the agency of Peter. But in doing that, we turn away from the deadly consequences of sin itself. Then we criticize a supposed action of Peter, but not the sin itself that is so rigorously disclosed. Incidentally, I also believe that this story cannot find a "following" in a bourgeois world because our hearts are not even divided when it comes to our dealings with money and possessions. Our hearts normally give the preference to property, and a liberated and liberating way of dealing with property is not at all, or scarcely ever, attempted.

Exclusion from the community of the saints (Acts 5:1-11) was, in the society of the time, not the only possible exclusion from a religious community, but probably it was the most radical. If we consider the intellectual-historical context it is important to observe that the Essene community in Qumran had specific rules for intimate common life, but also that they prescribed punishments for violation of those rules. On the one hand we read in 1QS 1:11-12, that all who enter the community should "bring their knowledge and their strength and their property into the community of God," but also in 1QS 6:24-25: "If a man is found among them who makes false statements regarding property, contrary to his own knowledge, he is to be put out from the purity of the many for a year, and he is to be punished with [the withdrawal of] a quarter of his food ration." This punishment is possible because a man is elected as overseer or manager, and not only is the property of those who enter the community turned over to him, but he also "maintains supervision over the income of the many" (1QS 6:20; cf. Josephus, *Bell.* 2.123). The overseer of the community is, according to 1QS 3:13ff., filled with the Holy Spirit; he knows the ordinances and can distinguish between the spirits of truth and falsehood. The punishment prescribed for a violation of the rules is a temporary exclusion from the community. According to Josephus,[53] this exclusion can also result in death, because the members of the community are bound by oath, for example, not to accept food from outsiders. Hence exclusion from Qumran could also mean starvation leading to death, if the person is not received back into the community before the conclusion of the punishment.

Ananias and Sapphira, by their own deed, distanced themselves from the community that lived in unanimity, from the "collective person," and thereby—because, in addition, the collective person was stronger than the two of them—they, as individualists, were destroyed. Carsten Colpe is right in saying: "Peter spoke no sentence and performed no miracle of punishment; he did not utter an excommunication or execute a first example of church discipline."[54] For him, Peter exercises the function of excluding Ananias from the community. The fact that this exclusion could lead to death does not justify us in regarding it as a punishment miracle.

To return to the text: the radical consequence of the couple's sinful deed is the death of both of them. First they are questioned about their action by Peter, one at a time. This can mean that all men and women are called to account for their deeds. Sapphira is questioned second. Three hours have passed since the scene with Ananias. Sapphira knows nothing about what had happened to him. She comes to the place where Ananias had been questioned. It is the place of the community assembly, where they worship together and assemble at the hours of prayer. We need not speculate about what those present are doing there and why Sapphira comes to that place.[55] The process of questioning is similar for Ananias and Sapphira, but there are some differences. Although Peter does not ask Ananias any question that requires a specific answer, Sapphira is addressed directly. Moreover, unlike Ananias, Sapphira has something to say. She is allowed to speak two words, and it is those words that reveal her complicity.

It seems useless to speculate whether Peter's question (v. 8) is meant to give Sapphira a last chance for repentance.[56] I do not know whether it is within the scope of this text to give anyone the chance to distance himself or herself from an action "after the fact."[57] The majority of exegetes interpret Sapphira's answer as a lie, whether they consider she had been given a second chance or not. This, they say, is her sin.[58] But seldom do they clearly explain in what this sin or lie consists. The emphasis is normally laid on lying to the apostle.[59] Thus Sapphira's sin is given a certain moral content; to put it another way, it is "moralized." The result is that, as I will describe later, the anti-patriarchal power within the statement of the text is silenced.

The text itself does not literally say that Sapphira lied. Nor is it expressly said that Sapphira and Ananias sinned. Their actions are to be understood from the context as sinful. Twice (but not in connection with the answer to the question) the text speaks of lying: in v. 3c and v. 4c. Ananias lies to the Holy Spirit, or to God—not to human beings—by keeping back a part of the proceeds of the sale. That is the sin of Ananias. But what is Sapphira's?

If the sum Peter mentions in v. 8 refers only to the amount of money that Ananias had laid at his feet, Sapphira's answer is untruthful.[60] In that case, she is lying to Peter. But that is not the sin that makes her liable to death. Her real guilt consists in her having been complicit in the action of her husband, which deserved punishment, and in trying to cover up both his action and her complicity by lying. Her true sin lies in her having played the role of accomplice without offering any resistance. Her genuine guilt is that she agreed with her husband, that she did not attempt to counteract in any way the deed she knew was taking place. Sapphira and Ananias had the opportunity to live in a non-patriarchal marriage (1 Cor. 7:29). Not only could Ananias have lived as if he had no wife, but Sapphira could also have lived as if she had no husband: For the statement in 1 Cor. 7:29 means that husband and wife are no longer to exercise power over one another by force. But Sapphira inserts herself, or rather reinserts herself, into a patriarchal marriage. She offers no resistance to her husband's decisions. Here, then, we have an example of how patriarchal marriage is an obstacle not only to the development of independent human personality, but also to the development of community life. The opportunity for a liberated life is rejected as both of the partners make themselves liable to death through their patriarchal act.

Luise Schottroff, in a study of the Pauline concept of sin, has clearly demonstrated that sin is a power that governs everyone.[61] That power can become concrete in sinful actions, but what is said about sin is conceived in a context of power relationships. Sin is the *ruler of the world.* In saying this, Paul was thinking of "governance within the dimensions of the *imperium Romanum.*"[62] Its rule appears like that of a *slaveholder:* people are its instruments. This rule can express itself as *demonic power:* those possessed are alienated from themselves. All three levels of domination belong together and cannot be sharply distinguished. Thus sin is a "comprehensive reign of terror."[63] Dorothee Sölle develops this insight from the New Testament systematically, asserting that sin, thus understood, is a state or condition[64] into which we are born and in which we live, independently of our own decisions. This reign of terror consists of two elements: "One . . . is fate, inheritance, involvement, social compulsion, the power of sin (the objective element)—and the subjective element is my will in this, the involvement of my own action, my freedom, my decision."[65]

The subjective response, which can also be understood as a decision to stand against this reign of terror, is not only possible; it is demanded. Christians "find themselves on the offensive" when they try "to make a liberated life in the community of the body of Christ a present reality."[66] They take a stand against the destructive rule of sin that is tangible in unjust human structures. They attempt to build a new life for everyone.

But even the community of the saints is not a place that is free from sin's reign of terror. Satan, the personification of sin, is a constant and enduring threat. He neglects no opportunity to express his power.[67] The story of Sapphira and Ananias testifies that even within the community of the saints the power of sin that rules over all of us is not yet entirely conquered. The subjective moment that assents to sin—Ananias's and Sapphira's decision—gives a visage to the objective side: the concealment of common property, which requires continually repeated lies in order to remain hidden and to continue its existence.

The author warns not only individual Christians against such a way of dealing with the foundations of the existence of a community of solidarity, but also the church as a whole. It is no accident that it is in this very context that the word ἐκκλησία is used for the first time in Acts. The word means—and this is Paul's vision also (1 Cor. 15:9; Gal. 1:13)—both the individual community and also Christians generally: "The individual congregation, in his usage, represents the church as a whole."[68] Hence this narrative is aimed at "the whole church and all who hear of these things" (v. 11), and it demands of its hearers and readers an attitude absolutely contrary to that of Ananias and Sapphira.

The text, as we have already emphasized more than once, reports that sin's reign of terror continues even within the circle of the saints, and that the wages of sin are here made concrete: death. One further aspect needs to be highlighted, if we are to do justice to the text and to the hope of many, even within the community itself. Sapphira and Ananias are buried. The community pays them a last service, a final work of love.[69] It does a deed of love for those who betrayed it. Something of ecclesiological and theological relevance is retained in this act of burial. First of all, the community does not completely exclude this couple. If it had done so, it would not have buried them. Second, with their burial they are handed over, or entrusted, to the final judgment of God. Their bones are not allowed to lie unburied, but are gathered together beneath the earth. Their eschatological resurrection remains possible, whether to salvation or damnation: the final word is left to God (Acts 2:29; Matt. 14:12; 1 Cor. 5:5).[70]

In summary we may say: this couple, Ananias and Sapphira, by their sin—the concealment that in turn demanded repeated lying—became subject to death, to total exclusion from the community of the saints. It need not have happened, if Ananias had not had a divided heart and if Sapphira had not been in agreement with him. From this dividedness arose the attempt to serve two contradictory gods. Their betrayal of the community of the saints is the expression of a lie not only to the Holy Spirit who dwells in the community (Acts 1:5, 8; 2:1ff.; 4:31; 5:32, and elsewhere) but also to God. The ecclesiological interpretation of this story is intimately connected to the pneumatological and theological understanding. Both of them, Ananias and Sapphira, broke the religious covenant. Both, through their sin, became worthy of death.

And yet the text makes a distinction between the sinfulness of the two partners. The character of Ananias's sinful deed is not the same as that of Sapphira. Although the consequences of the sin affect them both, the quality of their sinfulness is different. Ananias, and not Sapphira, had his heart filled by Satan. Ananias planned and carried out the deception. He thus lies to the Holy Spirit and to God. Sapphira, by her guilty knowledge, was complicit with her husband in testing the Holy Spirit. She sinned because she did not do anything to oppose her husband. In my opinion, *the substantial difference between the sinfulness of the two consists in this: while the "deed" of Ananias is characterized by self-assertion, that of Sapphira consists in a failure to define herself.* Her husband made a decision, and Sapphira went along with it. Peter's saying in Acts 4:19 and 5:28-29 would apply to her in this instance: that it is better to obey God and not human beings. Disobedience to her husband would have meant salvation for her, and a continued life in the community of the saints. Instead, the end of the story provides a concrete example of what Paul means when he concludes his description of the entanglement of sin and death with the words: "the wages of sin is death" (Rom. 6:23).

Summary. A Look Ahead

Acts 5:1-11 presents part of the story of a married couple in the Jerusalem community of the saints and thus, at the same time, part of the story of the community itself. The story of the couple belongs in this context because its initial statement connects with the preceding statement about the customary sale of goods. This practice presupposes a system of solidarity based on a very deep internal sense of community. It is founded on faith in the one Lord, the risen Jesus Christ. This unity is sustained by the gift and the presence of the Holy Spirit. The community is holy to the Lord. Injuries to this community are injuries to the Holy Spirit and to God's own self. These are presuppositions that are illustrated in the actions of Ananias and Sapphira.

For me, the following insights arise from this text:

It is not accidental that Sapphira is mentioned at the beginning of the pericope alongside her husband. Her naming here corresponds to a legal demand or presumes the existence of one. It is part of the Jewish law of private property, and especially the law of marital property, that every woman, when she enters into marriage, is to be assured a *kethuba* from her husband in the marriage contract. That means that he promises her a specific sum of money, to be given her in case the marriage is dissolved. The husband is responsible with his entire property, whether it be great or small, for his wife's *kethuba*. Therefore the wife must consent to the sale of real property. With her public consent, she renounces her right to her *kethuba*. Therefore Peter can say in v. 8 that both of them sold the field, and not only Ananias (as in v. 1). Verse 1 therefore tells us that Sapphira was prepared, for the sake of the community, to abandon her right to a more or less secure future.

The concealment can only be understood as such if we presume, in the case of this action, that even before the sale there had been an agreement about the surrender of the proceeds to the community. According to the concepts of the time, a portion can only be "held back" with respect to the property of another, common property, or goods that have been declared to be the property of the community. Peter explains Ananias's action by saying that Satan had filled his heart—his organ of volition and decision. But Satan can only find room in a heart that is not completely filled by something else. This can mean that Ananias was not wholeheartedly a member of the community. Peter's theological explanation implies that even Christians continue to be subjected to sin's reign of terror. Sapphira knew about her husband's guilty action, especially since it is expressly said of her that she was complicit in it.

Sapphira refused to set herself in opposition to the power of sin; this she did by functioning as a co-conspirator. She agreed with her husband, even after she had courageously renounced her *kethuba*. Complicity in this form is asserted in the New Testament only of this woman. It points to a system of patriarchal power that is here situated within patriarchal marriage. The husband does the action; the wife knows of it, but she does nothing to oppose this corrupt and corrupting deed. She takes her place within the patriarchal power system. In doing so, she becomes equally guilty and ultimately endangers herself as well. When there is danger to the community, the individual is also in danger.

By their sin of concealment, the couple becomes subject to death, the total exclusion from the community. The consequences of sin are the same for both of them, although they participated in the deed in different ways. Ananias's action is based on self-assertion, while that of Sapphira is founded in a lack of self-determination.

Their sudden death attests to their wrong behavior. Death is the negation of such behavior. In this story, a norm is established for the hearers: now they know what is to be done. If we read the story from the other side, it could mean this: In this story, women are shown an opportunity for liberation from death-dealing structures. They may—indeed they must—distance themselves from any such corrupt and corrupting decisions of their husbands. They are offered an opportunity for active disobedience. They should not be condemned with their husbands. They should struggle to reverse such decisions. In this story—in contrast to different warnings heard from the church[71]—they are not commanded to submit themselves to their husbands. Instead, they should resist them when they enter into corrupt and corrupting plans.[72]

Notes

1. It is evident from their names that Sapphira and Ananias were Jews: חֲנַנְיָה means "YHWH has mercy," and שַׁפִּירָא "the beautiful one." See Billerbeck 2:634.

2. Elisabeth Koffmahn, *Doppelurkunden,* esp. 104ff. The question of women's property rights in marriage was addressed by S. Krauss in *Talmudische Archäologie* 2:43ff., in the section, "Die Stellung der Frau (in der Ehe)" [The Position of Women (in Marriage)]. Rachel Biale, *Women and Jewish Law. An Exploration of Women's Issues in Halakhic Sources* (New York, 1984), 44ff., does not speak directly of marriage in discussing women's property rights. She does mention the socioeconomic circumstances surrounding marriage a number of times (pp. 55, 61, 86–87) and the making of a marriage compact (*kethuba*), but does not investigate this question of property rights in detail. See also, on this subject, Billerbeck 2:372ff.

3. E. Koffmahn, *Doppelurkunden,* 11.

4. E. Koffmahn, *Doppelurkunden,* 29. The double documents were a very ancient form for the legal confirmation of business arrangements among the Jewish people. Their existence can be demonstrated for the seventh century B.C.E., and Jer. 32:10-15 also attests that they had been known for a long time.

5. Thus E. Koffmahn, *Doppelurkunden,* 28–29. This may even have been the last symbolic form of resistance, since the duplicate documents were used in Masada up to the final days: see Koffmahn, 43ff., and elsewhere.

6. E. Koffmahn, *Doppelurkunden,* 109–10.

7. See the examples of duplicate documents cited by E. Koffmahn, *Doppelurkunden,* 114ff.

8. See E. Koffmahn, *Doppelurkunden,* 65, 104, 106; cf. also A. Gulak, *Urkundenwesen,* 37, 44–45, 52ff., 60, 67, 73, who frequently emphasizes that both the wife and the husband brought a dowry into the marriage. Thus for example Gulak quotes (p. 45) from y*Ketubot:* "It was taught: both the husband and the father set aside the dowry; but the husband does so in writing, while the (bride's) father does so only orally." Hence Gulak (p. 52) can speak of "mutual dowries."

9. *CPJ* 144 (first century B.C.E.) attests the fact that a divorced wife received her dowry of 60 drachmas, which, in accordance with the marriage contract, she had brought with her into the marriage; *CII* 763 (third century C.E.) reports that a wife had a grave marker prepared for herself, her husband, her son, and her daughter out of her dowry (ἐκ τῆς ἰδίας προικός). On divorce and the dowry that thereby came into the woman's possession, see Ross S. Kraemer, ed., *Maenads, Martyrs, Matrons, Monastics* (Philadelphia, 1988), 88; further information also in E. Koffmahn, *Doppelurkunden,* 110ff.

10. S. Krauss, *Archäologie* 2:43, says that slaves, real property, and movable goods could make up parts of a woman's dowry, if the father's means permitted.

11. Boaz Cohen, "Peculium in Jewish and Roman Law," *PAAJR* 20 (1951): 135–234, at 170, asserts that the wife's property was also controlled by her husband, and that this was meant to guarantee harmony in the marriage. For a discussion of the question of whether a husband could sell the goods that were his wife's property, see E. Koffmahn, *Doppelurkunden,* 104ff., esp. 108, with bibliography.

12. See examples and interpretation in E. Koffmahn, *Doppelurkunden*, 156ff.

13. Mur is the abbreviation for papyri from Wadi Murabbaʾat. All three are to be found in E. Koffmahn, *Doppelurkunden*, 116ff.

14. See E. Koffmahn, *Doppelurkunden*, 177.

15. See E. Koffmahn, *Doppelurkunden*, 185.

16. E. Koffmahn, *Doppelurkunden*, 179.

17. According to C. Brekelmans, "חֵרֶם," *THAT* 1 (1984): 635–39, this passage, in the Jewish context, reflects the original usage of the concept of חֵרֶם / ἀνάθεμα / "ban," and "the cultic usage of ḥrm . . . and the usage in the context of war were connected; in both it is a matter of the thing banned . . . belonging to YHWH, so that every offense against YHWH's right to possession of the ḥrm would bring harm to the community."

18. Josephus, *Ant.* 4.8.29.

19. τηρεῖν τὴν πίστιν κατὰ τὸν ὅρκον: see Titus 2:10, which concerns a similar matter (not military, but having to do with domestic administration), namely "not to pilfer, but to show complete and perfect fidelity."

20. Polybius 10.16.6; on this, see also 6.21.

21. Xenophon, *Cyropaedia* 4.2.42. See also, similarly, Plutarch, *Lucullus* 37; also Athenaeus 6.234.

22. Diodorus Siculus, *History,* 5.34.3.

23. See SIG 3.993. The same content—the contractually fixed sacrifice, which it is forbidden to hold back—is also in *IG* 4.841.

24. Aristides, *Apologia*, 15.4.

25. See Herbert Preisker, "κλέπτω," *TDNT* 3:754.

26. Cf. Werner Foerster, "ἁρπάζω," *TDNT* 1:472–73.

27. See, for example, Luke 10:27 (= Deut. 6:5); 12:34, 45; 16:10ff.; 22:3, 31-32; John 13:2; Acts 8:21-22; 11:23-24.

28. Quotations from Johannes Behm, "καρδία," *TDNT* 3:605–14, at 611–12.

29. Rudolf Pesch, *Die Apostelgeschichte*, EKK 5/1, 2 (1986), 1:198.

30. This interpretation is shared by Pesch, *Apostelgeschichte* 1:199 n. 21, and Luke T. Johnson, *The Literary Function of Possessions in Luke-Acts*, SBLDS 39 (Atlanta, 1977), 207–8. For the meaning and use of epexegetical καί, see BDR §442,9.

31. Johnson, *Function*, 207: "It is not just the unity of a human assembly which is threatened by conspiracy, but the Spirit of God Himself who creates that unity. An offense against the unity is therefore an offense against God."

32. For this interpretation, see Christian Maurer, "πράσσω," *TDNT* 6:632–44, at 639–40.

33. See, for example, Ernst Haenchen, *Acts*, 237; G. Schille, *Apostelgeschichte*, 149; in the same vein also J. Roloff, *Apostelgeschichte*, 94.

34. For discussion of "community of goods," see, for example, L. Schottroff and W. Stegemann, *Jesus*, 116–20; B. H. Mönning, *Die Darstellung des urchristlichen Kommunismus nach der Apostelgeschichte des Lukas*, diss. (Göttingen, 1978), esp. 42ff.; W. Schrage, *The Ethics of the New Testament*, 126–28;

G. Brakemeier, Der "Sozialismus" der Urchristenheit (Göttingen, 1988), 10ff., who in turn refer to other works.

35. R. Pesch, Apostelgeschichte 1:199.

36. That such a departure was not only possible, but really happened, is clear from Pliny, Epistulae 10.96.

37. J. Jeremias, Jerusalem I/2, 46 n. 4, where he also asserts that "Ananias's fault is not in his lie, but in the keeping back of the property dedicated to God." The study by B. H. Mönning, Darstellung, esp. 65ff. denies this. According to Mönning, Ananias and Sapphira's sin is this: "the sin of the pair (πρᾶγμα; v. 4b) [consists] in their untrue statements regarding the proceeds acquired by the sale of their field, and thus in lying to the Spirit" (p. 66). He further asserts on p. 68: "the pair's offense does not consist in not having given the apostles the full proceeds from the sale, but in the secret retention of part of it." It is interesting to observe that Mönning does not inquire at all about why the pair needed to lie, if not to conceal the offense (keeping back = "secret retention of part" of the money). He fails to observe the interrelation of the actions.

38. See, for example, 1 Cor. 7:29; differently Col. 3:18. For more detail, see pp. 16–23.

39. For a feminist discussion of shared responsibility, see especially Christina Thürmer-Rohr, Vagabundinnen: feministische Essays (Berlin, 1987), 38ff.

40. See, e.g., R. Pesch, Apostelgeschichte 1:202–3; H. Baltensweiler, "Wunder und Glaube im Neuen Testament," ThZ 23 (1967):255.

41. J. Roloff, Apostelgeschichte, 93; J. Comblin, Atos dos Apóstolos, 1:132.

42. R. Pesch, Apostelgeschichte 1:203.

43. See the summary of research in E. Haenchen, Acts, 239–41.

44. R. Pesch deserves commendation for honoring the many-sidedness of the narrative in his commentary.

45. G. Theißen, The Miracle Stories of the Early Christian Tradition, 109–10.

46. Ibid., 110.

47. Ibid., 109.

48. The expression "look, the feet of those who have buried . . ." was used in that period to describe the imminent approach of death to the person addressed. See Billerbeck 2:634.

49. E. Haenchen, Acts, 239.

50. If Peter's behavior is understood that way, then, as I have indicated above, we assign to him an authority that may well have been claimed by later popes. Then it is even possible, by means of a later exegesis oriented to church hierarchy, to use this narrative as the basis for a punitive canon law for those who assert themselves against the papal authority. In this light, Michel Clévenot's criticism of the aspiring spiritual leadership personified in Peter (Von Jerusalem nach Rom. Geschichte des Christentums im I. Jahrhundert [Fribourg, 1987], 86–87) is understandable, but inappropriate for this text. First of all, Ananias did not seek merely to deceive the leadership of the community, but the com-

munity of saints as a whole; second, Peter's action here is not a "religious fanaticism that propagates death in the name of God," but the uncovering of a socio-religious sin that in this case has radical consequences not because of the presence of Peter, but because of the presence of God in the community.

51. G. Schille, *Apostelgeschichte*, 155.

52. Jürgen Roloff, *Apostelgeschichte, 96*.

53. Josephus, *Bell.* 2.143.

54. Carsten Colpe, "Die älteste judenchristliche Gemeinde," 70.

55. According to Hans Conzelmann, *Acts*, 38, "the congregation seems to be always in session." G. Schille, *Apostelgeschichte*, 150, refers to possible holy days or the hours of prayer, "since it appears that prayers were held every three hours. Whether the community is always gathered together (and even in consultation) or whether it has just gathered (although in any case there has been a burial in the meantime)—of this, not a word is said." This is his summary of the commentators' discussion about the passage of three hours (v. 7).

56. There has been widespread discussion of the positive and negative possibilities. Let me mention just a few examples. The majority of exegetes answer in the negative: thus E. Haenchen, *Acts*, 238; G. Schille, *Apostelgeschichte*, 150; J. Comblin, *Atos*, 133. I. H. Marshall, *Acts*, 110, says that there was apparently no chance for repentance, but on p. 113 he writes: "Sapphira is given the opportunity to tell the truth and thus to show some sign of repentance from her former attitude." R. Pesch, *Apostelgeschichte* 1:200–201, interprets Peter's question in v. 8 as giving Sapphira another chance "to tell the truth and, in spite of her complicity (2), to distance herself from her husband's behavior—at least after the fact—and instead of 'agreeing with' him (9b) to become one with the community again (4:32)."

57. See R. Pesch's remarks cited in the previous note.

58. R. Knopf, "Apostelgeschichte," 21; E. Haenchen, *Acts*, 238–39; G. Schille, *Apostelgeschichte*, 150; J. Comblin, *Atos*, 134; H. W. Beyer, *Apostelgeschichte*, 38; R. Pesch, *Apostelgeschichte* 1:195–96, 201.

59. See, for example, H. W. Beyer, *Apostelgeschichte*, 38: "Certainly it is not, for example, the retention of part of the proceeds from the sale of the land that is the sin, . . . but the lie given to the apostles, and the hypocrisy." R. Pesch differs (*Apostelgeschichte*, 201), emphasizing that Sapphira's untruth in v. 8 "covers up for the wicked behavior of her husband and repeats the lie that is implicit in his action." In this opinion, Pesch distances himself from the dominant interpretation of this text.

60. The majority of commentators interpret τοσούτου as meaning the money presented by Ananias: R. Knopf, "Apostelgeschichte," 21; J. Roloff, *Apostelgeschichte*, 94–95; E. Haenchen, *Acts*, 239; R. Pesch, *Apostelgeschichte* 1:201; only I. H. Marshall differs (*Acts*, 113): "In fact the figure named by Peter in verse 8 might be the actual amount of the sale, in which case Sapphira's reply would be a confession." Unfortunately, he does not pursue the idea of this

confession and its possible consequences. Would Peter not have had to act differently if this were a confession of sin, and thereby necessarily also an expression of readiness to repent? For the use of τοσούτου as a *genitivum pretii,* see BDR §179, 1, and Jens-Uwe Schmidt, *Valenzorientierte Syntax des Griechischen,* 51.

61. L. Schottroff, "Schreckensherrschaft," 57ff.

62. Ibid., 60.

63. Ibid., 63.

64. Dorothee Sölle, *Thinking About God,* 54.

65. Ibid., 56. For more on "women's sin" and the way it is understood in the dominant currents of exegesis, see L. Schottroff, "Befreite Eva," esp. 56ff., 79ff.; and W. Deifelt, "Justificação," 16ff., both of whom refer to additional feminist literature in confrontation with the dominant theology.

66. Luise Schottroff, "Schreckensherrschaft," 71.

67. Rom. 7:8ff. See the interpretation and bibliography in Schottroff, "Schreckensherrschaft," 62.

68. J. Becker, "Paulus und seine Gemeinden," 124 (= "Paul and his Churches," 163).

69. On this, see my remarks on the works of the disciple Tabitha on pp. 36–41 below.

70. The religious significance of burial is indicated also by the practices of the burial societies that maintained their own communal burying grounds and were responsible for the interment of their members because they believed that this would give them a share in the future life. On this, see for example G. Heinrici, "Die Christengemeinde Korinths und die religiösen Genossenschaften der Griechen," 482; J. Becker, "Paulus," 116; E. Schüssler Fiorenza, *In Memory of Her,* 175–204.

71. See, for example, Titus 2:5; 1 Pet. 3:1; Col. 3:18; Eph. 5:22ff.

72. As Schleiermacher said in his *Catechism of Reason for Noble Women,* "You shall not bear false witness for men, you shall not gloss over their barbarism in word and deed." Quoted from Dorothee Sölle, *Thinking About God,* 67.

The Miraculous Story of the Disciple Tabitha (9:36-43)

Preliminary Observations

The narrative in Acts 9:36-43 is connected to the story of Aeneas by the indication of Peter's location. He is visiting the saints in Lydda, where he heals a sick man. This miracle causes many people from Lydda and the region of Sharon to turn to the Lord. Lydda is close to Joppa: the plain of Sharon extends from Joppa to Carmel.[1]

The use of the word ἐλεημοσύνη, "charity," at the beginning of the Tabitha narrative, and the information in v. 43 that Peter was lodging with Simon the tanner, are indications that Luke is also responsible for the compositional joining of the two stories of Cornelius and Tabitha. It is also said at the beginning of the Cornelius narrative (Acts 10:2) that he was devout and god-fearing, and that he had done many good works for the Jewish people; moreover, we are told again that Peter was lodging with Simon the tanner (vv. 5-6, 17-18, 32). In order that the two stories should agree in their location, the Tabitha narrative had to end with a reference to Peter's lodging with Simon the tanner. This compositional frame also makes it clear why Peter did not remain at Tabitha's house.

The framing technique indicates that Luke is using and combining traditions.[2] In this whole section it is evident that the narrative is growing. More and more details are added, reaching a climax with the Cornelius narrative, which is concerned with the difficulties involved in religious contacts between the Jewish and non-Jewish populations. The Cornelius narrative is the longest, most controversial, and most detailed, "conversion" story in Acts, because it is meant to witness to the lively and conflictual dialogue in primitive Christianity over the reception of non-Jews into the Christian community (although not without conditions: see 10:2, 34; 15:19ff.). In that respect, the Cornelius story is of central importance. But it is problematic when interpreters give less attention to the other two stories, of Aeneas and Tabitha, or when they are less highly regarded than the Cornelius story. It seems to me, however, that it is not appropriate to begin by comparing them with the Cornelius narrative, since the problems addressed are not precisely the same, nor can we make the same presuppositions in the one case as in the other.

It remains undisputed that the Cornelius narrative represents a central focus of the Lukan account, because it is here that the mission outside the limits of Judaism is said to begin. Nevertheless, it seems to me quite another thing to begin with the Cornelius story and from that perspective to regard the stories of Tabitha and Aeneas as a prelude[3] or introduction[4] to the story of Cornelius, because the use of such terms in this context seems dismissive. This is a tendency that appears repeatedly in the history of interpretation,[5] as well as in preaching.[6] In this process, not only is the emphasis shifted to the Cornelius story, but the spotlight on Peter's missionary activity serves to remove the focus from Tabitha. For example, it is striking how subtly Billerbeck (2:695) draws attention away from the works of Tabitha's lifetime by first describing the works of Cornelius. Then, in commenting on Acts 10:2, Billerbeck does not add further specific detail about good works and acts of charity, but points forward, with the result that interest is shifted from Tabitha and directed primarily to Cornelius.

I intend to concentrate on Tabitha. Beginning with her, and conscious that Luke had some purpose in arranging his material this way, I will look for information that will help me better to understand the story Luke has handed on to us. I will refer the results of my investigation to Tabitha so that I may approach more closely to her life and the effect of her works in community with the other saints and widows.

Interpretation of the Text

Here I will investigate all the information the text supplies about Tabitha, concentrating especially on her designation as a disciple devoted to good works. Then, in connection with her death, I will turn to the widows, because in retrospect they can open a door for me to Tabitha's life. In this context I will also investigate the resurrection miracle against its Jewish-(Christian) background. I will conclude with some summary considerations.

The Disciple Tabitha

First, the narrative is given a location: what is now to be reported takes place in Joppa (= Jaffa), a port city near Lydda. This is immediately followed by an initial description of Tabitha, the woman who makes the narrative possible, because without her none of this would have happened.

Something should be said here about the locale and history of the city of Joppa, because in my opinion it plays a vital role in the account. Joppa was a city in the Mediterranean coastal plain of Judea, about 14 kilometers from Lydda, which in turn is about 50 kilometers from Jerusalem as the crow flies. In the other direction, Joppa is about 50 kilometers from Caesarea. This geographical data is important to the story inasmuch as Joppa represents "the boundary of the Jewish region."[7] Thus in visiting the place Peter not only reaches this boundary, but he will pass beyond it, thereby carrying out part of the prophecy of Acts 1:8.

Since its conquest by Simon Maccabeus in 145 B.C.E. (1 Macc. 12:33; 13:11), Joppa had been a Jewish city. At this period it was an important port for the Jewish population. It remained overwhelmingly Jewish until the war, and this probably accounts for the fact that in the year 66 C.E. Joppa was a center of the Jewish revolt. That in turn was the reason why the Romans, marching from Caesarea under the command of Cestius Gallus, destroyed Joppa. Josephus says of the attack of the Roman army: "some of them made a brisk march by the seaside, and some by land, and so coming upon them on both sides, they took the city with ease; and as the inhabitants had made no provision aforehand for a flight, nor had gotten anything ready for fighting, the soldiers fell upon them, and slew them all, with their families, and then plundered and burnt the city. The number of the slain was eight thousand four hundred."[8] But that was not the end of the story of the Jewish city of Joppa. According to Josephus, it was also at a later date a place of refuge for the Jews who "had escaped out of the demolished cities," and who intended to establish a base there.[9] But when Vespasian heard of it, he sent soldiers to attack the city, and the Jews were unable to offer any resistance.

Our text, Acts 9:36-43, tells of events that took place in the first years of expansion of the Christian faith in Palestine: roughly 30-40 C.E.

But Luke wrote his account at a time when the Jewish-Roman war had already occurred. The destruction of the city and the massacre of the Jewish population must still have been quite vivid in the memories of the readers. Here it is said of this city that a certain woman lived there, and a group of widows nearby. What comes first is not the name of the woman; the text's initial statement is that there was a *[woman] disciple* (μαθήτρια) in Joppa. Although this feminine form is a hapax legomenon in the New Testament, we can infer from the way the text is written that she was not the only female disciple in Joppa. The Greek text indicates that "there was a *certain* [female] disciple,"[10] and not that she was ἡ, that is, *the only* [female] disciple. Verse 38 tells us that a number of disciples lived in Joppa. This expression will appear once again, quite clearly, in later Christian literature: in the Gospel of Peter 12:50, where in connection with the narrative of Jesus' resurrection the words "[female] disciple of the Lord" are applied as a designation for Mary Magdalene. Outside the biblical text the words μαθήτρια and μαθητρίς are seldom used; when they do appear, it is always in connection with a school.[11]

The word μαθητής[12] appears for the first time in Acts at 6:1 and is used until 21:16, but it occurs alongside other concepts that also serve to describe Christians, for example οἱ ἅγιοι, οἱ πιστεύσαντες, οἱ ἀδελφοί. It is not synonymous with the twelve apostles. Only rarely is it supplemented by any additional explanation (cf. 9:1; 21:16). According to K. H. Rengstorf, this is a sign "that when Ac. has the word for Christians, it is following a special usage which for its part derives from the way Palestinian Christians described themselves."[13] He also writes (p. 458): "we may take it that the simple תַּלְמִידִים was the original." That would mean that the meaning of the word could be derived from Jewish usage and thus describe discipleship in terms of the relationship between teacher and student. However, in the New Testament this designation not only represents the relationship between Jesus and his followers, and thus is used not simply for Christians, but also appears, for example, as a description of the relationship between Paul or John the Baptizer and their disciples. This is the case in Acts 9:25; 14:20; 19:1ff. The gospels also use this term to describe the disciples of John the Baptizer (John 4:1), those of the Pharisees (Mark 2:18; Matt. 22:16), and the disciples of Moses (John 9:28). Hence even within the New Testament it describes disciples within Judaism who need not necessarily have had Jesus as their master. In any event, in Acts the word normally refers to followers of Jesus, and probably to those of Jewish origin. Therefore we should consider whether the bearers of this title also understood it against the background of the designation תַּלְמִידִים— "student," "disciple," and so on—a concept that was otherwise familiar to them. In any case, there is also a rabbinic passage asserting that Jesus had תַּלְמִידִים;[14] in Jewish understanding, all disciples would devote themselves to the study of the Torah.[15] It is true that the rabbinic literature, so far as I am aware, makes no express mention of a female disciple (תַּלְמִידָה), but it does know of a woman who was learned in the scriptures. This was "Beruria (Valeria), the wife of R[abbi] Meir."[16]

We may conclude from these findings that the female disciple in Acts 9:36-43 was probably no different from all other disciples of Jesus. The tradition that Luke adopted, without changes, included no "limitations," and had no qualms about applying the word to women. In editing and arranging, Luke left the material intact. Discipleship included following Jesus, and was also characterized by confessing him as Lord, in word and deed.[17]

The narrative continues with a further description of the disciple: her name is Tabitha. Ταβιθά is an Aramaic name (תַּבְיְתָא / תַּבִיתָא) and means "gazelle," which is why it is translated into Greek as Δορκάς, "gazelle," or "deer."[18] The appearance of both names suggests that Luke wanted to address both Jews and Greeks, or that this disciple was known among people of both Jewish and non-Jewish origin. The name is also found in the rabbinic writings, in stories connected with Rabbi Gamaliel II from the year 90 C.E. Here it is always applied to female slaves, and in its masculine form to male slaves. According to y. Nid. 2.49d, 27 and Lev. Rab. 19.4, there was certainly at least one female slave with this name, while according to y. Nid. 1.49b, 43 all the slaves, male and female, in Gamaliel's house had the name.[19]

With regard to Tabitha, there have been repeated attempts to define her position "as a woman." Joseph Viteau[20] specifies it: There was a society of widows at Joppa, in which all the women were "professed widows" ("veuves de profession"). They worked for their living and devoted themselves to good works. Tabitha was one of them. I do not think this is a central issue; as J. A. McNamara correctly observes, the speculative pendulum can swing from one side to the other: "Tabitha may have been a widow; she could have been an unmarried virgin."[21] I suspect that the interest in defining Tabitha's "womanly" status reflects an agenda of the dominant exegesis, which tries to locate biblical women clearly within the framework of patriarchal familial structures. But the text in question is not interested in that agenda. It is more concerned with the social-missionary activity of the disciple Tabitha, independent of her status "as a woman."

The Works of the Disciple Tabitha

The description of Tabitha continues: "She was devoted to good works and acts of charity" (ἦν πλήρης ἔργων ἀγαθῶν καὶ ἐλεημοσυνῶν ὧν ἐποίει).

A brief glance at the commentaries shows that it is no simple matter to give a precise description of Tabitha's works. For example, in Biller-beck we read: "The so-called 'acts of charity,' גְּמִילוּת חֲסָדִים . . . such as visiting the sick, sheltering strangers, providing for poor couples about to be married, participation in wedding festivals and burials, consoling those in sorrow, and similar works [n. 1 refers to Matt. 25:35-36] are included, together with almsgiving (מִצְוָה צְדָקָה), among the 'good works,' מַעֲשִׂים טוֹבִים (= ἔργα καλά or ἀγαθά)"[22] that are also "laid down and commanded" in Scripture, and for that reason they can be counted "among the מִצְוֹת, the 'commandments' of the Torah." The notion of ἔργα ἀγαθά is thus a comprehensive concept within which all acts of love and mercy are subsumed. In this view, Acts 9:36b could repre-sent a confusion of ideas, inasmuch as exegetes have repeatedly trans-lated and interpreted ἐλεημοσύνη in Acts 9:36b as "almsgiving" (NRSV: "acts of charity"), which is thus placed alongside "good works" rather than being included within them.

The use of the concept of ἔργα ἀγαθά is fairly common in the New Testament. I will list some examples, each of which should be viewed within its own context: Rom. 2:7; 13:3; 2 Cor. 9:8; Eph. 2:10; Phil. 1:6; Col. 1:10; 1 Tim. 2:10; 5:10; 2 Tim. 2:21; 3:17; Titus 1:16; 3:1. The same idea is found in the related formula ἀγαθὸν ποιῆσαι, "doing good," in Mark 3:4; Luke 6:9; John 5:29; and similarly Rom. 2:10. These texts give a very clear picture of good works and those who practice them. With these, and probably many other texts, we may say that the perfor-mance of good works by human beings is seen as a sign, or even an image, of the mercy and love of God. They are commanded by God as a sign of genuine love of God, and God will reward them.

Obviously, the New Testament is also aware of "evil" works, which appear in a very negative light because, ultimately, they destroy one's relationship to God and other people. They are almost always described in contrast to good works: for example in John 3:19ff.; Rom. 13:11ff.; Heb. 6:1; 9:14.[23] This reference to works and the recognition of good and evil works is also found in the Letter of Barnabas (130–132 C.E.)[24]

at 4.1: "Let us therefore flee altogether from all the works of lawlessness (τὰ ἔργα τῆς ἀνομίας), lest the works of lawlessness overpower us," and at 4.9b-10:

> For the whole time of our faith shall profit us nothing, unless we now, in the season of lawlessness and in the offences that shall be, as becometh [children] of God, offer resistance. . . . Let us flee from all vanity, let us entirely hate the works of the evil way (τὰ ἔργα τῆς πονηρᾶς ὁδοῦ). Do not entering in privily stand apart by yourselves, as if ye were already justified, but assemble yourselves together and consult concerning the common welfare.

The existence of good works, their necessity, and the dangers that can be concealed in them are thus themes of Christian literature. However, it seems to me that the discussion and interpretation of good works in G. Bertram's article on work[25] is inadequate in view of the fact that in listing and interpreting "human labour and the work of man" he concentrates most of his attention on the negative and dangerous aspect.[26] This appears to result from an attempt to distinguish Christian from Jewish ethics, to the advantage of the former.[27]

Among good works, or included within the category as a whole, are acts of charity. The word ἐλεημοσύνη has the same roots as, for example, ἐλεέω, "to have compassion" (Rom. 12:8) and ἐλεήμων, "merciful" (Matt. 5:7), as well as ἔλεος, "mercy" (Eph. 2:4; Jas. 2:13). It could thus also be interpreted as "works of mercy." The LXX translates the Old Testament concept of חֶסֶד with ἔλεος. It describes an attitude "which arises out of a mutual relationship," a behavior that is "a helpful act corresponding to a relationship of trust."[28] This concept continues in the New Testament with regard to human behavior. A typical example is the action of the Samaritan in Luke 10:37: ". . . the demand for mercy is based on the divine mercy, as in Judaism."[29] The exercise of mercy should characterize people who act in the assurance of God's mercy. This is attested also by Didache 3.8 and 2 Clem. 4.3.[30] The concept of ἐλεημοσύνη appears in the LXX most often as a translation of the word צְדָקָה, "justice," or "righteousness."[31] God is on the side of the oppressed and suffering, does justice for them, does good things for them (Jer. 1:27; 59:16; Pss. 23:5; 102:6; Deut. 6:24-25; 24:13). Ἐλεημοσύνη is understood in this sense in Greek-speaking Judaism, except that the actors are not God, but human beings who are motivated by God's mercy. There is a new conception in Dan. 4:24 (LXX

4:27), where it is said that the king should atone for his sins through righteousness (צְדָקָה) and works of mercy (מְחֹן). It is striking that here one version of the LXX uses ἐλεημοσύνη for both Old Testament concepts, while another uses ἐλεημοσύνη for the first and οἰκτιρμός for the second. We may make a further observation about the Old Testament text: the two concepts are parallel and do not represent a contrast. Good works or works of mercy belong to righteousness; they are familiar in Greek-speaking Judaism and also in the rabbinic writings. Both can be attested without an intention to express two completely different concepts.[32] To conclude from this finding in the Jewish writings that, as regards the use of the word ἐλεημοσύνη in the New Testament, "ἐλεημοσύνη is found *only* in the sense of 'benevolent activity,' and always to the poor ('almsgiving')"[33] I regard as a twofold reduction of the concept. Furthermore, I see this as an interpretive attempt to derive a difference between Christianity and Judaism from this idea.[34] The danger of such a reduction, I think, is that one no longer sees good works or acts of charity as subsumed under the concept of righteousness, and that one also attempts to reduce good works to the giving of alms. I use the concept of "good works" or "acts of charity" here more in a Jewish-(Christian) sense that is inseparable from righteousness.

Acts 3:2ff. is, in fact, a demonstration that ἐλεημοσύνη is not restricted to almsgiving. The sick man hoped to receive ἐλεημοσύνη from those who are coming out of the Temple. Peter saw him and said: "I have no silver or gold, but what I have I give you; in the name of Jesus Christ of Nazareth, stand up and walk." A miracle has occurred. It may be that this healing is also part of the mercy for which the sick man hoped. We might make a similar examination of all the New Testament passages Bultmann lists[35] to support his assertion that the concept appears in the New Testament only in the sense of almsgiving. There is no compelling argument for the assertion that the word can only be used in that sense. Exceptions could be found in Luke 11:41 and 12:33, although there the text speaks of διδόναι ἐλεημοσύνην, and not, as elsewhere, of ποιεῖν ἐλεημοσύνην (= עָשׂה צדקה). Here we can more clearly understand the expression to mean "giving alms."[36] According to Billerbeck 2:188, this distinct use of the concept is meant to reproduce the Old Testament (ποιεῖν ἐλεημοσύνην) and rabbinic (διδόναι ἐλεημοσύνην) usage. We might then conclude that our passage would represent the Old Testament usage. That in turn need not mean that almsgiving is not included within the concept at all. It can very easily be included, but as a part of the whole, and not, as the tradition of interpretation of this text asserts, as the major aspect or even the whole idea. Luise Schottroff is correct in saying that "our German word for 'alms,' which the translators use at this point, contains false nuances: the crumbs that fall from the masters' tables are called alms. But in the Bible the works of righteousness are meant [by צְדָקָה and ἐλεημοσύνη]."[37]

Matthew 6:1ff. also locates works of mercy within the context of righteousness. It is clear that people had difficulty with the association of the two concepts from an early period, since various manuscripts read ἐλεημοσύνη in place of the word δικαιοσύνη in v. 1. This could mean two things: either that the connection between the two spheres was obliterated by the replacement of one by the other, or that at that time no sharp distinction was made between them.[38] In my opinion, Jesus was very close to his contemporary, Rabbi Hillel, in his concept of ἐλεημοσύνη. According to 'Abot 2.7, Hillel interprets Isa. 32:17 to mean that "righteousness" is understood as, or is equivalent to, "good works." The verse reads (NRSV): "The effect of righteousness will be peace" (וְהָיָה מַעֲשֵׂה הַצְּדָקָה שָׁלוֹם; LXX: καὶ ἔσται τὰ ἔργα τῆς δικαιοσύνης εἰρήνη). Hillel writes: "The more righteousness, the more peace." Hillel, and probably many others with him, thus understood the concept of good works in the context of righteousness much more broadly than, for example, Billerbeck 1:387 presumes when it reduces the concept to almsgiving.[39] In the same vein, Jesus apparently wanted to make clear the connection between righteousness and good works in Matt. 6:1ff. I think Billerbeck is right in saying that Matt. 6:1 is meant to be "a title for the whole section in vv. 2-18."[40] As a consequence, all the other actions (good works, prayer, fasting) are subsumed under the concept of righteousness. As regards the practice of good works, the text does not compel us to reduce it exclusively to almsgiving.[41]

Jesus may have thought more broadly. Incidentally, according to Matt. 6:1ff., Jesus does not deny that God will repay or reward good works, and does not even question the idea that God will repay. Jesus simply warns against "sounding the trumpet" to call attention to such works, that is, doing them to acquire respect for oneself. It is not the actions that are called into question, but a certain kind of self-satisfied and therefore disrespectful attitude on the part of the one doing them, whereby the action becomes an end in itself. We find the same warning in rabbinic texts.[42]

Thus a mere glance at the sources listed in Billerbeck 1:386–87 indicates that the concept of צְדָקָה is frequently understood as ἐλεημοσύνη. The concepts are equivalent, or at least are closely associated. Therefore ἐλεημοσύνη always means something more than simply almsgiving in the modern sense: it is to be understood in relationship to righteousness. In this connection, we may refer to Prov. 10:2 and Tob. 4:6ff.

Not least important in this context are the difficulties and dangers that can result when Christian theologians analyze Jewish charitable practices. This emerges clearly from the excursus on "Ancient Jewish Private Acts of Charity" in Billerbeck 4/1:536ff. The authors first list all the Jewish texts known to them in which there is mention of the practice of charity. In evaluating them, they write: "One may fully applaud ancient Jewish willingness to make sacrifices, but one must also admit that the manner in which it was practiced contained great dangers, first of all for the poor on whose behalf it was done. The certainly well-meaning readiness . . . to aid . . . the poor . . . was only too well designed to encourage, in many ways, a dismal and shameless practice of beggary."[43] It may certainly be true that this practice of charity encouraged beggars in that society. But, astonishingly enough, the New Testament exegetes fail to recognize that beggars have to place themselves in the streets in front of religious institutions not because they are shameless, but because they are poor. Poverty certainly does not exist because of the practice of charity, but because of unjust social and economic relationships. And the Jewish practice of charity did not exist in order to "encourage . . . a dismal and shameless practice of beggary," but to ameliorate suffering and hunger in some small way and thus to save lives. It is amazing that Christian theologians direct their attention primarily to these supposedly avoidable dangers, and thereby make this practice of charity taboo for Christians, all the more since they also connect it with Jews' "concept of reward," as in Billerbeck 4/1:552, where it is said that the greater mass of Jews were guided in their practice of charity mainly by the idea that God would repay them for it: there is a reward for every deed. Thus it is no longer the practice of righteousness or mercy toward others that is in the foreground, but one's own interest: "We see that there was scarcely any benefit that the Israelite did not hope to be able to acquire through almsgiving. That was the reason for the charitable acts of ancient Judaism, so gladly and frequently practiced."[44] Even when Old Testament or rabbinic texts[45] speak of the response of God to those who practice righteousness in the form of works of mercy, a Christian theologian may not treat such texts as if they yield a thesis like the one cited above. It is true that Jesus, like other Jews, admonished people to consider the manner in which they did their works of charity, but he did not challenge the works themselves, and he did not assert that his contemporaries were practicing them out of a hope of reward![46] These remarks on the twenty-second excursus in Billerbeck (4/1:537ff.) seem to me urgently required, especially in view of the fact that this literature is part of the standard set of materials with which exegetes and theologians work. It has left its mark, at least since 1928, on the existing traditions of interpretation, and it continues the trend of Christian anti-Judaism. After Auschwitz, Billerbeck should only be read with a deeply critical eye.

There is one point regarding the practice of works of mercy (when understood in terms of almsgiving) that I think deserves discussion. This is the question of whether those doing the actions saw or had no other opportunity to abolish hunger and misery.[47] In that respect, there is an important difference between people who give "out of their abundance" and those who "give their own life" (see Luke 21:1-4).[48]

Alms in the sense of "crumbs" are certainly not what is intended in Acts 9:36. We may clarify this in connection with v. 39. The interpretation of alms as crumbs, something left over that would otherwise be thrown away, comes from the perspective of the rich or well-to-do. But poor or poorer people also give aid and practice mercy, and in that case the flavor of "giving crumbs" is not present. There are clear examples: the poor widow in Luke 21:1-4 and Mark 12:41-44; Peter's words in Acts 3:2-6; compare also Tob. 4:6-11. In all these instances, people give what they have. For the widow it means that she gives her own life, what she has to live on. Rabbinic texts also refer to poor people who practice charity.[49]

The explicit description of Tabitha as a disciple devoted to good works can also be explained by the fact that this woman had not been forgotten by the early Christians in the course of the years. Her memory remained very much alive. The memory of a woman who used to bring people life through her works was retained. This vivid memory prevented her from being eliminated from written history. Any history that omitted a recollection of her would have lost credibility by doing so. The example of Tabitha must have served other people at that time—before and after its written transmission—as an incitement to action. Nowadays, and not only in the Lutheran tradition, we speak of these works only in whispers, and sometimes there is complete silence about them.[50]

The Death and Raising of the Disciple Tabitha

In this section I will treat the events portrayed in vv. 38-41 in connection with v. 37, for all the actions described depend on the assertion that Tabitha had died. Everything follows from this, and cannot exist without this statement about the death of Tabitha. Thus she is the one who sets the story in motion. She also puts other people in motion after her own death. It is through this setting-in-motion that, ultimately, the power of God comes to expression in her being raised to life.

Acts 9:37 first connects the following story to what has been said before. The formula "at that time" refers to the days when Peter was in Lydda. During that time Tabitha died of an illness. Unlike the illness in v. 33, which is followed by a healing, this one is not described by the text in detail. Not only the use of the concepts of ἀσθενέω ("be ill") and ἀποθνῄσκω ("die," "be dead"), but also the actions in the second part of v. 37 indicate that, in the understanding of the text, Tabitha was really dead.

The activity connected with the ritual of mourning is described as λούειν ("washing"). It appears with this meaning, as the washing of a corpse, only here in the New Testament.[51] This act is part of the Jewish ritual of mourning,[52] which also includes the loving deed of anointing the body and clothing or wrapping it (cf. Mark 15:46; Luke 23:53; John 19:39-40). But, for whatever reason, nothing is said of this here. It is needless to speculate whether placing Tabitha in the upper room[53] necessarily meant that her burial was delayed "because it was expected that Peter would bring help."[54] Even together with v. 35, this is not a necessary conclusion, because it is only at v. 38 that it is indicated that the disciples had heard of Peter's being in Lydda. Only when they learned of it did they send two messengers—in accordance with Jewish custom—with a request that he come at once. When they placed Tabitha's body in the upper room, they did not necessarily know that Peter was in the vicinity, and therefore they could not have acted with the latent idea that Peter would raise Tabitha. Placing the body in the upper room when an illness has resulted in death at home is rather a part of the Jewish (and Jewish Christian) rite of mourning.[55] There, according to v. 39, the mourning and weeping widows were gathered.

Only at v. 39 do we learn something about the presence of the widows and more detail about the people who lived with Tabitha, among whom were these widows. They are there in the upper room, mourning for Tabitha, when Peter enters. Weeping, they approach Peter and show him the tunics and other clothing that Tabitha had made during her lifetime. Only at this point, through the presence of the widows, do we learn something concrete about Tabitha's activity. The widows explain in a vivid manner, without words, something of what

was said about Tabitha in v. 36. Here part of her good works is made
tangible.

It is difficult to give a more precise description of the clothing that
the widows show to Peter. According to the text, it comprises both
underclothes and outer garments; the underclothes were probably of
linen.

The word χιτών is defined as follows in Genseler's *Griechisch-
Deutsches Wörterbuch*: "a woolen or linen, sleeveless robe, tunic, shirt,
worn by men and women next to the skin;" the ἱμάτιον is a "cloak,
dress, or robe, that is, a square or round-cut piece of cloth drawn from
the left arm backward below the right, with the end thrown over the
left shoulder." These definitions correspond to those in Bauer, Arndt,
Gingrich, and Danker's *Lexicon*. According to Liddell-Scott, the χιτών
was "a *woollen shirt* worn [by men and women] next the body; on
going out they threw a wide cloak over it, called φᾶρος, χλαῖνα, or
ἱμάτιον: the χιτών sometimes reached to the feet, and was then called
χιτὼν ποδήρης: with sleeves it was called χιτὼν χειριδωτος."

Only with the appearance of the widows in v. 39 do we obtain a
glimpse of an essential part of the work that women did. Tabitha worked
with textiles. To this point in the narrative, that aspect of her work was
invisible. The widows bring it to the fore. Tabitha did not give out
outerwear and undergarments as "alms." This is emphasized by the
text's assertion that she made the clothing herself. They are the work of
her hands. Tabitha was, according to J. Comblin, a "teceloa,"[56] which
means that she wove and finished cloth for garments.[57]

Verse 39 also tells us something about the social organization of the
widows. It is difficult to say whether these women no longer had families to which they could return after the death of their husbands. In any
case it is characteristic of Luke (and in this he carries on Old Testament
tradition) that he always depicts widowed women as being in a weak
socioeconomic position (cf. Luke 18:1-5; 21:1-4; Acts 6:1). Tabitha
made clothing for, or with, the widows. This also means that these
women had no other man who took care of them after their husbands'
death. Most probably they were widows who were alone and who, if
they were not themselves wealthy,[58] had need of others in order to go
on living. However, I do not believe that we can presume, solely on this
basis, that Tabitha was rich. The text's assertion that she herself made
clothes is a clear contradiction to that idea. Her good works included
her own activity; her works of righteousness were the expression of the
commitment of her whole person with everything she had: this must by

no means point to wealth or comfort.[59] Nor do I believe that there is reference here to an official, organized program for the care of widows, like that later established.[60] The idea that Tabitha "was commissioned . . . by the church at Joppa"[61] for her work can only be accepted if this does not refer to a fixed structuring of duties in the community, in which women's work was again established within the "household sphere." An interpretation in that sense makes it problematic to understand the actions of the widowed women and the saints as "unusual," in the sense that "this explains the *unusual concern* of the church at her death."[62] We need not even view Tabitha against the background of 1 Tim. 5:16 in order to see her as a true believer: Acts 9:36-43 by itself makes it clear that Tabitha was a woman who led a righteous life, keeping faith and works in harmony, and that no one saw any conflict in that. On the contrary: here the two are interdependent.

In vv. 40-41 the narrative tells of a whole series of actions: the widows show Peter their sorrow and some of Tabitha's good works. Peter hears and sees; perhaps he, too, is moved. But then follows what appears, at least initially, to be a callous act: Peter puts them all outside. The narrative continues: ". . . he knelt down and prayed. He turned to the body and said, 'Tabitha, get up.' Then she opened her eyes, and seeing Peter, she sat up. He gave her his hand and helped her up. Then calling the saints and widows, he showed her to be alive."

The story of Tabitha takes place in a Jewish town. The life-style of Tabitha and the community in Joppa is, according to vv. 36-39, also Jewish. In light of Tabitha's being raised, we must inquire about Jewish faith in the resurrection. What was its content? Are there similar resurrection stories in the Old and New Testaments? If so, do they match the Jewish resurrection faith?

These questions will be discussed here also in order to clarify whether these resurrection stories were understood at the time as resurrections within the framework of Jewish and Jewish-Christian resurrection belief, or more in the sense of therapeutic "awakenings."[63]

Jewish and Christian Belief in the Resurrection

Hope in the resurrection is a solid component of faith for many groups within Judaism. This is clearly and unmistakably expressed in the Jewish liturgical confession of faith. The liturgy for burial includes the doxology: "He [God] will raise you up. Blessed be He who keeps His Word and raises the dead!"[64] The second of the Eighteen Benedictions, which is prayed in the synagogue, says:

Thou, O Lord, art mighty for eternity,
thou reviver of the dead,
yea, master to save;
sustaining the living with loving-kindness,
reviving the dead with abounding mercies,
supporting the falling,
healing the sick
and releasing the captive,
yea, He keeps faith with them
that sleep in the soil;
Who is alike to thee?—
o wielder of powers;
Who can be compared unto thee?—
o king who brings death and life
and causes salvation to grow;
Yea, trusted art thou to revive the dead—
blest art thou, God,
reviver of the dead![65]

We find this faith in the Old Testament, for example in Daniel 12: the whole people shall awake, some to eternal life, others to eternal shame. This idea is found as early as Isa. 66:15ff. Moreover, the idea that God kills and gives life (again) can also be found, for example, in Deut. 32:39; 1 Sam. 2:6; 2 Kgs. 5:7. The thought is even more familiar to Jewish extra-canonical literature. According to 1 Enoch (167–64 B.C.E.)[66] the resurrection of the dead will occur on the day of divine judgment, when the Messiah will call forth the righteous and the saints (e.g., 22:1ff.; 51:1ff.; 90:33ff.; 91:7ff.; 92:1ff.; 100:1ff.). The day of judgment, when the resurrection is to happen, will come about in order to bring justice for those who have died long before (22:4). This day must come because of the existing unrighteousness and violence to which human beings are exposed. Because of their experience of injustice and the certainty of the coming day of judgment, people are called upon to practice justice. The suffering that exists, and the hope of resurrection, can thus move people to lead a righteous and merciful life. 1 Enoch 91:4-10 reads:

. . . do not draw near uprightness with an ambivalent attitude, and neither associate with hypocrites. But walk in righteousness, my children, and it shall lead you in the good paths; and righteousness shall be your friend. For I know that the state of violence will intensify upon the earth; a great plague shall be executed upon the earth; all (forms of) oppression will be carried out; and everything shall be uprooted; and every arrow shall fly fast.

. . .

When oppression, sin and blasphemy, and injustice increase, crime, iniquity, and uncleanliness shall be committed and increase (likewise). Then a great plague shall take place from heaven upon all these; . . . Then the righteous one shall arise from his sleep, . . .[67]

1 Enoch attests to a powerful hope in the resurrection, which also means rescue from situations of injustice for those who are affected by it. The hope of resurrection is thus a hope in God's redress.[68] This hope is always referred to a day that is to come. It is part of the messianic hope. It does not speak of a resurrection that has already happened, but only about the experience of suffering that calls out for resurrection.

Faith in the resurrection is witnessed by many Jewish writings from the first century B.C.E. to the first century C.E. that reflect lived experiences, both of justice and injustice, in the realm of eschatological hope as well.[69] Thus, for example, in the *Testaments of the Twelve Patriarchs* (first century B.C.E.):

And after this Abraham, Isaac, and Jacob will be resurrected
. . .
And those who died in sorrow shall be raised in joy;
and those who died in poverty for the Lord's sake shall be made rich, . . .
those who died on account of the Lord shall be wakened to life.
(*Jud.* 25:1-4)[70]

And then you will see Enoch and Seth and Abraham and Isaac and Jacob being raised up at the right hand in great joy. Then shall we also be raised, each of us over our tribe, and we shall prostrate ourselves before the heavenly king [who appeared on earth in the guise of a humble man; and all those who believed him on earth will rejoice with him]. Then all shall be changed, some destined for glory, others for dishonor, for the Lord first judges Israel for the wrong she has committed and then he shall do the same for all the nations. . . . if you live in holiness, in accord with the Lord's commands, you shall again dwell with me in hope; all Israel will be gathered to the Lord.
(*Benj.* 10:6-11)[71]

The assurance of resurrection for those who fear the Lord is also found in the *Psalms of Solomon* (first century B.C.E.). The righteous will arise, in contrast to sinners, that is, those who do not fear God.

The destruction of the sinner is forever,
and he will not be remembered when (God) looks after the righteous.
. . .
But those who fear the Lord shall rise up to eternal life,
and their life shall be in the Lord's light,
and it shall never end.

(*Ps. Sol.* 3:11-12)[72]

A general resurrection both of the righteous and the unrighteous on the day of judgment—some to condemnation, others to life—is further attested in Jewish pseudepigraphical writings from the first century C.E. The Syrian *Apocalypse of Baruch* (chs. 30 and 50–51) and the fourth book of the Sibylline Oracles offer a more precise idea of when and how this will happen:

. . . when the time of the appearance of the Anointed One has been fulfilled and he returns in glory, . . . then all who sleep in hope of him will rise. And it will happen at that time that those treasuries will be opened in which the number of the souls of the righteous were kept, and they will go out. . . . But the souls of the wicked will the more waste away when they shall see all these things.

(*2 Apoc. Bar.* 30:1-5)[73]

But when the judgment of the world and of mortals has already come,
which God himself will perform, judging impious and pious at once,
then he will also send the impious down into the gloom in fire,
and then they will realize what impiety they committed.
But the pious will remain on the fertile soil,
and God will give them spirit and life and favor at once.
All these things will be accomplished in the tenth generation,
. . .
The whole world will hear a bellowing noise and mighty sound.
He will burn the whole earth, and will destroy the whole race of men
and all cities and rivers at once, and the sea.
He will destroy everything by fire, and it will be smoking dust.
But when everything is already dusty ashes,
and God puts to sleep the unspeakable fire, even as he kindled it,
God himself will again fashion the bones and ashes of men
and he will raise up mortals again as they were before.
And then there will be a judgment over which God himself will preside,
judging the world again. As many as sinned by impiety,
these will a mound of earth cover,
and broad Tartarus and the repulsive recesses of Gehenna.

> But as many as are pious, they will live on earth again
> when God gives spirit and life and favor
> to these pious ones. Then they will all see themselves
> beholding the delightful and pleasant light of the sun.
>
> (Or. Sib. 4.41–44, 175–91)[74]

In the pseudepigrapha, the ideas about those involved in the resurrection are quite varied. Some writings envision a general resurrection, that is, that both the righteous and pious, on the one hand, and the unrighteous and godless, on the other, will be judged before God. Others think only of a resurrection of the righteous. All Jewish writings that acknowledge a resurrection see it being accomplished through a day of judgment. The rabbinic writings also continue this tradition, with all its variety.[75] Not least, New Testament texts also offer evidence of Jewish faith in the resurrection. Let me mention only Mark 6:14ff.; 9:31; 12:18ff.; John 11:23-24; Acts 23:6ff.; 24:15, 21.

In spite of the hope in the resurrection so widely attested in Jewish literature, I know of no writing in which anything is said of a resurrection before the day of judgment. Ideas of resurrection belong in the realm of eschatology, but a very concrete form of eschatology: "The resurrection [is] not a reunion of body and soul, but simply a renewed life of the whole human being and return to the community of the survivors on an earth that is purified of sin and freed from its consequences, but by no means spiritualized."[76] Jewish thought regards resurrection as part of a world that is fundamentally changed, liberated, and free from sin and misdeeds. The dead will not rise into the "old" world. Everything that previously caused suffering and pain will cease to exist. There will be a new heaven and a new earth.

This confident eschatological hope also shows that in their hope for the resurrection, oppressed people expressed their longing, and the necessity for a total alteration of their situation, in a variety of different ways. Thus expressions about the day of the Lord's judgment reflect fragments of contemporary life. There is a kind of hermeneutical circle in which life points to resurrection, and resurrection to the life that is to be constructed.

This idea, or rather this hopeful certainty that those who live righteously will experience the future resurrection as salvation, and not, like the unrighteous, as destruction, is part of the stuff of Jewish tradition. The promise of resurrection can therefore also give people the strength and will to practice justice and mercy. It seems to me an expression of

Christian prejudice when people say that Jews thereby attempted to buy resurrection. On the basis of the sources known to us, no one can deny that Jewish people expressed the will to live a righteous life out of gratitude and confidence in the resurrection, or the possibility of resurrection. They, too, demand righteousness out of their hope, or rather their confidence, in the resurrection.

Literary Parallels to Acts 9:40-41

As described above, belief in the resurrection is a part of Jewish faith; according to that faith, resurrection would occur on the day of judgment. This is presumed by all the authors we have cited. For that very reason, they do not mention the biblical "resurrection stories" that do not adhere to that theme. Jakob Kremer speaks very briefly of them and calls them "stories of people who have been revived." Hence they have no further place in his discussion of this topic.[77] The parallel texts to Acts 9:36-43 are not treated under the heading of "resurrection."

In the Old Testament there are at least two parallels to Acts 9:40-41: 1 Kgs. 17:17-24 and 2 Kgs. 4:18-37. In the New Testament we find Luke 7:11-17; Mark 5:21-24, 35-43 (= Luke 8:41-42, 49-56); John 11:1-44; Acts 20:9-12 as parallels. Thus, as far as I know, there are only seven stories of "reawakening." All of them are brought about by "men of God":

a) *Elijah:* 1 Kgs. 17:17-24, the story of the raising of the son of the widow of Zarephath. The special action is described in vv. 20-21: the prophet stretches himself out on the body, after first complaining to the Lord about the child's death. He lays himself on the child three times, saying: "O Lord my God, let this child's life come into him again." The life returns, and the boy revives.

b) *Elisha:* 2 Kgs. 4:18-37, especially 32-37, the raising of the son of the Shunammite woman. The special action is described in vv. 34-35: the prophet lays himself on the body, and it grows warm. Elisha does not speak a word to the boy.

The Old Testament reawakening stories have in common that both Elijah and Elisha go to the house of the dead person and lay themselves on the body. The second action appears to be a liturgical act; for Elijah prayer and touch belong together. After the reawakening, the prophet gives the living child to its mother. The mother responds with a confession or adoration of the God of the prophet, or of the prophet himself.

c) *Jesus:* Luke 7:11-17, the raising of the son of the widow of Nain. It is striking that according to v. 12 the dead man is already being carried out in his coffin for burial. In v. 14, Jesus touches the bier and says: "Young man, I say to you, rise!" The young man stands up and speaks.

Luke 8:41-42, 49-56, the raising of the daughter of Jairus, the ruler of the synagogue. Before the miracle, there is a discussion that clarifies the situation. Contrary to the opinion expressed in v. 49, that the girl is dead, Jesus says to the father in v. 50: "Do not fear. Only believe, and she will be saved," and in v. 52 he says to all those in the house: "Do not weep; for she is not dead but sleeping." Her death is asserted again in v. 53. Jesus' tenderness and sympathy for his companions form part of the fabric of the discussion. Then Jesus takes the little girl's hand (v. 54) and says aloud: "Child, get up!" (Mark 5:41: ταλιθὰ κοῦμ[ι]), whereupon her spirit returns and she immediately gets up.

John 11:1-44, especially vv. 17ff., the raising of Lazarus. According to vv. 17 and 39, the body had already lain in the grave four days. Jesus does not touch it, but he prays (vv. 41-42), and then cries out: "Lazarus, come out!" And it happens.

d) *Peter:* Acts 9:39-41, the raising of the disciple Tabitha in Joppa. Verse 37 asserts that she was sick and died. In v. 40, Peter acts: he kneels down, prays, turns to the body and says: "Tabitha, get up." Only after she sits up does he give her his hand; then he helps her to her feet and shows her to the others, alive.

e) *Paul:* Acts 20:9-12, the raising of the youth Eutychus in Troas. Verses 7-8 set the scene: people were gathered in the upper room, and Paul was preaching. Eutychus was sitting in a window, and fell asleep because Paul talked so long. Thus he fell from the window and died. Paul's action consists in his going down and bending over the body, taking it in his arms, and saying to the others: "His life is in him" (v. 10). He does not speak to the dead man.

We must now compare the parallel texts, first reiterating the similarities and differences between the two accounts in Acts: While Peter's action consists in speaking, Paul's is characterized by physical contact. Peter only touches Tabitha when she has already sat up. Paul speaks only to the other persons present. While Peter brings about the raising of Tabitha in private, Paul's action is done in public view. The result of Tabitha's reawakening is an increase of believers, while in the case of Eutychus it is only the comforting of those present. While for Tabitha the technical term ἀνίστημι, "rise up," describing a resurrection, is used, no such thing is said of Eutychus. Paul says nothing to the dead man, but he clasps him close and then observes that his spirit ("life") is in him. In the text itself it is not clearly stated that this is a scene of raising someone from the dead. The only symbolic action of Paul that might indicate this is in v. 10a: "Paul . . . bending over him took him in his arms." On the basis of the parallels in 1 Kgs. 17:21; 2 Kgs. 4:34-35, in which the prophet lays or extends himself on the body of the dead person, we may suppose that when Paul says "his life is in him," this is to be understood as the consequence of his action. That interpretation can be derived from 2 Kgs. 4:34, according to which, as the result of the prophet's action of stretching himself on the child's body, "the flesh of the child became warm." But on the whole the two narratives are very different, from the cause of death to the apostle's action. There is, however, a redactional basis for the parallel between the two scenes if we note that, in Acts, Peter and Paul appear equally adept in the accomplishment of miraculous acts.[78]

There are more substantial similarities to the Old Testament accounts of the raising of dead persons.[79] The death is "from natural causes." Elijah, Elisha, and Peter are sought and summoned, and they enter the house. Both in Acts 9:37 and in 1 Kgs. 17:19, the dead have been placed in the upper room (ὑπερῷον). The "miracle workers" withdraw, remaining alone with the dead. The public is kept outside while the action is taking place. All three stories include both prayer and touch as aspects of the action.[80] Both in Acts 9:40 and in 2 Kgs. 4:35, the first sign of the reawakening is the opening of the eyes (ἤνοιξεν τοὺς ὀφθαλμούς). All three of those raised are returned, living, to their mothers or those close to them. Only in Acts 9:42 is it said that the event has become known to a broader audience. Hence Peter can be seen as standing in continuity with the prophetic miracles of Elijah and Elisha; he moves within that frame of reference.

We can observe considerable verbal similarities between the reports of the reawakenings accomplished by Peter and Jesus; these same similarities can be seen for the two Old Testament texts. The fact that the raising of the young man at Nain is found only in Luke's Gospel can mean that Luke is making deliberate reference to the resurrection stories in the two books of Kings, and is also connecting them with the raising of Tabitha: Common to all these stories is the problem of those left behind, who from a social point of view are in need of assistance. The miracle is especially beneficial to them. The "liturgical" action is similar in all four cases. However, there is one clear difference: except in John 11:41-42, Jesus does not pray. In contrast to the other accounts of reawakening, which from the point of view of the history of religions are quite similar, a raising by Jesus is accomplished without recourse to prayer, while for Peter, Elijah, and Elisha, prayer is an essential part of the action. One possible interpretation would be that the power to raise the dead is present only in Jesus, while others require intercession; they are, so to speak, intermediaries at a time when the assurance of salvation in the name of Christ has become visible.

It is important to keep in mind that in all these resurrection stories the people who directly or indirectly hope for or request the miracle are part of the whole episode. There is no immediate contact between the dead person and the miracle-worker: in each case he is summoned by third parties, the friends or family of the one who has died. From this point of view, the relationship between the dead person and her or his friends and family is also part of the miracle.

All this gives us the following pointers toward our conclusion: Despite the importance of the resurrection miracles in the Old and New Testaments, especially in Acts, it is striking that the literature listed above on the theme of resurrection fails to mention the two reawakening stories in 1 Kings 17 and 2 Kings 4. I have found only one remark, in Jakob Kremer's work, to the effect that all the resurrection stories described refer to "revivification and return to the previous life."[81] It is true that such reawakenings were unusual even at that time, and were simply incredible to many people, but still they were "entirely within the realm of what could be seen as imaginable and as possible for God to do."[82] But in my opinion the very fact of return to the previous life makes it obvious that none of these reawakening stories describes the content of the Jewish or Jewish-Christian resurrection hope or faith, for that hope and faith were characterized particularly by the idea that the resurrection of all humanity would take place on the day of the eschatological judgment, and that on that day something entirely new would come into existence: there would be a new creation. The resurrected people are changed (cf. 1 Corinthians 15) and they rise into a new world. "Our" resurrections take place in the old world. The people who have risen return to their old relationships. Therefore we cannot really speak of resurrection in these cases, but at most of reawakening. In this regard I agree with Gerd Theißen that the reawakenings belong to the genre of healings. (See further details below.)

In concluding this part, let me indicate that at least one Jewish text indicates how the rabbis interpreted the story of the raising of the son of the Shunammite woman in 2 Kgs. 4:32-37. The rabbis did not see it as an example of the eschatological resurrection, for which they hoped and in which they believed; instead, they regarded it as an example of the fact that good and merciful actions could even make it possible for a dead person to come to life again. This reawakening happened "before its time," and thus is not the same as resurrection. The interpretation is as follows:

> R. Judah b. Simon [ca. 320] said to him: "Because it is written of her that 'she constrained him to eat bread' did she merit that her son should be brought to life again?" R. Judan [ca. 350] said in the name of R. Zeira [ca. 300] and R. Jochanan [d. 279] in the name of R. Simeon b. Yoḥai [ca. 150]: "Great is the merit of maintaining the needy, since it causes the resurrection of the dead to come before its time. The woman of Zarephath because she maintained Elijah was rewarded by having her son brought to life. The Shunammite because she gave food to Elisha was rewarded by having her son brought to life."[83]

The Miraculous Power in Relationships, or: Confronting the Traditional Interpretations

In what follows, two interpretations of Acts 9:36-43 will be presented in terms of two possible exegetical models. Then the miracle story as it stands will be subjected to a more thorough confrontation with miracle research.

First, the two interpretations of the story: one characterizes the interpretive tradition of many centuries, while the second attempts to introduce a new perspective. However, I find difficulties in both.

The first interpretation reflects traditional exegesis, and is exemplified by Alfons Weiser's essay, "The Role of Women in the Primitive Christian Mission." In the section on "The Work of Women in the Spread of the Gospel," he expresses the opinion that Tabitha exercised only a caritative office.[84] While he lists the many statements in the text itself, he does not interpret them, or does so only selectively. In this selective interpretation, Weiser first reduces the good works of Tabitha mentioned in v. 36 to the making of clothes. Then, in connection with this, he observes that both the description of Tabitha in v. 36b and the presentation of the clothing in v. 39c are Lukan redaction. Thus Tabitha's sociopolitical activity vanishes from the transmitted narrative, that is, from the tradition. He then follows with an explanation for Luke's additions: they are designed to show that Tabitha deserves a miracle. Thus only the miracle, and still more the miracle-worker, Peter, are central to the story.

Such an interpretation emphasizes precisely what the text does *not* say: That Tabitha's service was restricted to charitable work. Moreover, it reduces that work to the making of clothing for widows. The miracle is based on Tabitha's worthiness for being its recipient, with Peter the principal figure.

This kind of traditional interpretation is rightly criticized by Gerd Petzke.[85] He begins his own treatment with a more precise analysis of the concepts within the text, because it does not use words without a specific intention. In its context, each word has a single meaning. Petzke concentrates his attention especially on the description of the concept of "disciple." From it, and from the history of primitive Christianity, he correctly concludes that Tabitha's work was not only social, but also missionary. But he reads the text itself critically and skeptically, since for him it in fact reveals only the diaconal function of Tabitha. His fundamental criticism of the text is that Luke's redactional work has brought about, and even intended, a separation between mission and *diakonia*. This, he says, comes about when "the text restricts its description of Tabitha to her social function."[86] In my opinion, this critique does not do justice to the text. One of the premises of Petzke's work was that one should give close attention to the concepts Luke is handing on. There is general agreement that the description of Tabitha as μαθήτρια, "disciple," includes her within the work of proclamation. But, like most exegetes, Petzke ignores, in respect to this question, precisely what becomes even clearer on a closer examination of the further description of Tabitha in v. 36: Tabitha's missionary activity is not only presumed by the title "disciple," but is subsumed in the application of the concept of "good works," which at the time was a technical term.[87] This Jewish understanding corresponds to the early Christian experience that there was, as yet, no sharp distinction between "social work" and "missionary activity." Both could be carried on simultaneously, for example in the context of craft work within the working spaces of a house church.[88] This kind of inclusive work did not yet require any kind of special institutional framework. Such an understanding of a broadly conceived "social work" could, in fact, have the breadth Petzke misses in Acts 9:36-43: namely, that Tabitha did more in her working hours to promote the spread of the faith in Joppa than Peter did in passing through. Because Petzke also completely ignores Tabitha's craft work, an important entry to understanding the text remains closed to him, with the further result that, in his work, the widows take on a purely passive role.

From these two interpretations and my critique of them it becomes clear, I think, that interpreters of the text frequently confuse two levels: the statement of the text itself, and the interpretation of the text as such. I say this because the restriction of Tabitha's activity to charitable work is primarily a problem of interpretation. The source of the problem does not lie in Luke's redactional work, because informed hearers and readers of that time had no difficulty in understanding various aspects of Tabitha's work as soon as she was described: for them, the work of proclamation was already included in the concepts of "disciple" and "one who does good works."

It is striking that neither interpretation finds room for the topic of Tabitha's craft work, or for the central theme of relationship, which must have been very powerful since, ultimately, it brought about the miracle.

In my view, the whole event in Joppa is to be regarded as a miracle. I understand a miracle to be the expression of power in relationship.[89] I know of no miracle that happens outside a relationship. A close relationship between the people who participate in the miracle itself, or in the preparation for it, can be demonstrated at every point. On the one hand, there is the relationship between the persons who experience the miracle. This usually appears in the preparatory phase and at the end of the occurrence. It is a close, often even a dependent relationship of friends or relatives (e.g., Luke 7:2-10, 11-17; 8:41-42; Acts 9:38-39). Second, there is the relationship between the friends or relatives, or the subject, and the miracle worker. This is expressed in physical touch, in seeing, and in words (e.g., Luke 7:14; 8:43-48, 50; Acts 3:1-10; 9:40). Third, there is the relationship between the miracle worker and the divine power from which the miraculous power emanates. This is indicated by prayer and the invoking of the name of the god who brings about the miracle (e.g., Acts 3:6; 4:30; 9:40). Essentially, these and similar relationships can be observed in every miracle story; consequently, they are part and parcel of a miracle.

In Acts, the miracle stories are given an important place in order to show the great power of God, whose effectiveness is now being revealed through the apostles in the name of Jesus Christ. It is therefore all the more astonishing that there is no extensive study of this subject.[90] Erich Gräβer, in his review of Acts research, calls this "baffling."[91]

Frans Neirynck[92] summarizes the material on the treatment of miracles within the framework of major commentaries and monographs. His overview again shows that, at the level of content, very little is said about the narrative in Acts 9:36-43. There is more activity at the level of form criticism, and if anything is said about content, it focuses on the miracle workers and thus on the ultimate purpose of the miracle as part of the missionary work that is not only urged, but recognized by God. It is asserted that the special significance of the miraculous signs is that "in them is to be found an essential and indispensable part of the divine authentication of the apostles."[93] In this connection it is still more astonishing how frequently it happens that the narrative in Acts 9:36-43 is not only passed over without discussion, but even omitted altogether in essays that treat the theme of miraculous "resurrection" or "resuscitation."[94] In the commentaries, the parallels to other New and Old Testament resurrection stories are listed, but the narrative is seldom interpreted in and for itself.

The narrative in Acts 9:36-43 contains all three levels of the miracle-relationship, and yet it is this very aspect of relationship that disappears in commentaries on this story. One could get the impression that, in a literary-critical investigation, even the relationship between Peter and the raised woman vanishes, since interest is concentrated on the power that operates independently from above, or on the demonstration of a power that uses other people as instruments, rather than on the relationship that is empowered in and through other people.

I agree with Gerd Theißen's opinion that Christian exegetes use a variety of methods to minimize the miraculous element in the miracle stories.[95] Especially in the history of religions there is an apologetic attempt to embed Christian miracles in the world of ideas of that time, but simultaneously to distance them from that world. The result is that what is uniquely Christian is emphasized at the expense of other experiences. This can be seen with especial clarity in the question of the form and intention of the New Testament miracle stories: "It seems impossible to eradicate the view that ancient miracles outside the New Testament were described for their own sake, but that the New Testament miracles are in the service of an intention which includes more than miracles."[96] Another difficulty is created by attempts to minimize a miracle story historically. "This 'historical' underplaying of the miracles takes place in attempts to interpret the miracles in terms of their 'historical kernel.' It is claimed that the historical element in them is natural and that only interpretation turns this into a miracle."[97] Added to these is the minimizing of miracle stories by an interiorizing approach: "In this view the miracles themselves are not the point of the stories, which always carry a reference to something else."[98] Theißen believes that these last two aspects are not so problematic at present. I think otherwise, for with reference to the story of the raising of Tabitha, the commentators quoted often lay special emphasis on the "historical" kernel of the story, and are more interested in the ultimate goal of the miracle than in the miracle itself and its immediate effects on those concerned.

This can be illustrated most clearly in the work of J. Kreyenbühl,[99] whose emphases still find advocates today. He asserts:

> Simon Peter was staying in Lydda, apparently for missionary purposes. He traveled from there to Joppa and founded a community embodied by the charitable woman Tabitha/Dorcas. We certainly have no reason to doubt that there were women doing good works in the community at Joppa, who even today can serve as models for women's charitable organizations. But *the non-historical nature of the raising of Tabitha/Dorcas requires that we eliminate her as an individual person* and see her simply as the personification of the messianic community at Joppa, "which was devoted to good works and acts of charity." . . . Since we are not to think of a particular person, her death and reawakening, and yet it is impossible that the whole thing can be pure fable, . . . the *historical kernel* of the story is the fact that *Simon Peter* . . . achieved important missionary successes in Lydda, Joppa, and elsewhere, winning the people of the region to the new messianic movement by teaching the resurrection of believers through Jesus, the Messiah.[100]

In summary, this means first that the historical core of this miracle story is Peter's preaching of the resurrection in Joppa, with the Christian community being understood as the "daughter of the resurrection"; and second that the historical core (preaching) has been translated into a miracle story in which the "daughter of the resurrection" has become a charitable disciple of Jesus who falls sick and dies, and whom the preacher of resurrection then restores to life. This allegorizing makes possible and even demands the conclusion that the miracle story exists to call, or reawaken, the dead community to life through missionary work.

Rudolf Pesch also sees an "appeal to the community" in this story, but does not feel it necessary to deny the existence of Tabitha. According to him, the purpose of the story is to lead a dead community back to life.

> The fact that the raising of Tabitha is connected with her service to the widows in the community is not merely a feature associated with Luke's

interest in "pious care for the poor." It is an indication that the tradition knows that incidents of "raising the dead" cannot be individual miracles that are susceptible to being isolated from their context, but instead are "appeals" to the dead community in which the power to maintain life and intensify its social integration is in danger of disappearing.[101]

Gerd Lüdemann is not interested in the intention of the narrative; his concern is to determine whether it belongs to tradition.[102] He describes the "historical basis" as follows: for him, a visit of Peter to Lydda and Joppa is the historical core of Acts 9:32-42. Whether the miracle traditions arose in those places or were first associated with them by Luke is a question that remains unresolved. Ordinarily, miracle traditions were associated with leading figures in primitive Christianity. Thus on the one hand we cannot assert that these miracles really happened in those places, and involved Aeneas and Tabitha; on the other hand it cannot be denied that "Aeneas may have had a connection with Peter which can no longer be discovered. The same is true of Tabitha—though in her case that is less probable."[103] Here, a historical visit of Peter to Lydda and Joppa is posited, but his relationship to the people in those places is not acknowledged. The visit, and Peter's staying in those places, can be reconstructed. The miracle, on the other hand, cannot be substantiated.

It is thus possible to read this miracle story from a variety of perspectives, and in light of a number of different questions. In the process, it unfortunately happens that attention is seldom paid to the content and the meaning of such an event for those concerned. The same is true of the description by Gudrun Muhlack, according to whom the resurrection miracles in Acts (9:36-43; 20:7-12) have a compositional purpose for Luke: "Just as the miracle of raising a dead person represented a high point of Jesus' activity in Galilee, such a miracle forms the conclusion to both parts of Acts. Peter's raising of Tabitha is the last of his miracles described by Luke, and takes place shortly before the beginning of the Gentile mission. Paul raises Eutychus during a farewell meal in Troas; shortly afterward he begins his journey to Jerusalem."[104]

Muhlack's observation is correct. But it is questionable whether Luke intended to craft the various stories in such a precise way, or whether he thought in a "progressive" series at all. Finally, it is also questionable whether the author saw a qualitative difference, for example, between the miracles in Acts 3:1-10 and 9:36-43. In my view, both of these are high points in Peter's work and both, to an equal degree although with different effects, make possible a fullness of life.

In conclusion, let me make some remarks about the form-critical categorization of the text of Acts 9:36-43. It belongs to the genre of "miracle stories."[105] According to Gerd Theißen,[106] this genre has a structured form that can be subdivided into smaller units with reference to persons, motifs, and themes. From his inventory, we may conclude that Acts 9:36-43 has a number of *motifs*: first, the "appearance of embassies" (v. 38). Compositionally, this motif is part of the introduction. "The principal setting is healings, here particularly raisings of the dead (Mark 5:35; John 11; Acts 9:36-43) or healings of people close to death";[107] second, the exclusion of the public is part of "setting the scene." Compositionally, this motif should "normally directly precede the miracle proper";[108] third, healing and the raising of dead persons were effected by "touching." "The more intense the contact, the more vital force can be transferred: hence the contact with the whole body in the case of the dead. The slighter the healing contact is, the greater does the power which passes seem to be. . . ."[109] For this motif also, the context in the New Testament is always in the realm of healing; fourth, the "miracle-working word" is a word of power, here spoken by Peter. With its speaking, the miracle occurs; fifth, "prayer" or a gesture resembling prayer is frequently found "in healings by disciples (Acts 9:40, 28:8)";[110] sixth, the "recognition of the miracle" can also, as in this case, occur without the miraculous character of the event being underscored; seventh, the "demonstration" of the miracle occurs after the fact has been established: "In healings the newly acquired physical power is demonstrated by activity,"[111] which is here expressed in v. 40b by Tabitha's opening her eyes, seeing Peter, and then sitting up; eighth, the "dismissal" consists in giving those who have experienced the miracle to their friends or family, as here stated in v. 41. Compositionally, this motif belongs at the end of the narrative. "The context is almost always a healing."[112]

In this listing of the motifs appearing in Acts 9:36-43 we have repeatedly used the word "healing," which designates a miracle theme. It appears in Theißen's work because he assigns the raising of the dead to the theme of "healings."[113] Both the miraculous act of "healing" and the miraculous act of "exorcism" are "the exercise of a numinous power." But whereas in the second type there is a struggle, the first represents a restorative communication of strength produced by a word of faith and a healing touch. "The laying on of hands is thus a healing motif."[114]

In light of the results of Gerd Theißen's research on miracle stories, but perhaps already on the basis of what we have said about Jewish and

Christian belief in the resurrection, we can say of Acts 9:36-43 that it depicts a miracle story whose theme is a healing that was made possible by the power of relationship. The designation "healing" does not trivialize the meaning of the miracle. It simply helps us to understand the miracle of resuscitation more clearly. The miraculous power of relationship can extend even into death, but it cannot finally overcome death as an enduring counterforce, once and for all. Death continues to exist in the "old" world into which Tabitha and the son of the Shunammite were raised. Therefore the miracle is only therapeutic, and is not to be understood as resurrection in the eschatological sense.[115] This miracle has not made the "old" world new, but it can express the hope that, through the possibility of renewed living and lifegiving deeds by Tabitha and other saints, a new quality of power in relationship can be introduced into the "old" world. This is the place that needs to be impregnated with such a miraculous power.

The miraculous power of relationship reveals its might beyond the framework of the Tabitha story as well: The story of the raising of Tabitha comes to a literary end with the assertion in v. 41b that Peter showed her alive to the saints and widows. From there on, the story of Tabitha cannot be reconstructed. The future remains open. In retrospect, we may suppose that Tabitha would renew her works of righteousness, her craft work on behalf of the widows. The open end of the narrative, in my opinion, exists to bring the readers into the story and to allow them to discover and develop their opportunities for continued life on behalf of, and in community with, the socially disadvantaged. This is reinforced by the statement in v. 42. The immediate effect of this story is that many came to believe. These were not only the people who saw and were part of the miracle, because they were already part of the group of the saints. Verse 42 expands to encompass those who heard the story later. It is not the miracle itself, but the proclamation of the miracle that has a missionary effect. Through the spread of faith, the attraction of many women and men to Jesus Christ, the hope of the Christians of the time was expressed in a constantly growing community, in which widows and other single people, and those who are socially and economically abandoned, could find a non-patriarchal home.[116]

Summary Reflections

The narrative in Acts 9:36-43 presumes a Jewish-Christian community. We do not know how it originated: It could have been the fruit of the work of people driven out of Jerusalem (Acts 8:1), or the result of Peter's missionary activity. In any case it certainly appears that Peter had contacts and acquaintances there, perhaps especially Tabitha, since according to vv. 38-39 the messengers did not need to offer any further explanation to induce him to hasten to Joppa.

In this Jewish-Christian community worked a disciple named Tabitha. That title describes following Jesus, and includes the work of proclamation. Tabitha is a Christian. She lives a Jewish life. In describing Tabitha's style of life, Luke provides the best and most extensive proof that he did not regard Jewish spirituality either as offensive or as a barrier to faith in Christ. The example of a Jewish life lived by a Christian woman matches the example of the Gentile Cornelius. Jewish pious practices on behalf of the poor are neither challenged nor overthrown by this story. On the contrary: such a spirituality is both confessed and practiced by Tabitha, who is at the center of the story. A Jewish-Christian woman had no need to repudiate her roots.

The description of Tabitha's works in v. 36 is given a degree of concreteness by the appearance of the widows in v. 39. They tell us that Tabitha herself produced both outer- and undergarments during their time together. The widows, together with the clothing, witness to Tabitha. This concrete example of Tabitha's works is, in my opinion, not identical with the comprehensive concept of good works, but is to be understood as a part of the whole. Nor is this example to be interpreted as "almsgiving," because these are not crumbs from the table of the rich, but products of her own hands. Tabitha has put part of herself into this work, and thus gives of herself. In the clothing, the widows hold fast to the memory of Tabitha, whose work was done on their behalf.

The righteous works of Tabitha and the widows who shared in her work stood as witness for her. Only after this testimony does Peter undertake the actions that witness also to the power he has received from God. God affirms Tabitha's work by making it possible, through the mediation of Peter, for Tabitha to renew her life in community with the saints and widows. Tabitha is the center of this story also because, without her, the power of God would not have been attested in this manner. Without Tabitha and her life, outstanding for its righteous works, this story of reawakening could never have been, or at any rate it would not have been handed on to us in this way. Without her, too, we would know nothing about the existence of the widows, who only appear in the context of their life with Tabitha in Joppa. That is a question that seems scarcely to interest the exegetes.

The raising of Tabitha takes place in the absence of any onlookers. There are parallels to this in 1 Kgs. 17:19-22; 2 Kgs. 4:33-35. It is an action for which Peter, too, must be alone in order to receive the power to effect change. His power in relationship to Tabitha is a sign of his power in relationship to God. This last can be observed in his prayer, which is his first act. One could also say that God "stands up" for Peter and for Tabitha in and through this relationship. Through the relationship, Tabitha is raised up. The death of Tabitha had set a great many things in motion. The raising of Tabitha presupposes a lot of movement. Her reawakening is a sign of power in relationship: it shows how strong a power in relationship can be. It requires human cooperation: the two messengers who brought Peter, the widows who witnessed for Tabitha, Peter who says the powerful words to Tabitha. All of them together are the outstretched hands of God. All of them together are agents of the miracle. Each of them is indispensable to the whole relationship.[117]

From the point of view of Jewish and Jewish-Christian resurrection faith, we should not speak here of "resurrection," but of "reawakening" or "resuscitation." The former will happen at the end of time, the latter in this eon. The former presumes that everything will be made new; the latter occurs within the "old" situation. Acts 9:36-43, therefore, like the parallel biblical texts, represents a miracle story whose theme is a healing carried out in and through the power of relationship. This miracle did not make the "old" world new, but it can express the hope that the possibility for renewed, living, and life-giving deeds on the part of Tabitha and other saints can bring a new quality of power in relationship into the "old" world.

The miracle story in Acts 9:36-43 witnesses to the raising of a just woman. The raising of Tabitha could thus also be interpreted as God's "yes" to her Jewish-Christian way of life. Two effects of this story seem obvious to me: One is a consequence inherent in the story, namely that through this miracle God returned Tabitha to her service to the socially deprived. The second is the boundary-breaking affirmation in v. 42 that many, women and men, came to believe in Jesus when they heard of this miracle. They, too—like Tabitha—could put themselves in the service of the one God and, through their righteous works, become sources of life.

Notes

1. Cf. R. Pesch, *Apostelgeschichte* 1:319.
2. So also Gerd Lüdemann, *Early Christianity According to the Traditions in*

Acts, 123, who, however, in vv. 32-43 sees a historical basis only for Peter's presence in Lydda and Joppa.

3. See R. Pesch, *Apostelgeschichte* 1:320: "In the context, the miraculous healing of Aeneas and the raising of Tabitha are preludes to *the greater miracle: the conversion of the Gentile Cornelius."* Emphasis supplied.

4. Cf. J. Roloff, *Apostelgeschichte,* 158.

5. See, for example, R. Knopf, "Apostelgeschichte," 42, who thinks that Luke included the Tabitha narrative (which already existed in the tradition) at such length in his account in order to show how Peter "came into the vicinity of Caesarea, where in chapter 10 he undertakes the very important conversion of Cornelius." Cf. A. Loisy, *Actes,* 431; G. Schneider, *Apostelgeschichte* 2:46: "The two miracle stories in 9:32-35, 36-43 are both a topical and geographical introduction . . . to the Cornelius story." W. Schmithals writes (*Apostelgeschichte,* 98) that Acts 9:32-43 serves "to open the way for Peter to [make] the first Gentile conversion in Caesarea." J. Comblin represents the same point of view (*Atos* 2:187): "This narrative is placed here to introduce the great event of the reception of Cornelius by Peter. It serves to show how Peter came to be in the region of Caesarea." On the other hand, E. Haenchen writes with more subtlety (*Acts,* 341): "Now, what was Luke trying to tell his readers with these two stories [Aeneas and Tabitha]? The answer must differ according to whether one enquires as to the meaning of the individual stories or their significance in the context. The first relates the lesser miracle. . . . The second story he has left relatively untouched. It showed the reader that where miracles were concerned the Apostles could stand comparison with the great prophets of the Old Testament—indeed, . . . could do the same mighty works as their Master, if not mightier still!" But ultimately these stories remain within the context of the spread of Christian faith, a process that reaches its great climax in the story of Cornelius.

6. See for example, Werner Wiesner, "12. Sonntag nach Trinitatis. Apg. 9,36-42," in idem, *Göttinger Predigtmeditationen* II/3 (1947–1948), 62–64.

7. M. Hengel, "Der Historiker Lukas," 171.

8. Josephus, *Bell.* 2.508-9.

9. Josephus, *Bell.* 3.414-15.

10. For the use of τὶς + personal name, Acts 21:16 is of special relevance for the present passage, since there also one of the disciples is mentioned by name. The same is true of the emphasis on one among a number of god-fearers in Acts 22:12. See also Acts 10:5-6; Luke 23:26.

11. Diogenes Laertius 4.2; 8.42, where women are disciples of philosophical schools; see also Philo, *Deus imm.* 5; Diodorus Siculus, *History* 2.52.7. Cf. K. H. Rengstorf, "μαθητής, κτλ," *TDNT* 4:460–61, and G. Schneider, *Apostelgeschichte* 2:51.

12. Adolf von Harnack, *Mission and Expansion* 1:399-421, summarizes the various names for Christians, and also quite explicitly mentions Tabitha among

the disciples. Cf. also K. H. Rengstorf, "μαθητής," *TDNT* 4:415–61, and for its use in Acts, especially 457–59; however, it is striking that in this section, in listing all the "disciples" appearing in Acts, he does not mention Tabitha even once. This could be misleading, because an unsuspecting reader might conclude from it that there were no women among the disciples. It seems to me that in the section on pp. 457–59 Rengstorf should at least have indicated that he would give more detailed information about Tabitha at a later point, on the last pages of the article (460–61). Nevertheless, Tabitha was not mentioned by J. Jeremias, "Quellenproblem," 213–21, where he discusses an "Antiochene source" in Acts. One of its principal features is said to be the use of the word μαθητής; in addition, Peter does not appear. This source, probably written, would have included Acts 6:1—8:4; 9:1-30; 11:19-30/12:25; 13:1—14:28; 15:35ff. Everything else in the present text is said to be a Lukan insertion. But it is questionable, at least, to exclude Acts 9:36-43 from the source, considering that the concept of μαθηταί, said to be characteristic of the source, appears not once, but twice. It might at least be suggested that this part of the account—the presence of female disciples in Joppa—was contained in the source and that the addition of Peter, since he is not supposed to have been included in the source, could have been Lukan redaction.

13. K. H. Rengstorf, "μαθητής, κτλ," *TDNT* 4:458.

14. See Billerbeck 2:417; K. H. Rengstorf, "μαθητής," *TDNT* 4:435, 447.

15. Cf. K. H. Rengstorf, "μαθητής," *TDNT* 4:431–41, with list of sources.

16. Ibid., 461; cf. also Bernadette J. Brooten, *Women Leaders in the Ancient Synagogue*, 141; see the literature listed in both.

17. See further in K. H. Rengstorf, "μαθητής," *TDNT* 4:445–55. In my opinion, this author places too much value on distinguishing the usage in Judaism and Christianity. This leads to such statements as, for example, that the rabbis' disciples were members of a chain of tradition, while Jesus' disciples, in contrast, were his witnesses (cf. 453–54 and elsewhere). It does not seem to me that the two are mutually exclusive. The Jewish sources would have to be examined to determine more precisely whether they, too, do not contain a witnessing to their master. It remains an open question why Jesus' disciples should not also be regarded as the bearers of his tradition.

18. For the use and meaning of this name among Jews and Greeks, see Billerbeck 2:694; R. Pesch, *Apostelgeschichte* 1:322; see also G. Muhlack, "Parallelen," 65–66.

19. See Billerbeck 2:694, with literature. A woman named Tabitha who was very active in the work of prophetic preaching appears in *Apoc. Elijah* 34.

20. J. Viteau, "L'Institution," 532.

21. J. A. McNamara, *A New Song*, 34.

22. Billerbeck 6/1:559; cf. 536ff. It is very difficult, and perhaps impossible, to comprehend these two excursuses clearly and without ambiguity. It seems to me that the attempt to classify good works in Judaism within separate categories has resulted in a great degree of fragmentation.

23. See the further examples in G. Bertram, "ἔργον," *TDNT* 2:644. Unlike Bertram, I do not believe that one can simply classify such texts under the title "Man's work as sin and vanity," because they almost always refer not only to "evil" but also to "good" works side by side.

24. Cf. J. B. Lightfoot and J. R. Harmer, *The Apostolic Fathers* (London, 1891; repr. Grand Rapids, 1988), 271–72.

25. G. Bertram, "ἔργον, κτλ," *TDNT* 2:635–55, esp. 643–52.

26. Ibid. He subdivides section C under the following titles: "Human labour as a curse," "Man's work as sin and vanity," "The righteousness of works in later Judaism," "The righteousness of works and the thought of reward," "The work of man as a divinely given task," and "Word and act, faith and works."

27. See merely the last two pages of Bertram's article.

28. Quotations from R. Bultmann, "ἔλεος, κτλ," *TDNT* 2:479.

29. Ibid., 483.

30. The fourth chapter of the second letter of Clement to the Corinthians is an appeal to the practice of justice. Clement believes that it is not sufficient for the attainment of salvation to appeal to Christ as "Lord"; with reference to Matt. 7:2 he asserts that it is necessary to do justice. He extends the argument by attempting to make the concept of "justice" concrete: "So then, brethren, let us confess Him in our works, by loving one another, not by committing adultery nor speaking evil one against another nor envying, but by being temperate, merciful, kindly. . . . By these works let us confess Him, and not by the contrary."

31. R. Bultmann, "ἔλεος, κτλ," *TDNT* 2:485.

32. Ibid., 486.

33. Ibid. Emphasis supplied.

34. We may note this tendency in Billerbeck 1:387, as well: there we read that ἐλεημοσύνη means "human compassion or the human exercise of mercy, that is, almsgiving."

35. R. Bultmann, "ἔλεος," *TDNT* 2:486.

36. For the rabbinic use of עשׂה צדקה to mean "give alms," see Billerbeck 1:388; 2:188–89.

37. L. Schottroff, "Alles entscheidet sich," 11.

38. R. Bultmann's opinion is somewhat different: "ἔλεος," *TDNT* 2:486.

39. Cf. Billerbeck 1:386–87.

40. Ibid., 386.

41. On this, see Billerbeck 4/1, excursus on "Ancient Jewish Private Acts of Charity," where, for example at p. 537a there is reference to some characteristics of good works in rabbinic texts, but in the listing of texts on pp. 538–39 the use of the concepts is not so clear and uniform. Thus good works are spoken of in terms of works of love, and according to Billerbeck 4/1:536, these also include visiting the sick, hospitality to strangers, etc.

42. Ḥag. 5a (Billerbeck 1:391); *Sipre Deut.* 15.10 §117 (98b) (Billerbeck 4/1:545).

43. Billerbeck 4/1:546.

44. Ibid., 552.

45. See, for example, the texts listed by Billerbeck 4/1:552ff. and (!) 539ff.

46. See, for example, Matt. 6:1ff.; Mark 12:41; Ḥag. 5a (Billerbeck 1:391); Sipre Deut. 15.10 §117 (98b) (Billerbeck 4/1:545).

47. This is not the place for this discussion. For more detail, let me refer to H. Bolkestein, Wohltätigkeit, passim.

48. On this, see the Jewish literature on works of love listed below in n. 59.

49. On this, see Billerbeck 4/1:537ff.

50. T. Zahn, Apostelgeschichte 1:336ff., does not mention the works of Tabitha. He devotes his analysis primarily to the meaning of her name. The same is true of the commentary by R. Knopf, "Apostelgeschichte," 42, where it is also said that her resurrection is not very credible, but is a legend based on Mark 5:40-41.

51. For the anointing of a body—basically a second action in the ritual of mourning—see S. Krauss, Talmudische Archäologie 2:54ff.

52. On this, see the details in S. Krauss, Talmudische Archäologie 2:54ff. That the washing is part of the preparation for burial is clear from Shab. 23.5 (151a): "All the requirements of the dead may be done [on the Sabbath]: he may be anointed with oil and washed. Provided that no limb of his is moved." See Billerbeck 1:987. Luise Schottroff, "Mary Magdalene," 181–82, 200–201, has pointed out that this action was also practiced outside Jewish circles.

53. The concept of a ὑπερῷον or "upper room" appears otherwise in the New Testament only in Acts, at 1:13; 9:37, 39; 20:8. According to Acts 1:13 and 20:8, that was the place where the community assembled. This picture corresponds to the rabbinic idea that this place could be used, among other purposes, for assembly, prayer, and as a living room. On this, see Billerbeck 2:594.

54. R. Pesch, Apostelgeschichte 1:323. This is the usual interpretation.

55. For the mourning and watching over the dead in a house, see Luke 8:40-42, 49ff.; 2 Kgs. 4:19ff.; cf. S. Krauss, Talmudische Archäologie 2:54ff.

56. J. Comblin, Atos 1:187.

57. For more detail on this type of women's work, see below, pp. 99–101.

58. We know that in Roman law the dowry brought by a woman to her marriage was destined for her care after the death of her husband, should there be anything remaining of it, inasmuch as the dowry was used to pay the costs of the common household. See B. Kreck, Untersuchungen, 18–19. In Jewish law, after a husband's death levirate marriage (marriage to a brother-in-law) could be called upon. On the opportunities for a widow to marry, see S. Krauss, Talmudische Archäologie 2:53ff.; E. Koffmahn, Doppelurkunden, 26, 30, and pp. 2–6 above. But that most widowed women were in a situation of social need (greater than before) can be presumed simply on the basis of the ethical admoni-

tions to kindness and care for them. See G. Stählin, "χήρα," *TDNT* 9:440–65.

59. In *Pe'a* 4.19 (24) we read: "Charity צדקה (alms) and loving deeds are more weighty than all the commandments in the Torah; but charity is practiced toward the living, loving deeds for the living and the dead; charity is for the poor, loving deeds for the poor and the rich; charity with money, loving deeds with one's own self and with money." See Billerbeck 4/1:537.

60. In the third and fourth centuries there were fixed rules for the official care of widows; cf. G. Stählin, "χήρα," *TDNT* 9:460–61.

61. Ibid., 452.

62. Ibid. Emphasis supplied.

63. For more detailed information, let me refer to C. Thoma, "Auferstehung," 30–35; H. C. Cavallin, "Leben," 242–324; G. Stemberger, *Leib*, 5–119; J. Kremer, "Auferstehung," 7–164.

64. *Ber.* 7.5; cf. A. Oepke, "ἀνίστημι," *TDNT* 1:368–71, at 370.

65. S. Schonfeld, *The Standard Siddur-Prayer Book with an Orthodox English Translation* (London, 1976).

66. See the brief commentary and summary explanation of Enoch in P. Riessler, *Altjüdisches Schrifttum*, 1291–97; also H. C. Cavallin, "Leben," 252ff.

67. Translation by E. Isaac in James H. Charlesworth, ed., *The Old Testament Pseudepigrapha*. 2 vols. (Garden City, 1983–1985), 1:72.

68. See G. Stemberger, *Leib*, 45.

69. See C. Thoma, "Auferstehung," which offers a comprehensive overview.

70. Translation by H. C. Kee in Charlesworth, ed., *The Old Testament Pseudepigrapha*, 1:801–2.

71. Ibid., 827–28. Bracketed material according to the translation by M. DeJonge in H. F. D. Sparks, ed., *The Apocryphal Old Testament* (Oxford, 1984), 599.

72. Translation by R. B. Wright in Charlesworth, ed., *The Old Testament Pseudepigrapha*, 2:655.

73. Translation by A. F. J. Klijn in Charlesworth, ed., *The Old Testament Pseudepigrapha*, 1:631.

74. Translation by J. J. Collins in Charlesworth, ed., *The Old Testament Pseudepigrapha*, 1:385, 389.

75. See the citations in Billerbeck 4/1:1172ff.; on the whole question, see J. Kremer, "Auferstehung," passim.

76. G. Stemberger, *Leib*, 115.

77. J. Kremer, "Auferstehung," 10.

78. F. Neirynck, "Miracle Stories," 172ff., offers a survey of research on this topic.

79. See B. Lindars, "Elijah," 63ff.

80. G. Schille, *Apostelgeschichte*, 240, offers the following interpretation: "In place of a magical touch, simply turning toward the corpse is sufficient here; on the basis of 1 Kgs. 17:21 one might suppose that the motif of stretching

oneself on the corpse would have been offensive in the case of a woman."
Unfortunately, this author does not say what kind of offense he thinks might
have been given in this case.

81. J. Kremer, "Auferstehung," 10.

82. Ibid.

83. *Midr.* Song of Songs 2.5 (98a). See Billerbeck 4/1:567.

84. A. Weiser, "Frau," 169–70.

85. G. Petzke, "Diakonie," 238ff.

86. Ibid., 241.

87. See pp. 36–41 above.

88. For more on this subject, see chapter 5 below, on Priscilla.

89. For this concept, and for the theological meaning of power in relationship, see Carter Heyward, *The Redemption of God,* passim.

90. G. W. H. Lampe gives a general overview in "Miracles," 163ff.

91. E. Gräßer, "Acta-Forschung" (1977), 15–16: "Miracle stories have a
relatively large place in Acts. They are an important means for the demonstration of the mighty acts of God that are done through the hands of the apostles.
As a reporter on the literature on Acts, one is all the more baffled to find that
there is almost nothing written on this topic." See the literature listed there.

92. F. Neirynck, "Miracle Stories," 169ff.

93. K. H. Rengstorf, "σημεῖον," *TDNT* 7:242.

94. See, for example, J. Kremer, "Auferstehung," 8ff., who mentions this
story only once (p. 10), but does not discuss it further; the same is true of A.
Oepke's scholarly study of the word ἀνίστημι in *TDNT* 1:368–71. And because
in the narrative of Acts 9:36–43 (as also in vv. 32–35) the word σημεῖον is not
employed, it is not listed in K. H. Rengstorf's essay in *TDNT* 7:200–69.

95. G. Theißen, *Miracle Stories,* 291–302, lists three basic methods for this
minimizing, drawn respectively from the history of religions, redaction criticism,
and tradition criticism. He gives examples of each.

96. Ibid., 292.

97. Ibid., 298.

98. Ibid.

99. J. Kreyenbühl, "Ursprung," 267ff.

100. Ibid., 267–68. Emphasis supplied.

101. R. Pesch, *Apostelgeschichte* 1:325.

102. G. Lüdemann, *Traditions,* 122–23.

103. Ibid., 123.

104. G. Muhlack, "Parallelen," 56.

105. This assertion has offered no problem for scholars. See R. Pesch,
Apostelgeschichte 1:321: "The *narrative of the raising of a dead person* is
constructed according to the typical pattern of the genre, according to which the
miracle worker is brought to the house of the dead person."

106. G. Theißen, *Miracle Stories,* "Introduction," pp. 1–40.

107. Ibid., 50.
108. Ibid., 61.
109. Ibid., 62.
110. Ibid., 65.
111. Ibid., 66.
112. Ibid., 68.
113. Theißen says this explicitly in *Miracle Stories* 90, n. 25.
114. Ibid., 92. J. Roloff indicates (*Apostelgeschichte,* 160) that Tabitha was healed by Peter.
115. For that reason, this reawakening has no connection with the "false" idea of resurrection that was dominant, for example, in Corinth, and that referred only to a withdrawal from the world; it is this against which Ernst Käsemann so urgently warns (*Jesus Means Freedom,* 59–84).
116. With this interpretation of the miraculous event and the proclamation of the miracle in Joppa I am opposing the opinion of G. Petzke that the miracle "in our text by no means expresses the community's hope for change. Behind it is, instead, the patriarchally-influenced image of the spread of Christian faith through male, miracle-working missionaries."
117. The commentaries that interpret Peter alone as the miracle worker and the one on whom the whole event depends, of course, see the matter differently. See, for example, J. Roloff, *Apostelgeschichte,* 161; R. Pesch, *Apostelgeschichte* 1:323–24; G. Schille, *Apostelgeschichte,* 239–40.

3

Lydia and Her House
(16:13-15, 40)

Lydia is a woman with a central position in the Acts of the Apostles. She, together with Sapphira and the prophetic slave, is one of the few women in Luke's work who has a chance to speak. She does speak. And what she says is theologically significant. Lydia, like Priscilla, is described in terms of her profession. She is the only female god-fearer who is named in Acts. Her key position and particular importance for Acts are expressed in many ways, including the fact that she, with the other women gathered in the synagogue building, is the first person with whom Paul comes in contact on the soil of Macedonia, that is, in Europe. She is the first person in this region who gathers a house church in her own house. And yet she does not receive much honor. Her story, like that of Tabitha, is commonly treated in European exegesis as a "prologue" to the "real" conversion story, that of the Philippian jailer. Let me illustrate this tendency in the interpretations with a single example:

Gottfried Schille gives it as his opinion that Luke has transferred the Lydia story to another geographical location. There was a Lydia tradition, but originally it did not belong to Philippi; it was placed there by Luke. The reason why Lydia's story is not appropriate to Philippi, according to Schille, is that it is scarcely imaginable that there could be "two foundation stories for the church community in a single city."[1] What that really means is that only the jailer's story could be the "real" story about Philippi. Schille thus reduces the Lydia story to a "prologue" for the genuine Philippi narrative.[2] But it seems to me that in doing so the author fails to ask the most important questions, and therefore has no answers for them: Why would Luke have chosen precisely *this* story as a prologue? Why were the broader religious, economic, and political conflicts, together with the arrest of the Christian envoys and the story of the jailer, embedded in the story of Lydia?

The Women Who Were Gathered

On the sabbath day we went outside the gate by the river, where we supposed there was a [synagogue]; and we sat down and spoke to the women who had gathered there. (Acts 16:13)

Women have gathered. This is a unique statement in Acts, and in fact in the whole of the New Testament. It is true that there is a similar situation in the case of Tabitha, but only here is there a description of the gathering. It is truly astonishing that, within the framework not only of androcentric language, but of patriarchal relationships,[3] we learn something about the existence of a group of *women*. Here women have not been made invisible! And still more: part of the history of a group of women has been transmitted to us here. My goal in this chapter is to understand this story better.

Gathering

First let me inquire what is meant by the women's being gathered. Most exegetes overlook the importance of the fact that a group of women is gathered here, and turn their attention too quickly to Paul's activity, with the result that the women slip out of the picture. Apparently the interpreters are interested only in the missionary works of the apostles (in this case, Paul). But we should emphatically object to that kind of view of this story: Without the presence of these and similar groups, Paul could scarcely have missionized in the way he is reported to have done. On the other hand, we can say that without an account of the work of Paul and other missionaries, we would have no access to these women, and these fragments of the history of women would have been lost.

In order to clarify the importance of the women's being gathered, let us first analyze the verb συνέρχεσθαι, "gather," in connection with the other concepts of λαλεῖν, "speak," and προσευχή, "synagogue."[4] We will include the remarks of the commentators as well as material from outside the New Testament, including inscriptions, whenever possible. We can begin with the fact that it is unusual for Luke to give an account that focuses exclusively on women, or a group of women. The text gives us some important clues for the reconstruction of this group of women at Philippi: for example, it does not say that the women had met, but that they had *gathered* or *assembled*. What is the meaning of that statement?

To my knowledge there has been no extensive scholarly study of the verb συνέρχεσθαι.[5] Therefore we should introduce as many New Testament passages as possible to gain an overall picture of its semantic field. A look at these passages shows that the verb is used, fundamentally, in four different contexts of meaning:

First, the verb can describe a *judicial hearing* before a tribunal or before the Sanhedrin[6] (see Acts 22:30; 25:17; Mark 14:53; see also Acts 28:17, 20). This always refers to a gathering of high Roman or Jewish authorities to hear something from someone or to make a decision about something. This use of the verb is not relevant to our context.

Second, the verb appears when the subject is a particular *religious experience and faith-praxis*: On the one hand, people gather together because of good news given to them (Luke 4:18, the poor and the sick who want to hear of Jesus' words and deeds; Luke 5:15; Mark 3:20 in context; see also Acts 5:16 in context). They gather because they know that something is happening in a particular place in which they want to have a part and from which they expect something (healing, for example). Or, on the other hand, people are gathered in a particular place to hear and learn what God has to say to them (Acts 2:6, 11; 10:27; see 10:24, 33; John 18:20). According to these passages, people have gathered with a particular religious purpose. John 18:20 even makes it clear that the synagogue and the Temple are the places where "all the Jews come together." Jesus here speaks of a time in the past, but utters *this* statement in the present tense, probably because Jews were still gathering there.

Third, the verb appears only in Luke in connection with *discipleship and shared work*, which can also be expressed in traveling together. Luke uses the verb to describe the shared work of mission: for example, in Acts 10:45 (see 10:23b). Those who, according to this text, share in Peter's missionary work also belong, for example, to the community in Joppa (9:36-43). This use of the verb is still clearer in Acts 15:38 (see 15:37 and 13:13): According to 13:5-13 John Mark worked with Paul and Barnabas for some time and, for reasons not given, separated from them and returned to Jerusalem. He appears at Antioch again in 15:37-39, where Judas and Silas have also arrived, having been chosen by the community at Jerusalem and sent out with Paul and Barnabas. According to this passage, Paul refuses this time to travel and work with John Mark. We also learn of a "sharp disagreement" between Paul and Barnabas, so that they also separate: Barnabas takes John Mark with him, and Paul chooses Silas. Judas, Barnabas, and John Mark disappear from the author's view from this point on, but probably they continue their missionary activity, like many others before them (see 8:1-4; 11:19).

Luke makes a unique use of this verb in one other context having to do with discipleship and shared work: this is in regard to the people (women and men) who were with Jesus from the beginning (Luke 23:55; Acts 1:6, 21). Here it stands for intensively shared work with Jesus and as his disciples. It should be interpreted in the context of Luke 23:49; Mark 15:40; and Matt. 27:55-56.

Fourth, Paul uses this verb in 1 Cor. 11:17-34 and 14:23-26 as a "technical term for the coming together of the Christian congregation, especially to administer the Lord's Supper."[7]

On the basis of these passages we may observe that when a gathering of people is described with συνέρχεσθαι there is always the idea of a deliberate, purposeful gathering that also implies community (so especially Luke 23:55; Acts 1:6, 21; 15:38; Mark 3:20 πάλιν; John 18:20; see also 1 Cor. 11:17-34; 14:23-32).[8] Our women have therefore not met or gathered by accident. Because the gathering is always connected with a purpose, it remains to inquire why the women have gathered here.

In the context of a gathering made up exclusively of women, we learn that Paul and Silas, after seating themselves, talk to, or rather with the women. Because this circumstance seems to me to be important for understanding the women's being gathered together, I want to ask at this point whether the combination of words at the end of v. 13 is coincidental, or whether it can give us some definite information. I am referring to the expression καθίσαντες ἐλαλοῦμεν ταῖς συνελθούσαις γυναιξίν, "we sat down and spoke to the women who had gathered there."

The verb καθίζειν, "sit down," and similar words describe various situations in the New Testament: first, sitting on the throne of God or in the reign of God, but also sitting on the Roman judgment seat (Matt. 19:28; 20:21, 23; 25:31; Mark 16:19; John 19:13; Acts 2:30; 12:21; 25:6, 17); second, sitting down to work or to make decisions (Matt. 13:48; Luke 14:28, 31; 16:6); third, remaining in a given place (living somewhere for a period of time, in connection with religious aspects or purposes: Luke 24:49; Acts 2:2; 18:11). For our context the fourth use of the verb is important, especially since it is especially connected with *teaching* and *preaching*: Jesus sat down on the mountain and the μαθηταί, the "disciples" came to him, and he taught (διδάσκειν) them (Matt. 5:1-2); Jesus sat down in the house at Capernaum, called the Twelve together, and taught them (Mark 9:33-34; cf. v. 38: διδάσκαλε); after Jesus had sat down, he taught the ὄχλοι from the fishing boat (Luke 5:3); an Ethiopian eunuch was sitting in his chariot and reading from the prophet Isaiah when he invited Philip to climb up and sit with him. Philip then explained the pericope by preaching Christ to the eunuch (Acts 8:27-33), whereupon the eunuch asked Philip to baptize him. Καθίζειν also appears in the context of teaching and preaching in the *Temple* and in the *synagogue*: John 8:2 describes a repeated (πάλιν) scene in the Temple, that is, Jesus sat down and taught (see also v. 20); in Matt. 23:2 Jesus uses a highly symbolic expression when he says that the scribes and Pharisees sit on Moses' seat, that is, that they "have the office and the traditional authority to hand on Moses' teaching";[9] Luke 4:16-21 portrays the kerygmatic "premiere performance" of Jesus in his home town, for it says that *as was his custom* he went to the synagogue on the Sabbath and "stood up to read." After the reading he sat down (again?), and everyone waited for him to interpret what he had read. Acts also uses this word καθίζειν in the context of religious-liturgical praxis: for example, Acts 13:14-15 uses language similar to that in Luke 4:16-21 to describe Paul and Barnabas entering the synagogue at Antioch on the Sabbath. They sat down there, and after the reading of the law and the prophets Paul, having first been invited to do so, interpreted what had been read (vv. 16-41).

To understand the expression at the end of Acts 16:13 better, I want to look now at the other verb, λαλεῖν, "speak," primarily as used in Acts and especially where it refers to preaching:

1. Let me begin at 10:44 (see also the second description of the same events in 11:14-17). Here it is a question of Peter's preaching of Christ in Caesarea.

2. Λαλεῖν appears at least once in Acts as an expression for "distorted speech" that attempts to turn the disciples from the way they have chosen (20:30). This is said to be the talk of "teachers of error and false prophets"[10] who will appear in the community. Similarly, some of his people say of Stephen that he spoke against the law, against God and against the holy city (6:1-2; see vv. 8-15). Stephen's preaching,

which pointed to the fulfillment of Scripture (see 7:1-52) appeared in the eyes of the Sanhedrin as blasphemy against God.

3. In Corinth, after a conflict, Paul decides to separate himself from "the Jews," and says to them: "From now on I will go to the Gentiles" (18:6). But then he goes into the house of a god-fearer, and even the head of the synagogue becomes a believer and is baptized in the name of Jesus, together with all his household. This also tells us that Luke had no intention of describing a conflict with *the* Jews as a whole, for in vv. 9-10 Paul is urged by a vision of the Lord not to give up his preaching, "for there are many in this city who are my people," that is, the people of God in that city are very numerous. To the demand that he go on speaking and not be silent v. 11 adds that Paul stayed (sat down: καθίζειν) a year and a half in Corinth and taught the word of God among the people. It is also said of Apollos, a Jew, that he "spoke . . . and taught accurately the things concerning Jesus" (18:25), because he "had been instructed in the Way of the Lord." He began to speak boldly in the synagogue.

4. There are many passages in which λαλεῖν refers specifically to *preaching in the synagogue or in the Temple*. Acts 4:1 refers to a preceding speech by Peter in 3:11-26:[11] "While [they] were speaking to the people, the priests, the captain of the temple, and the Sadducees came to them, much annoyed because they were teaching the people. . . ." The same is confirmed by 5:20: after a conflict with the high priest and the Sadducees that ended in the apostles' imprisonment, an angel of the Lord says to them: "Go, stand in the temple and tell the people the whole message about this life." The apostles are supposed to continue speaking in the Temple (5:21; see also 4:17-21, 31). The apostles' customary activity in Jerusalem was then continued in the diaspora. Obvious examples are 13:5, 14-42; 14:1-7; 17:1-4, 10-15, and many more. According to Acts, Paul was not the first Jewish-Christian missionary in Antioch (see 11:19-22!). The sequence described in 13:14-42 should probably be presumed for 11:19-22 as well: 13:14-42 tells how Paul and "those with him" went to the synagogue on the Sabbath and sat down. The head of the synagogue invited Paul, after the reading of the law and the prophets, to speak a word of exhortation to the people. After he had given a long "sermon," he was urged (v. 42) to repeat his preaching on the following Sabbath. Here the word used is again λαλεῖν. However, on the next Sabbath Paul was contradicted, and Paul and Barnabas confirmed that the word of God had to be proclaimed first to the Jews (see v. 46). Then began a persecution, and Paul and Barnabas were driven out of Antioch (v. 50). They traveled next to Iconium,

where they "also" (as in 13:14) went into the synagogue and preached (λαλεῖν). Something similar is said of Apollos in 18:24-25.

We may conclude from this semantic discussion that whenever it is a question of religious praxis or matters related to faith, and whenever the location is a cultic place, the use of the verbs καθίζειν and λαλεῖν indicates that what happens here is teaching, interpretation and preaching of the Scriptures.

In Acts 16:13 there is only a brief notice of the "arrival" of the missionaries in Philippi on the Sabbath. We get no details at this point about the precise events, but this kind of reporting is nothing unusual in Acts. We find it also, for example, in 13:5 (Salamis); 14:1 (Iconium); 17:10 (Beroea); 17:17 (Athens); 18:4 (Corinth); and 18:19 (Ephesus). In those passages (except for 13:5), as in Acts 16:14-15, we learn only of the reaction to the missionaries' appearance in the synagogue. There is a slightly longer description in 17:1-3 (Thessalonica), where Paul's *customary* synagogue visits are described: Paul goes to the synagogue on three Sabbaths and speaks to the Jews there, interpreting the Scripture and explaining that it was necessary for the Christ to suffer and to rise from the dead. This, he tells them, is the Messiah, Jesus, whom he, Paul, is proclaiming to them (17:3). Luke is the only New Testament author to use the expression κατὰ τὸ εἰωθός, "as was his custom;" it appears in Luke 4:16 and Acts 17:2, describing in the first instance Jesus' custom and in the second Paul's, of going to the synagogue on the Sabbath and participating in the reading and interpreting of Scripture.

Most exegetes do not emphasize the combination of words at the end of v. 13, but some have written about the word λαλεῖν, for example in acknowledging a connection with v. 14 and asserting that the verb refers to preaching.[12] Alfons Weiser[13] reads it as "Paul's preaching," which the woman (*sic*) listened to and accepted because God opened her heart. Weiser concludes from this that in this expression Luke is indicating "why only Lydia and not the other women mentioned came 'to believe in the Lord'" H. W. Beyer[14] supposes that there were at least a few women at the Jewish place of prayer with whom the missionaries spoke about "religious matters," and Theodor Zahn[15] thinks that "the missionaries, after sitting down on the wood or stone bench in the place, spoke to them [the women]" and that after the entrance of "four strange, partly Jewish-looking [*sic*] men" there must have been many questions and answers, so that "the evangelical preaching, by Paul alone" grew out of all that. A. Wikenhauser[16] says that Paul proclaimed "his message" at the women's place of prayer, although it appears that there was no "proper Jewish service of worship" at the place.

The consequence of all this is that these commentators see Paul's initial appearance in Philippi as analogous to his activity in the other places where he preached or proclaimed the gospel. W. Schmithals[17] even asserts that we can discern "Paul's authentic missionary method" in Acts 16:13: it consisted in his seeking out a synagogue and initiating his preaching before Jews, god-fearers and proselytes. In this context, Theodor Zahn[18] even reads καθίσαντες ἐλαλοῦμεν as synonymous with διαλαλεῖν and διαλέγεσθαι, and on that basis equates the events in Philippi with those in Acts 17:2, 17; 18:4, 19; 19:8-9. But in spite of these initiatives, we should note that most commentators find difficulty in interpreting Acts 16:13-15. If they do not ignore altogether the fact that Paul also preached in that place, their interpretations are usually dependent on assumptions that are inadequate to the text, or discriminatory in nature. These assumptions are expressed, for example, in assertions like that mentioned above, that there were at least a few women in Philippi with whom the missionaries spoke about "religious matters." The reason for such statements will become clear in connection with the analysis of the word προσευχή, below; almost all the restrictive commentaries on this passage are connected with the interpretation of this concept.

In summary: It appears from the word analysis above that the missionaries spent their Sabbath in the same way as in the other places where, according to their custom, they participated in Jewish worship. We are talking about a liturgical action that presumed the existence of a Jewish community in the place: The missionaries only participate, and if they had not been there the liturgical action would have been carried out by someone else in that place, as usual. The difficulty in giving an "unproblematic" reading of this account, as we can observe in the history of its interpretation, lies, in my opinion, in the fact that the text speaks here of a gathering of women.

The Place of Assembly

The difficulty the commentators have in coming to terms with a gathering made up exclusively of women rests principally on the fact that these women are not assembled just anywhere, but in the προσευχή at Philippi. Everything that is said about the missionaries in v. 13b happens in that place. Here in Acts 16:13 we not only find a description of a gathering made up exclusively of women, but also the word προσευχή is used only here to describe the place where the action occurs (see also v. 16). This fact has largely determined the exegesis of this text.

An Overview of Interpretations

To begin with, the exegetical discussion seeks to clarify the meaning of προσευχή. This is not a new topic. Here I will present the statements of a number of exegetes in order to clarify how they deal with the question. The fundamental problem is whether the word stands for "synagogue," or for "place of prayer" or some other similar idea. We may summarize a number of observations based on the commentaries under four basic headings.

First, in some commentaries, the verdict remains *open:* H. J. Holtzmann[19] comes to an "either-or" position. He writes: "Either προσ[ευχή] is only a common expression for συναγωγή . . . or we should suppose that in cities where the Jews had no synagogue, they provided themselves with a place of prayer." The author then reaches the remarkable conclusion that "here, *as in Catholic churches*" there are "*always at least a few pious females.*" In drawing this conclusion, it appears, the author can scarcely bring himself to suppose that these "females" were the principal figures in Jewish Sabbath praxis in Philippi. G. Stählin[20] proceeds on the assumption that Paul looked for a synagogue in Philippi, as usual. But we cannot know whether the προσευχή he found was a "proper" synagogue. H. Conzelmann[21] knows that προσευχή can mean "synagogue." He finds it especially "strange" that "only women were there. Is the author thinking of a place for prayer out in the open?" This is a central question in all the interpretations.

Second, προσευχή is understood to mean *place of prayer,* or something similar. C. F. Nösgen[22] asserts that Paul and his companions expected to find a "place of prayer" outside the gate, near the river, because the Jewish community in Philippi was not very large. There would always be Jews and proselytes in such a προσευχή, but in this case the latter must be in the majority, "since there is special mention of the women." Unfortunately, the author does not pursue this argument. It is striking, however, that he presumes that men are also present. J. Felten[23] is aware that προσευχή is often used as a synonym for συναγωγή, but says that that is not the case here, because the Jews in Philippi had no synagogue. For him, a προσευχή is not even a building, "but simply some kind of walled or unwalled place in the open air, on the riverbank, where people prayed." Unfortunately we find no further citations here, either. Similarly, H. W. Beyer,[24] A. Wikenhauser,[25] W. de

Boor,[26] and G. Schneider[27] recognize that Acts 16:13-15 reflects Paul's usual procedure during his missionary journeys, but they argue that there was no synagogue in Philippi, and therefore the missionaries went to the river to find the Jewish place of prayer. For W. Schmithals, too, there was no synagogue in Philippi, because "apparently there were no Jewish inhabitants (cf. v. 20 [?!])" there.[28] The women were god-fearers who frequented the place of prayer.

Third, προσευχή is sometimes interpreted as a *synagogue*. E. Preuschen,[29] G. Hoennicke,[30] and O. Bauernfeind[31] assert that both custom and context require that we read the word here as synonymous with "synagogue." J. Schmid[32] also regards the προσευχή in Philippi, without reservation, as a synagogue. This can be concluded from his statement: "In New Testament times the synagogue was a solidly established and very common institution, both in Palestine and in the diaspora (cf. Acts 9:20; 13:5, 14; 14:1; 15:21; 16:13[!]; 17:1, 10, 17; 18:4, 19, 26)." Schmid thus equates the προσευχή in Philippi with all the other synagogues that appear in Acts. J. Munck[33] remarks very briefly that the προσευχή was "probably synonymous with a synagogue." R. Pesch[34] writes that the missionaries had inquired about the Jewish προσευχή in the days before the Sabbath. He then continues smoothly: "There was no synagogue *in the city*; therefore the missionaries go . . . outside the city gate . . . where they . . . supposed there would be a 'proseuche' = synagogue." It is also clear from the sentences that follow that he regards the προσευχή as a synagogue; I will return to this point later.

If we inquire about the reasons for these varying suppositions and assertions on the part of the commentators, we learn very little. Those who interpret the προσευχή as a synagogue point to other witnesses and literature.[35] Most of those who deny it give a variety of general reasons. For example, it is said that there were no Jews in Philippi, or that the Jewish community must have been very small.[36] A. Wikenhauser[37] thinks that we should conclude from 13:14-42; 14:1; 17:2, 10, 17; 18:4, 8; 19:8-9 that the word ἐλαλοῦμεν, which is used in 16:13, does not describe Paul's speeches in synagogues. Later he asserts that Paul begins "his preaching, as everywhere, in the Jewish community,"[38] but this could not have been in the synagogue because there simply was none in the city of Philippi. Wikenhauser admits that προσευχή means "synagogue [building]," but excludes that possibility for 16:13 because everywhere else in Acts Luke describes the place of assembly for worship as a συναγωγή. Therefore προσευχή "probably" means "nothing more than a (perhaps simple, but enclosed) place of prayer."

Fourth, there are a few interpretations that differ from all the preceding. H. H. Wendt[39] also prefers to read προσευχή to mean a place of prayer, and explains: Such places were sometimes buildings, sometimes open spaces, and were found "in those cities . . . where there were or could be no synagogues, *but they served the purpose of a synagogue.*" Unfortunately he does not say why and in which cities there could not be synagogues. At the same time, he does not deny that what happens in a synagogue would also take place in a προσευχή! T. Zahn does not deny this, either.[40] He also understands a προσευχή to be a house of prayer or place of prayer. He gives more particular attention to the question and argues that this was not an "ordinary" synagogue, because first, Luke and the other gospel writers used the word συναγωγή to describe "the buildings for worship in which the Jewish communities were accustomed to assemble to read Scripture, preach, and pray"; second, Luke always introduces "the individual synagogues that Jesus and the apostles visited . . . with the definite article, as the synagogue of the place in question." This presumes that there could have been only one synagogue in any given place. Consequently Zahn asks: "Why does he [Luke] express, through the use of προσευχή without the article, . . . the idea that there was such a thing in Philippi at all, if he wanted us to understand that this was the synagogue of the Jewish community in Philippi?" Finally, this must be connected with the fact "that only in this one passage does he indicate, regarding a Jewish place of prayer, where it was located within the city or its surrounding district." For Zahn, the purpose of Luke's expression is precisely to make a concrete statement that the Jewish place of prayer "was outside, on the river." Here, according to this exegete, everything was unusual, including the gathering! Nothing at all is said about the head of the synagogue as presider over the worship service, nor is there anything about his assistants. There are places to sit, "but *one almost has the impression* that it was only a few pious Jewish women and proselyte women who were accustomed to gather there." Finally, everything is said to point to the fact that Philippi had only "*small, undeveloped vestiges of the Sabbath service.*" Nevertheless, it was also customary, and attested, that Jews "were often accustomed to hold their *worship services*" outside the cities, by the water. The difficulty of understanding προσευχή in this context is especially evident in the case of Zahn. On the one hand, it cannot describe a space in which the Jewish communities celebrated their worship service (including Scripture reading, interpretation, and prayer), because Luke always uses the word συναγωγή for such a place.

On the other hand, it was customary for Jewish communities to hold services of worship in such places as well. In order to solve the problem, Zahn supposes that Philippi must have had a very underdeveloped, incomplete worship service, because no "proper" presiding officer was present. At the same time, Zahn does not deny that this was a Sabbath worship service.

We find a very different argument and result in the commentary by Jürgen Roloff.[41] He begins by remarking that "in this Roman city the connection with the synagogue, customary elsewhere," encountered "unusual difficulties" because the missionaries had to seek the Jewish house of God on their own, and when they went toward the river it was only because it was common for synagogues to be established in such districts! However, the commentator immediately poses the following question and provides an answer: "But was what they found there really a synagogue? It is true that the Greek word *proseuche* (= place of prayer) can also describe a synagogue; but *when only women* are mentioned as *being there*, this *scarcely* can indicate a *regular synagogue worship service,* for which at least ten men would have to be present."[42] Consequently, the προσευχή must here be understood as a "place of prayer under the open sky." G. Schille[43] also emphasizes the necessary presence or number of men at the synagogue service, but differently from Roloff. According to Schille, Luke himself has altered the tradition. Everything points to the fact that 16:13, like 13:14, is about Paul's customary practice. Therefore we should suppose that the προσευχή is a synagogue: "Luke is thinking of a synagogue in which the teacher sits (cf. Luke 4:20)." But the fact that only women were gathered there could then "be interpreted only as an exceptional situation, since synagogue worship could only be conducted when at least twenty men were present." Here, in contrast to Roloff's opinion, the necessary number of men has been doubled, although Schille does not say where he got this number. There is a fundamental difference between Roloff's and Schille's accounts: Schille can think of the assembly as an exceptional case, while Roloff does not even consider the possibility. We will return later to the problem of the necessary number of ten men as a precondition for constituting a synagogue worship service.

The principal reasons why the commentators think that the προσευχή in Philippi cannot be interpreted as a synagogue may be summarized as follows: first, there were no Jews, or very few, in Philippi; second, the word προσευχή is used in place of the usual συναγωγή; third, the only persons present are women. The first argument is very improbable on purely logical grounds, for if there had been no Jews or Jewish community in Philippi, why would the missionaries have been looking for a προσευχή, and how could they have found one? That method of procedure would by no means be applicable to Paul and his missionary methods. The second and third reasons must be examined more closely.

First we should note that many commentators attempt to answer the question of the purpose of such a προσευχή by use of the arguments mentioned above. That is, they ask why the women were there; consequently, the place and the women's gathering are made mutually interpretive. For most exegetes[44] (if they ask the question at all), the answer is simple: having decided that this passage is not about a synagogue in Philippi, they conclude that the προσευχή was the place where people gathered for prayer. They also think that women went there to pray. This is connected with their answer to the question of why the προσευχή was outside the city. Here, again, the answer is too facile: Because Jews were accustomed to making ritual ablutions before praying, the place of prayer (whether in the open air or not) was outside the city, at the riverside. According to this interpretation, the participation of the women in the religious activities of the Sabbath presents no problem: They perform the ritual washing (of the hands), and then they pray. In this connection, the thought process of the exegetes is important to note: these are the only two activities that could have taken place, because there were *no men* present. To put it another way: because there were no men in the group, they did not have a "proper Jewish service of worship."[45] The necessary conclusion these exegetes draw from their assumption that there was no "proper" synagogue in Philippi is that nothing happened here but ritual washing and prayers: No "proper" synagogue, no "proper" service of worship.

A second group of exegetes differs from those just named, but still does not consider the προσευχή in Philippi a synagogue: this group is represented by H. H. Wendt and Theodor Zahn.[46] Although they do not see the προσευχή in Philippi as a synagogue, they conclude that it served the purpose of a synagogue. Wendt does not explain this statement more fully, but Zahn believes that we are dealing with "small, undeveloped beginnings of a sabbath service." However, neither author inquires how this service, however "undeveloped," may have looked, since "only" women were gathered. Zahn tries to avoid this difficult situation by saying that "one almost gets the impression that only a few pious Jewish and proselyte women were accustomed to gather there." By this he means to say that some men were, in fact, present; therefore the sabbath worship service could be celebrated, however "unusual" the circumstances!

Finally, we should also inquire whether exegetes who think that the προσευχή in Philippi was a synagogue building draw any conclusions from that assertion, and if so, which. To begin with, no one except Rudolf Pesch addresses this question. Therefore the suggestion that we should interpret the exclusive presence of women, as mentioned in the text, is something fully new, and comes from Pesch alone.[47] First of all, this author quite correctly challenges the conclusion of many exegetes that the προσευχή in Philippi could not have been a synagogue because the text does not mention any men with whom the missionaries could have spoken. Then he introduces his own proposition: "one may also suppose that Paul and his companions *sat down with the women who had gathered outside the synagogue, and that their interest,* especially that of Lydia, *prevented them from going in to the synagogue service.*" This attempt at a solution again makes it clear (and nowhere else does R. Pesch display as much imagination as he does here) what great difficulties exegetes have in dealing with this little bit of information in Acts 16:13b. Pesch had previously (on p. 104) pointed to the similarity between the formulation of this verse and that of Acts 13:14, but at the same time he minimizes the force of this observation by asserting that in Philippi the missionaries sat down with the women *outside* the synagogue. He offers no reasoning or citations to support this statement. The presupposition, and at the same time the consequence of such an assertion is, in my opinion, that "inside," in the building itself, everything was going on in "normal" fashion: there we would find the men about whose presence our text is silent! The missionaries would have had no opportunity to preach to them because the women gathered "outside" prevented them from doing so.[48] If we wanted to carry this train of thought further, we could suppose that these women must have exercised a great deal of force to cause Paul to stop in response to their interest instead of following his traditional course on the Sabbath. But to speak seriously, Pesch's proposal has the following consequences: Apparently our women were not taking part in the Jewish worship service, because they were not in the synagogue at all. The question of what had brought them there and gathered them together remains open, since Pesch does not say explicitly what interest on the part of the women, "especially Lydia," would have been able to restrain the missionaries from entering the synagogue. It would seem that Paul must have found some interest in the matter as well.

A survey of interpretations clarifies how difficult it is to take a clear position on the question of what the προσευχή in Philippi is meant to be. As we have already noted, no New Testament texts can be adduced for direct comparison, because there is no parallel to the use of this term as a description of a place: it occurs only in Acts 16:13, 16. However, the word analyses above have already indicated some points of contact in combination with such terms as συνέρχεσθαι, καθίζειν, and λαλεῖν. We should not lose sight of those contexts.

Literary and Inscriptional Material

In the interest of further clarification of the meaning of the women's gathering and of the word προσευχή, we will take an interdisciplinary approach by examining extra-biblical sources[49] that, like Acts 16:13, use the word προσευχή. As with the biblical texts, we must here refer to secondary literature. I will list some literary and inscriptional sources.

Literary Evidence

In particular, we want to examine the sources to see in what context they use the word προσευχή and what they mean by it. "They had synagogues, and . . . they were in the habit of visiting them, and most especially on the sacred sabbath days."[50] Philo of Alexandria writes, in the *Legatio ad Gajum* 155–58, about the Jewish population of Rome whom Pompey had brought to Italy as prisoners of war and who had later been freed. Trastevere was the foreigners' district, on the opposite bank of the Tiber, and most of them had settled there.[51] In this context, Philo speaks of the προσευχαί of the Jewish people in Rome, where Jews gathered especially on the Sabbath, and where they were accustomed to interpret their laws. It is not surprising that Philo should speak of a number of synagogues in Rome; this is confirmed by other sources. For example, the grave inscription of a Gentile fruit seller speaks of a *proseucha* near the Republican Wall in Rome.[52]

Josephus also uses the word προσευχή to describe the synagogue building in reporting some episodes of Jewish intramural conflicts in Tiberias and Taricheae during the Jewish War: "On the next day . . . they all came into the Proseucha; it was a large edifice, and capable of receiving a great number of people."[53] In the same context he writes that a few days later, when he returned from Taricheae to Tiberias, the multitude had already gathered in the synagogue building,[54] and in *Vita* 293 he reports that, after arming himself because of the military situation, he also went into the synagogue: ἦλθον εἰς τὴν προσευχὴν. There he was able to participate in the Jewish service of worship.[55] The community present, that is, the people in the προσευχή, are described as σύνοδος, "assembly" or "congregation."[56] In this synagogue building they observe the νόμια ("laws" or "duties")[57] and the εὐχάς ("prayers");[58] that is, they celebrate the synagogue worship service. According to Vita 277–303, however, secular political problems were also discussed in the same place.[59] Josephus uses similar expressions in Antiquities 14.213–16 to describe the legal and religious relationship between the Jewish community in Delos and the Roman authorities at Paros. That community, which is here equated with a θίασος, a "collegium" or "society," is not to be forbidden to use its ancestral customs in worship, that is, to gather as prescribed by its laws. Similarly, the decree of Halicarnassus (on the southwest coast of Asia Minor) confirms what the Romans permitted the Jews to do, for in Antiquities 14.257–58 Josephus writes: ". . . we aim to follow the people of the Romans, . . . [therefore] we have decreed, that as many men and women of the Jews as are willing so to do, may celebrate their Sabbaths, and perform their holy offices, according to the Jewish laws; and may make their proseuchae at the seaside, according to the customs of their forefathers."[60] The decree of Sardis is similar:[61] Jewish men, women, and children shall be permitted to gather on the appointed days, and to do everything their laws prescribe. For that purpose, a place of their own choosing, fit for the purpose, is to be set aside for them, as a building and habitation (τόπον . . . εἰς οἰκοδομίαν καὶ οἴκησιν). In this context, and in parallel to Vita 277 (εἰς τὴν προσευχὴν μέγιστον οἴκημα), οἴκησις can very well mean a synagogue building or community hall.[62]

The references in Josephus are few, but they show that the word προσευχή was known to him, also, in reference to a synagogue. The concept is much more familiar to Philo of Alexandria, appearing especially in his descriptions of the persecutions of the Jewish men and women in Alexandria. Destruction and plundering of their holy places—their προσευχαί, of which there were many—were daily events, according to Legatio ad Gajum 132–38 and In Flaccum 6–7, 14, 41–54. We learn from Philo that the προσευχαί were buildings in which the Jews interpreted their laws and preserved their customs, where they worshiped God and resisted to the death the setting up of images of Caesar, which for them constituted blasphemy. In summary, we may say that in the passages cited both Philo and Josephus use the word προσευχή to describe Jewish holy places, that is, synagogue buildings.

Inscriptional Material

Numerous inscriptions and papyri show that the word προσευχή was common in the Greek-speaking diaspora at least from the third century B.C.E. until the second century C.E.[63] The oldest attestations of the existence of synagogue buildings, and also of the use of the word προσευχή in the diaspora, come from Egypt: from Shedia near Alexandria (*OGIS* 726) and from Arsinoë (Crocodilopolis) in Fayum (*CPJ* 3.1532A). The inscriptions list personal names and give a very precise dating for the existence of these synagogues: during the reign of King Ptolemy III Euergetes and Queen Berenice (246–221 B.C.E.). These inscriptions thus indicate the time when the buildings were erected, and constitute the oldest witnesses known to us for the existence of προσευχαί in the diaspora. However, the use of the word προσευχή to describe a synagogue building is not restricted to that time period, as can be illustrated in the case of Arsinoë, where two further witnesses from different centuries also speak of the Jewish synagogue or synagogues there. Neither of these is a Jewish witness; both are legal documents of the city, from which we may conclude that the word προσευχή was known not only to the Jews themselves, but also among their non-Jewish fellow citizens, and that it was used as a precise designation for a Jewish synagogue building.

The Arsinoë papyri include one from the end of the second century B.C.E., describing the land surveys in Arsinoë-Crocodilopolis (*CPJ* 1.134). The precise location of the προσευχή is indicated. It was bordered on the north by a "holy or sacral garden" (ἱερὰ παράδεισος) belonging to a woman named Hermione; on the south the προσευχή bordered a "fallow piece of ground" (χέρσος) owned by Demetrius of Thrace. To the west was the "town boundary" (περίστασις πόλεως, i.e., Pomerium), and to the east was the "canal or ditch of Argaitis" (Ἀργαίτιδος διῶρυξ). The following may be emphasized here: (a) This προσευχή lay on the fringe of the town, near the water; (b) there would appear to have been other sanctuaries there as well, inasmuch as the papyrus mentions two ἱερὰ παράδεισοι, one belonging to the synagogue itself, the other to Hermione; and (c) this is most probably the same προσευχή that is mentioned in *CPJ* 3.1532A.[64] The other Arsinoë papyrus (*CPJ* 2.432) is from the year 113 C.E. It documents the source of water and the bills for certain public installations during the reign of the emperor Trajan. Among the various buildings listed are the following: the "baths of Severianus," the "street well," the "Macedonians' well," and "the brewery of the Sarapeion." Alongside these "public" institutions, two Jewish synagogues are also mentioned: a προσευχή Θηβαίων and an εὐχεῖον.[65] What is especially striking in this papyrus is that the water bills for the synagogues are higher than any of the others, even including the bathhouse. Each synagogue had to pay 128 drachmas per month, while the costs for the bath were only 72 drachmas and 18 oboli per month. Another difference is found in that, whereas all the other institutions had to pay a fixed, daily tax, so that the monthly bill constituted a sum of the individual days on which water was used, the synagogues had to pay a fixed monthly rate. A. Fuks[66] offers a series of suggestions to explain this situation. It could be that these different measures were not related to the exact quantity of water used, but that the tax was based on a special classification of customers, so that (as in the case of the synagogues) the same sum of 36 drachmas and 9 oboli had to be paid monthly for all the wells and fountains alike. But, according to Fuks, we would have to conclude from this that the various customers were assigned a rate corresponding to their average water usage, and in that case the amount of water used would still be the measure by which they were billed. If that were so, the synagogues would be the most extensive users of water in the whole metropolis of Arsinoë. The question necessarily arises: why and for what purpose did they use so much water? Fuks's answer is based on certain insights derived from Jewish sources:

> The Jews of the period to which our papyrus [CPJ 2.432] belongs were particular about the observance of the religious prescriptions concerning ceremonial purification and personal hygiene. There were connected with synagogues special arrangements for washing. . . . Also, sometimes there were boarding-houses connected with synagogues. . . . One has therefore to reckon with additional water for daily purposes.[67]

But Fuks does not consider this a sufficient reason for the synagogue water bills to be so much higher. He therefore adopts the suggestion of A. C. Johnson,[68] which probably approximates the ordinary situation during the Roman era (113 C.E.). He proceeds on the assumption that "the ghetto [i.e., the Jewish section of the city] may have got its daily supply at the temple fountain." That would mean that the water bills would cover not only the water used by the two synagogues for religious purposes, but also the daily usage of the whole Jewish population in Arsinoë. From that we could conclude that the synagogues were, at least in part, centers of daily Jewish life and communal organization.

This example from Arsinoë-Crocodilopolis thus illustrates the fact that the word προσευχή was used without exception, in both Jewish and non-Jewish sources extending over a period of several centuries, as a designation for the synagogue building, the Jewish place of prayer in the Greek-speaking diaspora. That building was the common gathering place for a minority group attempting to maintain its identity in the diaspora. Such a religious and cultural center may in fact have included "a school, a hostel, a dining hall, even a kitchen,"[69] as we have already indicated in our discussion of *CPJ* 2.432.

Additional examples may be introduced to expand our understanding of Acts 16:13-16 within the context of its contemporary situation. These examples clearly show that the people who have left us indications about the conditions of their lives in these different sources had no difficulty in speaking of a προσευχή as something they had built or developed themselves, either in whole or in part. There are, for example, the numerous inscriptions concerning the building of a προσευχή, many of which are dedicatory, indicating who built the προσευχή (or caused it to be built), where, and at what period. Most of the known inscriptions are from Egypt in the second and first centuries B.C.E. Here are some examples:[70]

1. In Schedia, near Alexandria, Jews under King Ptolemy III Euergetes and Queen Berenice (246–221 B.C.E.) built their synagogue and dedicated it to the royal couple.[71]

2. In the same period, the Jewish community at Arsinoë-Crocodilopolis built a synagogue and dedicated it to the same royal pair (*CPJ* 3.1532A). The text is almost identical with that of the inscription just cited, and everything indicates that the two of them are the oldest evidence known to us of the existence of synagogue buildings in the diaspora.

3. A century later we find an inscription indicating that between the years 143 and 117 B.C.E. an (entry) gate and synagogue were built in Xenephris in lower Egypt.[72]

4. At the same time, Jews in Nitriai dedicated their synagogue and its furnishings to the royal couple, Ptolemy and Cleopatra, whom they called "benefactors."[73]

5. Also from the second century B.C.E. is a badly damaged inscription found in Hadra, near Alexandria.[74]

6. *CPJ* 3.1443 represents an inscription from the synagogue at Athribis. The period of its origin is uncertain, but the names of King Ptolemy

and Queen Cleopatra, to whom it is dedicated, point to the second or first centuries B.C.E.[75]

7. Another inscription from Athribis, from about the same time, indicates that a family has added a colonnaded vestibule to the synagogue building.[76]

8. There is documentation for a synagogue building in the southwest quarter of the city of Alexandria (Gabbary) in about 37–36 B.C.E.[77]

9. Finally, there is an inscription of unknown origin from the first or second century C.E., according to which a family has built the synagogue.[78]

On the basis of such inscriptional evidence for the use of προσευχή and the archaeological and historical commentary on it by the editors of various collections of inscriptions, there can be no doubt that in every case it refers to a building in which the Jewish communities of the diaspora gathered. Most of the evidence is from Egypt, and it is also the oldest. But there are inscriptions from elsewhere: (a) Two from Pantikapaion on the Black Sea, from the year 81 C.E., document the manumission of slaves. They indicate that the προσευχή was also the place where slaves were set free.[79] (b) In addition, we have inscriptional evidence from Delos from the first century B.C.E.: dedicatory inscriptions were found within a humble group of houses, including *CII* 726 (Ἀγαθοκλῆς καὶ Λυσίμαχος ἐπὶ προσευχῇ) and another inscription discovered in the years 1979–80 (Οἱ ἐν Δήλω Ἰσραηλῖται . . . κατασκευάσαντα καὶ ἀναθέντα ἐκ τῶν ἰδίων ἐπὶ προσευχῇ τοῦ θεοῦ . . .),[80] which apparently refer to a synagogue building. (c) Josephus reports on events in the synagogues at Tiberias and Taricheae (*Vita* 277–82). (d) The popular decree of Halicarnassus permitted the Jewish congregation to build a synagogue near the water (Josephus, *Ant.* 14.257–58). (e) Philo reports on the Jewish prisoners of war transported from Egypt to Rome and later released, and describes their synagogue buildings in Rome (*Leg. Gaj.* 155–57). (f) *CII* 1.531 is a tomb inscription referring to the synagogue at the Republican Wall in Rome.

Preliminary Conclusions and Food for Thought

The evidence for the use of προσευχή found in Egypt and other places within the Greek-speaking diaspora permits us to draw the following conclusion: The προσευχή in Philippi that is mentioned in Acts 16:13-16 can be no different from all the other προσευχαί mentioned in the literary and inscriptional evidence. They are all synagogue buildings in which the Jewish community of a particular town or city gathers, primarily on the Sabbath, to worship God. This has been asserted by other scholars in similar fashion.[81] Speculations about why Luke uses the word προσευχή, which was common in his time and place, only in Acts 16:13, 16 in place of συναγωγή, which he uses everywhere else, bring us no farther. It is not true to say that the location of the προσευχή outside of the city of Philippi was something exceptional: the description of the place in Acts 16:13, ἔξω τῆς πύλης παρὰ ποταμόν, "outside the gate by the river," has almost identical parallels in other sources.[82]

Thus the statement of Acts 16:13 is not a single, isolated instance in its contemporary situation, nor is it by any means contradictory to that situation. The best answer to the speculative proposals mentioned above seems to be that Luke's report rests on a source, and that it transmits the content of the source virtually without alteration.[83] According to this source, then, women were gathered on the Sabbath in the synagogue at Philippi, and the missionaries, after seating themselves, interpreted Scripture for them. But, although this statement of the text corresponds to the circumstances of the period, many exegetes have difficulty with it. They assert that if only women were gathered, this could not have been a synagogue in which divine worship was celebrated.

This is a conclusion drawn from rabbinic sources. Thus, for example, Jürgen Roloff[84] rests his argument on Billerbeck,[85] who cites, for example, Megilla 23b: "The introduction to the shema is not repeated, nor does one pass before the ark, nor do [the priests] lift their hands, nor is the Torah read [publicly], nor the Haftarah read from the prophet, . . . save in the presence of ten." Billerbeck, in interpreting his sources, always speaks of "ten persons," who make up the "minyan." The sources say nothing about "ten men." Thus the עֵדָה, the "congregation," presumes a minimum of "ten [persons]."[86] But Roloff interprets this passage, and Billerbeck's comment, to refer expressly to "ten men," without whom no regular service of worship could have been held.[87] In referring to rabbinic sources we should be aware that they do not present a unified picture. B. J. Brooten has presented sources that give us knowledge of the presence and leadership of women in the Jewish synagogue, showing that rabbinic sources also contain information about women's active participation in religious life.[88] For example, there are two basic statements about the participation of women in the reading of the Torah in the Sabbath service:[89] according to Megilla 23a and 24a, minors and women may be counted among the מנין שבעה (the seven who read the Torah aloud in worship). That is the first part of the statement in Megilla 23a. But the second part restricts the first and contradicts it, because it says that women should not read (publicly) from the Torah. Such contradictions should not be elided, because they can shed light on the history of the wealth of conflict and debate within the Jewish community over the process by which religious norms of behavior were to be discussed and finally laid down as rules. In any case, women could study Torah, and demonstrably they had leadership functions in the synagogue.[90] And as far as the "minyan" is concerned, B. J. Brooten bases her statement on a whole variety of sources and interpretations when she says that "the rabbinic inclusion of women in the quorum of the seven attests to a more ancient tradition, later suppressed, according to which women were allowed to read from the Torah in public."[91]

In light of the reflections presented above, there is no compelling reason to restrict the participation of the group of women in Philippi in the Sabbath activities to ritual washings and (probably silent) prayers. On the contrary: Acts 16:13-15 can serve precisely as an "attestation of women's presence at Jewish worship services."[92] Our text, in fact, says nothing against women's participation in the Sabbath service; on the contrary: the word study (συνέρχεσθαι + καθίζειν + λαλεῖν) at the beginning of this chapter has shown that the whole story permits us to discern in it the Sabbath practices of the synagogue.[93] The process of patriarchalization, in Christianity as in Judaism, certainly ran a multifaceted and tension-filled course to the point at which certain rules and norms were fixed (and even beyond that point). And the contradictions within the Pauline literature[94] regarding the participation of women in worship and community life are matched by similar contradictions in the rabbinic sources.

Reconstructing the Story of Lydia

Acts 16:13-15 should be regarded as a source for investigation of women's participation in Jewish (Sabbath) religious praxis and the history of women in general. Therefore I want to give attention to this woman who belonged to that group of women, and who herself is more precisely delineated. The details of the story concern her social, economic, and religious circumstances. According to Acts 16:14-15:

> A certain woman named Lydia, a worshiper of God, was listening to us; she was from the city of Thyatira and a dealer in purple cloth [porfirópo-lis]. The Lord opened her heart to listen eagerly to what was said by Paul.

When she and her household were baptized, she urged us, saying, "If you have judged me to be faithful to the Lord, come and stay at my home." And she prevailed upon us.

I intend to examine some of the significant attributes of Lydia, as delivered to us by Luke, in order to reconstruct at least part of her story. They depict Lydia in her religious, social, and economic surroundings, and they can give us clear evidence about her origins. In this reconstruction I will make use of historical sources and refer to the results of historical and New Testament scholarship.

"A Worshiper of God"

According to Acts 16:14, Lydia was a worshiper of God (σεβομένη τὸν θεόν).[95] This designation connects Lydia with the synagogue context and with the Sabbath service. It directs our attention more broadly to a particular religious group attached to Judaism: the "god-fearers."

According to a general consensus in New Testament research, the god-fearers were Gentiles attracted to Judaism, but unconverted, not having been circumcised. As associates of or sympathizers with Judaism, they participated in synagogue worship, kept the Noachic laws, and practiced religious monotheism.[96] This consensus rests primarily on the classic work of K. G. Kuhn, whose summary definition of the group follows:

> More numerous [than the proselytes] was the group of Gentiles who attended synagogue worship, believed in Jewish monotheism, and kept some part of the ceremonial law, but who did not take the step of full conversion to Judaism by circumcision. As distinct from proselytes these were called σεβόμενοι or φοβούμενοι τὸν θεόν.[97]

It appears from this that the god-fearers were more numerous than the proselytes because they did not have to be circumcised—and yet they continued to be regarded by both the Jews and the proselytes as unclean (because they were uncircumcised), and therefore as less than their equals, as inferior.[98]

It is striking that scholars' definition of proselytes, σεβόμενοι, and φοβούμενοι applies only to males, since circumcision is regarded as the principal sign of full or less than full adherence to Judaism. These scholars mention women only in passing, but they also assert that there were more women proselytes than men. Women are mentioned in connection with circumcision, as is clear from the following statement, which has been foundational for New Testament research:

> . . . Josephus's information about proselytes in the Jewish-Hellenistic diaspora [reflects] the fact [!], attested elsewhere, . . . that the Jewish mission enjoyed its *principal success among women.* This can be explained in part, at least, by the circumstance *that for them conversion to Judaism was easier than for men, because neither circumcision nor sacrifice was required of them.*[99]

And yet it appears that women were more numerous than men not only among the proselytes (of whom circumcision was required), but also among the "god-fearers" (of whom no circumcision was required)![100] This fact alone must cast doubt on the category of circumcision as decisive for full adherence to Judaism. As a category of explanation, it is sexist and unjust toward women. And yet "god-fearing" women in the New Testament are continually described in scholarly writing according to the model of "god-fearing" men, especially Cornelius. The same is true of Lydia: exegetes attempt to explain the description of Lydia as σεβομένη τὸν θεόν by equating it with the description of Cornelius in Acts 10:2 as εὐσεβὴς καὶ; φοβούμενος τὸν θεόν. We may mention R. Pesch as an example: in treating Acts 16:14[101] he asserts: "She [Lydia] was one of the 'god-fearers' (*cf. at 10:2*) in Philippi." The reference to Acts 10:2 is unequivocal. In commenting on this passage, he writes: "The Roman officer Cornelius . . . [belongs] to the group of 'god-fearers,' who were attached to the synagogue, but had not completed their conversion to Judaism through circumcision."[102]

But besides circumcision there were other important characteristics that designated a proselyte. They must be taken seriously if we are to understand the role of women in this religious movement. The marks of a male proselyte were circumcision, baptism (= ceremonial bath), and the presentation of a sacrifice in the Temple.[103] It is said that women were not required to bring a sacrifice.[104] From this it is concluded that for female proselytes baptism was "the only act of initiation,"[105] and it alone characterized them as initiates. The "god-fearers" are said to have been exempted from fulfilling this condition. However they, together with the proselytes, must certainly have participated at least in the "instruction,"[106] which then brought them into a common association. When Josephus writes ". . . let no one wonder that there was so much wealth in our temple, since all the Jews throughout the habitable earth, and those that worshiped God, nay, even those of Asia and Europe, sent their contributions to it, and this from very ancient times,"[107] the σεβόμενοι τὸν θεόν[108] are certainly included in the presentation of sacrificial offerings.[109] What ultimately separated male proselytes from male "god-fearers" was baptism and circumcision: among women, the only difference was baptism.[110]

The substantive formed from the verb σέβεσθαι (τὸν θεόν) is used in the New Testament only by Luke, and only in the book of Acts. That book speaks of the σεβόμενοι only after the description of the first missionary journey of Paul and his companions, and it is not used again after the end of the second missionary journey. More precisely, the word appears for the first time at 13:43 and for the last time at 18:7; moreover, it is mainly used *in connection with the synagogue:* 13:43; 16:14; 17:4, 17. After Paul (and Barnabas), at the request of the leaders of the synagogue, had explained the law and the prophets in the synagogue at Pisidian Antioch, many Jewish men and women and σεβομένων προσηλύτων followed them (13:43). It is difficult to decide whether these are "god-fearers" (specifically addressed in vv. 16 and 26 as φοβούμενοι τὸν θεόν), or proselytes, emphatically described as "pious."[111] In Thessalonica, also (17:1-4), Paul went to the synagogue on the Sabbath, as was his custom, and on three successive Sabbaths explained the Scripture to those present, applying his interpretation to the fulfillment of Scripture in Jesus' messiahship. Some of those present believed what Paul said and became his and Silas's followers. In Athens as well (17:16-17), Paul goes to the synagogue and speaks to and with the Jews and devotees he finds there, although there is no report of success or lack thereof with respect to the Jews and others present, because the text immediately (from v. 17b onward) shifts attention to the events on the Areopagus.

The scenes in 13:50 and 18:7, which do not take place within the synagogue itself, are nevertheless associated with the events in the synagogue.

Paul was asked to speak the word of the Lord in the synagogue at Antioch a second time. This took place in the presence of almost the whole city (13:44ff.). After the controversy between Paul and his fellow Israelites in Antioch, Jewish men and women aroused the devout women of high standing and the leaders of the city and provoked a persecution against Paul and Barnabas (v. 50). Something similar happened in Corinth, where the missionary activity of Paul was at first persuasive among the Jews and Greeks (18:4-5), but again led to conflicts, at which point he announced that he would go to the Gentiles (v. 6).

Instead, however, he goes to the house of the "god-fearer," Titius Justus, next door to the synagogue. It is also reported that the head of the synagogue believed in the Lord, with his whole household and many Corinthian men and women, and they all were baptized (vv. 7-8).

In light of the passages from Acts just adduced, we may conclude:

First, σεβόμενοι (τὸν θεόν), often mentioned in association with Jews, appear only from the point at which Paul and his fellow missionaries have begun "to go into the synagogue" in the cities of the diaspora where there are existing Jewish communities with which non-Jews are associated. They do not appear again after Acts 18:7. It is not accidental that after Acts 19:8 (Ephesus) we no longer read of Paul's going into the synagogues.[112] Σεβόμενοι, then, are usually mentioned in connection with the synagogue and are associated with the synagogue in some way.

Second, we cannot deduce from these passages in Acts that god-fearers were generally despised or regarded as inferior by the Jews because the males in the group were not circumcised.[113]

Third, the complete expression σεβομένη/σεβόμενος τὸν θεόν appears only twice: in 16:14 for Lydia, and in 18:7 for Titius Justus. Otherwise we find only the adjective without the accusative. Whether the simple adjective always means "god-fearers," persons associated with Judaism, is questionable insofar as it is used in a general sense as a "typical expression of Greek piety."[114] According to Acts 19:27, Diana is also worshiped (σέβεσθαι), which shows that the simple verb or its substantive form need not always refer to those associated with Judaism. In the expanded expression, the accusative serves to designate the deity who is worshiped. Since terms like θεός, θεός ὕψιστος, or κύριος were regarded in the Greek-speaking diaspora as designations of the Jewish god,[115] there can be no doubt that σεβομένη/σεβόμενος τὸν θεόν means "worshipers of [the Jewish] god," the more so when such expressions appear in connection with the synagogue.

Fourth, it is not easy to discern the social status and economic-political connections of the σεβόμενοι (τὸν θεόν) from the passages in Acts where the term appears. It appears to me that it is incorrect with respect both to method and to the content of the material to make Acts 13:50 a rule governing all the others, because this fails to take into account the emphasis in the text, namely that "devout women *of high standing*" are the subject, and not *all* devout women in general. I also see it as methodologically problematic to interpret all "god-fearers" in analogy with Cornelius, that is, to take Cornelius as the typical example representing all statuses. Christian exegetes believe that Christianity recruited very strongly from the ranks of the "god-fearers," who are supposed to have been of considerable significance for Judaism, both economically and in terms of local politics. Christians are thought to have brought Jewish enmity upon themselves by attracting these people away from Judaism. Folker Siegert writes: "Women of high standing among the god-fearers appear with remarkable frequency in Acts [the reference is to 13:50; 16:14; 17:4, 12]. The Jews had . . . particular success among women: those of high standing were especially useful to them in local politics and economically as well. That is why the bitter enmity of the Jews repeatedly lashed out at the Christian missionaries."[116] Rudolf Pesch formulates his interpretation as follows, in commenting on Acts 17:4: "The fact that the missionaries enticed women from prominent circles away from the synagogue is an understandable reason for Jewish 'jealousy.'"[117] He also writes, with regard to Acts 17:12: "Again the synagogue (cf. 4c) has women 'of high standing' (cf. Luke 8:3 [!]; Acts 13:50) among the god-fearers, who are now converted [to Christianity]."[118] We need not contest the fact that there were rich women with influence in local politics who often espoused the Jewish religion and used their position to lend it political and economic support. Many such women are documented in the literature and in inscriptions.[119] But to generalize from that fact to the idea that god-fearers belonged exclusively or overwhelmingly to the upper classes is, in my opinion, not a correct conclusion from the evidence. Acts, in fact, mentions devout women of high standing only in 13:50 and 17:4, 12. These passages attest that devout women from the upper classes did not always and everywhere attach themselves to the (Christian) missionaries.[120]

It is evident from both inscriptional and literary material that women were particularly inclined to accept and practice the Jewish religion. A story recorded by Josephus[121] tells us that almost all the women of Damascus,[122] Queen Helena of Adiabene, and the "women that belonged to the king" in Charax Spasini on the Persian Gulf[123] had converted to Judaism.

Although the words σεβόμενοι and φοβούμενοι (τὸν θεόν) do not appear in inscriptions, to my knowledge,[124] the Latin concept of *metuens/metuentes* can be regarded as synonymous with σεβόμενοι or φοβούμενοι.[125] Appearances of these words can not only support the existence of the "god-fearers," but also substantiate the thesis that it was especially women who adopted the Jewish religion, for the existing tomb inscriptions, with one exception, also mention the names of those who have died. They are Larciae Quadrati(llae),[126] Maiania Homeris,[127] a woman whose name is lost,[128] Aurelia Soteria,[129] and Aelia Criste, mentioned alongside Aelius Priscilianus (her husband).[130] One inscription retains the name of an Emilio Valenti.[131] Apart from these inscriptions, so far as I know, there are no others that mention *metuens/ metuentes*. Of six inscriptions, four name only women, one names a married couple, and one a man. But if the Latin word *colens* (*deum*) can also be regarded as a synonym for "worshipers of god,"[132] we have a further indication of "god-fearers." Again it is a woman, Julia Irene Arista, who is named.[133]

The inscriptions mentioned above give us clear information only about the gender of the "god-fearers." In my opinion, these inscriptions permit no absolute certainty or general conclusion regarding the economic or sociopolitical status of the "god-fearers."[134] At best, something more concrete can be drawn from texts. But even when the text gives key information about a "god-fearer," no all-encompassing thesis can be derived from it,[135] because "there is no historical information to show that the god-fearers appeared within the life of the Jewish or Gentile society as a circumscribed, cohesive group, so that one could speak of them as a [social] class."[136]

The text of Acts 16:14, unlike all the other passages that mention σεβόμενοι (τὸν θεόν), takes pains to describe certain qualities of the devout Lydia, and it does not—as do 13:50; 17:4, 12—say that she was "well-to-do" or "of high standing," but speaks very simply and at the same time in detail of her profession and place of origin. In order to be able to better describe her socioeconomic situation, we will, in what follows, investigate her work world.

It is difficult to ascertain from the sources why more women than men accepted and practiced the Jewish way of life.[137] Luise Schottroff has shown that the Jewish religion must have offered women—as in the case of the "king's women" in Charax Spasini—"a possibility to express the identity of women as a group, an identity that did not exist before."[138] Indeed, in that religion also it is demonstrable that women could share in leadership functions.[139]

Lydia's Employment

The text says of Lydia that she was a πορφυρόπωλις. The word is universally translated as "dealer in purple cloth." The text itself tells us nothing further about that profession. We may suppose that in that place and context further explanation was unnecessary, since the profession was known. But what kind of work did Lydia do, and how was it regarded? First we will consider the commentaries, and then the literary and inscriptional material.

A Review of New Testament Commentaries

Current New Testament exegesis has a distinct idea about this profession. Observations are not focused on the precise meaning of the job itself, but on what can be deduced from it about the social position of Lydia. Thus at the end of the last century J. Felten[140] categorically asserted that Lydia was well-to-do, "since dealing in purple required a substantial capital because of the costliness of the material, and she [Lydia] exhibited a great degree of hospitality (see v. 15)." Other exegetes have followed this and similar statements.[141] Only a few fail to draw like conclusions from this description of Lydia's profession.[142] Gottfried Schille is the only commentator of this century who does not presume Lydia's wealth as a given: "It is not evident that Lydia was wealthy."[143] The argumentation and the evidence produced is fragmentary on both sides; some do not even bother to offer any argument. When some point out that there were purple dyeing works or a "purple industry" in Thyatira, they apparently do so in order to give a "solid" basis to the presumption of Lydia's wealth and to explain it through this circumstance. Expressions like "having a great deal of capital at her disposal," "luxury goods," and "lucrative business" quickly follow.

Overall, the traditional exegesis has failed to ask what kind of work Lydia really did. With the exception of Schille, the interpreters simply presume that work with purple dye, or purple goods, had made Lydia a rich woman. We will now test this presumption by examining the meaning of the statement that Lydia was a πορφυρόπωλις from Thyatira.

Lydia's Origins

The text finds it important to emphasize that Lydia came from Thyatira. In seeking further information about Thyatira, I will concentrate principally on business and trade in that place.

Thyatira: A Long Lydian Tradition of Textile Work

It appears from the inscriptions cited in the following notes that there were a great many workers of both sexes in the Lydian city of Thyatira who were organized into guilds. There were bakers,[144] potters or ceramists,[145] tanners,[146] leather workers and shoemakers,[147] blacksmiths,[148] linen weavers,[149] wool spinners,[150] tailors,[151] and finally dyers.[152] The last three categories describe workers who were especially representa-

tive of the Lydian region. Textile work, especially making and working
with woolen stuffs, is also attested in Ephesus[153] and Philadelphia.[154]

It is true that the inscriptions *CIG* 3496 and 3497, which attest the
presence of βαφεῖς, "dyers," in Thyatira, are from the time of
Caracalla,[155] when the dye works and clothing manufactories had already been in the hands of the Roman empire for some time and were
under the emperor's direct control.[156] But Thyatira had been famous
from earliest times for its textile production and the dye works associated with it.[157] It is all the more amazing that there are no inscriptions
from Thyatira that mention, for example, πορφυροβαφεῖς, "*purple* dyers,"[158] but only βαφεῖς, "dyers." This detail has been overlooked or
suppressed by the commentators, although in my opinion it is important. If these inscriptions make no special mention of purple dyers, this
means that a variety of colors were made there, and not uniquely purple
dye.

Lydia comes from a region known for the production of dyed wool
and woolen clothing. No one denies that work with wool was an activity typical of women.

"She kept house, she made wool."

Dyeing was part of the production and preparation of wool. It is even
said that the dyeing of wool was a Lydian invention.[159] The invention of
linen weaving is also ascribed to Arachne, who was a Lydian.[160] It is no
accident or poetic invention that Lydian women were repeatedly mentioned in connection with textile dyeing.[161]

Making wool thread and cloth and working with them had been a
typical work of women from the most ancient times, as is clear from
part of the tomb inscription of Claudia in Rome: *domum servavit,
lanam fecit* ("she kept house, she made wool").[162] Here as in Prov.
31:10-31 (LXX), we find an expression of the ideal of womanhood
that, like the myth of Arachne, sheds light on concrete conditions: a
γυναῖκα ἀνδρείαν, a "capable woman," should or does produce, among
other things, textiles and clothing for everyone's use, that is, for herself
and all the members of her household. She makes them with her own
hands, of wool and flax; she dyes the cloth purple and spins it. This
"capable woman" is not one of the poor (31:20), but she herself has no
slaves. She works with her own hands. Words derived, for example,
from ποιεῖν ("to make," "to manufacture"), χεῖρας ("hands"), ἐνδύειν
("clothe") appear with remarkable frequency in Prov. 31:10-31. In this
passage πορφύρα, "purple," refers to clothing or material made and

dyed by the housewife herself, and used for her own and others' clothing. She is able to enjoy the results of her own labor: 31:31 emphasizes this fact. Cicero also knows of a woman named Lamia in the city of Segeste on the northern coast of Sicily (in this case, a wealthy woman) who, like the women of other households, makes wool and produces purple-dyed cloth and clothing.[163]

Proverbs 31:10-31, CIL 1.2.1211, and Cicero all show that the work of making textiles was at first restricted to the household or extended family. But even when it was for the most part produced in business establishments, it remained mainly a woman's task,[164] so that the imperial clothing factories from the third century onward were still known as *gynaecea/gynaeciarii*.[165] It is therefore historically correct to read the inscriptions that speak of βαφεῖς as referring to *female* dyers as well as men. In this connection, we can already anticipate what is to come by saying that in the exercise of this profession, women were not restricted to the household as the place of their activity.

Wherever textiles were produced and used in the manufacture of finished products, dye-stuffs were highly important: "Dye-stuff plays a major part in the coloring of textiles; in all cases it is a question of organic dyes. In antiquity, this special application was restricted primarily to coloring materials extracted from plants."[166]

The Business of Purple Dye and Purple Cloth

What was understood at that time under the designation "purple"? How was purple cloth produced and sold? It is important to observe how differently work was evaluated in those times. Here again, we must consult both literary and inscriptional material.

The Many Shadings of a Concept

The word πορφύρα, Latin *purpura*, has three principal meanings. Its first reference is to a type of sea snail. There were two kinds:[167] the κῆρυξ (*bucinum, murex*) and the πορφύρα (*purpura, pelagia*). From the latter the original, animal purple dye was extracted: the second reference of the word is to this dye, and the third meaning of the word is the dyed material itself, purple cloth.[168]

The word appears in biblical texts, mainly in its third meaning as purple cloth or clothing: 1 Macc. 4:23 (LXX); Luke 16:19; Mark 15:17, 20. Revelation 17:4; 18:12, 16 also indicate, in my opinion, that there were different types and qualities of purple cloth.

First Maccabees 4:23 says that, after the battle, Judas despoiled the vanquished and took away χρυσίον πολὺ καὶ ἀργύριον καὶ ὑάκινθον καὶ πορφύραν θαλασσίαν καὶ πλοῦτον μέγαν as booty. This is always translated as: "they seized a great amount of gold and silver, and cloth dyed blue and sea purple, and great riches." The sequence of the listing is according to the value of what was taken. Another meaning for ὑάκινθον is "jacinth" (a semiprecious stone);[169] in that case the text would read "and they seized a great amount of gold and silver, jacinth, sea purple, and great riches." Or it may be that ὑάκινθον is intended to draw a clear distinction between plant and animal purple dye; that is, the text would be speaking of dye extracted from the hyacinth (blue) and from sea creatures (purple).[170] The phrase πορφύραν θαλασσίαν is, in any case, quite specific and indicates that there were other types of purple that were not made from animal dyes.

Whereas Rev. 17:4; 18:12, 16 distinguish the types of purple in a series ordered according to value, using different terms for each (πορφύρα, κόκκινον), the situation in other texts is more complicated because the same word, πορφύρα, is used to describe items of different value. This can be illustrated by looking at Luke 16:19 and Mark 15:17, 20 in their respective contexts. Whereas the wearing of purple in Luke 16:19 can be a sign of wealth, this is not the case in Mark 15:17, 20. There the persons involved are common soldiers, and their action in clothing Jesus in a purple cloak is symbolic and intended to ridicule Jesus. That the word πορφύρα was used without always referring to a symbol of luxury status is clear from these same passages in Mark. It is made still more obvious by Matthew's correction of this story: Matt. 27:28 refers to a χλαμύδα κοκκίνην, a "soldier's purple [or scarlet] cloak." Matthew makes an alteration here to make clear what πορφύρα means: that there were many types and qualities of purple subsumed under the same heading. Matthew is making an effort to be specific at this point.[171]

The Manufacture of Various Kinds of Purple Dye and Purple Cloth

The word πορφύρα (*purpura*) does not always refer to the original dyestuff extracted from snails or to the cloth dyed with that substance; it can also describe colors and colored materials that merely resemble the original.[172] Two processes quite frequently used to produce an imitation of the original purple have been known for a long time:[173] first, various types of purple dye extracted from snails are mixed to produce, among other things, a cheaper "genuine" purple; second, certain plants were also used to produce a purple color. For Pliny it is a matter of course that in wool production both animal dyes (that is, those extracted from snails) and plant dyes will be used.[174] Among the colors for various purposes that he mentions, he also distinguishes individual types and qualities of animal purple obtained by particular combinations,[175] all of which he ultimately categorizes among the artificially produced colors.[176] This artificial purple is not only "diluted," but is also produced by "re-adulterating nature's adulterations."[177] The different types and qualities of purple are also associated with particular localities. Thus, for example, there was the good, original purple produced especially in Tyre (in Asia), Meninx (in Africa), Laconia (in Europe), and Puteoli (in Europe).[178] It appears from Pliny, *Naturalis Historia* 35.45, that there was an inferior, cheaper type from Canosa (in Apulia). Prices differed accordingly, with the cost of a pound varying from 1 to 30 denarii.[179]

In Lydia it seems that purple dye was produced in many cities, including the capital at Sardis, being derived from *coccum*[180] and even from saltpeter (*nitrum*) dried in the sun.[181] In Hierapolis in Phrygia, where there were both πορφυροβαφεῖς and ordinary βαφεῖς,[182] it was also possible, because of the character of the water, to extract a famous purple dye from roots that are no longer known today.[183] Thus there was purple derived from plants; the color was not inferior to that extracted from animals, and it was used for the dyeing of wool. Pliny writes:

> Moreover, we know that clothes are dyed with a wonderful dye from a plant, and, to say nothing of the fact that, of the berries of Galatia, Africa, and Lusitania, the "coccum" [*granis coccum*] is specially reserved to color the military cloaks of our generals, Transalpine Gaul can produce with vegetable dyes Tyrian purple, oyster purple, and all other colors.[184]

Among the plants used for the production of purple vegetable dye were ὕσγη (*granis coccum*), ὑάκινθος or hyacinth (= *vaccinium* or "blueberry"), and ἐρυθρόδανον (*rubia* or "madder").[185] It appears from *Naturalis Historia* 35.45 that both the animal and vegetable dyes were called "purple," for in Puteoli purple was produced from the juice of *hysginum* ("crimson") and *rubia* ("madder"). *Rubia* was used for a number of purposes: in addition to its medicinal use it served "to dye wool and to tan leather."[186] Pliny remarks elsewhere that this plant is known "only to the avaricious herd [*sordido*]," namely for the dyeing of wool and leather.[187]

This purple extracted from plants was also used for slaves' clothing.[188] Cicero reports, in addition, that the beds in slaves' sleeping chambers bore the purple coverlets of Gnaeus Pompeius.[189] He is also aware that not all purples are the same: for example, he knows that the original type comes from Tyre, but that there is also a *purpura plebeia*.[190] The distinction among types of purple is also found in Quintilian, who makes use of the symbolic quality of the color to describe the art of oratory and the clothing then associated with it;[191] he is also aware of "adulterations" or imitations of the genuine, animal purple.[192]

Thyatira is mentioned for its dyeing establishments both in literature and in inscriptions. Nowhere, however, is it said that purple extracted from animals was involved in those operations. Since the evidence does not emphasize this, it appears more likely that the dye works in Thyatira produced vegetable purple. Mention of wool production accords well with the existence of dye works, since both operations were ordinarily carried on in tandem. Because the inscriptions at Thyatira make no mention of πορφυροβαφεῖς, scholarly discussion outside the New Testament field has assumed that the dyers in Thyatira extracted their purple dye from *rubia*.[193] The theologians M. Clévenot and C. J. Hemer similarly assert that "In Lydia . . . the city of Thyatira was known for the madder root that grew in its fields, while sheep and goats provided the necessary material for the production of cloth and wool blankets."[194] "Its [Thyatira's] purple dye came from the madder root rather than the marine *murex*, and the use of this substance is attested in the district until the present century."[195] On the basis of this information that purple dye and cloth were made in Thyatira from madder roots, we can understand why K. Schneider[196] does not include Thyatira in a long list of cities in which animal purple was produced and utilized: he is primarily concerned with the production of *animal* purple, but not with *vegetable* purple dyes.

Nevertheless, I believe we may be quite certain about the basis of purple production in Thyatira. In spite of the opinions of Clerc, Clévenot, and Hemer,[197] it appears to me that there is no absolutely clear evidence, and for that very reason we may not presume beforehand that it is a question of superior products or luxury articles. In light of the sources that have come to light, indeed, it is historically very probable that the purple of Thyatira was made from vegetable materials. This, and the vegetable-mineral mixed purple, were also produced in the *purpurariis* (*officinis*), as we see from Pliny, *Naturalis Historia* 35.44–46, and 9.140–41. But the fact that purple dye was extracted, for example, from madder roots is not merely something derived from the evidence of ancient writers and artists. People are still working with the same substance today.[198] Hence, to say that the βαφεῖς, the "dyers," in Thyatira were solely *purple* dyers is a historical misunderstanding or a simplification of the manifold range of methods available at that time for the production and imitation of dye-stuffs. This simplification can also be observed in New Testament exegesis. In my opinion, it is used to lend support to the idea, current in today's wealthy Western world, that Lydia, the first Christian in "Europe," was herself a wealthy woman.

Was Lydia a European Wholesaler?

There is no literary or inscriptional evidence for the existence of specialized wholesale merchants in Thyatira who devoted themselves to the sale of products such as purple dye or purple cloth. It was different, for example, in Tyre, where there were ἔμποροι and ναύκληροι (*mercatores*), "wholesalers," who subsequently settled in Puteoli and Rome.[199] Hence it is also not particularly remarkable that historians only mention Lydia at the point when they treat βαφεῖς, "dyers;"[200] they put Lydia in the context of the dyers' trade. Dio Chrysostomus[201] asserts that it is much cheaper (costing only two or three minas) to buy καλὴν πορφύραν, "good purple-dyed material" direct from the dyers.[202] This also agrees with the Latin word *purpurarius/a*, the Latin equivalent of πορφυρόπωλης/ις, referring to people who work both in dyeing and in the sale of the dyed products.[203] We will refer to this inscriptional usage again later.

This work brought Lydia, who grew up in the Lydian tradition of wool production and wool working, to Philippi. How and from whom she learned this work can be guessed in connection with her religious adherence.[204] Lydia is further evidence that women's work with textiles did not remain confined to the household, but that they took to the road or were compelled to travel in order to sell what they produced. Lydia is not an isolated example. We find inscriptional evidence of a married couple on the island of Cos in which both the man and his wife had the same job description as Lydia.[205] However, the Latin equivalent, *purpurarius/a*, is much more common.[206] It is striking that in most cases the inscriptions mention not individuals, but whole groups. Most of these groups are made up of women and men,[207] but women were apparently numerous, and often constituted a majority within the group, as *CIL* 6.984, 9848 attest.

"DIRTY WORK." A passage in Cicero (*De Off.* 1.42, 150–51) clearly reveals the estimation of various professions and occupations that existed in the society of the time, as set down by Cicero. He here lists the occupations worthy (*liberales*) of a free person and those that are unworthy (*inliberales*) and filthy (*sordidi*); in doing so, he reflects "the ideas of a powerful elite."[208]

> . . . ungentlemanly and sordid are the earnings of hired hands who are paid for their physical efforts rather than their skill; for the very wages they receive are a token of slavery. Retail dealers are little better, for they have little to gain unless they are pretty dishonest, and deserve no credit if they are. The occupation of a craftsman is also to be scorned, for what well-born man could possibly spend his time in a workshop (*officina*)?

Honorable and worthy of free persons are professions like medicine, architecture, teaching, and wholesale trade combined with the possession of large landed estates:

> Those professions which require skilled training, or fulfil a useful function, such as medicine, architecture or the teaching of the liberal arts, are reputable for those whose station in life they suit. The career of a merchant (*mercatura*) is only to be despised (*sordida*) if pursued on a small scale, but if it includes large and valuable transactions and imports from all over the world . . . it is not so much to be condemned; in fact, if those who indulge in it become satisfied or at any rate are prepared to be content with their profits, and retire from the harbor to their country estates just as they had frequently retired to the harbor from the sea, this seems to be entirely commendable. But of all the sources of income the life of a farmer (*agri cultura*) is the best, pleasantest, most profitable and most befitting a gentleman.

Cicero here represents the common, dominant opinion and thus supports Roman patriarchy, the system of the *pax Romana*.[209] The dichotomy and dualism between "spiritual" and "physical" on the one hand, and on the other hand (although connected with it) between worthwhile and less worthwhile work is striking in this passage from Cicero. Everything that demands either "practical" or "philosophical" wisdom (*De Off.* 1.43, 153), and whatever brings a great deal of profit, he regards as worthy and honorable (*honestus*). Everything that demands work with the hands and does not bring much profit is considered despicable and filthy (*sordidus*).

Cicero's reflection of the dominant opinion seems illustrative to me because it applies not to wholesale merchants, but to the making of goods for sale and the business of dealing in those goods on a small scale. Work with purple was normally done in workshops (*purpurariis officinis*).[210] According to Cicero, this was dirty work, so we may suppose that the workers were looked down upon. This attitude had concrete effects, which can be illustrated by two examples: first, the inscription *CIL* 1.1413, according to which a certain workshop of this kind was outside the city of Rome, in the Via Salaria; second, Plutarch[211] writes that a person should always pursue only the best, rejoice over what is beautiful, and eagerly imitate the deeds of noble men in order to act just as they do. But then he speaks of tasks in which there is no desire to do likewise, rather the contrary: "Often we take pleasure in a thing, but we despise the one who made it. Thus we value aromatic salves and purple clothing, but the dyers and salve-makers remain for us common and low craftspersons [because they do work that is unworthy of a free person]."[212] Dirty work done in dye works and tanneries also had to be conducted outside the city because of the stink it produced.[213] According to Pliny,[214] the production of purple cloth by the use of vegetable dyes is also a filthy (*sordidum*) job. On this basis, we can discern a deeper meaning in Acts 16:13: synagogue buildings were located in the vicinity of the people who belonged to them.[215] Moreover, a good deal of water was needed for working with purple.[216] Thus the information contained in ἔξω τῆς πύλης παρὰ ποταμόν, "outside the gate by the river" (Acts 16:13) may refer not merely to the common practice of locating synagogues near water,[217] but also to the fact that Lydia and her household conducted their business, which was socially despised as dirty work, outside the city and near the water that was so abundantly available in Philippi.[218]

THE WORK OF SLAVES AND FREED PERSONS. The production and processing of textiles was not only typical woman's work; it was done primarily by slaves and freed persons.[219] According to *CIL* 1.1413; 6.4016, 9847; 14.473, also, *purpurarii* were slaves or freed persons.[220] We may infer from *CIL* 1.1413 that the group of people freed at the same time continued under the authority of the *patronus*; apparently they are still working for him.[221] It also appears from *Digesta* 38.1.45 that *purpurarii*, to the extent they could be said to be *negotiatores vestiarii*, were also slaves who, after being freed, could only continue their work in the same place and in the same town without the consent of the *patronus* who freed them if their liberator suffered no economic or social injury (*laesio*) as a result. There was a long history of experience behind this law. It makes clear why so many small merchants had to take to the road, and why they could not continue to practice the trade they had learned as slaves in their homeland or hometown after they had been freed,[222] or how it happened that, even as freed persons, they had to continue performing the same services (to the extent that they continued in the same trade after being liberated) for the one who had released them.[223] Thus according to *Digesta* 38 and the experiences on which it was based, freed persons continued to be very closely tied to the one who had freed them, especially from an economic point of view. Had there been no such connections, or had they been rare, the legal texts extending to the end of the imperial period would not have treated them so consistently and in such detail, nor would they have needed to establish legal norms for such a relationship, as is the case in the texts in question.[224] We may also consider Luise Schottroff's observation regarding Lydia's work within this context: "In general, the manufacturing and the sale of dyed products were done by the same people. That means the dye-house was operated by an owner with several employees. These employees both worked in the dye-house and sold the wool."[225] In line with this, we could suggest at this point that Lydia was an employee in one of the many dye works in Thyatira.

Retail trade as well, especially in connection with the production and processing of textiles, was characteristically the work of freed persons.[226] But even though slaves and freed persons are inscriptionally attested as *purpurarii,* this does not prove that Lydia was one of them. It is something that must still be considered.[227] In any case, her name indicates that she had been a slave at some point: "Lydia" is an *ethnicon,*[228] but originally *ethnica* were more appellatives than personal names. They were applied especially to slaves and hetaerae because they described special features of their origin, nationality, and thus particular racial or ethnic characteristics that served to single out their bearers. It was possible for an *ethnicon* to become a personal name, so that freed persons continued to bear the *ethnicon* as their own name. This is revealing in the case of Lydia.

At this point some reflections on the relationship between the large, organized dyer guilds and the Roman authorities are in order. The βαφεῖς, or some of them, may well have been faithful participants or collaborators in the *pax Romana.* This was the case for the majority at least from the second century C.E. onward, as *CIG* 3497 from Thyatira indicates: Titus Antonius Claudius Alpheus Arignotus, to whom the inscription is dedicated, was the commander of a number of military troops and, as such, also held many religious offices in the service of the state. We cannot draw a general conclusion from this that at an early period all dyer organizations were always subservient to the Imperium Romanum and followed its orders in all things, including in matters religious. This was, in fact, the norm even for organizations of ordinary people, primarily in the *collegia,* but it was not the everyday rule of life. There were also a great many *collegia illicita.* In addition, we know that there were frequent imperial interventions in the *licita,* and that the *illicita* existed at least for that length of time and could frequently organize themselves in opposition to the *pax Romana,* as long as they were not discovered.[229] Obedience to and compliance with all official regulations was not the rule, as, for example, another inscription from the same period as that of the βαφεῖς in Thyatira shows. The people mentioned in this inscription[230] are a counter-example to those named in CIG 3497, because here it appears that the purple dyers in Hierapolis celebrated the feast of unleavened bread (ἐν τῇ ἑορτῇ τῶν ἀζύμων). They were therefore Jews who did not bow to at least one essential ideological component of the *pax Romana,* namely the religious.

Lydia's House

Having considered the women's place of assembly and Lydia's profession, I now turn to the next piece of information in the text. Acts 16:15 uses the word οἶκος twice: Lydia's "house" is baptized along with her, and she has a house of her own. The same word here refers to different things: first it applies to people who are connected with Lydia, and then to a place, namely her dwelling.

Hellenistic Greek usage comprehended a number of meanings under the term οἶκος, so that the same word could, for example, describe a variety of locations and relationships. This word includes meanings ranging from "cave," "cabin," "tent," "temple," "dwelling," and "house" to "household," "wealth," and "family property."[231]

Was Lydia a Widow, or the Presider over a Congregation?

It is difficult to determine exactly what is meant by the word "house" in this verse. H.-J. Klauck makes it a principle of interpretation to extract the meaning of οἶκος only from its individual occurrences within the context of the text itself, to the extent that the context offers clues to the word's meaning.[232] He himself applies this rule to Acts 10:7 and 16:5: here he finds that the word serves to denominate the members of a household named by means of this "house" formula, namely those of Cornelius and Lydia.[233] Acts 10:7 makes it clear that the house of Cornelius includes at least two household slaves and a pious soldier, all of whom are mentioned concretely in the Cornelius story. In the case of Lydia, it seems that Klauck cannot deduce anything from the context; nevertheless, he asserts that Lydia was "an independent businesswoman, possibly a widow"; her house must "with some certainty [have included] servant women and slaves who [were] indispensable in her mercantile business."

Like Klauck, Peter Stuhlmacher[234] takes as his rule that "[it can] only be determined from the context who belongs to the οἶκος (οἰκία) and who does not," because the οἶκος does not always represent the same group of people, but can refer to others. Unlike Klauck, however, Stuhl-macher draws the following conclusion from the application of his thesis: Whereas in Acts 10:1-8, 24-48 we can learn who the probable members of Cornelius's household were (v. 7), this is impossible in the case of Lydia. From these two texts (Acts 10:1-8, 24-48; 16:5) we can derive only one common aspect, namely that neither of them contains any mention of children.

The discussion remains controversial. The examples just given show how difficult, if not impossible, it is to determine from the text who and what constituted Lydia's house. However, New Testament scholarship has not been lacking in suggestions. Lydia is everything from a "wealthy and independent woman," probably head of an extended family,[235] to a "widow in charge of an orderly household."[236] C. F. Nösgen produces a reason why Lydia is to be thought of as a widow: "Nothing is said about a man; the text appears to speak of her [Lydia's] οἶκος in v. 15 at the time of the baptism. Thus it appears that Lydia is a widow."[237] This manner of speaking makes it clear that critics always expect or presuppose that the word οἶκος will refer to the situation that was the rule in that era as well: A man is head of the house. This thesis is then regularly applied to all texts in which οἶκος appears. From that point of view, and in any reading guided by this thesis, Lydia must necessarily be a widow. But it appears to me that Lydia's house is a direct contradiction to these patriarchal ideas, whereby the man plays the role of husband, father, and master, and in which wife, children, and slaves are part of the property of the house, that is, of the man.[238] It is only in the context of this or a similar view of things that a statement like "[t]he house and family are the smallest *natural* groups in the total structure of the congregation"[239] can be considered to be true.

The dominant interpretation of this story reveals the difficulties that confront us in considering the matter of Lydia's house. "This exegetical history does not try to hide its intentions: The first female Christians had to be from the upper middle class; they were not allowed to question the patriarchal family and the patriarchal organization of religion."[240] I want to inquire whether Lydia's house can be understood in some other way than in the exegesis that has dominated until now. In the following sections it will repeatedly appear that Lydia was a very important person, the head of a worshiping community.

"My House" — A Community of Work and Faith

Work with purple cloth required a considerable number of hands. No doubt Lydia, too, found a large number of people "indispensable" for carrying out her job. However, that does not necessarily mean that they were Lydia's slaves.[241] Luise Schottroff has correctly shown that "[e]ven the lowly could, under certain circumstances, have a female slave,"[242] but she also concedes that we are not compelled to make that assumption in this case. The text gives no indication of this, nor of the existence of a patriarchal "family." The inscriptional evidence discussed above (on pp. 105–109) shows that, normally, a group of women and men worked together in the production of purple cloth. They traveled together and sold the products they had made. In many cases, as illustrated especially by *CIL* 1.1413; 6.4016, 9847–48; 14.473, these were a group of slaves or freed persons and their companions.

The women gathered in the synagogue, or some of them, may have been part of Lydia's house. We may suspect this from the text, to the extent that it continues to describe the episode begun in v. 13. We may speculate that this was an exclusively "female household," but that must remain open. Certainly such a thing is historically possible: At that time there were a number of women's groups who, for example, "accepted the Jewish religion on their own accord and practiced it . . . without male leadership or any other form of legitimization."[243] The existence of women's houses is also attested for Naples by *IG* 14.760.[244] Therefore I think we are justified in supposing at this point that Lydia's house was composed primarily of women.

In this connection, and on the basis of the many inscriptions mentioned above, we may also consider whether the other women who worked with Lydia in Philippi were foreigners, like Lydia herself. *Purpurarii* were mainly freed persons who settled in other cities to do their work, normally in small groups; in such groups, women were frequently in the majority.[245] This association and shared work was a form of organization practiced by common people who were attempting, together, to earn a subsistence income and at the same time to shape their social and religious lives in common.[246] Slaves and freed persons were almost entirely organized in *"collegia"* and "houses," and it was not exceptional for one of them to be found at the head of the group, for example as its *patronus* or *patrona*.[247]

The common notion that Lydia's house was very large and that her business had "brought her a substantial fortune," that is, that she had enjoyed "economic success,"[248] is unpersuasive for two reasons: On the one hand, at that time there was no large-scale textile production.[249] On the other hand, it cannot be demonstrated that people who worked in the production and sale of purple goods ever played an important economic role in Philippi; there is only one *purpuraria(ii)* inscription at Philippi (*CIL* 3.664).[250] From what has been said thus far, we are more inclined to conclude that Lydia's work was a subsistence occupation for herself and her house.

Another consideration is important at this point. In the New Testament period there was a strict dividing line between the upper and lower classes that was difficult to cross. We really cannot speak of a "middle class" in the present meaning of the term.[251] Craftspeople and small merchants were also part of the *plebs urbana*. Even when they had a "better" economic status (in comparison, say, to beggars), so that they even employed a few slaves or freed people, they were socially despised by the upper classes. In the eyes of the upper crust, their economic position was insignificant.[252] This contempt for ordinary working people on the part of the upper classes was based, as we have seen, on their "dirty," "undignified," and "ignoble" professions, as seen from the point of view of the upper classes. In addition, this contempt was partly motivated by the fact that a considerable number of the people practicing those trades and professions came from the East.[253]

On the basis of these observations, we may offer the following considerations: It is possible that there were slaves in Lydia's house, and it is probable that the income of her house made possible a better economic state of things than the lot of beggars. But still, as foreigners from the East who carried on a despised trade and also practiced the Jewish religion in that Roman colony, they belonged to the *plebs urbana*, the common people. As such, they were required at all times to work with their hands to earn their income and livelihood, and they were (as was customary with this kind of work) quite possibly not permanently resident in Philippi. They are not to be equated with the great merchants of the period.[254] These latter sold the goods produced on their estates by slaves, and thus concentrated the wealth in their own hands; among many other products, they also sold πορφύρα (see Acts 18).

"Come to My House" — A House Church at Philippi

Acts 16:12-15, 40 is a detailed narrative of the steps in founding a Christian house church. It seems to me that the narrative, so rich in detail about the lives of women (or one aspect of their lives), is pointed toward such a foundation. To put it another way, it seems to have been important to the author, through this narrative, to give a more precise description of the leader or presider over this house. It became increasingly important to me to inquire more penetratingly into the question of the author's precise emphases. In investigating the concrete meaning of the description of Lydia, I have also been confronted with other women who did the same or similar kinds of work and belonged to the same religious community. Lydia thus led me to other religiously committed working women. She opens a door to an important aspect of the history of women, a history that for the most part has been lost, hidden, or veiled, and continues to be obscured. Lydia was not an exceptional woman in her time, who then capped the story by adhering to Christianity because she was also looking for something "better" in her religious life.

The implications of the descriptive terms applied to Lydia and her environment give us access to her social world. But certain key words Luke uses also sketch the social and economic location of this community. Luke does not speak of just any people who went to the synagogue on the Sabbath and listened to the words of Paul's proclamation, accepted baptism, and confessed the Jewish-Christian faith. These were women who had done hard and difficult work, women who, even before the arrival of Paul, had led a religious life in common. They were women for whom it was a matter of life and death to be together, who drew from their Jewish religion the strength for their daily lives. This religion had offered them "a possibility to express the identity of women as a group, an identity that did not exist before"[255] because Judaism, like other eastern religions, "gave women a higher standing in comparison to the subordinating roles they had in state religion, and . . . allowed women to participate in leadership functions." It was important to the author to hand on this traditional foundation story in such a way that it was still possible to discern the social location of this house community within the overall sociopolitical constellation.

Let me now turn to the question of the theological, missionary, and organizational elements[256] in a house church/community like this one.

Lydia's Fidelity

The founding of this house church in Philippi takes place, according to the text, not primarily at or because of the baptism of the members, but only afterward. Acts 16:15 reads: "When she [Lydia] and her household were baptized, she urged us, saying, 'If you have judged me to be faithful to the Lord, come and stay at my home.' And she prevailed upon us." The expressions we find here are peculiar; in context, I think, they make a powerful statement. They include, for example, παρακαλεῖν, "to urge," "to entreat," "to demand"; κρίνειν με πιστὴν . . . εἶναι, "to judge [someone] faithful [etc.]"; and παραβιάζεσθαι, "to prevail upon," "to constrain," "to compel."

The decision to enter Lydia's house cannot be made by Lydia herself, in the final sense, but depends on the missionaries' judgment. Lydia invites them, however, and offers them the means of decision, which in her case is itself a judgment. They are to decide about her fidelity to the Lord. That fidelity may be a precondition for baptism, or something constituted by it, since κρίνειν is in the perfect tense and therefore describes something that has already occurred. We may suppose, then, that in baptizing Lydia the missionaries have already made a positive judgment about her "fidelity." The founding of the house church is therefore only to be understood as a direct consequence of her baptism to the extent that the positive judgment about fidelity to the Lord, that is, Lydia's faithfulness, belongs to and is a part of baptism. But if Lydia is true to the Jewish Jesus Christ preached by Paul and his companions, she is so within a society that owes fidelity to the Roman emperor, and her fidelity is a subversion of the dominant order.[257] The fidelity of Lydia's house to the Jewish Lord represents a simultaneous infidelity to the Roman emperor and his officials. The two are mutually exclusive.[258] The founding and existence of this house church rest on Lydia's fidelity, which then appears also as a precondition or component of baptism. Essential to this fidelity are obedience, trust, and hope—or, to put it another way, a sweeping, hopeful trust that also dares obedience to a God who stands in relationship to human beings (in this case, Lydia and her household) and gives them a share in God's salvation.

Rudolf Bultmann[259] attempts to distinguish points of unity and diversity between "faith" in the Old and New Testaments. Obedience, fidelity, trust, and hope are of central importance in both the Old Testament and the New, and are even closely connected. It remains problematic, however, that Bultmann exalts "Christian" faith over against "Jewish" faith. For example, in discussing Old Testament motifs in Judaism's idea of faith, he writes with regard to these different "elements" of fidelity, obedience, trust, and hope, that "to the degree that it looks to the future generally, [this faith] is also belief in retribution in a more general sense."[260] In attempting to distinguish between Judaism and the Old Testament, he writes: "As a result of the canonization of the tradition in Scripture, *obedient faithfulness* acquires the character of *obedience to the Law*. That is to say, it is no longer in the strict sense faithfulness to the experienced acts of God in history, with trust in His future acts therein."[261] And in this instance prejudice plays a major role: the idea of inspiration of Scripture is said to limit "the work of the Spirit to the past" and restrict "God's dealings to past history," resulting in "a despising of the natural conditions of life."[262] Jewish faith, "in so far as it hopes for God's acts," now remains oriented to miracles; trust is reduced to a "surrender to suffering," and hope is directed to "supernatural eschatological events, and God's judgment is . . . [thought of as] the eschatological forensic act."[263] The whole polemic ends with the assertion that "Belief in retribution is also *belief in merits*,"[264] which locates the whole discussion within the context of divine grace and works.

After Bultmann has listed the various nuances of the later history of Old Testament and Jewish tradition within "general Christian usage," he makes the following assertion: "To be distinguished from all the senses under 1. is the specifically Christian use of πίστις. . . πίστις is understood here as *acceptance of the Christian kerygma*. It is thus the *saving faith* which recognizes and appropriates God's saving in Christ."[265] It is also said here that the elements of "[o]bedience, trust, hope and faithfulness" are implied, but "the primary sense of πιστεύειν in specifically Christian usage is acceptance of the kerygma about Christ."[266] When this kerygma is accepted, of course, confident hope is less prominent, because Christian belief "looks primarily to what God has done, not to what He will do."[267] This, however, is all the more difficult to understand since the kerygma contains not only what God has done through Jesus, but also what God will continue to do,[268] and that implies ongoing, confident hope, because faith does not represent something finished and complete, but continually changes and draws new strength from the content of the kerygma.[269]

In my opinion, the "acceptance of the kerygma about Christ" does not exclude fidelity and is not dispensed from it. Through a public confession of faith, the believer enters into a relationship of fidelity with God, which includes a just relationship with other human beings. Infidelity toward God means at the same time mistreatment of and contempt for other people, fellow servants of God. This is clear from the parables that deal with service or care for others.

Matthew 24:45, for example, presents a faithful, good servant. (Luke 12:42 replaces πιστὸς δοῦλος with πιστὸς οἰκονόμος, but parallels it with δοῦλος in v. 43). This servant has the duty to give his fellow servants their food (portion of grain) at the right time. The one whom the Lord sees doing this will be blessed. But a bad servant who thinks that the Lord is long in coming and begins to beat and mistreat his fellow servants, thus revealing his true character, will be punished. Because the believer has received something from God,[270] she or he pledges faith to God with the obligation to remain faithful to God and to stand in a just relationship to other human beings. In this relationship, for example, believers do not seek their own good, but what is useful for all. Both aspects, the pledge and act of fidelity toward God and a just relationship toward and among human beings, are combined in the unified "moments" of faith, including obedience to God's order of things. If these ties are broken, the just relationship with other people is also ruptured, and vice versa. The fact that πιστός, πιστή includes a public confession of faith is clear, for example, from John 20:27-28. This confession, which is exclusive in the sense that it allows for and serves no other masters or mistresses, leads or can lead to persecution and martyrdom, as appears from Rev. 2:10-13.[271]

The first letter of Clement also knows and uses the word πιστός to describe the union between faith and mutual human relationships. In the letter to the community at Corinth an apparent distinction is made among different "Christian community categories" (1 Clem. 48.5: "Let [one] be faithful, let [one] be capable of uttering 'knowledge,' let [one] be wise in judging arguments, let [one] be pure in conduct") but this does not mean that one who believes cannot also be "pure in conduct." In this connection, it is important to note the emphasis on the fact that all are obligated in Christ "to seek the common good in preference to [one's] own" (1 Clem. 48.6: ζητεῖν τὸ κοινωφελὲς πᾶσιν, καὶ μὴ τὸ ἑαυτοῦ).

Πιστός with the dative appears in the New Testament, apart from Acts 16:15, only in Hebr. 3:2, where Jesus is described with this word as faithful to the one who made him. However, there is a similar use of the verb πιστεύειν with the dative in Acts 5:14 and 18:8.

The god-fearer Lydia, who accepted Jewish faith and thus also shared the Jewish messianic hope with other women in Philippi, believed in response to Paul's words that her hope had been fulfilled. She confessed this Messiah and had herself and her own people baptized in his name, thus entering into a relationship of fidelity with him that excluded other masters.[272] It seems to me that it is precisely in light of and against the background of this relationship of fidelity in the context of the political situation in the Roman colony of Philippi that we should understand the information in Acts 16:15 that Lydia constrained the missionaries to come to her house and remain there.

"She Urged Us . . . and Prevailed upon Us."
A Theological Anchor for a Praxis of Solidarity

The text concludes by noting that Lydia "prevailed upon" or "compelled" the missionaries (to stay at her house). This follows the theological judgment that she is faithful to the Lord. The expressions used in the text permit a glimpse of a turbulent situation behind the words. It appears to be transparent to the urgency of the moment and to latent conflicts. The expressions used give the impression that the situation in Philippi was not innocuous. Apparently time is pressing. A foreign working woman in a Roman colony exerts intense pressure on the missionaries to remain in her house.

The word παραβιάζεσθαι appears only one other time in the New Testament, in Luke 24:29. The disciples met the Risen One on the road to Emmaus, but did not recognize him. After they had described to this stranger the events connected with the crucifixion of Jesus, "they urged him strongly, saying, 'Stay with us, because it is almost evening and the day is now nearly over.' So he went in to stay with them."

These two passages should be studied more closely so that we may better understand this "urging" or "compulsion" and its possible consequences. As far as I am aware, the verb παραβιάζεσθαι is used outside the New Testament[273] primarily to describe events in which a life-threatening situation is averted, or can be avoided, or threatens to happen in the future. There can be compulsion:

1. *To accept gifts or similar things:*
a. After Genesis 32 has told how the relationship between Jacob and Esau was destroyed, and that there is danger of a struggle between the two groups associated with them, Gen. 33:1-17 reports an encounter between the two men that turns out peacefully after all. Jacob had

prepared for this meeting by taking with him gifts ("oxen, donkeys, flocks, male and female slaves," 32:5; cf. 33:8) to present to Esau in case he may find favor in his eyes. This did happen, but Esau refused to accept the gifts, saying: "I have enough, my brother; keep what you have for yourself" (33:9). Finally, Gen. 33:11 reports that Jacob successfully "urged" Esau (פצר + ב, LXX βιάζεσθαι) to accept the gift bestowed by divine favor (ברכה, LXX τὰς εὐλογίας).

b. After the prophet Elijah "ascended . . . into heaven" (2 Kgs. 2:11), his disciples went to Elisha, offering to seek Elijah on the mountains and in the valleys, where perhaps the spirit of the Lord had cast him (v. 16). Elisha refuses, and the prophet's disciples feel compelled to urge him to give his consent or approval (v. 17: ב + פצר, LXX παραβιάζεσθαι).

c. After Naaman the general had been healed of leprosy by Elisha, he desired to give him a gift with a blessing (ברכה, LXX τὰς εὐλογίας). Elisha refused. Naaman urged him (2 Kgs. 5:16: ב + פצר, LXX παραβιάζεσθαι). Still, Elisha did not accept.

d. The Hebrew Bible also uses the verb פרץ, which the LXX translates with βιάζεσθαι, in 2 Kgs. 5:23; 1 Sam. 28:23; 2 Sam. 13:25, 27, to mean "to urge someone to accept something."

2. *For the provision of accommodation and shelter in houses*:

a. Gen. 19:1-14 describes the events that took place in Sodom before its destruction. Lot was sitting at the gateway (πύλη) of the city in the evening, and saw that two messengers or "angels" were entering the gate. He immediately went to meet them and said: "'Please, my lords, turn aside to your servant's house and spend the night, and wash your feet. . . .' They said, 'No; we will spend the night in the square.'274 But he urged (פצר ב, LXX καταβιάζεσθαι) them strongly; so they turned aside to him and entered his house; and he made them a feast, and baked unleavened bread, and they ate." The story has proceeded peacefully enough up to this point, but with v. 4 and the arrival of the "men of Sodom" begins a text of terror275 such as we might have anticipated, especially for the women who are first mentioned at this point. The "men of Sodom" demand that Lot hand the (young) messengers over to them so that they may have sexual intercourse with them (vv. 5 and 8, with ידע in 5). Lot refers to pederasty as רעע (*hifil*), "acting wickedly." He begs the "men of Sodom" not to act wickedly toward the two messengers, and offers them his two daughters as "substitutes": ". . . do to them as you please;

only do nothing to these men" (v. 8). At the end of the verse, Lot explains why he urged the messengers to lodge with him: namely, so that nothing evil should happen to them. They could have gone to the town square, but there they would have been exposed to abuse. After Lot offers to hand over his daughters, the men of the town utter threats against him and there is a brief, violent struggle between him and the assailants. In the struggle over the messengers, the "men of Sodom" also put pressure on Lot (NRSV: "they pressed hard against the man Lot," v. 9). We can see here an important *difference between the two instances of "urging" or "putting pressure on" someone:* while Lot uses pressure to offer protection to the messengers, the "men of Sodom" use it as a means to snatch the messengers from that protection. Lot also gives an explanation for his urging the messengers to stay with him: "(for that reason [i.e., so that nothing evil should happen to them]) they have come under the shelter of my roof" (end of v. 8). But this means that Lot urged them because he was aware of the danger that only becomes obvious with the arrival of the "men of Sodom."

b. In Judges 19:1-30 we find a case of pressure (ב + פצר, LXX βιάζεσθαι) put on a son-in-law by his father-in-law. The son-in-law is pursuing his concubine, who has fled to her father's house, and the father-in-law pressures the son-in-law to spend the night there. He stays in the father-in-law's house with his concubine for some nights, and finally starts for home. The important verses in this story, as regards pressure to the spend the night, are vv. 11-26. Beginning at v. 15, the story is very similar to that in Genesis 19. It is dangerous—even for men (and especially strangers?)—to spend the night outdoors, in the "open square." In v. 20 an old man who finds them there says: ". . . do not spend the night in the square" and takes them to his house. Then the "men of the city" come and behave like the men of Sodom in Genesis 19. The old man's offer (v. 24) is also similar to that of Lot, but with the major difference that in Judges 19 the offer is partly accepted: here the man seizes his concubine and thrusts her outside to the "men of the city," who then rape her and go away (v. 25). The story continues with the violent consequences for the woman and others.

Here we note first of all that protecting men from pederasty and putting pressure on them in order to shield them, thus placing oneself in danger, by no means implies, in the instances cited, that a more just condition is thereby created: for the sake of protecting the men, women are (and must be) sacrificed. One sexual act cannot be replaced by another. The rape of women cannot be substituted for pederasty as if nothing had happened (Judg. 19:26-30). There can be no legitimate theological justification offered to explain such acts of violence and abuse.[276]

Second, we must also observe—and this is the crucial point as regards the investigation of the meaning of παραβιάζεσθαι in these passages—that as long as there are guests in the house, the hosts are responsible for their protection. While they are in the house, nothing must happen to them. The guests are under the protection and shelter of the host.

3. *As a Response to Proconsular Power*:

a. *Mart. Pol.* 3.2 speaks of Germanicus as someone to be imitated because of his constancy (ὑπομονή). In acting against the Christians, in this case against Germanicus, the proconsul hoped to persuade them to renounce Jesus Christ. To avoid this, Germanicus wished to die more swiftly, and so, when he was in the arena, he dragged the wild beasts toward himself.[277] As the crowd saw it, they shouted: "Away with the atheists! Let search be made for Polycarp!"

b. However, rather than Polycarp, another man appears in *Martyrdom of Polycarp* 4: one Quintus, a Phrygian, who "when he saw the wild beasts, [and what was happening in the arena] turned coward. He it was who had forced himself and some others to come forward of their own free will." The proconsul persuaded this Quintus to swear the oath and offer incense, that is, to apostatize from the faith. The process seems to have been quite similar to the proconsular procedures in the trials of Christians in Bithynia under the governorship of Pliny the Younger.[278]

The following reflections are in order: Quintus is described by scholars as an "apostate," and as someone who may have been close to the later figure of Montanus.[279] However, in my opinion, he and his actions need not be understood as though he was attempting to hasten his execution by submitting himself (and others) to judgment. It is possible that he did so out of fear, hoping to find favor and receive mercy without having to deny Jesus, for ultimately, according to the text, the proconsul had to go to great lengths to bring Quintus to his denial. It seems to me that this also reveals the hopeless situation of Christians in face of proconsular power. Those who voluntarily surrendered were judged in just the same way as those who were accused by others.

These two examples describe situations of persecution in which the victims of proconsular power were coerced or put under pressure. Without these trials and the punishment of the arena no one would have thought of urging himself or herself and others to "voluntary" surrender, perhaps in the hope of pardon. The examples also show that in this context of martyrdom the issue was one of reactions to a powerful art of persuasion exercised by the Roman authorities.

The juxtaposition of the examples in *Mart. Pol.* 3.2 and 4, it seems to me, is not for the purpose of lending more luster to Germanicus in contrast to the "apostate" and "traitor" Quintus. There is no idea here of postulating and documenting a certain type of Gentile attitude by way of example. I believe that it is, instead, a portrayal of various facets of one and the same reality: the situation of persecution. The same set of circumstances can evoke different reactions. These two examples are meant to encourage people subjected to fear and despair, persecution and torture that are difficult to withstand. Christians should resist as long as possible. The advice at the end of *Martyrdom of Polycarp* 4, not to praise people who "voluntarily" surrender themselves, is thus not to be understood as "antinomian." It is intended to teach others to learn from Germanicus, and to practice, in the heart of danger, persecution, and martyrdom, the virtue of ὑπομονή, "patient hope" or "the power of resistance."[280] Christians should not let themselves be coerced by what are often tangible, concrete, hopeless situations to act in ways that help neither themselves nor others. They should resist as long as they have the strength. Moreover, it seems to me that those who submit under torture to things they do not otherwise say or practice are not "failures."

The verb παραβιάζεσθαι also appears frequently outside the New Testament canon in its Latin equivalent, *cogere*.[281] Pliny,[282] for example, writes to a friend who had "released" a freedman, or from whom the freedman had escaped, pleading with him to forget his anger and to receive his freedman back without torturing him. Pliny is severe toward the freedman, warning him to improve his behavior. To his friend, Pliny describes his intervention on behalf of the freedman as urgent pressure or coercion: "I'm afraid you will think I am using pressure, not persuasion (*non rogare, sed cogere*), if I add my prayers to his [i.e., those of the *libertus*]." It is true that this letter from Pliny the Younger is similar to Paul's letter to Philemon, but there are important differences. For example, Paul presents himself as δέσμιος Χριστοῦ Ἰησοῦ, while Pliny is a governor in the Roman imperial service; in Philemon it is a case concerning a slave, Onesimus, that is at issue, while Sabinianus has to do with an unnamed freedman.[283] Paul treats the slave Onesimus as his child (in this case, that means his manner is full of love), while Pliny is severe and threatening toward the freedman; although Paul knows that he can use his apostolic authority to order Philemon to do his duty (ἐπιτάσσειν σοι τὸ ἀνῆκον), he restricts himself to a frequently repeated but urgent plea (παρακαλῶ). Pliny also makes a deliberate contrast between the meanings of *rogare* and *cogere,* knowing that in the future he will make other requests of his friend, while in the case of the freedman he asks only this one time. For that reason he emphasizes that in reality he is not merely making a request of his friend, but is pressuring him. He thereby indicates that, at this point, he can make use of his proconsular power and the force necessary to coerce someone in a legal matter.[284]

As another example, Cicero[285] at one point describes the oppressed situation of the population of Lampsacus, an important city in Mysia, under Cornelius Verres. In their customs and discipline, this was one of the mildest of peoples. But politically, the inhabitants were allies (*socii*) of the Romans. De facto, they were Roman slaves who were petitioning for self-government. The Romans' injustices and crimes were so enormous that they forced the population to a desperate decision: perhaps death would be preferable to such mistreatment. In this situation, Cicero warns those in authority not to coerce their allies and other foreign nations to seek refuge elsewhere or to withdraw (from the alliance?) to wherever they would flee in their desperation.[286] He further states that the people's resentment against Verres could not be lessened by any means, since for his addressees also, no matter their status, the Roman laws would not serve them in opposing Verres, and consequently they could draw no hope from them. Cicero asserts: "You forced those unhappy and unfortunate beings, as if there were no hope for them in our laws and law-courts, to fall back upon force and armed violence."[287] He thus offers us impressive examples of the way in which people oppressed by Roman officials were or could be ultimately coerced into seeking refuge, or a place of safety, where they could defend themselves against that power.

In summary, the texts show that the word παραβιάζεσθαι (*cogere*) is used primarily (a) for the acceptance of gifts accompanied by blessings, i.e., when someone is released from a life-threatening situation and therefore feels so obligated to give thanks that he or she brings pressure to bear to coerce the acceptance of the gift; (b) in cases when protective shelter is sought and offered, and (c) in describing the reactions of people who are subjected to proconsular trials or proconsular power.

When the LXX translates the Hebrew ב + פצר with παραβιάζεσθαι or (κατα)βιάζεσθαι, this means that in the first century C.E. this word presents a precise description of the matter summarized here, and that it was generally understood by all.

On the basis of the textual evidence, the following conclusions can be drawn regarding this concept, which appears in the New Testament only in Luke 24:29 and Acts 16:15.

In the passages cited from Pliny and Cicero, coercion or pressure is to be seen as an act of proconsular or military power. It proceeds from people with official power within the Roman empire. In the New Testament passages, on the other hand, it comes from people who derived their power from faith, that is, from their fidelity to the crucified and risen Lord. *Martyrdom of Polycarp* 4 shows the negative consequences for Christians of the pressure put on the victims of judicial process by the proconsul. The pressure described by Luke has a completely different effect. While in the former instance, pressure or coercion is a means applied with the result of producing either martyrdom or apostasy from Christian faith (in order to avoid martyrdom), in Luke it serves for the protection of those concerned. In the houses of Lydia and the Emmaus disciples, those abiding there because of the pressure exerted upon them are to be provided with hospitality and protection.[288]

With the explanatory phrase "because it is almost evening," Luke 24:29 hints at a danger similar to that in Judg. 19:1-26, but in my opinion Luke 24:29 should be read in the larger context of the scenes of crucifixion, burial, and resurrection. On the road to Emmaus, the Risen One encounters two disciples, but they do not recognize Jesus. They continue on the road together. When they reach the town, Jesus intends to go on; because he is living as a stranger in Jerusalem (παροικεῖς 'Ιερουσαλήμ, 24:18) he probably has no fixed residence in the vicinity. I find this detail, which is emphasized in the story, important: namely, that he is a stranger in the city; for this can hint that he, too, is from Nazareth and a friend and follower of the Crucified, especially since he knows a great deal about Christ and his crucifixion (24:25-27). Luise Schottroff indicates that "the Romans considered Jesus' crucifixion a political act,"[289] and in such cases burial rites and mourning were forbidden. If people were caught carrying out such a ceremony, they would be punished. This must have been even more dangerous for Jesus' followers than for members of the family, inasmuch as "showing any kind of behavior [e.g., burial or weeping] that would reveal one as a follower of Jesus could have been a dangerous act of solidarity that might have led to being crucified oneself."[290] Precisely in this broader context of the crucifixion and "disappearance" of the crucified Jesus of Nazareth, every stranger in the city would have appeared suspect to the Roman soldiers, who were watching everything and everyone,[291] and undoubtedly denouncing people as well. The guard was probably augmented during the night, which only enhanced the danger for those who wanted to move about freely. In order to protect the stranger they met on the road to Emmaus from these dangers, the disciples pressed him to come into their house and remain with them.

In Lydia's case, the pressure she applies is a sign of her solidarity. She certainly knows the conditions in the Roman colony of Philippi, and the attitude of the Roman authorities toward Jews (Acts 16:19-24). In this situation, her pressing invitation is an attempt to aid the missionaries by taking precautions for their protection. At the same time, she has to be ready to answer to the city authorities for giving them her protection. Should a conflict arise between her guests and the Roman authorities, her house would be drawn into a dangerous situation.[292] It is possible that in this case Lydia was unable to offer the protection provided by law, inasmuch as Paul (differently from the situation in Acts 17:5-9) finds it necessary to appeal to his own rights as a Roman citizen.[293] The action of Lydia and the others is to be understood, against the background here developed, as "hospitality,"[294] which included the provision of protection for her guests. To put it another way: hospitality is not abrogated when there is danger, but only at that moment proves itself to be genuine hospitality.

A hermeneutical and theological reflection is appropriate at this point. It was not only because Lydia was a Christian, and not only from the moment when she became a Christian, that she revealed her gratitude through hospitality; for Lydia is not the first in this field, nor is she the exception. As a woman who reveres God, she stands within a tradition in which non-Jewish women adhered to Judaism, practicing its way of life and also, when the situation required it, supporting and sheltering Jewish women and men in danger. Two examples appear to me to be revealing as regards this attitude, and their significance extends beyond the external characteristics of the "god-fearers":

First, an inscription[295] found in the Jewish catacombs on the Via Nomentana in Rome upholds the memory of Julia Irene Arista, "who worshiped the power of God and kept fidelity to the sheltered seed, the Law, in a righteous way." This god-fearing woman has kept the Law, and the concept of *fides,* "fidelity," appears as well. Her way of life is

Jewish, and her fidelity to the Jewish God corresponds to her keeping of the Law, which is intended to create just relationships among human beings.

Second, Josephus[296] describes how the male inhabitants of Damascus behaved toward the Jewish population both before and after the defeat of the Romans. These men shut the Jews up in the gymnasium because they appeared suspicious. Moreover, the men of Damascus wanted to kill the Jews. It is only when this plan is described that the women of Damascus appear. The text continues: "yet did they [the men of Damascus] distrust their own wives, which were almost all of them addicted to the Jewish religion; on which account it was that their greatest concern was, how they might conceal these things from them." Josephus goes on to say that then 10,500 unarmed Jews were immediately and swiftly slaughtered. This parenthetic remark about the women of Damascus is very revealing: The men kept their decision secret from the women, *because they were afraid of them*—and probably they were feared because they had adopted the Jewish religion. Still more, they were feared because, on account of their faith, they would have made some move in opposition to their men's decision! Otherwise, there would be no sense in the men's anxiety here. Moreover, the description of the women of Damascus makes it clear that solidarity with the Jewish suspected and persecuted population was a sign of a kind of "hospitality." It is a loss to history that Josephus reports nothing about the women's reaction to the slaughter of the Jewish inhabitants by the men. Apparently it was a subject that did not interest him.

Lydia's House: A "Contrast Society" in a Roman Colony

Lydia's story, partly told in and reconstructed from Acts 16:13-15, is relevant for both Jews and Christians from a religious-historical point of view, but also with respect to social-political questions. A woman, Lydia, is the head of a house. Normally, the *pater familias* ruled over wife, children, and slaves, and the governing structure of the state—in this case, the Roman state—was anchored in this family structure. In Acts 16:13-15 we find nothing either about a *pater familias* or about the kind of rulership that is based on scales of subjection and that lives and survives through them because it forces other people into dependency and keeps them there, exploiting and oppressing them.[297]

Luke not only knows of this independent woman, Lydia, who provides shelter for other people in her house. He also tells of other women who house people in cases where there is no mention of a *pater familias* or any other man. For example, Luke 10:38 speaks of Martha, who received Jesus into her house. Luke uses here the same verb, ὑποδέχεσθαι, "to receive as a guest," as in the description of Jesus' reception by Zaccheus (Luke 19:6) and of Paul's lodging with Jason (Acts 17:7). Luke makes no distinction among these instances, but some manuscripts do: in the case of Martha, and only there, they add an explanatory note that Martha received Jesus *into her house*. It is important to insist that women, independently of men, received other men into their houses. This is certainly unusual in a patriarchal society,[298] but according to Luke's reporting it did occur. Thus in the Jesus movement, and in the beginnings of the Christian mission, there was no place for the patriarchal political governance exercised elsewhere; social compulsions to subordination were eliminated in the solidaristic praxis of the humble.[299] In these houses a place was created for women and men in which they could live by other standards, in mutual service, directing their energies to the end that no one need suffer want.

Lydia's house became a center of Christian life in Philippi. In this house church, as in others, we may suppose that people lived according to the baptismal confession of Gal. 3:28. Thus they also were continually striving to overcome the patriarchal relationships that pervaded all areas of life. Even if they did not exercise active, face-to-face confrontation with the existing order of power, they were nevertheless living a life contrary to Roman customs: a life resting not on dominance, but on κοινωνία, "community," "participation," a life in which despised and humbled people were transformed into a people in solidarity with one another, mutually encouraging one another in the faith that gives strength for endurance.[300] Because, for example, there is no longer a *pater familias,* there is no more patriarchal and hierarchical subordination, and all can be equal sisters and brothers. This really does lead to "a relativizing of domestic power relationships and thus of the 'house' as a social unit."[301] To the extent that the fidelity of the early Christian house church belongs to the Jewish Lord Jesus Christ, the crucified and risen one, fidelity is withdrawn from the Lord Emperor, and his claim to lordship over all spheres of life is denied. In the last analysis, then, this is a practice of resistance.[302] This house church in Philippi can also serve as a model for a "contrast society"[303] on a small scale. Such an understanding fits within the framework of the conflicts between Paul and Silas and the imperial authorities in this Roman colony. Acts frames those events within the story of Lydia. In a society in which only dominance-minded men appear in leading political and economic roles, as is clear in Acts 16:16-39, this framing story of Lydia surrounding the events is subversive. Among its subversive features is the "fact that [in it] sexes and classes are treated as equals."[304]

Challenges to a Feminist Interpretation of Lydia. Summary and Outlook

The story of Lydia in Acts 16:13-15 has, throughout centuries of interpretation, received cursory treatment from theologians writing biblical-exegetical commentaries. In the process, as this chapter has shown, particular ideas about the social, economic, and religious allegiances of Lydia were passed on from commentator to commentator. When Lydia was introduced to congregations or groups outside the commentaries, it was always against this background: that is, Lydia's image was mediated by this history of interpretation. Questions about her work, and thus about the conditions of her life, were simply not asked. I have become better acquainted with Lydia and her work through my examination of extra-biblical literary and inscriptional sources. The conditions of her life, in her own milieu, are no longer so foreign to me. Historical reconstruction has also made her community praxis and her theology clearer to me: they have taken on sharper contours. A social-historical, feminist liberation theological analysis of biblical texts can aid us to approach nearer to the theological statements to be found in a particular context, and to give precision to them.

For centuries, Lydia and her story were defined by men's historical writing, from Luke to the latest commentators. Recently, this picture of research has begun to change. Women are taking up the task of uncovering the figures and stories of women in the Bible, and Lydia has received renewed attention. I will only review at this point the extent to which feminist theologians have concerned themselves with Lydia, and the question whether and to what degree they have distanced themselves from the dominant scholarship.

Luise Schottroff[305] points out that in the dominant interpretation throughout history Lydia has been declared to be a well-to-do woman, partly in order to affirm that the first Christian women were members of the upper middle class: "The fact that women work, and under very hard conditions at that, is rendered invisible [in the dominant exegesis]. Also, no one takes time to ask what a woman does who sells purple fabrics."[306] The demand for a social-historical analysis has arisen out of this state of scholarship. Thus Bernadette Brooten[307] and Luise Schott-roff[308] formulate a task for feminist liberation theological exegesis: inquiring especially and minutely about women's work and reconstructing it to the extent possible, with the aid of new sources and techniques drawn from other scholarly fields. By means of this research and analysis, Schottroff, in her essay on Lydia and other studies, reveals the latent, unspoken tendencies of the dominant exegesis. She knows the power and force of this tradition of interpretation; it is made clear once again in the fact that even critical feminist theologians succumb to the dominant interpretation, especially as regards social-historical questions.

Valerie A. Abrahamsen[309] has devoted her efforts to a study of the development of and different trends in the history of Christian and non-Christian women in Philippi. Her whole project and her conclusions are good, and are instructive for future research, but it seems to me that they lack precision in some details. It is probably for that reason that Lydia appears in her work in a very unfavorable light. To begin with, she assumes that Acts 16 as a whole (the description of Paul's missionary work in Philippi) is probably fictional. Thus, as so often occurs in the dominant exegesis, whose theses she adopts on this point,[310] she makes a direct comparison between the "genuine" Paul (or accounts of Paul) in the Pauline letters and the "ungenuine" or "less genuine" Paul of Acts. One result of this is that, for example, she contrasts Evodia and Syntyche (Phil. 4:2) with Lydia. For her—even though the story is supposed to be "fictional"—Lydia is a "domestic," married woman[311] who was obedient to Paul, while Evodia and Syntyche, "two rival missionaries,"[312] made a lot of trouble for Paul because, it seems, both of them had more influence in Philippi than Paul. In contrast, Luke presents the "fictional" Lydia as "a devout follower of Paul, not a schismatic," who presents no danger, but rather is a "less threatening 'type' of Christian woman."

Ruth Albrecht and Franziska Müller-Rosenau[313] adopt a critical stance toward the dominant tradition of interpretation. They point out, for example, the difficulty that exegetes have, in approaching the story of Lydia, in not immediately "seeking to define women through men;" this same difficulty emerges in the interpretation of the place of assembly and Lydia's station in life (as a widow, etc.). But in the matter of social and economic questions, these authors remain captive to the conclusions of the same dominant exegesis they have criticized, and do not challenge them.

Susanne Heine devotes several pages in her book to Lydia and the god-fearers.[314] She writes about Lydia in her chapter on "Paul the Scapegoat," in which she defends Paul against feminist criticism. On the whole, her description of Lydia and the god-fearers does not differ from that in the dominant interpretations. Heine correctly proceeds on the premise that ". . . women in particular . . . felt particularly attracted by the Christian missionaries." She wishes to demonstrate the reasons for this "from the formation of the community in Philippi." On the one hand, this author, inspired by the example of the women of Damascus, asserts that, as far as the god-fearers are concerned, it was especially "pagan women" who "felt attracted by the Jewish faith and particularly by the ethical implications of the law," because "the immense brutality of a political system" called for "an alternative." On the other hand she continues:

> The "case" of Lydia is symptomatic, for she was not the only one among the godfearers who took this course. The opening up of the Christian mission to Gentiles resulted in the surrender of many Jewish elements which were impossible for the godfearers: circumcision, the observance of ritual laws and the strict observance of the precepts of the law expounded casuistically by the Jewish scribes. Therefore women like Lydia must have found Christian faith even better and more in accord with their hopes.[315]

Here it is obvious that Heine is dealing uncritically with the conclusions of scholarship about the effects and the evaluation of the "Christian" mission among the god-fearers; she offers no challenge to them. But we must point out the following: This author asserts that Christian faith must have seemed better to women. However, the issue with regard to the missionary movement in the first century was not the evaluation of religion according to a certain yardstick, but the acknowledgment of the fulfillment of Jewish messianic hopes. The author offers no critical comment either on the commentators' shared ideas about the προσευχή or on their routine estimation of Lydia's socioeconomic status. According to her, women were gathered together for prayer, and the well-to-do Lydia was among them. Heine's understanding of the text is, in large measure, a repetition of the dominant consensus.

I have inquired about Lydia's work and her conditions of life because, in my opinion, they are of critical significance for her religious life. Social-historical examination of a text has theological relevance to the extent that it seeks to illuminate what theological statement or praxis can be found in it, for whom, and in what historical situation. Therefore it is of fundamental importance to approach the situations in which faith experiences have been and are being lived, and to pay closer attention to the people who have acquired and are acquiring particular theological insights.[316] In this way, we can get closer to the people themselves. Thus work with biblical texts can also support and encourage women and men today in their efforts toward more just, non-patriarchal relationships. The story of Lydia can and does give us strength, for it, too, tells us of a woman whose power came to expression in her relationship to God and to other women and men. This implies the construction of conditions that, within the house church also, are founded not on hierarchical relationships, but on the leadership of equals.[317]

Notes

1. Gottfried Schille, *Apostelgeschichte*, 343–44 in context.
2. Ibid., 342.
3. On the existence and use of androcentric language in a patriarchal society, see my sixth chapter below. For further information, see especially E. Schüssler Fiorenza, *In Memory of Her*, 26–36, 41–67; eadem, "Women," 155; L. Schottroff, "Mary Magdalene," 169–71; eadem, "Critique," 35–36.
4. On this see also below at p. 78–92.
5. J. Schneider devotes a very small section to this verb under "ἔρχομαι" in *TDNT* 2:684, but does not discuss this passage.
6. See R. Pesch, *Apostelgeschichte* 2:240ff.; W. Stegemann, *Synagoge*, 47.
7. J. Schneider, "ἔρχομαι," *TDNT* 2:684.
8. The only time that people do not know why they are gathered is in Acts 19:32. This remark is emphasized by the author in order to accent the confusion of the gathering. Thus the emphasis favors the idea that this is an exceptional situation.
9. Thus J. Schniewind, *Matthäus*, 226.
10. See R. Pesch, *Apostelgeschichte* 2:205.
11. Solomon's Portico (see also 5:12) was part of the Temple precincts (cf. John 10:23) and was a customary gathering place for the Jerusalem community; see R. Pesch, *Apostelgeschichte* 1:152; further also Josephus, *Bell.* 5.185.
12. Thus, for example, G. Schneider, *Apostelgeschichte* 2:214.
13. A. Weiser, *Apostelgeschichte* 2:432.
14. H. W. Beyer, *Apostelgeschichte* (1947), 101.
15. T. Zahn, *Apostelgeschichte* 2:573–74.
16. A. Wikenhauser, *Apostelgeschichte*, 188.
17. W. Schmithals, *Apostelgeschichte* 2:149–50.

18. T. Zahn, *Apostelgeschichte* 2:574, n. 86.
19. H. J. Holtzmann, *Apostelgeschichte*, 107. Emphasis supplied.
20. G. Stählin, *Apostelgeschichte*, 217.
21. H. Conzelmann, *Acts*, 130.
22. C. F. Nösgen, *Apostelgeschichte*, 308.
23. J. Felten, *Apostelgeschichte*, 312–13.
24. H. W. Beyer, *Apostelgeschichte* (1947), 101.
25. A. Wikenhauser, *Apostelgeschichte*, 188.
26. W. de Boor, *Apostelgeschichte*, 294.
27. G. Schneider, *Apostelgeschichte* 2:214.
28. W. Schmithals, *Apostelgeschichte*, 149–50.
29. E. Preuschen, *Apostelgeschichte* 1:101.
30. G. Hoennicke, *Apostelgeschichte*, 91.
31. O. Bauernfeind, *Apostelgeschichte*, 208.
32. J. Schmid, *Lukas*, 90.
33. J. Munck, *Acts*, 161.
34. R. Pesch, *Apostelgeschichte* 2:104–5. Emphasis supplied.
35. Thus, for example, E. Preuschen, *Apostelgeschichte*, 101; R. Pesch, *Apostelgeschichte* 2:105, n. 3 refers to M. Hengel, "Proseuche," 157ff., and to Safrai and Stern, *People*, vols. 1 and 2, pp. 159–60, 466, 490, 913, but gives no direct sources. See also T. Zahn, *Apostelgeschichte*, 571, n. 82, with reference to E. Schürer, *Geschichte* 2 (4th ed.): 500, 517–18, to Philo, *Flacc.* 6.7.14, and to Josephus, *Vita*, 277, 280, 293.
36. See W. de Boor, *Apostelgeschichte*, 294; C. F. Nösgen, *Apostelgeschichte*, 308; J. Felten, *Apostelgeschichte*, 313.
37. A. Wikenhauser, *Geschichtswert*, 330.
38. A. Wikenhauser, *Apostelgeschichte*, 188.
39. H. H. Wendt, *Apostelgeschichte*, 345–46. Emphasis supplied.
40. T. Zahn, *Apostelgeschichte*, 570–72. Emphasis supplied.
41. J. Roloff, *Apostelgeschichte*, 244. Emphasis supplied.
42. Roloff (p. 244) supports this opinion by citing Billerbeck 4:153.
43. G. Schille, *Apostelgeschichte*, 341.
44. See H. H. Wendt, *Apostelgeschichte*, 345; H. J. Holtzmann, *Apostelgeschichte*, 106; E. Preuschen, *Apostelgeschichte*, 101; W. Schmithals, *Apostelgeschichte*, 149; A. Wikenhauser, *Apostelgeschichte*, 188; J. Roloff, *Apostelgeschichte*, 244.
45. A. Wikenhauser, *Apostelgeschichte*, 188; see also J. Roloff, *Apostelgeschichte*, 244.
46. H. H. Wendt, *Apostelgeschichte*, 345–46; T. Zahn, *Apostelgeschichte*, 570ff. For more detail, see nn. 37–38 above.
47. R. Pesch, *Apostelgeschichte* 2:104–5. Emphasis supplied.
48. W. de Boor, *Apostelgeschichte*, 294, would have made similar suggestions except that he had a more "reverent" starting point: according to him, Paul had originally intended to go to the Macedonians and help them (Acts

16:9-10), but "what good are a few pious women outside the city? . . . Paul is completely present for them. This is what it really means to be *led by God*, namely that one can *abandon all one's great plans and devote oneself* completely and collectedly *to small and unimportant things*" (emphasis supplied).

49. Some exegetes refer to secondary literature in this context: see n. 35 above.

50. Philo, *Leg. Gaj.* 156: ἠπίστατο οὖν καὶ προσευχὰς ἔχοντας καὶ συνιόντας εἰς αὐτάς, καὶ μάλιστα ταῖς ἱεραῖς ἑβδόμαις. With regard to the plural form of προσευχή, A. Pelletier, "Legatio," 179 n. 8, notes that at the time of Augustus there were supposed to have been four in Rome.

51. On this, see L. Cohen, *Philon*, 215 n. 4, on §155; see also P. Lampe, *Christen*, 26ff.

52. *CII* 1:531. For the "synagogues [communities] of foreigners from the same locality" in Rome, see especially P. Lampe, *Christen*, 367–68; Martin Hengel, "Proseuche," 172–73.

53. Josephus, *Vita* 277: κατὰ τὴν ἐπιοῦσαν οὖν ἡμέραν συνάγονται πάντες εἰς τὴν προσευχὴν μέγιστον οἴκημα καὶ πολὺν ὄχλον ἐπιδέξασθαι δυνάμενον.

54. Ibid., 280: συναγόμενον ἤδε τὸ πλῆθος εἰς τὴν προσευχήν.

55. Ibid., 293–95.

56. Ibid., 279–80.

57. Ibid., 279, 295.

58. Ibid., 195.

59. For further detail, see M. Hengel, "Proseuche," 177, 181; Billerbeck 2:742; 4/1:115ff.

60. Josephus, *Ant.* 14.257–58: κατακολουθοῦντες τῷ δήμῳ τῶν Ῥωμαίων . . . δεδόχθαι καὶ ἡμῖν Ἰουδαίων τους βουλομένους ἄνδρας τε καὶ γυναῖκας τά τε σάββατα ἄγειν καὶ τὰ ἱερὰ συντελεῖν κατὰ τοὺς Ἰουδαικοὺς νόμους, καὶ τὰς προσευχὰς ποιεῖσθαι πρὸς τῇ θαλάσσῃ κατὰ τὸ πάτριον ἔθος.

61. Ibid., 14.261: . . . συνερχομένοις ἐν ταῖς προαποδεδειγμέναις ἡμέραις πράσσειν τὰ κατὰ τοὺς αὐτῶν νόμους.

62. On *Ant.* 14.261, see the commentary and interpretation by Ralph Marcus, *Josephus* 7:589, note e.

63. For a fuller interpretation, with extensive citation of sources and literature, see M. Hengel, "Proseuche," 157–84; see also Billerbeck 4/1:115ff.; S. Safrai, "Synagogue," 908–44; M. Stern, "Diaspora," 117–83.

64. Further information, commentary and comparative arguments are presented in M. Hengel, "Proseuche," 158–59, and still more specifically in V. A. Tcherikover, *Corpus* 1:247ff., in his commentary on *CPJ* 1.134.

65. The εὐχεῖον seems to be a unique synonym for προσευχή. This is also Martin Hengel's interpretation ("Proseuche," 158), as well as that of A. Fuks (*Corpus* 2:220ff., in his commentary on *CPJ* 2.432, with bibliography), and of V. A. Tcherikover (*Corpus* 1:8, in the prolegomena to the Ptolemaic period).

This papyrus is also a concrete example of the existence of a number of synagogues in a single town; for "synagogues belonging to people of a single nation," see also nn. 50ff.

66. See A. Fuks, *Corpus* 2:221.
67. Ibid.
68. A. C. Johnson, *Roman Egypt* (1936), 647, quoted in Fuks, *Corpus* 2:220–21, n. 2.
69. A. T. Kraabel, "Synagogue," 502.
70. Further and more precise information and bibliography may be found in M. Hengel, "Proseuche," 157ff.
71. *OGIS* 726 (= *CPJ* 3.1440).
72. *SB* 5862 (= *CPJ* 3.1441).
73. *CPJ* 3.1442.
74. *SB* 589 (= *CPJ* 3.1433).
75. *CPJ* 3.1443.
76. *OGIS* 101 (= *CPJ* 3.1444).
77. *OGIS* 741 (= *CPJ* 3.1432).
78. *SB* 6832.
79. *IosPE* 2.52–53. On this, see also A. Deissmann, *Licht*, 80; M. Hengel, "Proseuche," 174, with the literature cited.
80. Both inscriptions quoted from L. M. White, "Synagogue," 139–40. See also the fuller information and bibliography there, and see, in addition, M. Hengel, "Stobi," 161; idem, "Proseuche," 167.
81. Thus S. Safrai, "Synagogue," 913–14, 920; M. Stern, "Diaspora," 160; J. Schmid, *Lukas*, 90; M. Hengel, "Proseuche," 175; Billerbeck 2.742. See, in addition, Carl Schneider, "κάθημαι," *TDNT* 3:440–44, at 443–44: "Jesus (Lk. 4:20) and Paul (Ac. 13:14; 16:13) sat at synagogue worship"; W. Schrage, "συναγωγή, κτλ," *TDNT* 7:798–852, at 808, 814.
82. Josephus, *Ant.* 14.275–76; Philo, *Leg. Gaj.* 155–56; *CPJ* 1.531; see also S. Safrai, "Synagogue," 937–38, where he asserts that "in the diaspora, synagogues were often outside built-up areas . . . outside the towns, or by the sea or the lake"; on this, see also M. Hengel, "Proseuche," 176–77; W. Schrage, "συναγωγή," *TDNT* 7:814–18; W. Elliger, *Paulus*, 48ff., also speaks of the synagogue in Rome, which—as was the case in Philippi—was permitted to be built outside the *pomerium*. According to Elliger, one could suppose regarding the location of the synagogue at Philippi that the place had a "triumphal arch," described as a πύλη, associated with the founding of the Roman colony and located outside the old city walls. Between those old walls and the "triumphal arch" was the *pomerium*. Thus the προσευχή could have been outside the *pomerium* and near the arch, on the west side and close to the river Gangites. However, there have not yet been excavations in that area. On this, see also V. A. Abrahamsen, "Women," *JFSR* 3:17–30.
83. Thus also M. Hengel, "Proseuche," 175; B. J. Brooten, *Women*, 140. On this subject, see also S. Krauss, *Synagogale Altertümer*, esp. 11ff., 281ff.

84. J. Roloff, *Apostelgeschichte*, 244.

85. Billerbeck 4/1:153.

86. On this, see also S. Krauss, *Synagogale Altertümer*, 100, who emphasizes that it was only at a later period that the number was limited to ten persons. To begin with, "minyan" meant the whole congregation: "every praying congregation of ten persons, without exception." According to idem, pp. 103ff., at a later time this number was reduced to ten men.

87. Thus also H. Haag, "Minjan," 235–42.

88. See the examples and interpretation of such rabbinic sources in B. J. Brooten, *Women*, esp. 90ff., 139ff.; see also Billerbeck 4/1:157ff.

89. See Brooten, *Women*, esp. 94ff.

90. On this, see Brooten, *Women*, esp. 35ff., 73ff.; L. Schottroff, "Leaders," 73–75. For the study of the Torah, see the remarks in ch. 2 above (Tabitha), pp. 33–36; also the Talmudic expression in Sotah 21b: "Rabbi Eliezer says: whoever teaches his daughter Torah, teaches her obscenity." On this, see A. Ohler, *Frauengestalten*, 215.

91. B. J. Brooten, *Women*, 94.

92. Ibid., 140.

93. On this, see also L. Schottroff, "Leaders," 64–65. She further emphasizes that the text of Acts 16:13-15 says nothing to indicate that this gathering of women was not a "fully valid" worship service. She then continues, on the basis of the traditional interpretation of this text: "The contempt for women, discussed in a different context as a problem of Judaism, is in reality Christianity's own contempt for women. Sources are reinterpreted simply because they do not fit one's own Christian idea of women."

94. Cf. Rom. 16:1-16 with 1 Cor. 11:2-16; 13:13b—14:40. For more detail, see, for example, L. Schottroff, "Critique," 35–59, esp. 48–51.

95. We know that under Antiochus III (223–187 B.C.E.) 2,000 Jewish families were deported from Mesopotamia and Babylonia to Phrygia and Lydia, with the result that many Jewish women and men settled in Thyatira. There was also a synagogue (συμβαθεῖον) in that city: see *CIG* 3509, and J. Keil, "Thyateira," 658; Shimon Applebaum, "Organization," 469. In addition to the required military service, many of these people were occupied in agricultural activities, especially in the vineyards; but they were also well acquainted with methods of purple production. For historical information on the settlement of Jews in Thyatira, see M. Stern, "Diaspora," 143ff.; S. Applebaum, "Legal Status," 431; idem, "Economic Status," 715; M. Noth, *Geschichte*, 315ff. For the connection between the Jewish population and the production of purple goods, see K. Schneider, "Purpura," 2009.

96. So, for example, M. Simon, "Gottesfürchtige," 1060ff.; K. Lake, "Proselytes," 74–96, at 88; E. Haenchen, *Acts*, 346, in treating Acts 10:1ff.; G. Schille, *Apostelgeschichte*, 242, in treating Acts 10:1ff.; R. Pesch, *Apostelgeschichte* 1:336, in treating Acts 10:1ff.; K. Romaniuk, "Die 'Gottesfürchtigen,'" 69–91,

at 72ff. On the topic of "god-fearers," see also F. Siegert, "Gottesfürchtige," 109–64; K. G. Kuhn, "προσήλυτος," *TDNT* 6:727–44; K. G. Kuhn and H. Stegemann, "Proselyten," 1248–83; W. Foerster, "σέβομαι," *TDNT* 7:168–72. Critical of this consensus are F. Siegert, "Gottesfürchtige," 109–64, and esp. A. T. Kraabel, "Disappearance," 113–26, who even denies their existence.

97. K. G. Kuhn, "προσήλυτος," 731; see also K. G. Kuhn and H. Stegemann, "Proselyten," 1260.

98. M. Simon, "Gottesfürchtige," 1068; G. Schille, *Apostelgeschichte*, 242.

99. K. G. Kuhn and H. Stegemann, "Proselyten," 1263. Emphasis supplied.

100. Ibid., 1265–66.

101. R. Pesch, *Apostelgeschichte* 2:105. Emphasis supplied.

102. R. Pesch, *Apostelgeschichte* 1:336.

103. K. G. Kuhn and H. Stegemann, "Proselyten," 1274–75; M. Simon, "Gottesfürchtige," 1965; K. Lake, "Proselytes," 77–79, where he also counts "instruction" among the characteristic marks and attempts (p. 77) to define it: "the nature of this instruction was probably left to individual rabbis in the earliest period and afterwards became standardized, but no written record exists." This instruction is supposed to have been called "the two ways," as well, and to have been partly retained in the Christian *Didache*. Although its content cannot be more closely defined, according to Lake such a formative instruction must have existed because "Jews and Gentiles were both intelligent groups and neither would wish to make converts or to be converted without some understanding of the questions involved" (p. 78).

104. K. G. Kuhn and H. Stegemann, "Proselyten," 1263, but no source is given for this assertion.

105. K. Lake, "Proselytes," 78.

106. On this, see n. 96 above, and those passages that deal specifically with the Noachic commandments (e.g., F. Siegert, "Gottesfürchtige," esp. 120ff.) and participation in synagogue worship. Some aspects of the Noachic covenant are reflected in Acts 15:19-20, 29.

107. Josephus, *Ant.* 14.110: θαυμάσῃ δὲ μηδεὶς εἰ τοσοῦτος ἦν πλοῦτος ἐν τῷ ἡμετέρῳ ἱερῷ, πάντων τῶν κατὰ τὴν οἰκουμένην ᾽Ιουδαίων καὶ σεβομένων τὸν θεόν, ἔτι δὲ καὶ τῶν ἀπὸ τῆς ᾽Ασίας καὶ τῆς Εὐρώπης εἰς αὐτὸ συμφερόντων ἐκ πολλῶν πάνυ χρόνων. F. Siegert quotes this passage in "Gottesfürchtige," 127, where (n. 1) he remarks that this income "refers both to the regular contributions collected from every Jew (and proselyte) through a system of taxation, and which a non-Jew could not give . . . , and also to voluntary offerings that anyone could present."

108. On the σεβόμενοι τὸν θεόν, see R. Marcus, "Sebomenoi," 247ff., where the author takes up and discusses the argument among scholars about whether these are two different groups or only different designations for the same Jews. Marcus concludes, on the basis of an analysis of the grammar and content, that they are really two different groups. Josephus was thus acquainted with god-

fearers as well. In this, Marcus also argues against A. T. Kraabel, "Disappearance," 113ff.

109. On the god-fearers' presentation of sacrificial offerings, see F. Siegert, "Gottesfürchtige," 143, n. 3.

110. A. von Harnack, *Mission and Expansion*, 1:12, even asserts with regard to acceptance into Judaism: "Immersion was more indispensable than even circumcision as a condition for entrance." Unfortunately, he alludes to no sources to which we might refer in order to pose a more definitive challenge to the category of "circumcision" as it is posited by scholars.

111. R. Pesch, *Apostelgeschichte* 2:41, alludes to the exact opposite: that is, he asks whether we should not understand τῶν σεβομένων προσηλύτων as "god-fearers" because nothing was previously said about proselytes. According to him, "'proselytes' should then be seen as a Lukan addition in light of 13:46-47 . . . , as if in the first place it was only a question of Jews (whether born such or having become Jews by conversion)." For G. Schille, *Apostelgeschichte,* 297, it is here a matter of an "imprecise way of speaking." However, while considering whether "proselytes" could be an "early gloss," E. Haenchen takes the opposite position in *Acts* 413, n. 5: "σεβομένων προσηλύτων only makes sense if σεβόμενος denotes not, as in 13:50, 16:14[!]; 17:4; 17:17 and 18:7, a Gentile frequenting the synagogue without accepting the whole of the law, but a devout person—in this case a proselyte—who has accepted circumcision and the whole of the law."

112. On this, see also A. T. Kraabel, "Disappearance," 120.

113. Against M. Simon, "Gottesfürchtige," 1086; G. Schille, *Apostelgeschichte,* 242.

114. W. Foerster, "σέβομαι," *TDNT* 7:168–72, at 168.

115. F. Siegert, "Gottesfürchtige," 142.

116. Ibid., 136.

117. R. Pesch, *Apostelgeschichte* 2:122.

118. Ibid., 125.

119. On this, see, esp. B. J. Brooten, *Women,* 144ff.; L. Schottroff, "Leaders," 63–75.

120. There is more on this subject in ch. 6, with respect to these passages, and also in L. Schottroff, "Leaders," 60–75. Schottroff also points out (p. 66), that in Christian research on this topic "[a]nti-Judaism, contempt for women, and contempt for religion are often closely related." F. Crüsemann, "Fremdenliebe," 11ff., had earlier pointed out how often scholarship has fallen prey to the hidden dangers of an anti-Jewish reading of the whole phenomenon of the "god-fearers."

121. Josephus, *Bell.* 2.560; *Ant.* 20.17–53, 92–96.

122. On this, see further on pp. 117–25.

123. See the commentary on Josephus, *Ant.* 20.34–38 in L. Schottroff, "Leaders," 68–71. An English translation of the passage is in R. S. Kraemer, *Maenads,* 257–61.

124. A. T. Kraabel, "Disappearance," 113ff., discusses excavations at six different synagogues in the Jewish diaspora (Dura Europos, Sardis, Priene, Delos, Stobi, and Ostia) and concentrates especially on the examination of the more than one hundred inscriptions found there. No σεβόμενοι or φοβούμενοι are mentioned in them; however, there are ten instances of θεοσεβής, "but as an adjective describing Jews, usually Jewish donors" (p. 116).

125. Thus, for example, K. G. Kuhn and H. Stegemann, "Proselyten," 1265ff.

126. *CII* 1.285 = *CIL* 6.29759.

127. *CII* 1.524 = *CIL* 6.29760.

128. *CII* 1.529 = *CIL* 6.29763.

129. *CII* 1.642 = *CIL* 5.88.

130. *CII* 13*.

131. *CII* 1.5 = *CIL* 6.31839.

132. For example, the *Novum Testamentum Latine* uses the expression *colens deum* in Acts 16:14; 18:7.

133. *CII* 1.72.

134. K. G. Kuhn and H. Stegemann differ (pp. 1265–66). They assert that inscriptions mentioning "god-fearers" (*metuentes*) name no slaves, although there are two of the latter among those called "proselytes" in the inscriptions (*CII* 1.256: a man named Nikete; *CII* 1.462: a woman named Felicitas). For that reason these authors prefer not to see the "socially better placed" among the proselytes, but among the "god-fearers." G. Theißen, *The Social Setting of Pauline Christianity*, 102–4, also simply paraphrases without qualification the assertions of dominant scholarship, as represented, for example, by K. G. Kuhn and H. Stegemann. Nevertheless, we should ask whether *CII* 1.256 and 462 are really about a slave man and a slave woman, since the word *patronus/a* (synonymous with προστάτης/ις) is also a religious expression. For this, see esp. Rom. 16:2 and B. J. Brooten, *Women*, 62–63, where she is discussing "mothers of the synagogue." She establishes the identification between the characteristics of πατήρ καὶ πατέρων on the basis of their parallel use in the inscriptions *CII* 619d and 619c, and asserts: "It is probable that in the Diaspora the line separating synagogue leadership from civic leadership was rather fluid." On this, see also *CII* 1.84f., 94f. According to K. E. Georges, *Lateinisch-Deutsches Handwörterbuch* (1841), moreover, *patronus/a* does not describe a slaveholder, but rather the master of a freed person! On this, A. Graeber, *Untersuchungen*, 14, remarks that even freed persons could be *patroni*: "patroni could be persons from all social classes" (p. 99).

135. This occurs repeatedly in the commentaries, where there is constant reference to the "god-fearer," Cornelius (Acts 10:1ff.) as an example.

136. F. Siegert, "Gottesfürchtige," 125; more at 130.

137. Somewhat vague reasons (if any) are given for their attachment or conversion to Judaism. Thus, for example, K. G. Kuhn and H. Stegemann, "Proselyten," 1259: "their [the Jewish missionaries'] preaching of the one, true

God, who is invisible and is not worshiped in images, and is the creator of heaven and earth, together with the practical application of Jewish religion to a happy, moral life distinguished Jewish propaganda from other religions, and must have been particularly attractive"; F. Siegert, "Gottesfürchtige," 164: "The successful attraction of Judaism at this period [from the second century onward] may well have been so great just because, through the acceptance of the god-fearers, even outsiders were given a share in the hope of the Jewish religion."

138. L. Schottroff, "Leaders," 70.

139. See, for example, B. J. Brooten, *Women*, 139–40; L. Schottroff, "Leaders," 73–75. Cf. also Juvenal 14.96ff., who says that women are also occupied in studying Scripture.

140. J. Felten, *Apostelgeschichte*, 300.

141. See E. Preuschen, *Apostelgeschichte*, 101–2; T. Zahn, *Apostelgeschichte*, 574–75; A. Wikenhauser, *Apostelgeschichte*, 188; G. Stählin, *Apostelgeschichte*, 217–18; W. de Boor, *Apostelgeschichte*, 294; J. Roloff, *Apostelgeschichte*, 244: he also asserts that there was a purple *industry* in Thyatira; W. Schmithals, *Apostelgeschichte*, 150; A. Weiser, *Apostelgeschichte*, 2:422. According to R. Pesch, *Apostelgeschichte* 2:105, Lydia was engaged in "importing luxury articles to Europe," and this was the basis of her wealth.

142. See H. H. Wendt, *Apostelgeschichte*, 346; C. F. Nösgen, *Apostelgeschichte*, 309; O. Zöckler, *Apostelgeschichte*, 228; H. J. Holtzmann, *Apostelgeschichte*, 106–7; J. Munck, *Acts*, 161; O. Bauernfeind, *Apostelgeschichte*, 208; G. Schneider, *Apostelgeschichte* 2:214.

143. G. Schille, *Apostelgeschichte*, 341.

144. οἱ ἀρτοκόποι = *pistores*, CIG 3495.

145. οἱ κεραμεῖς = *figuli*, CIG 3485.

146. οἱ βυρσεῖς = *coriarii*, CIG 3499. See also Acts 9:43.

147. οἱ σκυτοτόμοι = *sutores*, Bull. de Corr. hell. 10 (1886): 422 n. 31; J.-P. Waltzing, *Etude historique* 3:59, no. 162.

148. οἱ χαλκεῖς χαλκότυποι = *aerariorum fabrorum*, Bull. Corr. hell. 10 (1886): 407 n. 10; J.-P. Waltzing, *Etude historique* 3:59, no. 163.

149. οἱ λινουργοί = *lintearii*, CIG 3504.

150. οἱ λανάριοι = *lanarii*, Ath. Mitt. 12 (1887): 253 n. 13; J.-P. Waltzing, *Etude historique* 3:60, no. 165.

151. οι ἱματευόμενοι = *vestiariorum*, CIG 3480.

152. οἱ βαφεῖς = *tinctores*, CIG 3496, 3497, 3498, and Bull. Corr. hell. 11 (1887), 100 n. 23; the latter in J.-P. Waltzing, *Etude historique* 3:59, no. 164; see also pp. 57–58.

153. οἱ λανάριοι (wool spinners), inscription in J.-P. Waltzing, *Etude historique* 3:47, no. 140.

154. οι ἐριούργοι (wool workers), CIG 3422. See also J.-P. Waltzing, *Etude historique* 3:51, no. 146.

155. See the commentary of J.-P. Waltzing, *Etude historique* 3:55ff. CIG 3497 specifically mentions only the name of Alphenus Arignotos, but he lived in

the time of Caracalla and did military service under him. For this, see the words used to describe him in this inscription.

156. See, for example, M. Besnier, "Purpura," esp. 771ff.; K. Schneider, "Purpura," esp. 2012ff.

157. In his commentary on *CIG* 3496, J.-P. Waltzing (*Etude historique* 3:57, no. 157) also mentions Acts 16:14 and, with reference to the description of Lydia's profession, remarks: "La *teinture rouge* de Thyatire était renommée [the red dye of Thyatira was famous]" (emphasis supplied).

158. In Thessalonica: *IG* 10.291, according to which Menippo, also called Severo, comes from Thyatira; in Hierapolis: five inscriptions collected by J.-P. Waltzing, *Etude historique* 3:36ff.

159. Pliny, *Naturalis Historia* 7:196: "inficere lanas Sardibus Lydia [invenerunt]" (Dyeing woolen stuffs [was introduced] by the Lydians at Sardis).

160. Ibid.: "linum et retia Arachne [invenit]" (Linen and nets [were introduced by] Arachne). For Arachne, the weaver, whose father also dyed wool, see also Ovid, *Metamorphoses*. 6.5ff.

161. For the importance of Lydian women who are celebrated in poetry for their textile work and dyeing, see Homer, *Iliad* 4.140–41; Claudian, *Raptus Proserpinae* 1.269ff.; Val. Flacc. 4.367ff.

162. *CIL* 1.2, 1211. On this, see S. B. Pomeroy, *Goddesses,* 199.

163. Cicero, *In Verrem* 4:59.

164. On this, see S. B. Pomeroy, *Goddesses,* esp. 199–200, 247; L. Schottroff, "Lydia," 132; A. H. M. Jones, "Bekleidungsindustrie," 157ff.

165. On this, see esp. J.-P. Waltzing, *Etude historique* 2:232ff.; H. Gummerus, "Industrie," 1514ff.; A. H. M. Jones, "Bekleidungsindustrie," 161.

166. R. König, commenting on Pliny, *Naturalis Historia* 35.29ff., p. 174.

167. Pliny, *Naturalis Historia* 9.130–31.

168. See M. Besnier, "Purpura," 770. See also K. Schneider, "Purpura," 2001; H. Blümner, *Technologie,* 225–26, and even BAGD, 694.

169. See Rev. 21:19-20.

170. For the use of hyacinth as a source of purple, see H. Blümner, *Technologie,* 234, 247.

171. E. Lohmeyer, *Matthäus,* 387: "a scarlet cloak represents the king's purple robe." He thinks (see n. 3) that the differing use of the words is a "sign of [Matthew's] independence" of Mark. "Mark's use of 'purple' refers to the purple cloak . . . that was part of the regalia of Hellenistic rulers; obviously the soldiers did not have such a cloak on hand to use in their taunting play, and they . . . must have made do with a purple substitute. The model for Matthew's scarlet cloak was probably the *sagum* of the Roman lictors, something the soldiers could easily have obtained." With regard to the terms used by Mark, E. Lohmeyer writes (*Markus,* 340): "this may have been a soldier's threadbare cloak."

172. See, e.g., Cicero, *In Verrem* 5.31, 86, 137; *Orationes Philippicae* 2.85, where he speaks of the purple-colored cloaks of men of rank; for the technical

processing of heavy materials and different mixtures and the resulting products, see the commentary and remarks on Aristotle, Περί χρωμάτων and other works, e.g., those of Plato, in K. Prantl, *Aristoteles. Über die Farbe.* See also L. Schottroff, "Lydia," 131–32.

173. For further details, see M. Besnier, "Purpura," 774ff., and esp. H. Blümner, *Technologie,* 230ff. Both authors offer extensive bibliography.

174. Pliny, (*Naturalis Historia* 8.187–99), in a long discussion of the characteristics of sheep, mentions the dyeing of wool at 8.193, promising to expand this information elsewhere: "de reliquarum infectu suis locis dicemus in conchyliis maris aut herbarum natura" (We will discuss the dyeing of the other sorts in their proper places under the head of marine shellfish or the nature of various plants). (All Pliny quotations are from the LCL edition: *Pliny. Natural History. With an English Translation.* 10 vols. [Cambridge, MA, 1961–62].)

175. See esp. Pliny, *Naturalis Historia* 9.129-35.

176. Ibid., 35.30.

177. Ibid., 9.139; see also 35.46.

178. Ibid., 9.127; 35.45. Also in Cicero, *In Verrem* 5.146, *purpura Tyria* is listed among other valuable gifts.

179. Pliny, *Naturalis Historia* 35.45. For prices in different times and the corresponding qualities, see also ibid., 9.137; Dio Chrysostom, *Orationes,* 66; and on this subject K. Schneider, "Purpura," 2006–7.

180. For details on this, see B. Büchsenschütz, *Hauptstätten,* 84ff., with bibliography.

181. Pliny, *Naturalis Historia* 31.110, 113.

182. See the inscription of the βαφεῖς in J.-P. Waltzing, *Etude historique* 3.37, no. 123; see also n. 122 there, and n. 158 above.

183. Strabo, 13.4.14; on this, see M. Clerc, *De rebus Thyatirenorum,* 94 n. 1; B. Büchsenschütz, *Hauptstätten,* 84.

184. Pliny, *Naturalis Historia* 22.3: "Iam vero infici vestes scimus admirabili fuco, atque ut sileamus Galatiae, Africae, Lusitaniae granis coccum imperatoriis dicatum paludamentis, transalpina Gallia herbis Tyria atque conchylia tinguit et omnes alios colores." There was a wide selection of possibilities: see also Pliny, *Naturalis Historia* 16.32; 26.103; 13.136–37; 32.66. See also B. Büchsenschütz, *Hauptstätten,* esp. 84ff.

185. In addition to the literature already cited, see Pliny, *Naturalis Historia* 16.77; 19.47; 21.170; 24.94; H. Blümner, *Technologie,* 242, 247. See also Francesco Bianchini, et al., *Simon and Schuster's Complete Guide to Freshwater and Marine Aquarium Fishes,* American ed. by Michael K. Oliver (New York, 1977), 68ff.

186. Pliny, *Naturalis Historia* 24.94.

187. Ibid., 19.47.

188. Ibid., 16.77.

189. Cicero, *Orationes Philippicae* 2.67: "conchyliatis Cn. Pompei peristromatis servorum in cellis lectos stratos videres." However, K. Schneider,

"Purpura," 2011, speaks of freed persons rather than slaves. This text from Cicero was quoted by Quintilian (2.8.4.25) in the first century C.E. as an example of the emphasis used in an oration: that is, the emphasis consists in stressing the fact that slaves have purple-colored bedcovers in their chambers, even such as were used by Gnaeus Pompeius!

190. Cicero, *Pro Sestie* 19. See also Cicero, *In Verrem* 2.176, where he mentions a number of types of imported goods on which, unless they are antiques, no tax is to be paid. Purple is fourth in the list after gold, silver, and ivory, and is followed by a series of other items.

191. For the garb of an orator, which bore a purple stripe, see Quintilian 2.8.5.28; 2.11.3.138–39. For the purple cloak of a gentleman, see also Cicero, *In Verrem* 5.31.86.137.

192. See Quintilian 2.12.10.75; 2.11.1.31; cf. 1.1.2.6.

193. M. Clerc, *De rebus Thyatirenorum*, 93: "Thyatireni autem tinctores non purpura, nec cocco, sed *rubia* ad inficiendas vestes usos esse." Similarly also J.-P. Waltzing, *Etude historique* (see n. 152 above): he does not speak of *purple* produced in Thyatira, but very specifically of *"red dye."*

194. M. Clévenot, *Jerusalem*, 100. In spite of his accurate observations on the production of purple, his interpretation of Acts 16:14-15 remains for the most part captive to the dominant opinion.

195. C. J. Hemer, *Acts*, 114.

196. K. Schneider, "Purpura," esp. 2001–17. The same is true of the listing of principal cities in which purple dyeing took place in H. Gummerus, "Industrie," 1467. See also J. Keil, "Thyateira," 657ff., where there is only general discussion of βαφεῖς and textile production.

197. See nn. 193ff. above.

198. See, for example, the remarks and recipes in G. Fieler, *Farben der Natur;* P. Weigle, *Naturfarben;* E. Bächi-Nussbaumer, *So färbt man mit Pflanzen.*

199. *CIG 5853.* On this, see also J.-P. Waltzing, *Etude historique* 4:100; 3, no. 1699; see 441ff. with commentary.

200. See, e.g., J.-P. Waltzing, *Etude historique* 3:57, at the commentary on no. 157 (= *CIG 3496*); M. Clerc, *De Rebus Thyatirenorum*, 94.

201. Dio Chrysostom, *Orationes*, 66.4.

202. This does not require us to substitute βαρβάροι for βαφεῖς, as, for example, M. Besnier, "Purpura," 776, does.

203. H. Blümner, *Technologie*, 239; M. Besnier, "Purpura," 771; K. Schneider, "Purpura," 2001.

204. On this, see n. 95 above.

205. *CIG 2519.*

206. See, e.g., *CIL* 1.1413 (= Dessau 3.9428); 2.2235; 5.1044, 7620; 6.4016, 9843–48, 32454, 33888; 9.5276; 10.540, 1952; 11.1069a; 14.473, 2433 (= Dessau 2.7597); Dessau 2.7598.

207. *CIL* 1.1413; 2.2235; 5.1044; 6.4016, 32454; 14.473, 2433.

208. L. Schottroff, "Patriarchatsanalyse," 11. In this study, the patriarchal system represented by Cicero is illustrated and compared with the world of the New Testament.

209. Quotations from *De Officiis* are taken from *Cicero on Moral Obligation. A New Translation of Cicero's "De Officiis,"* trans., introduction, and notes by John Higginbotham (London, 1967). On the reign of terror that was the *pax Romana*, see in detail K. Wengst, *pax Romana*, 23ff., and frequently elsewhere; on Roman patriarchy and its various aspects, see L. Schottroff, "Patriarchatsanalyse," 1ff.

210. See, e.g., Pliny, *Naturalis Historia* 9.129; 35.46.

211. Plutarch, *Pericles,* 1.3–4.

212. Plutarch, *Pericles,* 1.4: Πολλάκις δὲ καὶ τοὐναντίον χαίροντες τῷ ἔργῳ τοῦ δημιουργοῦ καταφρονοῦμεν, ὡς ἐπὶ τῶν μύρων καὶ τῶν ἀλουργῶν τούτοις μὲν ἡδόμεθα, τοὺς δὲ βαφεῖς καὶ μυρεψοὺς ἀνελευθέρους ἡγούμεθα καὶ βαναύσους.

213. L. Schottroff, "Lydia," 132; B. Büchsenschütz, *Hauptstätten,* 90ff. This consideration also applies to Acts 9:43.

214. Pliny, *Naturalis Historia* 19.47.

215. P. Lampe, *Christen,* 27, 31, 367, and elsewhere.

216. For the importance of water in dye works, see J.-P. Waltzing, *Etude historique* 3:37, inscription no. 123; B. Büchsenschütz, *Hauptstätten,* 84; L. Schottroff, "Lydia," 131–32.

217. See pp. 87–90 above, and S. Krauss, *Synagogale Altertümer,* 281ff.

218. The lesser springs in Philippi, as well as the swampy area south of the city, supported a rich plant life. On this, and the minerals that were also found there, see Pliny, *Naturalis Historia* 16.133, in context; 18.155; and 31.106 also report on the *nitrum agrium* present in the marsh. For the use of *nitrum* in the production of mineral purple dye in Lydia, see also 31.113. There is more detail on the marsh and the plants of Philippi in W. Elliger, *Paulus,* 34–35; Johanna Schmidt, "Philippoi," 2207.

219. See, for extensive information, S. B. Pomeroy, *Goddesses,* esp. 198–202, 247–48; A. H. M. Jones, "Bekleidungsindustrie," 164, says, for example, that the work in the *gynaecia* was done by slaves.

220. On this, see also M. Besnier, "Purpura," 778 (see nn. 202 and 203 above). According to R. Günther, *Frauenarbeit,* 127–28, CIL 6.9846 contains "a list of *libertae,* all of whom are summarily described as *purpurar(iae).* Analogously, we may suppose that these were assistants who had been testamentarily liberated."

221. This situation also agrees with Pliny, *Epistles* 9.21.

222. CIL 6.9845, for example, speaks also of a *hospes,* a "stranger," who lived in other cities in order to work there. For the immigration or movement of workers from the East to Rome, see esp. Juvenal, *Satires* 3.61ff.

223. *Digesta* 38.1.23, 34, 38. According to *Digesta* 38.1.35, freedwomen were no longer compelled to continue working for the one who had freed them

after they reached the age of 50. On the rarity of women's reaching that age, see, for example, G. Alföldy, "Freilassung," 351ff.; on working for the *patronus/a*, see N. Brockmeyer, *Sozialgeschichte*, 113. P. Csillag, "Arbeit," 173–74, states, on the basis of legal texts on the origin of workers, that freed persons had to continue performing for the *patronus* the trade they had learned.

224. See, for example, the various legal rules for manumission and the relationship between *liberti* and *patroni* in *Digesta* 38 and 40. On this subject, and especially the economic connections, see, for example, G. Alföldy, "Freilassung," 360ff.

225. L. Schottroff, "Lydia," 132.

226. G. Alföldy, "Freilassung," 362.

227. Thus already E. Schüssler Fiorenza, *In Memory of Her*, 178; see also L. Schottroff, "Lydia," 132. On this, see R. Günther, *Frauenarbeit*, 127–28.

228. On this, see E. Fraenkel, "Namenwesen," esp. 1643ff.

229. See the vivid descriptions in Tacitus, *Annales* 14, 17, and the further information in A. H. M. Jones, "Wirtschaftsleben," 62.

230. In J.-P. Waltzing, *Etude historique* 3:41–42, no. 128.

231. These meanings are taken from H.-J. Klauck, *Hausgemeinde*, 15; and O. Michel, "οἶκος, κτλ," *TDNT* 5:119–59, at 119–20.

232. H.-J. Klauck, *Hausgemeinde*, 19.

233. The two examples given here and their citations will be found in H.-J. Klauck, *Hausgemeinde*, 52.

234. P. Stuhlmacher, *Philemon*, 74, in context.

235. See J. Roloff, *Apostelgeschichte*, 244–45.

236. Thus T. Zahn, *Apostelgeschichte* 2:574; so also R. Knopf, *Apostelgeschichte*, 70.

237. C. F. Nösgen, *Apostelgeschichte*, 309.

238. Homer, *Odyssey* 1.397. On the ideological and political function of these kinds of patriarchal ideas and relationships, see esp. E. Schüssler Fiorenza, *In Memory of Her*, 251–66, with listing and discussion of ancient literature; and L. Schottroff, "Patriarchatsanalyse," 1ff. Striking in this context is J. Comblin's remark (*Atos* 2:66): "Que a família toda accompanhe o chefe de família concordava plenamente com o costume antigo," especially since it was not usual, precisely in the context of the time, for a woman to be the "head" of a family, whom all its members followed!

239. O. Michel, "οἶκος," *TDNT* 5:130; emphasis supplied. For a feminist critique of patriarchal domination (and ideology) propagated by ancient philosophers for the benefit of the state and then carried forward and developed by a state and church that rested on patriarchal forms of dominance, see E. Schüssler Fiorenza, *In Memory of Her*, esp. 260–66; L. Schottroff, "Patriarchatsanalyse," 1ff.

240. L. Schottroff, "Lydia," 134.

241. Thus H.-J. Klauck, *Hausgemeinde*, 52. Several commentators also hold the opinion that Lydia had a large number of slaves: e.g., E. Haenchen, *Acts*, 499; W. de Boor, *Apostelgeschichte*, 294–95.

242. L. Schottroff, "Lydia," 133.

243. Ibid.

244. For the "women's guilds," see the materials in J.-P. Waltzing, *Etude historique* 4:205, 254ff.

245. See pp. 105–109 above.

246. These organizations were later subjected to legal regulation; they are described in historical research as *collegia*. For the legal regulation of the *collegia licita et illicita*, see the laws later recorded in *Digesta* 47, 22; for the date of origin of these legal texts, see S.-A. Fusco, "Rechtspolitik," 254ff.; on the organization of those who for the most part were common people, see J.-P. Waltzing, *Etude historique* 1: esp. 52ff., 90ff., 128ff., 332ff.; 2: esp. 247ff.; A. H. M. Jones, "Wirtschaftsleben," 58ff.; H. Gummerus, "Industrie," 1492; V. Weber, "Geschichte," 247ff.; T. Mommsen, "Lehre," 65–66; more in A. Graeber, *Untersuchungen*.

247. For the existence of such organizations and for slaves and freed persons in leading positions in such groups, see *CIL* 14.251; E. M. Staermann, "Klassenkampf," 319, 323ff.; A. H. M. Jones, "Wirtschaftsleben," 59–60, 73; A. Graeber, *Untersuchungen*, 13ff., 104–5.

248. These phrases are found in H.-J. Drexhage, "Wirtschaftliche Stellung," 41.

249. See T. Pekary, *Wirtschaft*, 93–94. Only later, in the fourth and fifth centuries, could one speak of mass production: when, for example, the *gynaecia* were imperial factories, the state had a monopoly on the clothing industry and ordinary people were forced into the apparel factories to produce garments for the imperial armies and the court. On this, see esp. J.-P. Waltzing, *Etude historique* 2:232ff.; A. H. M. Jones, "Bekleidungsindustrie," 161; V. Weber, "Geschichte," 252; I. Hahn, "Freie Arbeit," 145ff.

250. We should note that this inscription is badly damaged; it is no longer possible to determine whether it concerns one or several persons, or a workshop. In any case, it is striking that neither P. Collart, "Philippes," 712ff., or J. Schmidt, "Philippoi," 2206ff., or W. Elliger, *Paulus*, 23ff., gives any information about the existence of or the economic significance that might have attached to *purpurarii* in Philippi. This is all the more astonishing because they all mention Acts 16:12-15 and list the inscriptional materials in which *purpuraria(ii)* are found. More significant economically in Philippi were agriculture and minerals.

251. For more detail, see G. Alföldy, "Freilassung," 87, 94ff.; T. Pekary, *Wirtschaft*, 107ff.; N. Brockmeyer, *Sozialgeschichte*, 108ff.; L. Schottroff, "Gerechtigkeit," 322–23.

252. Quintilian 1.12.16–17 shows that trades like Lydia's were despised by the upper classes, even though they brought in more money than the profession

of a rhetor. On this situation and the insignificant economic status of craftspeople and merchants, see also A. H. M. Jones, "Hintergund," 345, 358; G. Alföldy, "Freilassung," 118ff.; P. Huttunen, *Social Strata*, 124ff.; C. L. Lee, "Unruhe," 78–79; P. Lampe, *Christen*, 158–59, where the passage cited in n. 124 (*Digesta* 33.1.45) should be corrected to *Digesta* 38.1.45.

253. Juvenal, *Satires* 3.62ff. For more detail, see T. Pekary, *Wirtschaft*, 99; G. Alföldy, "Freilassung," 100–101, 120; also C. L. Lee, "Unruhe," 78–79, where he addresses the fact that traders and craftspeople were almost completely unable to profit socially or personally from their slightly better economic situation.

254. Such people were, for example, emperors, senators, knights, and the like. On this, see T. Pekary, *Wirtschaft*, 93; G. Alföldy, "Freilassung," 89, 103. For the distinction, including the linguistic distinction, between different kinds of merchants, major and minor traders, see P. Huttunen, *Social Strata*, 108ff., esp. 124ff.

255. L. Schottroff, "Leaders," 70; the following quotation is from the same essay, p. 74. On the role of the Roman state in the system of patriarchy, see eadem, "Patriarchatsanalyse," 1ff.; S. B. Pomeroy, *Goddesses*, esp. 150–63; E. Schüssler Fiorenza, *In Memory of Her*, esp. 260–66; eadem, *Bread Not Stone*, 70–77.

256. These, plus the sociological, are the elements listed by Peter Stuhlmacher, *Philemon* 75, as those to be treated in connection with this topic.

257. Thus also M. Clévenot, *Jerusalem*, 103. On the demands of the emperor, including the religious, see K. Wengst, *Pax Romana*, esp. 63ff.

258. See the parallels in Matt. 6:24; James 4:4.

259. Rudolf Bultmann and Artur Weiser, "πιστεύω, κτλ," *TDNT* 6:174–228, esp. 199–202.

260. Ibid., 200; the author refers to Billerbeck 3:190–91.

261. Ibid., 201; throughout this section the author refers to A. Schlatter, *Glaube*, esp. 9–40.

262. Ibid., 201.

263. Ibid.

264. Ibid.

265. Ibid., 208.

266. Ibid.

267. Ibid., 209.

268. Ibid.

269. See the very similar remarks in ibid., 212–13.

270. For the word πιστός, πιστή in Greco-Roman usage as an expression of a "relationship of 'mutual' creditworthiness" in which the partners are unequal to the extent that one owes something to the other, see M. Clévenot, *Jerusalem*, esp. 112.

271. On Christian public confession of faith and its consequences, see, for example, W. Stegemann, *Synagoge*, esp. 24ff., according to which faith-confes-

sion as such is not the speaking of a "credo," but a statement of belonging that endangers the life of the member outside the community and can have forensic consequences.

272. Luke is aware that the emperor was called κύριος by his officials: Acts 25:26. Domitian, for example, also wished to be called and worshiped as κύριος and θεός, at which point we see an expression not only of the claims to rulership, but also of the religious aspects of the *pax Romana*. On this, see K. Wengst, *Pax Romana*, esp. 63ff. See also *Mart. Pol.* 8.2, according to which the trials of martyrs included a challenge from the Roman authorities to the Christians to save themselves from martyrdom by, among other things, calling the emperor "Lord."

273. The LXX, for example, renders the verb ב + פצר, "to urge, compel" as used in the Hebrew Bible, with παραβιάζεσθαι or (κατα)βιάζεσθαι.

274. According to Gesenius, the first meaning of רחב is an open square, to be found in the larger towns and cities, especially near the gates or in front of the temple, where the people gathered and where strangers and travelers could spend the night.

275. For a feminist interpretation for and by women of this and other texts of terror, see Phyllis Trible, *Texts of Terror* (Philadelphia, 1984), esp. 64–91. I cannot enter into this theme fully at this point, but the story indicates what the offering of shelter can (although must not necessarily) mean for the women in the house if danger arises from without. For a justified critique, let me refer to the very fine work of Phyllis Trible just mentioned.

276. Apart from Phyllis Trible, the commentators do not even raise this issue. H. Gunkel, *Genesis*, 208–9, rightly emphasizes, with regard to Gen. 19:6-8, the protection that the host is required to provide, but with respect to Lot's offer he writes: "he *nobly* prefers to *sacrifice* the *honor* of his own daughters. We are meant to think: this is a *man of honor*, who holds the law of hospitality sacred! He deserves to be rescued!—Of course, this sacrifice of his own daughters appears *to us modern people* [!] in a different light [Gunkel does not specify what kind of light!]; but an ancient Israelite regards the surrender of one's own daughters for the sake of visiting strangers as admirable magnanimity. . . . That Lot's offer is by no means a 'sin' (against Franz Delitzsch) is also clear from the fact that the 'men' consent to it; they wait to see the extent of the Sodomites' vice and of Lot's hospitality" (emphasis supplied). It is worth asking why this remarkable talk of "sin" occurs here. From a male perspective, is there no "sin" if an action is not criticized or refused? Gerhard von Rad, *Genesis*, 218–19, also sees this as a case of the "sacredness of hospitality": "The surprising offer of his daughters must not be judged simply by our Western ideas. [?] That Lot intends under no circumstances to violate his hospitality, that his guests were for him more untouchable than his own daughters, must have gripped the ancient reader. . . ." H. W. Hertzberg, *Josua, Richter, Ruth*, 251–52, regards the description in Judg. 19:22-26 as a "disgusting scene." The sacrifice of a virgin daughter

(but not that of the other man's concubine!) serves as "a testimony to the most self-sacrificing hospitality." Finally, the man's dealing with his concubine seems "to us highly ignoble. . . . Throughout, we should note that in these expositions the violation of the duties of hospitality is regarded as a worse sin than unbridled lust. It is different, of course, when the woman succumbs to the violence of the wild mob. Now it is a case of blood-guilt demanding retribution."

277. Other translations are similar: e.g., G. Rauschen, *Märtyrerakten*, 298: "He violently agitated the beast against him." However, ἑαυτῷ ἐπεσπάσατο τὸ θηρίον προσβιασάμενος can also mean "he violently dragged the wild beast toward him."

278. Pliny, *Epistles* 10.96.

279. See, e.g., H. von Campenhausen, "Bearbeitungen," 18ff.

280. For this interpretation of ὑπομονή, see L. Schottroff, "Befreite Eva," 88ff.

281. I will restrict myself here to two examples that seem to me important in this context.

282. Pliny, *Epistles* 10.21.

283. This letter shows that a freed person was still under obligations to the *patronus* or *patrona*.

284. For this matter, and other information regarding Pliny's letter, see R. Gayer, *Sklaven*, esp. 258ff.

285. Cicero, *In Verrem* 2.1.32.81–82.

286. Ibid., 2.1.32.82: Nolite, per deos immortales, cogere socios atque exteras nationes hoc uti perfugio, quo, nisi vos vindicatis, utentur necessario.

287. Ibid.: cum coegeris homines miseros et calamitosos, quasi desperatis nostris legibus et iudiciis, ad vim, ad manus, ad arma confugere.

288. In this connection, see Acts 17:7-9.

289. L. Schottroff, "Mary Magdalene," 171–72. For the general context and development of capital punishment under the Romans, see also T. Mommsen, "Todesstrafe," esp. 441–42.

290. L. Schottroff, "Mary Magdalene," 172, with sources and additional literature.

291. In this regard, see, e.g., Tacitus, *Annales* 6.19.

292. See, e.g., Acts 17:5-9. For hospitality, "care and protection of guests," see esp. R. Leonhard, "Hospitium," esp. 2496; according to this, in a conflict situation a host must "stand by [a guest] before the court" and also acted as a mediator in business affairs. See also R. Leonhard, "Ius," esp. 1220ff.; T. Mommsen, *Römische Forschungen*, 326ff., where he describes the Roman law of hospitality. According to him, there was both a private, individual rule of hospitality and a public law established at the local level. In both cases, the strangers who were sheltered had a right to legal protection. Both the guest and the host carried with them a *tessera*, a "sign of the host/guest" which they prepared in duplicate, and which must be shown to the authorities on demand

as a guarantee. In this way, strangers were afforded the protection of the law. Moreover, in these circumstances strangers were also invited or accepted into the household community; this included the religious aspect, with participation in cultic ceremonies. For the responsibilities and dangers of the host's role, see also L. Schottroff, "Lydia," 133–34.

293. See also A. Ohler, *Frauengestalten*, 206.

294. This is the common interpretation by the commentators, to the extent that they address this question. See, e.g., H. H. Wendt, *Apostelgeschichte*, 348 ("with feelings of gratitude"); J. Felten, *Apostelgeschichte*, 313–14; H. J. Holtzmann, *Apostelgeschichte*, 106; W. Schmithals, *Apostelgeschichte* 2:150. More recently, commentators describe Lydia's action as "offering lodging": e.g., J. Roloff, *Apostelgeschichte*, 245. However, the most common interpretation of the pressure applied by Lydia opines that the missionaries did not wish to accept her invitation, but eventually made an "exception" in Philippi, although they normally earned their living by working with their own hands. See, for example, A. Wikenhauser, *Apostelgeschichte*, 188–89; E. Haenchen, *Acts, 495*, says that they could not refuse her request, although in n. 3 he asserts: "They [the missionaries] had probably up to this time lived in an inn at their own expense." In my opinion the text says nothing about this topic—i.e., that they had to be pressured because they ordinarily supported themselves; for in other cases, including those of Priscilla and Aquila (Acts 18:2), Jason (Acts 17:5-9) and Simon the tanner (Acts 9:43), when missionaries are given shelter, this idea does not arise (even in the minds of the commentators).

295. CII 1.72: Iul(iae) Irene Aristae m[at]r[i] Dei virtut[em e]t fidem sationis conservatae iuste legem colenti Atronius Tullianus Eusebius v(ir) o(ptimus) filius pro debito obseq[uio. A](nnos) XLI. The translation is by the Latin teacher Iris Mücke. See above, pp. 93–98 on "god-fearers."

296. Josephus, *Bell.* 2.560–61, in context. On this, see also L. Schottroff, "Leaders," 72.

297. For these structures of family and state, which were connected with one another and mutually influenced one another, see esp. S. B. Pomeroy, *Goddesses*, 150–63; and E. Schüssler Fiorenza, *In Memory of Her*, 245; K.-H. Bieritz, "Rückkehr ins Haus," 115ff.

298. For more detail, see R. J. Cassidy, *Jesus*, 34–37.

299. R. J. Cassidy, *Jesus*, 37–40. For the solidarity of the humble, see K. Wengst, *Demut*.

300. This formulation rests on Jas. 1:3. In Phil. 3:21, Paul speaks very concretely of "our humble bodies" and the hope for a transformation of our situation based on the transformation of Jesus (cf. Phil. 2:5-11).

301. K.-H. Bieritz, "Rückkehr ins Haus," 121.

302. On the different forms of Christian resistance, see the thorough discussion in W. Schäfke, "Widerstand," 460ff.

303. I adopt this concept from K.-H. Bieritz, "Rückkehr ins Haus," 123.

304. M. Clévenot, *Jerusalem,* 103.

305. L. Schottroff, "Lydia," 134.

306. Ibid.

307. B. J. Brooten, "Frauen," 86, in context.

308. L. Schottroff, "Vergessene," 685ff.

309. V. A. Abrahamsen, "Women," *JFSR* 3, esp. 17–20.

310. She adopts the theological opinions, for example, of W. C. van Unnik and H. Conzelmann (see her n. 3 in this context), without entering into or even making reference to the scholarly discussion, for example, between H. Conzelmann and R. J. Cassidy, *Jesus,* esp. 7–19 and 128–30; according to the latter, this whole story should not be regarded as "fictional," in particular because of the location in Philippi.

311. V. A. Abrahamsen, "Women," *JFSR* 3:18, 20.

312. V. A. Abrahamsen, "Women at Philippi" (SBL paper): 8; the following quotations are from the same location.

313. R. Albrecht and F. Müller-Rosenau, "Lydia," 246ff.

314. Susanne Heine, *Women and Early Christianity* (1987), 83–86. All quotations from those pages.

315. Ibid., 84.

316. This is the starting point for E. Schüssler Fiorenza's feminist theological hermeneutics of liberation. See her *In Memory of Her,* 68–95; eadem, *Bread Not Stone,* 65–92. For hermeneutical questions about the relationship between a social-historical situation and the theological formulations expressed therein, see also Milton Schwantes, *Teologia,* 4ff.

317. On this, see further L. Schottroff, "Lydia," 135–36, and E. Schüssler Fiorenza, *In Memory of Her,* esp. 140–51.

4

The Prophetic Slave in Philippi (16:16-18)

The group of assembled women in which Lydia appears leads us into Philippi. Through them, we come into contact with what appears, on the whole, to be a well-ordered world: for example, Lydia's work creates no conflict with the missionaries, but appears rather in a positive light. Acts, in speaking of her work as a dyer and seller of purple, and in the attitude it displays toward her, presents a picture that deviates from Aristotelian and Ciceronian positions, according to which this and similar types of work are despised by the upper classes as "filthy."[1] But the story of Lydia, by itself, gives only an incomplete picture of the daily life and working conditions of women; the story of the slave girl should therefore be read as a supplement to it, because it broadens our view of the everyday situation from a social-historical perspective.

Slaves and freed persons, most of them from the East, propagated their eastern religions wherever they went, or where they were brought or transported.[2] Acts speaks, in connection with religious activities, and independently of Paul's missionary work, of women from the East who are connected with the synagogue or "place of prayer." In this context, a slave girl appears. Women are the active subjects here. A slave girl as religious protagonist is nothing exceptional in Philippi, as will be shown. The unnamed slave girl in Acts 16:16-18 opens for us a social-historical route of access to the broader contexts of religious and public life in Philippi.

Active participation of slaves and freed persons in religious life is inscriptionally attested at Philippi. Among the many deities worshiped

151

there was, for example, Silvanus,[3] the most popular slave god of ancient Rome. He was honored in Philippi also by independent religious groups (*collegia*) of slaves and freed persons, as well as by the poor among those born free.[4] The inscriptional material shows the great number of slaves and freed persons in Philippi, and at the same time reveals that it was not true in every case that the sacred cultic duties or care of the shrine of the god was carried out by better situated or wealthy persons. In the cult of Silvanus, both the priests and the adherents (*sacerdotes* and *cultores*) were made up of the lower orders listed above.[5]

The cultic *collegia* could be composed of equals, but Acts 16:16-18 shows us a different picture when it describes the relationship between masters and their religiously gifted slave girl. This needs to be pursued in detail.

Religious Gifts, Economic Exploitation, and Dependency

First we must inquire about the living conditions of the slave girl and her importance for her masters at that time. We must give a closer definition of her religious activity. Here the words the text uses to describe her role give us clear directions. The account in Acts 16:16-18 can be divided as follows:[6] First, the encounter between the missionaries and the slave girl (v. 16); second, the action of the slave girl (v. 17); third, Paul's reaction (v. 18).

The Encounter (Acts 16:16)

> But one day, as we were going to the synagogue, a slave girl met us. She had a "Pythian" spirit and brought her owners a great deal of money by her prophecies.[6a]

This verse offers a variety of information: where the encounter took place, and who met whom. From the outset, the slave girl is depicted in an active role. She makes the first move: "[she] met us." At this point we must investigate the rest of the author's description of the girl.

A Profitable "Animate Property"

Three important pieces of information are given about this woman: she is a slave (παιδίσκη). She has a "Pythian" spirit (πνεῦμα πύθωνα). She has several owners (κύριοι). Her prophecies garner them a good deal of profit (ἐργασίαν πολλήν). The assertion that she is a slave corresponds to the idea that she is legally at the disposal of her owners. The statement that she has a "Pythian" spirit means that she prophesied or uttered oracular statements. The owners' profit is the heart of the matter. The structure of v. 16 thus indicates, and this is the author's emphasis, that the whole of the profit gained from their slave's religious gifts and her work accrues to the owners. It is just this profit, or the loss of it, that links this story to the unit that begins with v. 19. Ἐργασία, "profit," is the reason the legal owners of the slave took action when the expulsion of her "Pythian" spirit cost them the source of their gain.

Slaves called παιδίσκη are attested in great numbers in the documents of that period.[7] It is all the more surprising, therefore, that in scholarly studies of the word παῖς and related terms the παιδίσκαι are mentioned only in passing, if at all.[8] The information in vv. 16 and 19 that the slave girl had a number of owners matches the testimony of many contemporary documents.[9] Ownership of slave women could be parceled out among a number of people. In such cases, children born of the slave woman belonged to the owners "in the same proportions."[10] If slaves were included in legal transactions—for example, if they were rented—the owners had a right to a deposit. If a slave belonged to a number of owners, "each of them may demand his or her share of the deposit."[11] Slaves could even be bequeathed in partial shares to several persons. The owners had the right "to make use of the physical and intellectual abilities of the slave as they wished."[12]

Acts 16:16-19 sketches a picture of the slave problem that is realistic for its time. Slaves were "animate property" belonging to their legal owners, and "not only [the] master's slave but wholly [the] master's property."[13] As κτῆσις or κτῆμα, "property," a slave was a valuable tool. He or she (incidentally, in the Roman empire slaves were usually foreigners) was legally an *instrumentum* and *res* for the owners. They had no rights, and although they were productive property they owned nothing of what they produced or earned.[14] What they brought in or produced belonged, both legally and factually, to their owners. N. Brockmeyer shows that, even though some protective laws were passed in the first century C.E., slaves continued to be regarded as *instrumentum* until the fourth and fifth century, and as such "they had not improved in their legal, and thus in their social and probably also their economic status."[15]

Acts 16:16 also memorializes one of these tools of value to her owners from that ancient time. This slave girl brings her owners a great deal of profit by means of her prophecies. Prophecy is this slave's τέχνη, her "art" or "craft." This gift made her very valuable to her owners. What, more precisely, was this prophetic gift?

A Pythian Protagonist

According to the account in Acts, all the events related in Acts 16:19-40 came about because of the religious action in Acts 16:16-18. The unnamed slave girl had a "Pythian" spirit. The linguistic and lexical shaping of the text itself, as we shall see, awakens Pythian associations and suggests religious ties between the event reported here and the Delphic oracle. This has been observed by some exegetes: for example, the phrase πνεῦμα πύθωνα in Acts 16:16 refers not only to the serpent, or "Python," but directly to the Delphic oracle.[16] The phrase is also connected directly to, or identified with Apollo.[17] Many exegetes refer to the statement, unique to Plutarch,[18] that in his own time ventriloquists were called "Pythones," and draw from it a general conclusion that the name given to the spirit should be seen as designating a ventriloquist or medium.[19] Plutarch (De def. or. 9) is writing about an argument between the philosopher-theologian Cleombrotus and the academic philosopher Ammonius, who was also Plutarch's teacher.[20] At Ammonius's suggestion, they have been discussing whether the existence of oracle shrines and people who make oracular utterances is really necessary, since God causes his voice to be heard even in oracles that are not consulted, such as flowing water, and since the essence and power of the divine can show themselves in nature and in inert matter. In this connection, Plutarch asserts that he knows of ventriloquists called "Pythones." Plutarch himself had been a priest at Delphi;[21] he was not speaking against the existence of oracle shrines. And even if the oracle culture of Pythian prophecy was not as flourishing in his time as previously, it was never extinguished.[22] The fact that the Pythia no longer spoke in verse in Plutarch's time indicates, rather, that the oracle culture had spread over a wider area and was present even in places where there were no oracle shrines.[23]

Regarding the expression "Pythian spirit": the slave girl is not called a "pythona"; and Luke does not speak here as, e.g., in Luke 7:21; 8:2 of an unclean or evil spirit, nor are these connotations latent in the story. The description of the spirit serves, instead, to indicate the slave girl's religious and cultic allegiance.[24] The spirit in Acts 16:16 is not just any spirit. There had been a dragon or snake called "Python" that guarded an oracle near Delphi; it was killed by Apollo because he "wanted to take possession of the region, the sanctuary, and the prophetic activity."[25] Apollo thus acquired the epithet "Pythios,"[26] and established his oracle or sanctuary there (the "Pythian oracle"). Pythian Apollo, with his prophetic Pythia, was known also in Macedonia, Phrygia, and Lydia as the most important oracular god.[27] His prophetic seer was called "Pythia," and she received a πνεῦμα in order to prophesy.[28] This function could only be exercised by "virgins," old and/or widowed women.[29] It is also said of the Pythia that she would grow up in the home of poor peasants (ἐν οἰκίᾳ γεωργῶν πενήτων), inexperienced and uninformed;[30] that is, she would come from poor circumstances. Although the Pythia was the principal person in this religious event—without her, after all, there could be no oracular utterance—she was always only "the mouthpiece of a male deity,"[31] who, as a medium, had little influence on the interpretation of her prophecies: at the oracle shrines, this responsibility belonged to the priests.

The following aspects of this historical background appear to me relevant for an interpretation of Acts 16:16-18: Derived forms of πυθ- always appear in connection with the Delphic oracle, and ὁ Πυθών, –ῶνος[32] may represent either a designation of the place or of the dragon or serpent. But since, according to the myth, the animal itself had no prophetic power, or at any rate did not confer it on anyone, but only fulfilled the function of a guardian at the oracle Pythos (and, moreover, since the serpent had long ago been killed by Apollo), the form in Acts 16:16 probably does not refer to the animal. Here, in fact, the slave girl's ability to prophesy is characterized particularly by the fact that she possessed a "Pythian spirit." We should also observe that the slave girl herself is not called πύθωνα; if this were the case; we could simply equate her with a "ventriloquist." But it is precisely this combination of πνεῦμα πύθωνα and μαντεύεσθαι, and the reasons given above, that permit, or even demand, that we see this prophesying in connection with cultic activities related to Delphic Apollo. Apollo was, among other things, the god of "mantic," the oracular god who gave the Pythia the gift of prophesy through reception of the prophetic spirit. Wherever a Pythia appears, there is also talk of μαντεύεσθαι and the concepts derived from that verb.[33]

The verb μαντεύεσθαι is a hapax legomenon in the New Testament. That is, in accord with its historical roots, it appears only in this "Pythian" context. The following observation is connected to this fact: namely, that the woman, the prophetic παιδίσκη in Acts 16:16-18, has no name. That is not generally the case of "Lukan" slave women, as we see from the naming of the slave Rhoda in Acts 12:13; but in a Pythian context it is not unusual:

> General information about the person of the P[ythia], her outward appearance, her origins or other circumstances of her private life are scarcely ever given. Nor is the case any better as regards any sort of historical-biographical details about individual seers. . . . She [Pythia] remains the instrument of revelation. The result is anonymity in principle, whereby her sacred title replaces her proper name.[34]

Thus what is said about the prophetic slave girl in Acts 16:16 accords with what was usual in the religious-historical context of the time (as described in detail above). The information in our story enables us, on the basis of the testimony and evidence collected here, to establish a religious-historical reconstruction of the slave girl's religious adherence. In all probability, she was a Pythia,[35] of the type who apparently uttered her prophecies not at a fixed oracular shrine, but "on the move."[36] This accords with the appearance of the slave girl in Acts 16:16-18.

The Action of the Slave Girl (Acts 16:17-18a)

> While she followed Paul and us, she would cry out, "These people are slaves of the 'Most High' God, who proclaim to you the way of salvation!" And[37] she kept doing this for many days.

In vv. 17-18a, what had been hinted in v. 16 is made concrete. The slave girl prophesies; she speaks an oracle. She prophesies while, or after, following Paul and Silas.

From Encounter to Discipleship

We are prepared for the slave girl's mantic utterances by her following the missionaries, and even before that by her deliberate encounter or confrontation with them. This is expressed in the verbs ὑπαντᾶν, "to meet," "to encounter," and κατακολουθεῖν, "to follow" (including "to follow as a disciple"). It is therefore probably correct to say with Theodor Zahn that "the one who comes to meet them becomes their follower."[38] Because of this combination of verbs, it is appropriate to inquire into their use in the New Testament.

The verb κατακολουθεῖν, "to follow," is a composite, here with the same sense as the simple ἀκολουθεῖν.[39] It appears only twice in the New

Testament, and only in the Lukan work: at Acts 16:17 and Luke 23:55. The subjects of the following in both cases are women, and solely women: here the slave girl, and in Luke the women who followed Jesus from Galilee. In distinction to Luke 23:55, here the woman who follows, the slave girl, speaks for herself.

The verb ὑπαντᾶν, "to meet," "to encounter," appears ten times in the New Testament, but only in the Gospels and Acts. Two subject groups can be identified: "possessed" people, and those who are not "possessed." The verb appears in connection with exorcisms, but also to describe ordinary, everyday encounters:

1. *The verb ὑπαντᾶν in narratives preparatory to exorcisms*:

In the Gospels, this verb is used in Matt. 8:28; Mark 5:2; and Luke 8:27, all in the same story: it describes the encounter between the Gerasene and Jesus.[40] We are told that this person was troubled by an "unclean spirit," and that other people could also be in danger if they came close to him (Mark 5:2-5). He also suffers physically from this possession. In the encounter, the man kneels or bows down before Jesus. Three actions are described (Luke 8:28; Mark 5:7; cf. Matt. 8:29): First the man asks a question ("what have you to do with me/us?"), then makes a confessional statement ("Jesus, son of the 'most high' [ὕψιστος] God"), and concludes with a request ("do not torment me"). The request is immediately followed by a reason: "for Jesus had commanded the unclean spirit to come out of the man" (Luke 8:29; Mark 5:8). This plea, with the attached reason, expresses the torment that an exorcism causes in a possessed person. It is also important that, after the encounter and exorcism, the narrative turns again to the person who had undergone the exorcism: in Luke 8:35-36 the healed man joins Jesus in meeting the crowd of people, who experience shock and fear.

In Acts 16:16, the slave girl goes to meet the missionaries and attaches herself especially to Paul, who later drives the "Pythian" spirit out of her. Unlike the exorcism story, this one has nothing further to say about the slave girl, the no-longer-possessed person, after the exorcism. She disappears from the scene, and there is no crowd which could experience fear or awe because of the exorcism. The only people whose story continues are the owners, who have been injured by the exorcism and now proceed to accuse the missionaries.

2. *In the description of everyday encounters*:

The passages in question are the encounters of Jesus with the disciples (Matt. 28:9; John 11:20, 30; 12:18); of a master and his slaves

(John 4:51); and the description of enemies' meeting in war (Luke 14:31).

For our passage it is important to note that, while the synoptic encounter story in Mark 5:1-20 speaks of "unclean spirits" or "demons," Acts 16:16 tells of a mantic spirit, i.e., a spirit of divination, which is not described in those or similar terms. Whereas the other exorcism stories mentioned above are interested in the unique, one-time nature of the encounter, our text emphasizes that the first, perhaps accidental, encounter became a discipleship lasting many days. While in the other narratives the exorcism took place at the first encounter, in this story it occurs only after the slave girl has appeared many times. Her behavior was mantic, not marked by fear like that of the man with the "unclean spirit" at Gerasa. I will return to the effects of the exorcism below.

In order to interpret this passage, we must investigate in this context the way in which the "Pythian" spirit expressed itself through the slave girl. According to the text, the girl, having attached herself to the missionaries, spoke her oracle out loud.

The verb (ἀνα)κράζειν, "to cry out," "to say out loud," which also appears in Acts 16:17, is part of the linguistic field describing mediation between the divine and the human.[41] To determine its use here more precisely, we need also to look at the passages in the Gospels in which the verb appears in connection with "spiritual" or "demonic" actions. It is noteworthy that in the Gospels this verb, in the sense under consideration here,[42] also describes the reactions of (unclean) spirits and demons toward Jesus. In the synoptics, (ἀνα)κράζειν appears as follows in combination with πνεῦμα or δαίμων/δαιμόνιον:[43]

• Mark 1:23-24 presents an ἄνθρωπος ἐν πνεύματι ἀκαθάρτῳ in the synagogue who cries out, asking Jesus his intentions and acknowledging him as the Holy One of God; Luke 4:33 reads: ἄνθρωπος ἔχων πνεῦμα δαιμονίου ἀκαθάρτου.
• Mark 3:11 speaks of the πνεύματα τα ἀκάθαρτα who flee from Jesus when he is healing people, shouting, "You are the Son of God!"; Luke 4:41 has δαιμόνια.
• Mark 5:5-7 describes the reaction of the ἄνθρωπος ἐν πνεύματι ἀκαθάρτῳ described in v. 2 to the presence of Jesus; he shouts, calling Jesus "Son of the Most High [ὕψιστος] God." See vv. 8 and 13; Luke 8:27: ἀνὴρ ἔχων δαιμόνια; in v. 29 Luke speaks of a πνεῦμα ἀκάθαρτον. Thus the two expressions are parallel; Matt. 8:28ff. talks of δύο δαιμονιζόμενοι and οἱ δαίμονες.[44]

- Mark 9:26 tells of the <u>crying out</u> and the expulsion by Jesus of the spirit that, according to vv. 17 and 25, is a πνεῦμα ἄλαλον and κωφόν, a "spirit that keeps [the child whom it has possessed] from speaking and hearing." (Matt. 17:14-18 reports the healing of an "epileptic" boy, from whom Jesus also expels a δαιμόνιον; Luke 9:37-43 tells of the healing of a boy possessed by a δαιμόνιον or πνεῦμα ἀκάθαρτον that causes him suddenly to begin shrieking.)

Now let us investigate the particular usage of the verb (ἀνα)κράζειν in Luke-Acts. In Acts, only κράζειν is used (not ἀνακράζειν); it appears eleven times:

- In 7:47; 19:28, 32, 34; 21:28, 36 it represents the tumultuous <u>shouting</u> of a <u>crowd</u>.
- In 7:60 it is <u>Stephen</u> <u>crying out in a loud voice</u> in prayer.
- In 14:14; 23:6; 24:21 it is the <u>shouting</u> of <u>Paul</u> (and Barnabas) against the tumultuous outcry of the crowd, in order to say something important.
- In 16:17 it is the <u>crying out</u> of the <u>slave girl</u> in the Pythian spirit.

In the Gospel of Luke, κράζειν appears only three times:

- In 9:39 a spirit (πνεῦμα) seizes a <u>child</u> and makes him <u>shriek</u> all at once. (V. 42 calls this same spirit, from whom Jesus heals the child, δαιμόνιον and πνεῦμα ἀκάθαρτον.)
- In 18:39 a <u>blind man</u> <u>shouts,</u> asking Jesus to help, i.e., heal him.
- In 19:40 it is said that the <u>stones</u> will <u>shout out</u> if the disciples are silenced.

The verb ἀνακράζειν is used five times in the New Testament, three of them in the Gospel of Luke:

- In 4:33 an ἄνθρωπος ἔχων δαιμονίου ἀκαθάρτου <u>cried out</u> with a loud voice in the synagogue and <u>confessed</u> Jesus of Nazareth as the Holy One of God (Mark 1:23).
- In 8:27-28 an ἀνὴρ ἔχων δαιμόνια <u>shouted</u> when he saw Jesus and <u>named</u> him as "Son of the Most High [ὕψιστος] God." In v. 29, δαιμόνια is paraphrased with πνεῦμα ἀκάθαρτον (Mark 5:2, 7).
- In 23:18 "they all," i.e., the <u>whole crowd,</u> <u>shouted</u> to Pilate to seize Jesus and release Barabbas.

In summary, we may say that in the Lukan corpus the verb (ἀνα)κράζειν is used frequently outside the "demonic" or "spirit" realm. It thus does not represent a particular type of action, and is certainly not reserved for the mad ravings of persons possessed by evil spirits or demons.

An analysis of the use of the word πνεῦμα in "demonic" and "spirit" passages will permit a further conclusion about the passage in question.

Πνεῦμα is used very differently in the Gospels and Acts. According to Eduard Schweizer[45] it refers to demonic and human spirits as well as to the power of God at work in the community. In Luke's view, Jesus is Lord of the spirit. Interestingly, of the twenty-three πνεῦμα-passages in Mark, for example, fourteen contain the equivalent expressions πνεῦμα ἀκάθαρτον and δαίμων or δαιμόνιον.[46] These words appear very frequently in Luke's work also, but not as often as in Mark.[47] It is therefore all the more striking that it is not said of the spirit in Acts 16:17 (in spite of the efforts of many exegetes)[48] that it is ἀκάθαρτον ("unclean") or a δαίμων ("demon")! Hence Luke, or his source, did not unequivocally equate a mantic, divining spirit with an unclean or evil spirit.

A Pythian Revelation, or:
The Content of the Prophecy

The content of the slave's mantic speech is: "These people are slaves of the God 'Hypsistos' [Most High], who proclaim to you the way of salvation!" This statement is a designation of the identity of the missionaries. What or who was the God "Hypsistos," whose slaves the missionaries are said to be, and whose way of salvation do they proclaim? Does the speech correspond to the reality of who the missionaries were? We must examine this question here.

Δοῦλοι τοῦ θεοῦ ("Slaves of God")

The phrase δοῦλος τοῦ θεοῦ was also used in connection with the oracle of Delphic Apollo. It is said of one Ion, who belonged to the god, that he was δοῦλος του` θεοῦ.[49] We should also note that this description comes from an eastern context and was imported into the West. It is also found in Acts,[50] which describes prophets on the Old Testament model: "We have basically the same usage in Ac. 16:17, where the παιδίσκη . . . in Philippi describes Paul and his companions as δοῦλοι τοῦ θεοῦ τοῦ ὑψίστου."[51]

The designation δοῦλοι τοῦ θεοῦ by itself, however, does not adequately describe its subjects and their deity. The important detail of the description of the god must also be considered. The missionaries are not slaves of just any god, but of God the Most High ("Hypsistos").

Θεὸς ὕψιστος ("God the Most High")

The epithet "God Hypsistos" is well attested in written materials. The whole body of literary and inscriptional evidence will not be investigated here, as it has been treated elsewhere.[52] I will concentrate on the materials that are Jewish in origin or reveal Jewish influence, because the context of Acts 16:16-18 permits the conclusion that this is a Jewish epithet (e.g., the association with the προσευχή; cf. also vv. 20-21). The inscriptions in which this designation appears are for the most part those related to manumissions and dedications of buildings and other things. However, we must also treat Old Testament texts in their LXX form.

INSCRIPTIONAL MATERIAL. Basilius Latyschev[53] has published two almost identical manumission inscriptions from Gorgippia on the Bosphorus, from the year 41 C.E. Both say that the event they attest is dedicated to the god "hypsistos."[54] Both concern slaves[55] who have been freed because of vows sworn by their owners. There has already been extensive discussion of the question whether the religious statements in these inscriptions refer to the Jewish god or to "pagan" deities.[56] When the inscriptions were first published, in 1860, the editor, Stephani, declared that they were Jewish.[57] For Latyschev, on the other hand, and on the basis of another inscription that concludes with the words ὑπὸ Δία Γῆν Ἥλιον ("by Jupiter, the Earth, the Sun")[58] and thus is undoubtedly "pagan," inscriptions nos. 400 (= CII 1.690) and 401 (= CII 1.78*) are also to be regarded as "pagan": "Titulum non Iudaeorum esse . . . sed ethnicorum."[59] It appears to me that both explanations are very reductionist in their effect, because they confuse two groups, both of which appear in inscription no. 400. It is one thing for a manumission to be made, and another for the freed person to be dedicated or donated. The one freeing the slave may be a non-Jew who nevertheless, because of a vow, has dedicated the freed slave to a *proseuche,* that is, in effect, to a Jewish congregation. The document is therefore syncretistic only to the extent that here different deities are named, corresponding to different groups of believers. The deities themselves, however, are not confused. The inscription is dedicated to the god "hypsistos," but the emancipation was done in the name of other gods. The slave woman was the property of "pagan" people, and is now turned over to Jewish people. The freed woman is released and handed over to the *proseuche* because of a promise whose content is not communicated.

In summary: The inscription is syncretistic to the extent that it depicts different deities and religious groups, but that need not mean that the groups themselves are syncretistic. In this regard we should say, with Emil Schürer, that the inscription is "just as 'pagan' as it is Jewish. . . . The formula saying that the slave woman is to be free ὑπὸ Δία, Γῆν, Ἥλιον is pagan. . . . This description of the deity [θεῶι ὑψίστωι παντοκράτορι εὐλογητῷ] is purely Jewish, *and utterly foreign to extrabiblical usage.*"[60]

The expression θεὸς ὕψιστος is also very frequently found in *proseuche* building inscriptions. It is important to note that these attest to an official use of the term among Jews. In Atribis (lower Egypt), for example, the master of the guards and the Jewish population of Atribis built a synagogue in the time of Ptolemy and Cleopatra and dedicated it to the θεὸς ὕψιστος.[61] Regarding these building inscriptions, we should say with Martin Hengel[62] that the term προσευχή and the dedication to the God "Hypsistos" show that the whole building is a synagogue, and thus also attest the official Jewish use of this expression. The epithet (θεὸς) ὕψιστος is also attested in the context of the Jewish synagogue at Delos, in this case in personal dedications.[63]

The phrase also appears, quite significantly, in a series of inscriptions from the first century C.E. found in Gorgippia on the Bosphorus, where θεὸς ὕψιστος is connected with the expression ἀδελφοὶ σεβόμενοι.[64] The ἀδελφοὶ σεβόμενοι θεὸν ὕψιστον are *collegia* not only for religious purposes, but also, for example, for the cultivation of gymnastics and the care and upbringing of children, since there are numerous mentions of the γυμνασιάρχης ("gymnasiarch") and a νεανισκάρχης or "teacher" as officials. Here it is important to note that the technical term σεβόμενοι τὸν θεόν is connected with the name of the θεὸς ὕψιστος. The whole attests to people on the Bosphorus who had adopted elements, at least, of Judaism and integrated them into their way of life. The designation θεὸς ὕψιστος allows us to conclude without any doubt to the existence of a Jewish community in that place.[65]

Two very impressive grave inscriptions show the divine title "hypsistos" in connection with phrases from the psalms. They are from the first century B.C.E. and were found in Rheneia, then the meeting place on Delos. The stelae are 40–50 centimeters tall and 30 centimeters wide. An upraised pair of hands is carved above the inscription.

Both these inscriptions (*CII* 1.725a and b) treat the same topic: the murder of young women is lamented and condemned, and there is a petitionary prayer to God for revenge and protection. Unfortunately,

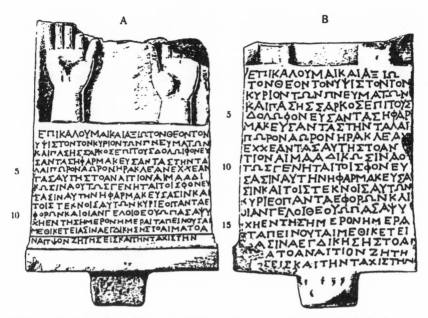

The front and back sides of a marble stele from Rheneia containing a prayer for vengeance for the Jewish woman Heraklea of Delos, ca. 100 B.C.E. From Gustav Adolf Deissmann, *Licht vom Osten*, 352. Bucharest Museum; reproduced with permission of the Austrian Archaeological Institute.

the superscription of this prayer is not preserved. Since there are numerous inscriptions erected by women, many of them mothers,[66] we may suggest that this inscription may also have been set up by the mothers or parents of the murder victims. The prayer reads:[67]

> I call on and appeal to God the Most High (ὕψιστος), who is the Lord of spirits and of all flesh, regarding those who treacherously killed or poisoned the unhappy and all too soon departed Heraklea, and who unjustly shed her innocent blood: that the like may happen to her murderers or poisoners, and to their children. Oh Lord, who sees all, and you angels of God! You to whom all life at this day humbles itself with entreaties for protection, that you would revenge innocent blood and call it home by the swiftest way.[68]

This prayer for revenge has some points of contact with two other, non-Jewish inscriptions.[69] In them also there is prayer to the gods (the sun god, Nemesis, and others, including the "hypsistos") for the revenge of the deaths of young people; they also have the upraised pair of hands.

However, I believe that the contacts with LXX usage are much stronger: the manner of addressing God as "hypsistos" (Sir. 46:5; 47:5); naming God as "the all-seeing one" and "God of spirits and all flesh" (2 Macc. 3:31; Num. 16:22; 27:16). The idea of revenge in this prayer is theologically relevant. It contains echoes of Old Testament and New Testament witnesses in its plea to God to avenge the blood of innocent victims (Joel 3:21; Ps. 79; Deut. 32:35, 43; 2 Kgs. 9:7, etc.: see below). These people were deliberately murdered, and this formulation (δολῶ) is used in a forensic sense (see Exod. 21:14; Deut. 27:24). The idea, and the belief in divine vengeance are Jewish traditions that are also found in the New Testament (Luke 11:48-49; Rev. 6:10). It is associated with the idea of humbling oneself, which can also imply fasting, in order to obtain the fulfillment of the request (Lev. 16:29, 31; 23:27, 29, 32; Isa. 58:3, 5; Jdt. 4:9; Ps. 34:13).[70] The inscriptions and the biblical witnesses indicate that belief in the Jewish God, who is also called "hypsistos," is belief in the one God to whom people who experience violence, wrong, and injustice can appeal for divine vengeance.

IN THE SEPTUAGINT. The epithet θεὸς ὕψιστος corresponds, in the usage of the LXX, to the Hebrew Bible's אל עליון, and is used there only in this sense. In the Old Testament, אל עליון as a predicate for God appears primarily in the later books and the apocrypha.[71]

It is possible that the divine predicate אל עליון had a polytheistic background, which can be demonstrated, for example, in the Old Testament texts.[72] However, this does not mean that the epithet is in itself polytheistic: in Gen. 14:18-24 the name appears as synonymous with "YHWH" as creator of heaven and earth; Ps. 96:9 places this god "above all gods;" in Pss. 46:3; 82:19 he is ruler over the whole earth; in Ps. 56:3 he is the god of the oppressed and offers them his protection (Ps. 90) and demands that his faithful people should create justice for the poor and suffering (Ps. 81:3-16); according to Pss. 77:35, 56; 49:14; 106:11 his commandments are to be kept for the sake of this justice. According to Dan. 3:93ff. (LXX), the slaves of this God are called παῖδες τοῦ θεοῦ ὑψίστου. Wisdom also asserts of herself that she comes from the mouth of the "hypsistos" (Sir. 24:3).

As this epithet also appears together with, or as synonymous with other divine predicates used to designate Israel's God, there can be "no doubt that it refers to the God of Israel."[73] Since it is used almost exclusively in the later writings of the Old Testament, we may conclude that it "corresponds to the ideas of its environment and is therefore especially" suited "to the Jewish diaspora."[74] "This divine predicate, mediated by Judaism, also penetrates the Hellenistic sphere and becomes a common designation for the God of the Jews."[75] This matches the fact that the LXX always translates אֵל עֶלְיוֹן with θεὸς ὕψιστος. New Testament authors follow this usage, and it remains quite clear that the reference is always to the Jewish God.[76]

IN THE NEW TESTAMENT. In the New Testament the word ὕψιστος as a term for God appears only nine times[77] and is used almost exclusively by Luke. There appears to be an affinity to the language of the LXX, which uses this word only for the God of Israel, YHWH.[78] The use of the word in the New Testament can be seen as further evidence of the maintenance of Jewish traditions in the diaspora. This term for the Jewish God is spoken in Acts 16:17 by a "pagan" girl. On the basis of the inscriptions cited above (in the context of "syncretism"), we may suppose that the slave girl refers to this Jewish God and no other.[79] She used the expression with precision, so that her words must have had a transparent clarity in the Roman colony of Philippi, especially since even Roman authorities made use of this expression to describe the Jewish God.[80] According to New Testament evidence also, this epithet was used to describe the Jewish God; it must have been very well known.

Interim Reflections

The religious giftedness of the slave girl is characterized in Acts 16:16 as a "Pythian" spirit that enabled her to prophesy. The owners of the slave girl profited from this gift of their "ensouled property," that is, they made a good income from the mantic speeches of their slave. The slave girl herself must have profited only indirectly from her work, insofar as, because of it (that is, through the money she earned) she was cared for and probably not mistreated by her owners, since an injury to the slave could also have had direct impact on her gift of prophecy, and hence on the owners' profits. Ultimately, her religious gifts were at the service of the economic gain of the slaveholders.

In light of the arguments, evidence, and reasoning presented above,[81] I think we may say that πνεῦμα Πύθων, a New Testament hapax legomenon, is a "πνεῦμα of inspiration"[82] from a religious-historical point of view. The inspiration or "possession" evidenced here is mantic. That sphere, the realm of "divination," points to the Delphic oracle of Apollo, together with its female priests, the Pythias,[83] who received the mantic spirit. In this realm, "The supreme and (historically) most important result of the spirit's working is the giving of oracles."[84] In all probability, the slave girl is understood to be a "Pythia" who also uttered her prophecies at a distance from the sacred oracle shrine. However, in all cases of πνεῦμα the rule is that the spirit is not at the command of the human being, but the reverse: "For the theme and content as well as the source of the experience of the spirit . . . is always something divine or a god, especially the most 'spiritual' of the gods, Apollo."[85] There is thus a strict, though in this case passive (as far as the human being is concerned) connection between the deity and those who receive the spirit. But to the extent that in this conception of the passive mantic "possessedness" of human beings they are "only" filled with "the god or the spirit" and as such in their divinations and prophecies are simply a "ministering organ"[86] of the superior god, they do not cooperate in any active, decision-making way in the deed they carry out.

Acts 16:16-19 attests that the slave girl's work in the religious sphere is exploited by her owners. At the same time, that work unites her, through her mantic powers, with the deity whose spirit she has received. The theological relevance of this story consists, in my opinion, in the fact that this deity, whose mouthpiece she is, is unable to deliver the slave girl from her slavery—at any rate, there is no evidence of it in our text. Even if the owners and the slave practiced the same religion, and thus could participate equally in the same religious community, there is an absence of any power to overcome social conflicts: the barriers between exploiter and exploited are not removed.[87]

On the other hand, as I see it, we should emphasize the slave's special gift of prophecy. Her gift enabled the slave to reveal the identity of the missionaries. She, or rather the spirit speaking through her, was aware that the men who went to the synagogue day by day served the Jewish God "hypsistos," the Most High God, who was known and worshiped throughout the world.[88] By her prophecy, the slave gives renewed expression to the identity of the missionaries within the Roman colony at Philippi, and in doing so she proves that her gift is genuine and not "deceptive."[89] Her appearance in Acts 16:16-18 is an example of her gift and her craft, which nevertheless hold her ensnared, like so many others, in the nets of exploitation, for her owners are very capable of making economic use of religious gifts.

In her physical and spiritual imprisonment, the slave girl prophesies; by doing so she brings great joy to many people and does a great deal of good.[90] It is not typical for her to make negative or ominous predictions.[91] Hence in her surroundings she could not be evaluated as someone who possessed an evil or unclean spirit! Yet Acts 16:18 reports that at some point, after the slave girl had been following the missionaries for many days, Paul began to find the situation insupportable. This does not mean that he regarded the spirit as evil or unclean, but his annoyance resulted in the expulsion of the mantic spirit. We must now inquire about this exorcism and its consequences. One question, however, we should keep in mind: would it not have been possible for the slave girl to be liberated from the exploitation of slavery without the destruction of her gift?

Religious Exorcism and Economic Damage to Property

After the slave girl had exercised her mantic gift for many days, Paul became annoyed and expelled the spirit that was at work in her. Here again, it is clear from Paul's action that the slave girl is not understood to be the subject of the mantic activity, for Paul does not address her. Instead, he turns directly to the Pythian spirit and orders it in the name of Jesus Christ to come out of her. This also presumes that the spirit not only knows the missionaries' religious allegiance, but also is aware of who Jesus Christ is. The exorcism is immediately effective. Thus we need to inquire about Paul's reaction, and then about the owners' response. In the former case we also need to ask whether and what similarities and differences exist between Acts 16:18 and other exorcism stories. In the second case we must determine whether and what legal consequences followed Paul's action, which then becomes the basis of the owners' accusation.

Paul's Reaction (Acts 16:18b)

Now that we have investigated the content of the slave girl's prophecy, we must ask about Paul's reaction, for the very reason that the content of her mantic utterances was true. Did Paul find this disturbing? If so, why? The troublesome question at the bottom of all this is based on the opinion of exegetes that "demons" could not tell the truth, or that the truth on the lips of "demons" was a provocation. In addition, we should ask how the owners of the slave girl reacted to Paul's intervention (vv. 19-24).

Paul's "Annoyance"

But Paul, very much annoyed, turned and said to the spirit, "I order you in the name of Jesus Christ to come out of her."

Before I inquire in detail about the exorcism, I would like to investigate the meaning of Paul's "annoyance" in connection with the exorcism, and what could have been its cause—to the extent that it can give us some indication of the reasons for the exorcism.

The verb διαπονεῖσθαι, "to be annoyed" appears only twice in the New Testament, in Acts 4:2 and 16:18. Acts 4:1-2 reports that Peter and John were speaking to the people (cf. 3:9, 12) after Peter had healed a lame man. This healing caused wonder and amazement among the people and gathered a large crowd, to whom the apostles were preaching. Then "the priests, the captain of the temple, and the Sadducees" came, annoyed because Peter and John "were teaching the people and proclaiming that in Jesus there is the resurrection of the dead." Here we have a clear statement of the reason for their annoyance. In the eyes of those who are annoyed, Peter and John have invaded their area of responsibility: the priests were in charge of teaching the people in the temple, the captain of the temple was responsible for keeping order within the temple precincts, and the Sadducees did not believe in the resurrection of the dead (Acts 23:8). These seem to be the principal reasons why the three groups are annoyed with Peter and John.[92] The result of this offense on their part is that Peter and John are imprisoned overnight.

It is evident from the context in Acts 4:2 that annoyance is a reaction: in the first place, to deliberate or inadvertent interference by others in the area of responsibility of those who are annoyed as a result, and precisely because the "intruders" have thus attracted considerable attention among the people and brought many to believe. On the other hand, it is also a reaction to the content of what the "intruders" are saying; in the case of Acts 4:2 (in context) this does, in fact, indicate differences—in this instance, with regard to the resurrection of the dead.

But why was Paul annoyed, as is said in Acts 16:18; what was the reason for his reaction? On the basis of the text, two possibilities suggest themselves: the mantic utterances of the slave girl, and the "many days" during which she spoke them.

Review of Research

The action of following for many days, combined with the mantic utterances of the slave girl, are almost universally treated by exegetes as a continual strain on the missionaries. Theodor Zahn, whose interpretation of the event may stand as representative for many, imagines the scene as follows:

> On seeing the missionaries, she [the slave girl] does not continue on her way past them, but stops and lets them pass by her, *certainly not without taking a good look at them,* then turns around and attaches herself to them, primarily to P[aul], crying loudly and continually: . . . *Because* she repeated this for many days afterward (v. 18), P[aul] did not see this as a welcome testimony to the truth he represented, but as an *undesirable distraction.*[93]

Zahn emphasizes the text's statement that "she kept doing this for many days," which for him represents the principal reason for Paul's reaction, and also justifies it. He does not question her prophecy: the slave girl's words are true. Paul is not said to have been disturbed by what the woman said, but by her repeated action. We should take note of this: according to Zahn, what is annoying is not the statement, but the woman's appearance over many days. Unfortunately, he does not say or even hint why he thinks Paul would have felt annoyed by it.

According to Gottfried Schille's opinion, Luke himself considers the slave girl's very words, i.e., her "demonic utterance,"[94] a continual annoyance. "The presence of a demon" in itself "arouses the resistance of the exorcist," independently of what the "demon" says. For that very reason, the statement about continual annoyance as contained in the Lukan report—with which Luke attempted "to make Paul's attitude understandable for the reader"—in no way matches the description in v. 16, which is thus superfluous.

Schille shares this opinion with a great number of exegetes who regard the religious phenomenon described in vv. 16-18 as "demonic and unclean," as we will see hereafter. It is precisely in this evaluation of the religious-historical information that the exegetical opinions achieve their harshest tone, and their assertions culminate in a kind of religious language that is equally harsh in its sense of superiority. On the one hand the exegetes unanimously admit that other spirits or demons also acknowledge the power of the (Jewish) God and even confess that same God, but on the other hand they describe that very ability as, in their opinion, impossible: "In the Gospels demons also speak objective truth (Mark 1:24; Luke 4:41, etc.), but they are not *allowed* to continue speaking."[95]

Practically speaking, the whole body of exegetical interpretation of this story in Acts 16:16-18 is subsumed under that motto. Even in his translation of v. 18b, for example, Otto Bauernfeind gives expression to his conviction: "But Paul was annoyed (in fact by this hypocritical satanic praise, whose purpose was obvious)."[96] However, he does not explain how it was that this supposed purpose was made obvious. He simply goes on to assert that, while what the slave girl said was the truth, "here truth is, rather, a guise for malice."[97] This assertion also remains unexplained. Werner de Boor writes similarly.[98] First he makes a general acknowledgment that it was especially "people possessed by occult powers who felt attracted by Jesus' disciples," and then says that Paul was not interested in the slave girl and her prophecy, because he knew who was behind it all: Paul "will not tolerate any advertisements for Jesus's cause from the devil." Finally, Jürgen Roloff[99] interprets the matter as follows: The slave girl's words show that in Philippi, apart from Lydia, it is only the "demon" who knows the truth about Paul and Silas, because "the demon is able to reveal hidden truth." He continues: "Of course, in the mouth of the demon these words are not a confession of faith, but a provocation." Consequently, Paul is challenged to show his power. His superiority is then made clearly evident by the very fact that "Paul's calm" stands "in sharp contrast to the restlessness [?] of the demon," i.e., before the latter annoys him (v. 18b).

Evaluation and Interpretation in Light of the Text

The text itself provides us with none of the criteria for interpretation that the exegetes impose on it. As we have seen, the interpreters begin very quickly to operate with ideas like "demon," "devil," and the like, equating them with the πνεῦμα πύθων in Acts 16:16. Their approach to the various "spirit" stories shows little subtlety throughout. However, in my opinion there is a great difference, from the point of view of intellectual and spiritual history, between an "evil" or "unclean" spirit, a "demon," and a mantic or divining spirit, in particular because of the effects of their actions (see pp. 156–60 above). The former cause sickness, torture, and fear, while the last enables mantic speech. Clarifying this question within the context is different from asking how outsiders evaluate these different "spirit" actions: in this latter respect it may be that, from a Jewish-Christian perspective, and primarily in Christian exegesis, a mantic spirit can be defined as "evil" or "unclean." In the following section I will describe my opinion of why Paul was annoyed in this story.

Exorcism as Damage

When Paul becomes "annoyed" he reacts by turning to the Pythian spirit and driving it out of the slave girl. It is obvious that this action has not only a religious, but also a legal significance. First let us look at some other exorcism stories in order to see whether they make a statement in common with that in Acts 16:16-18. Then I will address the legal question of damage to property and inquire about the possible consequences of this action for Paul.

Comparison with Other Exorcism Stories

As in most exorcism narratives,[100] the verb ἐξέρχεσθαι is used to describe the command ("go out," "come out") and the effect ("it came out").[101] In the synoptics this is "the characteristic word for the 'going forth' of demons from those possessed by them."[102] The verb is used not only for the departure itself, but also, as synonymous with ἐκβάλλειν, for the *command* to depart.

There are a number of *differences*: First, whereas in the Synoptic exorcism stories Jesus himself is the subject and miracle worker characterized by the first person singular pronoun, here Paul is the subject who does the action. Nevertheless, the use of the formula "in the name of Jesus Christ" retains Jesus as the one who does the miracle. Second, in the Synoptics, a dialogue or dispute between Jesus and the spirits or demons occurs at their first and sole encounter. Here it only happens after "many days." Third, ordinarily we learn of the demons' or spirits' reaction as they depart, e.g., "crying with a loud voice, [it] came out of him" (Mark 1:26). Nothing is said about this in Acts 16:18. Fourth, for the most part, in the Synoptics we learn of a positive or astonished reaction of other people to the miracle that has been done. The stories thus serve also to spread the message of Jesus. Here there is no acclamation.

Thus precisely those features that characterize a miracle (the second, third, and fourth) are absent from this story; it is only said that the spirit immediately departed, without uttering a sound. However, there is another exorcism story in Acts (at 8:7) that does contain these three characteristics; thus the form is known to the author of Acts. Therefore we may say that Acts 16:18 is not simply a report of a successful exorcism by the missionaries. On the contrary, here the exorcism is followed by something unusual: instead of admiration, astonishment, and conversion, what ensues is a Roman legal accusation against the missionaries, the content of which must still be examined.

The authority of Jesus' disciples is characterized by the formula "in the name of Jesus Christ." Thus Acts 16:18 is a concrete example of Jesus' promise in Mark 16:17: "by using my name they [i.e., believers] will cast out demons . . . ,"[103] the difference being that here there is no question of a demon. Here Paul is accorded the power that, according to Mark 9:18-29, Jesus' disciples were unable to exercise. Paul is, so to speak, Jesus' representative; he takes his place and uses his name "successfully." This is ultimately an "act of power"[104] on the part of Jesus' disciples, who are empowered by him to do these things, as in Acts 3:1-9; 5:1-12; 9:33-42, and elsewhere.

Jesus showed through his exorcisms that he is also master of the spirits or demons, who obey his word of command. The demons are strong; they cause afflictions and diseases in those they possess. But Jesus is "the Stronger, who penetrates into the house of the strong man"[105] and conquers him. Jesus enters into combat with the demons.[106] The exorcisms thus represent a divine power struggle, and this is equally true when disciples do such deeds in the name of Jesus.

I believe that Acts 16:18 also represents a "battle of the gods." It takes place between Paul and the slave girl as representatives of different gods, Jesus the Jewish Messiah and, probably, Apollo. It is not said that the struggle was intentional, at least not before Paul reacted with annoyance. Had it been meant from the beginning to end in a conflict between different divine powers, Paul would have had to react earlier, perhaps on the very first occasion, as is attested in other exorcism narratives. I believe it only becomes a "battle of the gods" when Paul detects some kind of competition or danger in the power of the religiously gifted slave girl. It may have consisted in the fact that Paul could not deny the slave's power to divine the truth. It would seem that her daily appearance over a long period of time made her a precursor of Paul: that is, she prepared the way for the missionaries and announced their coming. It may be that people were turning to the prophetic slave girl to learn more about the missionaries and the "way of salvation" they preached.[107] Thus it may have happened that the slave girl's speech turned the spotlight more on her than on the missionaries. At that point, the missionaries may have categorized her appearance much the way the learned people in Jerusalem did that of the "intruders" in Acts 4:1-22. This is not to exclude the possibility that the slave girl's loud announcements may also have constituted a danger for the missionaries, for the very reason that the words she used revealed the missionaries' identity and could have aroused suspicion that they were prosely-tizing among the Roman population of the colony.[108]

In summary we may reiterate: In the exorcism stories in the Synop-tics and in Acts 8:7, the spirits expelled are always "unclean" or "evil." They cause illness, isolation, and physical pain in the people in whom they dwell. The story in Acts 16:16-18 is not about this kind of spirit who causes illness and pain, and who now is exorcised. We should further observe that it is not the "Pythian" spirit who enslaves the woman. It is her owners who enslave her and who profit financially from her ability to prophesy. Nevertheless, the spirit that is expelled from her has kept the slave girl in her state of slavery; it does not reveal itself within this situation of enslavement as a liberating spirit.

Previous Interpretations

The story in Acts 16:18 about the exorcism done by Paul in Philippi has been given a Christian theological explanation—or rather, justification—in the Christian tradition of interpretation. The exegetes attempt to establish a reason for the exorcism in the following ways (see also above, p. 170):

Rudolf Pesch considers the slave girl's power of divination "a morbid capacity" or "a morbid religiosity,"[109] but does not explain why it is "morbid." I think that in these and similar interpretations everything that is "pagan"—and thus inferior to what is "Christian"—is consid-ered "morbid." Indeed, after Pesch, for example, has interpreted the slave girl's following of the missionaries over a period of many days as an "irritation," he concludes that "after some days of calm patience, Paul reacts with 'annoyance' (cf. 4:2) and accepts the challenge to dem-onstrate the *superiority* of the servants of the true God *over the ghost of pagan religiosity.*"[110]

I. H. Marshall unmistakably equates the Pythian spirit with an "evil spirit," interpreting the slave girl's ability as similar to that of a ventril-oquist and attributing to her the gift of clairvoyance, which in turn is said to be something evil.[111] Paul had not discovered this on the first day, but after the slave girl has appeared for a number of days in succession he discovers "that she was in the grip of an evil *spirit.*" According to Marshall, the fact that Paul did not immediately discern what was at work in her is the reason why he tolerated the slave for days on end.

Otto Bauernfeind regarded the prophetic slave girl as a disturbance to Paul's missionary activity; thus the exorcism serves to clear the way for Paul. This can be deduced from his remark that, as a result of Paul's successful exorcism, the slave girl "utters no more μαντεία; Paul's way is clear again."[112] In Bauernfeind's opinion, Paul risked everything in driving out the "Pythian" spirit, referring thereby to the missionaries' imprisonment (vv. 23-40). Bauernfeind also asks whether the sacrifice Paul made was appropriate to the matter at hand, and thus probably to the mission itself. He thinks that Paul was fully aware of the potential consequences of his action from the beginning, which certainly seems to correspond to the accusation in vv. 20-21.

For a great many exegetes, the exorcism is a liberation, often even a healing of the slave girl. It should be noted that in this interpretation the slave is usually regarded as sick.[113] W. de Boor, for example, asserts that the slave girl was "like a Pythia in miniature,"[114] a normal phenomenon of religious life. On the other hand, however, he indicates afterward that she had been sick in some way, because she was now free and her health was not of interest or value to her owners.[115] Elisabeth Schüssler Fiorenza also considers the slave's state of possession as a sickness, for she says that Paul healed her and interprets this as liberation.[116]

Legal Aspects of Damage to Property

On the basis of historical and legal information I agree with Elisabeth Schüssler Fiorenza to the extent of saying that, by the act of exorcism, Paul made the slave girl worthless to her owners. In this way "Paul interfered with the property rights and ancestral laws of the household."[117] This is a new insight in the history of the exegesis of this text. The question is not about Paul and the "irritation" and "interference" posed for him by the slave girl. Legal issues are raised instead, and this is a line of questioning that keeps the slave girl in the center of the picture. As soon as I attempt to place her at the center, I must assert that the whole story of the events in Philippi, as reported in Acts 16:16-40, is far from being a story of her liberation. In fact, the slave girl is not liberated from her concrete state of slavery. Paul's action makes her a piece of damaged property in the eyes of her owners. This is the first conclusion to be drawn from the story in light of the legal facts of the case. Therefore it is not sufficient simply to say that Paul's action made the slave girl worthless to her owners. We must also ask about the legal consequences of such an action.

When the slave's power of divination is withdrawn as a result of the exorcism performed by Paul, she loses her value. As far as her owners are concerned, a valuable "tool" has been damaged. Acts 16:19 shows, with unmistakable clarity, that this "tool" has been damaged by being deprived of her τέχνη. The first consequence of this kind of damage to their property is the owners' loss of a significant source of income. Since slaves were "legally the property of their owners,"[118] and as such also a source of income, the damage done to these owners' property has resulted in the loss of one such source.

Hence Paul's religious actions have caused economic loss to these owners. But what will happen to the damaged property? Owners had no obligations to their slaves,[119] other than to feed them and keep them healthy enough to work. As "instruments of production,"[120] they were to be kept in a condition to produce. Should the property be damaged by a third party, the law is very clear about what is to be done, but it is concerned with the owner, not with the property itself: the owner must be compensated. Before considering the means, let me indicate the presuppositions behind this kind of legal arrangement. They can be described as follows:

> As a piece of property, the slave is no longer subject to the whim of just anyone, but exclusively to that of his owner. *Damage done to him by a third is no longer a matter of legal indifference, but is damage done to his owner.* At the outset, he enjoyed no legal protection against mistreatment by the owner; he was secured against excessive mistreatment only by the owner's own interest, since in damaging the property the owner would be damaging himself.[121]

The slave girl in Acts 16:16-18, who was legally a piece of property, was in this case damaged not by her owners,[122] but by a third person, namely Paul. According to Roman law, Paul had thereby done injury to the owners themselves, by damaging their property. Ultimately, the religious act of exorcism proved economically unfavorable to them. Paul has thus interfered directly in Roman legal arrangements. He has to answer to the owners for his action. The religious conflict is expressed in a legal dispute, or rather, in a legal accusation.

The Owners' Reaction (16:19-21)

> But when her owners saw that their hope of making money was gone, they seized Paul and Silas and dragged them into the marketplace before the authorities. When they had brought them before the magistrates, they said, "These men are disturbing our city; they are Jews and are advocating customs that are not lawful for us as Romans to adopt or observe."

Political Charges Brought Against Paul and Silas

Acts 16:19-40 describes a legal procedure deriving from Roman law. The fact that the slave girl's owners turn to the Roman authorities with their complaint and advance charges against the missionaries allows us to conclude that they were Roman citizens who had recourse to Roman law. Two questions need to be clarified at this point: What does Roman law envision in cases where a third party has damaged the property of another? What is the meaning of the political and police procedures adopted in vv. 20-24?

Legal Consequences of Damaging Others' Property

In light of the incidents reported, we should expect that charges of property damage would be brought, and a demand made for restitution. Here we will attempt a legal-historical reconstruction and contrast it with the political nature of the actual charges. I will inquire what could have happened to Paul and, still more important, what could have happened to the slave girl as a result of the property damage inflicted. In fact, the slave girl disappears from the narrative; my attempt at reconstruction is done in memory of her. Her fate should be remembered.

There was a special section of Roman private law dealing with cases of individual offenses.[123] From the time of the Lex Aquileia (286 B.C.E.), the digests included a basic rule for damages done to someone through injury to (or destruction of) slaves or other property. This rule of law[124] applies especially to the killing of another person's slaves and four-footed herd animals, and to all other damages done to someone by the burning (*urere*), breaking (*frangere*), or tearing (*rumpere*) of property. Since all these last three could refer to acts of torture resulting in bodily injury or mutilation, slaves could also be the objects of these actions. As regards punishment, we observe that it always involves payment of a fine. If there has been a killing, the fine corresponds to the "highest value of the object [!] during the past year," and for all other damages the law assesses "the fine according to the value *in diebus triginta proximis*, i.e., . . . within the last thirty days before the deed."[125] The payment of the highest value of a slave makes it clear that she or he had lost his or her real value for the owner, that is, had been made unusable. The one who caused this damage must pay what the slave was worth before the damage or killing, in order that the owner can replace her or him with another of equal value. Thus the payment results in "restitution" to the owner. But what happens to the one who was injured? It seems to me that there can be no "restitution" of the damage done to him or her. The payment of the full value to the injured owner settles matters between debtor and creditor, and the creditor probably has no further claim on the property whose value has been restored.[126] The latter, it would seem, can remain in the possession of the debtor; the result, then, is an indirect transfer of property, or purchase of freedom in the case of a slave.

I have found no examples in the legal literature referring, for example, to damage to "spiritual" or "intellectual" property, but we may draw some conclusions by analogy. In the present case it is not a matter of physical, but of "spiritual" damage. After the expulsion of her "Pythian" spirit, the slave girl could no longer do her job. The primary damage done by the exorcism was not to her body, but to her spirit. According to the text, Paul did not even touch the girl, and yet his actions made her unemployable according to her accustomed gifts. It seems to me that this fact is important for the legal consequences, inasmuch as the Aquileian rule was expanded and extended to cover cases in which damage was done in such a way "that the one acting does *no immediate* physical damage to the injured object, but acts on another person or thing that then, in turn, causes the damage."[127] The doer of the deed, Paul in this case, certainly caused the damage, since without him it would not have happened in this way. This is the Roman "principle of indebtedness,"[128] and in this way Paul had made himself liable under Roman law. In just such cases involving liability incurred without direct physical contact with the damaged object, that is, in cases involving this expansion of the Aquileian principle, a charge is to be brought before the praetorium.[129] In any event, the charge reported in Acts 16:19-24 should be regarded as a civil procedure, since the praetor was responsible for legal disputes between Romans and non-Romans.[130] The observation that this is a civil trial accords with the passages from *Digesta* 9.2. cited above. In addition, we should note that all Roman civil judgments involve monetary fines.[131]

Let me introduce at this point an excerpt from one of Cicero's legal orations[132] to clarify the question of compensation for damage done to a piece of property belonging to several owners. This was a case of a slave owned by two men.[133] The slave had artistic talents, and thus did a type of intellectual work. Fannius, the original owner, lent the slave Panurgus to the actor Roscius so that the slave could be trained for the stage. Roscius made it a condition that he would share in the profits to be gained from Panurgus's subsequent stage work. Thus a partnership was created between Fannius and Roscius, based on the artistic activity of Panurgus. But when Panurgus was at the height of his stage success, he was killed by Flavius, depriving Fannius and Roscius of an important source of income. Roscius brought charges against Flavius to recover damages. During the trial, and without informing Fannius, Flavius bought Roscius off with a worthless piece of land, but set the value of the land very high: 100,000 sesterces. When Fannius learned of it, he demanded that Roscius pay him 50,000 sesterces, and when the latter refused, an arbitrator was brought in to bring the parties to a discussion intended to satisfy everyone. Fannius then sued Flavius, who tried to escape trial by paying Fannius 100,000 sesterces. Fannius did not share the money with Roscius; instead, four years after the murder of Panurgus he again sued Roscius for the 50,000 sesterces he had demanded earlier. In the new trial, Cicero appeared on behalf of Roscius. We do not know how it came out, because a large part of the oration is lost. But this example shows something of the operation of partnerships or associations based on the work of slaves. Something similar would have applied to the slave girl and her owners in Acts 16:16-24, and a demand for compensation of damages could also have been raised against Paul.[134]

Police and Political Measures

Under Roman law, Paul (and Silas) should also have had to pay a fine in this case. However, the text says nothing about it. It shows us a new scene in which the owners of the slave girl seized Paul and Silas and dragged them to the marketplace before the authorities, presenting them to the magistrates. What is described in vv. 20-24 is within the realm of municipal law.[135] The στρατηγοί or "magistrates" (duumviri iure dicundo) are the two highest officials in a Roman colony. They have jurisdiction over the city government and over judicial proceedings. The ῥαβδοῦχοι are the lictors in service of the municipal magistrates. Among their duties are "bringing persons before the bar as well as arrest and scourging: a set of duties that the ῥαβδοῦχοι carry out with some exactitude in the context of Acts."[136]

According to A. N. Sherwin-White, Acts 16:19-21 represents a "formal indictment before the municipal magistrates."[137] The latter were there to preserve "Roman order" within the colonies as well. The starting point for the police and political conflict was a charge, in this case resulting from the conflict between the missionaries and the owners of the slave girl, who had suffered economic loss as a result of the missionaries' action. The charge brought by the owners has to do with "distur-bance," supposedly resulting from the action of Jews (Paul and Silas) in advocating foreign customs.

The charge of advocating foreign customs that Romans may not adopt or observe is political: it is an accusation of offending against the Roman *mos maiorum*,[138] that is, of causing uproar in the city by pro-moting foreign customs. Among "foreign" Jewish customs were "for-bidding military service, celebrating the Sabbath, observation of the food laws, and maintaining a separate court system."[139] It is also possi-ble to subsume Paul's action, i.e., exorcism, under the umbrella of "ad-vocating foreign customs," because if the result of the exorcism done by Paul is concrete damage to property, this ultimately means that Paul has violated Roman property laws. He has offended against Roman custom, that is, against the Roman laws regarding property, and thereby also against the Roman state religion, which was intimately connected with those laws.

In this connection we should observe the following detail of this text: This is the first report in Acts of Paul and Silas being brought before Roman authorities. It is possible that, by calling them Jews, Luke at-tempted to give a Christian apologetic twist to the story: it was not Christians, but Jews who were disturbing the city.[140] But I think another detail is more important: exegetes have correctly pointed out the wide-spread anti-Judaism in the Roman colony of Philippi, especially strong among the veterans of the Roman army.[141] This information, which also appears in this text, is all the more important because the measures taken against Paul are not, as elsewhere, initiated by Jews, but by Roman authorities. Paul himself attests to this treatment (1 Thess. 2:2; 2 Cor. 11:25). The anti-Jewish attitude and the behavior of the people and their rulers in Philippi found their first expression in the conflict between Paul and the slave girl's owners. What I think needs to be emphasized, however, is precisely that this anti-Judaism was the normal context within which, for example, Lydia and the other women who assembled in the προσευχή were living. For them, danger was always latently present. It has already been pointed out that women were not spared the application of such measures.[142] It is apparent from Phil. 1:30 that such dangers, and probably the police and political measures associated with them, continued to exist after Paul; that is, they were an ongoing threat to the community.

As a result of the police measures and the political conflict, the slave girl and her fate disappear from the perspective of the story, and yet she is the starting point for the narrative and the key figure around whom the conflict revolves. Hence the constabulary-political scene is "strongly interlocked" with the exorcism and with the slave girl.[143] At this point, I want to reflect on her fate.

An Opportunity for Liberation.
Summary Prospects

In my opinion, we ought not to see the act of exorcism from the outset as a "liberation" of the slave girl—as I have already said.[144] When the mantic abilities that brought profit to her owners were removed, she certainly lost her economic interest for her owners, and with it their special regard for her. It is well known that slaves who, for example, had artistic abilities regularly enjoyed favor in the eyes of their owners; they were treated better than other slaves who did not possess such talents.[145]

As a result of Paul's actions, the slave's property value was diminished; accordingly, Paul had to be called upon to make restitution to the owners. The conclusion that follows, I believe, is that here we cannot speak primarily or immediately of the liberation of the slave girl. The "restitution" could legally be made to the owners, but not to the slave girl, because the slave was totally at her owners' disposal, and not her own. It was thus not enough to deprive the owners of their source of profit, thus removing the slave girl from her previous way of life. She had to be given a new opportunity for life, a new and qualitatively different beginning. Only then could we speak of liberation, of the establishment of a new sphere of existence. Simply to abandon the damaged property, after it has served its purpose by revealing Paul's power, the strength of his faith, and the power of God working in him, would certainly not constitute a concrete sign of a praxis of liberation in solidarity with the oppressed. It seems to me that we can only speak of liberation when, historically, an opportunity for freedom is both envisaged and available for reconstruction. Then there would be a chance for "restitution" to the slave girl, who has been deprived of her art—even if, according to the text, a legal "restitution" to the owners did not have to be made. This freeing of the slave girl—a historical possibility—I will adopt as a hypothesis; it rests on the witnesses that document this as existing practice. Let me review the evidence.

The word προσευχή in Acts 16:16 is not a superfluous element in the text.[146] Instead, it is the element that unites the two stories not only literarily, but also historically. The information that the missionaries went frequently to the προσευχή should not present any particular difficulties for a socio-historical interpretation of this text. We have already demonstrated in detail[147] that a προσευχή served a number of community functions, even apart from the Sabbath context of worship. It could be the gathering place for a minority group in the diaspora even during the week, serving as a school, a source of water, a place for community meals, or even a place of lodging. Thus even during the week Paul could have met people there and spoken with them about the "way of salvation." The slave girl joined in this daily movement, following the missionaries on their route. Perhaps her following them was also motivated by a hope of liberation, for it was well known in the world of that time that this place, in addition to its routine uses, offered not only asylum[148] for tortured and mistreated slaves, but even the opportunity for them to gain freedom.[149] Thus the Jewish προσευχή was known and even famous for being a place of liberation. Understandably enough, slaves often sought out such places and made efforts to remain there. To many of those in slavery, they represented the hope of liberation.

Manumission inscriptions attest the practice of liberating slaves in the προσευχή. This practice in the Jewish communities of the diaspora was adapted from the "sacral release" practiced in sacred, non-Jewish temples in the larger environment.[150] Three or four inscriptions from the first century C.E. attest the Jewish adoption of this traditional practice.

B. Latyschev (*Inscriptiones* 2:52)[151] reproduces a manumission declaration from Pantikapaion from the year 81 C.E. The document was given by the Jewish woman Chreste and contains the statement that she is freeing her slave Heraklas. This action takes place in the προσευχή, "in the synagogue," before the assembled community (συναγωγή) and in consequence of a vow (κατὰ εὐχή[ν]). The second inscription[152] is badly damaged, but the legible lines very closely resemble the one just mentioned: this manumission also takes place in the synagogue in consequence of a vow; the difference is that someone is freeing not just one, but many slaves. Both inscriptions have an additional, very striking characteristic: The people freeing the slaves are Jews. The slaves are released from all previous obligations, but the manumission bears a condition or request on the part of the liberators: those who have been freed should undertake an obligation not to separate themselves from the προσευχή. On the contrary: they should go there regularly and practice the Jewish religion.[153] The third inscription[154] attests that the one freeing the slave was not a Jew, but that the act of manumission was done in the name of God the Most High (ὕψιστος) and in the synagogue. The liberated slave woman is brought as a votive offering to the προσευχή.

Latyschev (*Inscriptiones* 2:401) edited another manumission document in which the act of manumission is also done in the name of God the Most High. In it, a slave woman is liberated by a man and his sister because of vows they have made. Since the inscription is only partially preserved, it is not clear whether this action also takes place in the προσευχή, or whether the freed slave may have been given to the synagogue. However, in light of the other documents treated above, it may be supposed that this was the case.

These "sacral" manumissions were acknowledged as legally equal to the "profane" variety.[155] The acknowledgment was also documented and guaranteed by the person freeing the slave. Emil Schürer writes regarding the inscription in Latyschev, *Inscriptiones* 2:52 (and what he says here can be applied to all other similar declarations of manumission): "The purpose of the documentary declaration is to secure the slave's freedom, even in case of the death of the owner."[156] In the case of a manumission in the synagogue, or the gift of a freed person to the synagogue community, the precondition is that the community is prepared to assume the status of patron to the manumitted slave or slaves; that is, the liberated person or persons are placed under the protection of the community, which takes responsibility for them.[157] There were also cases in which the synagogue, that is, a Jewish congregation, paid the redemption price for a manumission.[158]

In light of what has been learned about the conditions of the time, I conclude that we can only speak of the liberation of the slave girl through Paul's action if, on the basis of the common practice of the time, we can also reckon with the possibility of such a "sacral" manumission in this case. If Paul was legally obligated to compensate the owners, this would correspond, de facto, to a redemption or purchase, because the owners would presumably no longer have had access to the piece of property whose value had been restored to them. For the slave girl, the exorcism constituted a worsening of her situation, inasmuch as she no longer possessed the gift that had been her life's security. For her, there could only have been the opportunity to create a new way of life if, for example, the Jewish Christian community in Philippi took her under its protection, accepting her into a community of sharing.

In the letter of Bishop Ignatius of Antioch to Polycarp, the bishop of the community at Smyrna, two matters are addressed in the ethical parenesis beginning at 4:1: There are slaves in the community, but they "must not be overanxious to gain their freedom at the community's expense" (4:3: μὴ ἐράτωσαν ἀπὸ τοῦ κοινοῦ ἐλευθεροῦσθαι). On the other hand, this admonition demonstrates that slaves expected to be released, or rather have their freedom purchased, from the funds of the community; presumably this expectation was met in a number of communities.

Whether this is what happened, or whether the slave woman was accepted into the community of the saints in Philippi, is something we can no longer determine. It remains, however, a historically possible hypothesis that what followed corresponded to a practice that is attested for that time by multiple witnesses. If it also happened in Philippi, then this slave girl should be counted among the brothers and sisters in Acts 16:40, the people who gathered in Lydia's house. The thesis is also favored by the fact that, according to the testimony of Paul, the Christian community in Philippi had very close connections with slaves and freed persons: in Phil. 4:22 Paul sends greetings to the community in Philippi from all the saints, and especially from those who belong to "the emperor's household." The phrase ἡ οἰκία Καίσαρος does not refer to the members of the imperial family in the narrower sense. It is a terminology that refers to slaves and/or freed persons of the imperial family.[159] Such persons are frequently attested to in inscriptions: they are always women and men who served in the imperial household, and they were to be found not only in Rome, but throughout the empire. They also formed *collegia* in order to organize their religious life and to provide for the burial of deceased members and their families. Many of them worshiped Silvanus, the slave god.[160] It appears from Phil. 4:22 that some of them had been converted to the Christian God: now they belonged to a Christian community of equals. The fact that they in particular send greetings to the community in Philippi is, in my opinion, a sign of their close mutual connections.

Thus Phil. 4:22 can reflect the possibility that the slave girl was accepted into the community at that time and was able to participate in its life. But if that was not the case, we must suppose that the slave girl had a very difficult time of it with her owners after being deprived of her prophetic power. She had become worthless to them. She no longer deserved to enjoy any kind of special regard, and would be treated like any other slave. Perhaps she now had to undertake the "normal" hard labor of slaves. However that may have been: Without considering the concrete effects of the exorcism, we surely ought not to undertake to talk about a "liberation" of the slave girl at Philippi.[161]

Notes

1. On this, see pp. 98–109 above, with bibliography.

2. See Tacitus, *Annales* 2.85.4, and the description, in terms of the history of religions, by F. Bömer, *Untersuchungen*, 188ff.

3. Silvanus, Hercules, and Mercury (*CIL* 3.1.633); Diana (*CIL* 3.1.634, 635, 636); Mater Deorum (*CIL* 3.1.639); Minerva (*CIL* 3.1.640); Athena (*CIL* 3.1.642). For more on deities in Philippi, see J. Schmidt, "Philippoi," 2241ff.; S. Pelekanidis, "Kultprobleme," 393–97; P. Collart, "Philippes," 726ff.; V. Abrahamsen, "Women at Philippi," *JFSR* 3 (1987):17–30, esp. 20–23.

4. As Silvanus was never a god of the upper classes, there was never a civic cult in his name, nor were there official cultic societies, in which citizens alone could participate, while slaves were excluded. For the non-admission of slaves to official cultic societies, see R. Gayer, *Sklaven,* 56.

5. On this, see also F. Bömer, *Untersuchungen,* 82, 191ff.; J.-P. Waltzing, *Etude historique* 1:260ff.; in addition, see R. Gayer, *Sklaven,* 56–57. Unfortunately, there are no women's names in the inscriptions listed in n. 3 above.

6. There is a good, detailed outline in A. Weiser, *Apostelgeschichte* 2:419.

6a. The translation follows the author's version and varies from NRSV in essential points related to the interpretation.

7. See, e.g., PSI 601.12, where it is mentioned that the owners of the slave girl must feed her (see R. Taubenschlag, "Sklavenrecht," 155–56, n. 6); P. Cairo Gen. 2.59142 mentions slave women in the wool trade (see J. Hengstl, *Papyri,* no. 117); see H. Thierfelder, *Unbekannte antike Welt,* "Weber," 121 n. 19, who collects instances in which slave women in the textile industry are mentioned. They even do business for themselves: in PSI 709 a slave woman makes a lease agreement with a free man; in *BGU* 727 a slave woman and her free husband arrange a loan with a third party. According to *Inst.* 3.163ff. we may conclude that slaves were, in such instances, carrying on business for their owners.

8. For example, it is striking that in A. Oepke's article, "παῖς, κτλ," *TDNT* 5:636–54, he only gives the usage of the masculine form. He describes the various lexical meanings of παῖς ("child," "son," "boy," "servant," "slave"). Under the overarching masculine παῖς he also mentions, by way of exception, a παιδίσκη, but she plays no role in the discussion. He then enters into a fuller discussion of the meaning "child." O. Cumont, "Παῖς," 2429ff., and A. Hug, "Παῖδες," 374, proceed in a similar manner, beginning clearly and concretely with a discussion of "temple slaves" (ἱεροὶ δοῦλοι, ἱεροὶ παῖδες), but then in the course of the study concentrating only on gymnastic education and the participation of the παῖδες in contests. A. Brelich, *Paides e Parthenoi,* thoroughly

investigates the question of the religious activities of children and virgins, but restricts the discussion to their participation in rites of initiation.

9. See esp. R. Taubenschlag, "Sklavenrecht," 148ff., 152.

10. R. Taubenschlag, "Sklavenrecht," 148. The author introduces sources according to which sale contracts should guarantee in addition that the children born to the slave woman at home would also belong to the buyer.

11. R. Taubenschlag, "Sklavenrecht," 152–53.

12. Ibid.

13. Aristotle, *Politics* 1.1253b; 1254a: κτῆμα δὲ ὄργανον πρακτικόν. See H. Klees, "Herren und Sklaven," 188, who also comments on this and other passages. See esp. also M. I. Finley, *Sklaverei*, 86ff., who contends against other scholars who attempt to minimize the offense of slavery by referring to the later notion that the slave was, ultimately, a human being. Finley asserts: "As a commodity, the slave is property. At least since Westermann's writings at the beginning of this century, some sociologists and historians have made a sustained effort to deny the significance of this simple fact, on the grounds that the slave is also a human being, or that the rights of the owner were often restricted by law. All this appears to me inessential: the fact that a slave is a human being has nothing to do with the question whether he [or she] is counted as property or not; it only reveals that he [or she] is a special form of property, namely, as Aristotle says, 'animate property' (*Politics* 1253b 32)."

14. N. Brockmeyer, *Antike Sklaverei*, 8–9, 164, and elsewhere.

15. Ibid., 213, where he collects a variety of studies and laws on the status of slaves.

16. W. de Boor, *Apostelgeschichte*, 298.

17. O. Bauernfeind, *Apostelgeschichte*, 209, quoting from a letter received by A. Wikenhauser from A. Abt: the πύθων is said to have acted as a ventriloquist, and to his knowledge is "none other than Apollo, or better still the ancient earth spirit who was replaced by the Delphic Apollo, taking over its oracle and name."

18. Plutarch, *De defectu oraculorum* 9: εὔηθες γάρ ἐστι καὶ παιδικὸν κομιδῇ τὸ οἴεσθαι τὸν θεὸν αὐτὸν ὥσπερ τοὺς ἐγγαστριμύθους, Εὐρυκλέας πάλαι νυνὶ δὲ Πύθωνας προσαγορευομένους, ἐνδυόμενον εἰς τὰ σώματα τῶν προφητῶν ὑποφθέγγεσθαι: "For it is a very childish and silly thing, to suppose that the God himself does, like the spirits speaking in the bowels of ventriloquists (which were anciently called Euryclees, and now Pythons), enter into the bodies of the prophets. . . ." Translation by Robert Midgley, et al., in William W. Goodwin, ed., *Plutarch's Morals* (Boston, 1870) 4:13.

19. See, e.g., T. Zahn, *Apostelgeschichte* 2:576–77, with listing of biblical-literary material; E. Haenchen, *Acts*, 495; A. Weiser, *Apostelgeschichte* 2:425–26; J. Roloff, *Apostelgeschichte*, 245; Billerbeck 2:743; R. Pesch, *Apostelgeschichte* 2:113 n. 23 no longer even refers to the question of the Delphic oracle, and immediately reduces the whole matter to Plutarch's statement.

20. For the professions and characteristics of Cleombrotus and Ammonius, see Plutarch, *De defectu oraculorum* 2 and 4.

21. I. Becher, "Plutarchos," 439. On the mantic in Plutarch's writings, see F. Pfeffer, *Mantik*, esp. 96ff.

22. See, e.g., Plutarch, *De defectu oraculorum* 8–11; Origen (*Contra Celsum* 3.25); and John Chrysostom (*Hom. 29 in Epistulam ad Corinthos Primam*). These last two authors are very polemical, speaking also of an erotic relationship between the Pythia and Apollo. However, according to W. Fauth, "Pythia," 546, they thereby furnish proof that "there was never any real doubt in antiquity about the inspiration of the P[ythia]. . . . The harshness of the polemic is understandable if we consider that, precisely in its erotic aspect, less developed minds could scarcely avoid a comparison between the divine *pneuma* [spirit] at Delphi and the Christian *pneuma hagion* [Holy Spirit]." Origen, *Contra Celsum* 1.70; 4.3.7 does not hesitate to contrast the Pythia "as the voice of the Delphic *numen* to the Jesus received through the *pneuma hagion* as the voice of the Christian God" (W. Fauth, "Pythia," 547). See also H. Koester, *Introduction to the New Testament* 1:171–73.

23. Plutarch, *De Pythiae oraculis* 17. There are two possible reasons why the Pythia no longer speaks in verse: because she cannot approach the place where the deity dwells, or because the *pneuma* is extinguished and its power of inspiration has vanished (ἢ τῆς Πυθίας τῷ χωρίῳ μὴ πελαζούσης ἐν ᾧ τὸ θεῖον ἐστιν, ἢ τοῦ πνεύματος παντάπασιν ἀπεσβεσμένου καὶ τῆς δυνάμεως ἐκλελοιπυίας). See the commentary on this subject in W. Fauth, "Pythia," 535.

24. This is clear in other Lukan passages as well, e.g., "filled with the Holy Spirit," Luke 1:15-17; 4:1; Acts 2:4; 4:8; 9:17, etc.; contrast references to "unclean" or "evil" spirits that enslave human beings: Luke 7:21; 8:2; Acts 5:16; 19:12-20.

25. In Höfer, "Pythia," 3402, 3405 we read that there was another legend according to which Apollo and Artemis killed the Python: Ἀπόλλων καὶ Ἄρτεμις ἀποκτείναντες Πύθωνα.

26. Höfer, "Pythia," adduces a mass of epigraphical material, esp. 3371ff.

27. See the epigraphical proof in Höfer, "Pythia," 3371, 3374, 3386ff. Under Hadrian and Caracalla this city cult was also established in Thyatira. See M. Clerc, *De rebus Thyatirenorum*, 84. The cult of Apollo is also inscriptionally attested at Philippi: see J. Schmidt, "Philippoi," 2241–42, and cf. n. 3 above.

28. In order to prophesy, the Pythias had to receive πνεύματα and be filled with them. These πνεύματα did not always have the same name or designation. For the different designations, see W. Fauth, "Pythia," esp. 534ff.; also F. Pfeffer, *Mantik*, esp. 96ff.

29. Höfer, "Pythia," 3381-82. W. Fauth, "Pythia," 542ff., produces literary material to support the assertion that the Pythias always had to be παρθένοι, "virgins." However, this designation is not intended to describe "either the age or intact physical condition" of the priestesses, as was also the case in other religions.

30. Plutarch, *De Pythiae oraculis* 405CD.

31. S. B. Pomeroy, *Goddesses*, 33; however, W. Fauth, "Pythia," 531–32 opposes this kind of statement by emphasizing "the unanimous acknowledgment, in antiquity, of the authority of Apollo and of the one who proclaimed him." This, however, does not change the fact that the prophetess could not decide how to interpret her oracle.

32. S. Lauffer, "Pytho," 571, uses the expression "secondary construction" to describe this form, because there are no "*ethnica*, personal names or other derivatives of Πυθών." This would indicate that this form was an old and well-known secondary construction from the original form Πυθώ (the place where the serpent guarded the oracle, and where it was killed by Apollo).

33. See W. Fauth, "Pythia," 516–17 and elsewhere, with further bibliography; Höfer, "Pythia," 338ff.

34. W. Fauth, "Pythia," 518.

35. W. de Boor, *Apostelgeschichte*, 298, speaks of a "Pythia in small format."

36. Plutarch, *De Pythiae oraculis* 17, informs us that in his time oracles were also uttered outside the oracular shrines. For him, this is a sign that oracle culture was no longer so highly respected as previously. See above, n. 22.

37. The particle δέ is not adversative here, but rather a clarification or explanation: whereas v. 17 affirms what the slave girl did, v. 18a makes it clear how long she went on doing it; no contrast is effected. For this usage of δέ, see BDR §447.8. In this respect, I think, Acts 16:18a is similar to Philemon 2, 8c.

38. T. Zahn, *Apostelgeschichte* 2:577, n. 98.

39. G. Kittel, "ἀκολουθέω," *TDNT* 1:210-16 does not mention this composite verb in the context of his article, although he analyzes other terms for "following" from the stem ἀκολουθεῖν. These include, e.g., the verb συνακολουθεῖν, which Luke uses at Luke 23:49, and I believe is directly parallel to κατακολουθεῖν in Luke 23:55, although Kittel thinks that in this case the word "signifies only 'external accompanying,'" even though everywhere else it refers to those who accompany Jesus. BDR §193.1 also fails to mention the verb κατακολουθεῖν in its listing of verbs stemming from ἀκολουθεῖν, often used with the dative and having the meaning "to follow" (ἀκολουθέω, ἐξ—, ἐπ—, παρ—, σύν—).

40. According to Matt. 8:28 there are two δαιμόνιοι, "demons"; in Mark 5:2 a man ἐν πνεύματι ἀκαθάρτῳ, "having an unclean spirit"; and in Luke 8:27 a man who had δαιμόνια, "demons" or πνεῦμα ἀκάθαρτον, "unclean spirits" (v. 29).

41. According to W. Grundmann, "κράζω," *TDNT* 3:898–903, at 898, within the history of Hellenistic Greek religion this verb has "religious significance in the sphere of the demonic."

42. The verb (ἀνα)κράζειν is also used in other, non-demonic spheres to describe the reactions of people who, for example, look for help from Jesus: see Matt. 9:27; 15:22-23.

43. In the following list, the subjects are in Greek, and the actions they perform are doubly underlined. In the subsequent lists, the subjects will be either in Greek or, if in English, are underlined once.

44. People possessed by demons and people who are healed proclaim who Jesus is. They preach, even against Jesus' will (Luke 4:34, 41; 8:28). According to G. Friedrich, "κῆρυξ, κτλ," *TDNT* 3:683–718, "we are not to compare it with the preaching of the disciples after their sending. As preaching it has no more significance than the fact that the demons name the name of Jesus and make him known to those around" (p. 708). Then, with regard to Acts 16:17 he writes (n. 50): "The demons naturally do not wish to preach, but try to assert themselves by naming the name."

45. E. Schweizer, "πνεῦμα, E: 'The New Testament,'" *TDNT* 6:396–451.

46. Ibid., 396.

47. A review of the concordance is sufficient to establish this.

48. See the review of research on pp. 168–70.

49. K. H. Rengstorf, "δοῦλος, κτλ," *TDNT* 2:261–80, at 264.

50. See, e.g., Acts 2:18; 4:29.

51. K. H. Rengstorf, "δοῦλος," 273.

52. See the further reference to other material, primarily that which attests "pagan" usage of this expression, e.g., in E. Schürer, "Die Juden," 209ff.; G. Bertram, "ὕψος, κτλ," *TDNT* 8:602–20, at 614–20.

53. Basilius Latyschev, *Inscriptiones*, 2:208–9.

54. See Basilius Latyschev, *Inscriptiones* 2:400 (= *CII* 1.690) and 2:401 (= *CII* 1.78*) in the appendix.

55. There are a number of inscriptional attestations to the emancipation of slaves in the name of the θεὸς ὕψιστος: see the citations in E. Schürer, "Die Juden," 209ff.

56. For the use of the predicate ὕψιστος (with or without Ζεύς or θεός) by "pagan" authors, and in inscriptions, see E. Schürer, "Die Juden," 209ff.

57. See E. Schürer, "Die Juden," 204.

58. From the French translation in J.-B. Frey, *CII* 1.500.

59. "The titles are not Jewish . . . but Gentile"; B. Latyschev, *Inscriptiones* 2:209, in his commentary on inscription no. 400.

60. E. Schürer, "Die Juden," 204ff. Emphasis supplied. On the following pages, the author presents an extraordinary amount of inscriptional and literary, as well as biblical material attesting that this combination of words can only be Jewish.

61. *CPJ* 3.1443. See pp. 87–90 above, where a number of *proseuche* building inscriptions dedicated to the θεὸς ὕψιστος are listed.

62. M. Hengel, "Proseuche," 167.

63. See *CII* 1.727–30, and, for the evaluation of the expression in question as a Jewish witness to the Jewish God: A. T. Kraabel, "Synagogue," 491–92; L. M. White, "Delos Synagogue," 139–40.

64. B. Latyschev, *Inscriptiones* 2:449, 450, 452, 456.

65. See the fundamental analysis and interpretation by E. Schürer, "Die Juden," 217ff.

66. See, e.g., *CII* 1.474–75, 494, 637.

67. *CII* 1.725. The reproduction is from A. Deissmann, *Licht vom Osten,* 352.

68. See *CII* 1.725a in the appendix. The translation is derived from J.-B. Frey, *CII* 1.724. *CII* 1.725b has the same content, but in lines 5–6 speaks of another murdered young woman named Martina.

69. Inscriptions and commentary in J. Bergmann, "Rachegebete," 507–8.

70. The linguistic and theological contacts with the Old Testament are treated and discussed in detail by A. Deissmann, *Licht vom Osten,* 354ff., and J. Bergmann, "Rachegebete," 509–10.

71. The passages are listed by E. Schürer, "Die Juden," 214ff.

72. G. Wehmeier, "עֶלְיוֹן," *THAT* 2:286: "The polytheistic background of this predicate appears, in fact, in Ps. 97:9, where the superiority of Elyon 'above all gods' is emphasized. Significantly, Elyon as a predicate for God appears, apart from Genesis 14, only in poetic texts in which the use of material from outside Israel was more permissible."

73. Ibid., 286.

74. Ibid., 287.

75. Ibid., 290.

76. See ibid., 290; E. Schürer, "Die Juden," 214ff. thinks that even if there is inscriptional material referring to other gods, e.g., Ζεὺς ὕψιστος, within the framework of the biblical world θεὸς ὕψιστος must always refer to the Jewish God. On this, see also G. Bertram, "ὕψιστος," *TDNT* 8:614–20.

77. Mark 5:7; Luke 1:32, 35, 76; 6:35; 8:28; Acts 7:48; 16:17; Heb. 7:1.

78. G. Bertram, "ὕψιστος," *TDNT* 8:617–18.

79. Among those who hold a different opinion are, for example, W. Elliger, *Paulus,* 67–69. Even if this epithet is a "common designation for the God of the Old Testament," Elliger wishes to argue that Acts 16:17 refers to a "not precisely defined syncretistic deity." Thus he concludes that the formulae "theos hypsistos" and "way of salvation" can be differently interpreted, depending on the context in which they are found. This can be established for inscriptional material, but, as we have already seen, when it is a question of biblical use of this expression it can refer only to the Jewish God.

80. Josephus, *Ant.* 16.6.2 says that Augustus permitted the Jews to make use of their own customs according to their laws, as was the case under Hyrcanus, the high priest of God the Most High (ὕψιστος): ἐπὶ Ὑρκανοῦ ἀρχιερέως θεοῦ ὑψίστου. Thus also Philo, *Leg. Gaj.* 23; 40. For more on this, see E. Schürer, "Die Juden," 215–16.

81. See above, pp. 154–56.

82. This expression is derived from H. Kleinknecht, "πνεῦμα," *TDNT* 6:332–59, at 343–44.

83. See the details and literature in ibid., 345–52.
84. Ibid., 345.
85. Ibid., 347.
86. Ibid., 347, here making use of Platonic expressions. On this, see also n. 31 above.
87. See R. Gayer, *Sklaven*, 54-64.
88. For the missionaries' Jewish identity, see below.
89. See E. Haenchen, *Acts*, 495 n. 4, where he criticizes exegetes who think, for example, that she was an impostor.
90. H. Kleinknecht, "πνεῦμα," *TDNT* 6:347, with bibliography.
91. For the varying content of the questions addressed in writing to the Pythias, see, e.g., the papyrus materials in K. Preisendanz, *Papyri* 2:156–57, 204–5, and elsewhere.
92. See also R. Pesch, *Apostelgeschichte* 1:164, for a similar interpretation of their annoyance.
93. T. Zahn, *Apostelgeschichte* 2:577. Emphasis supplied. In n. 98 the author had already noted that the aorist κατακολουθήσασα, which he thinks more appropriate here, makes "the one coming to meet them into a follower."
94. G. Schille, *Apostelgeschichte*, 345. The next quotation is from the same source.
95. H. Conzelmann, *Acts*, 131; see G. Schneider, *Apostelgeschichte*, 215.
96. O. Bauernfeind, *Apostelgeschichte*, 207.
97. Ibid., 209.
98. W. de Boor, *Apostelgeschichte*, 298.
99. J. Roloff, *Apostelgeschichte*, 245.
100. For their characteristics, see G. Theißen, *Miracle Stories*, esp. 43–72, and above, pp. 53–60.
101. See, e.g., Mark 1:25-26 (Luke 4:35-36); 5:8, 13 (Matt. 8:32; Luke 8:29, 33, 38); 7:29-30; 9:25-26 (Matt. 17:18); Luke 4:41; 8:2; Luke 11:14; Acts 8:7.
102. J. Schneider, "ἔρχομαι, κτλ," *TDNT* 2:666–84, at 679.
103. But contrast Mark 9:18 and also 9:38.
104. C. J. Hemer, *Acts*, 434. This author lists the miracle stories in Acts in ten categories, drawing a very sharp line, for example, between the Pentecost events, the visions, and the healing miracles. For the theme of the empowerment of the disciples and victory over demonic powers, see O. Böcher, *Mächte*, esp. 54ff.
105. E. Stauffer, "ἐπιτιμάω," *TDNT* 2:623–27, at 626.
106. Ibid. See also E. Lohmeyer, *Markus*, in the interpretation of Mark 1:21-31.
107. For the "way," see also Acts 9:2; 19:9, 23; 22:4; 24:14, where this expression quite clearly refers to the followers of Jesus. The fact that pious Jews were also described in this expression appears from Acts 2:28; 13:10; 18:25-26. As these groups have their "way" (of the Lord; of salvation), so also non-Jewish

peoples have their own way (Acts 14:16). For the possibility of such inquiries being addressed to the Pythias, see n. 91 above.

108. For the prohibition on proselytizing among Romans, see G. Schille, *Apostelgeschichte*, 346, with citations of literature. A. N. Sherwin-White, *Roman Society*, 79, also discusses Acts 16:19-24 and summarizes: "officially the Roman citizen may not practise any alien cult that has not received the public sanction of the State, but customarily he might do so as long as his cult did not otherwise offend against the laws and usages of Roman life, i.e. so long as it did not involve political or social crimes."

109. R. Pesch, *Apostelgeschichte*, 2:113 and 114.

110. Ibid., 2:113. Emphasis supplied. See the very similar interpretation in J. Roloff, *Apostelgeschichte*, 245–46; however, he does not describe the power of divination as morbid.

111. I. H. Marshall, *Acts*, 268–69. The following citations are from this location. C. J. Hemer, *Acts*, 437, also understands this to be an "evil spirit."

112. O. Bauernfeind, *Apostelgeschichte*, 209.

113. Thus, e.g., H. W. Beyer, *Apostelgeschichte* (1947), 101–2; W. de Boor, *Apostelgeschichte*, 299; W. Schmithals, *Apostelgeschichte*, 2:150. E. Haenchen expressed his opinion against this dominant opinion quite early: see his *Acts*, 495 n. 9: "We should not speak of a 'healing.' . . . Luke neither considered the slave girl sick nor did the thought of help enter as a motive for the act. Modern psychology has no place here."

114. W. de Boor, *Apostelgeschichte*, 298, n. 364.

115. W. de Boor, *Apostelgeschichte*, 299: "What did the health and freedom of a slave girl matter to them [the owners]?"

116. E. Schüssler Fiorenza, *In Memory of Her*, 265.

117. Ibid.

118. H. Klees, *Herren und Sklaven*, 32.

119. *Digesta* 50.17.22; see the commentary in N. Brockmeyer, *Antike Sklaverei*, 8ff.

120. This is N. Brockmeyer's description of the legal situation of slaves (*Antike Sklaverei*, 9), on the basis of the corresponding texts in the *Digesta*.

121. E. Hölder, *Institutionen*, 117. Emphasis supplied.

122. For the absoluteness of the way in which slaves were at their owners' disposal, and therefore their total surrender to the owners' power to punish, see the review of research in N. Brockmeyer, *Antike Sklaverei*, 111ff., 125.

123. According to M. Kaser, *Privatrecht*, 205ff., these were essentially: deprivation of goods (*furtum*); damage to property, i.e., slaves and objects (*damnum iniuria datum*); personal injury (*iniuria*); and theft (*rapina*) and the like.

124. For the Lex Aquileia, see *Digesta* 9.2 and the individual crimes treated there. For this question I refer especially to M. Kaser, *Privatrecht*, 205ff.

125. M. Kaser, *Privatrecht*, 205. The author refers to Roman legal texts, e.g., *Digesta* 9.2.1 for killing. On the question of compensation for damages, see also A. Ehrhardt, "Studien," 87ff.

126. The literature I consulted has given me no satisfactory answer to this question. It should be investigated further; here we must be content to draw a conclusion from the legal texts.

127. M. Kaser, *Privatrecht*, 206. For the Lex Aquileia, see above.

128. M. Kaser, *Privatrecht*, 146–47.

129. According to M. Kaser, *Privatrecht*, 14, the praetor "as the one responsible for ordinary disputes under civil law . . . was not a jurist, but a politician who, in the course of his career, was called to a year's service in charge of civil (and punitive) legal procedures." According to T. Mommsen, "Strafrecht," 222–23, the functions of the representative for legal procedures in Italic prefectures (*praefecti iure dicundo*) included both legal processes between Romans and those between Romans and non-Romans.

130. Acts 16:20-21 makes it clear that the charge is brought against non-Romans. Only at 16:37 do we find an assertion that Paul is a Roman citizen. For the areas of responsibility of a *praetor urbanus* and a *praetor peregrinus*, see M. Kaser, *Privatrecht*, 310ff.

131. On this, see D. Liebs, *Recht*, 185–86; cf. also 180. Regarding judgments in civil trials, the author writes on p. 186: "Inevitably, the judgment was for a sum of money, the value of the object under dispute." A. Ehrhardt, "Studien," 125, also asserts that "in classical trials, we know that there were only monetary judgments." For the monetary fine in the case of a slave who had been killed, see also *Digesta* 6.1.17.

132. Cicero, *QRosc.* 1ff.

133. F. C. Wolff, *Reden*, 118–19, says in his introduction to the "oration for the actor Quintus Roscius" that the two owners (Roscius and Fannius) had set up a partnership in the slave Panurgus and made their living from the income acquired by the slave's labor.

134. For the various *actiones*, "legal procedures" in cases of property damage, and the rules for compensation, see D. Liebs, *Recht*, 178ff.; M. Kaser, *Privatrecht*, 30ff.; A. Ehrhardt, "Studien," esp. 85ff. For the legal status and treatment of Romans and non-Romans by the authorities, see also K. Wengst, *Pax Romana*, 94ff.; T. Mommsen, "Rechtsverhältnisse," 87ff.

135. On this, see T. Mommsen, *Staatsrecht* 1:812, in context; H. Conzelmann, *Acts*, 131–32; W. Elliger, *Paulus*, 53ff. All agree that the words ἄρχοντες, "rulers," "authorities," and στρατηγοί, "magistrates," both refer to the same group of officials; the second is the more precise designation. For the Roman authorities in Philippi, see also Collart, "Philippes," 719, with a list of inscriptional sources.

136. W. Elliger, *Paulus*, 55.

137. A. N. Sherwin-White, *Roman Society*, 79. T. Mommsen, "Strafrecht," 89–90, also asserts that such a procedure is within the competence of the "municipal authorities of the empire."

138. On this, see W. Elliger, *Paulus*, 56ff., with literature. See also E. Haenchen, *Acts*, 496; R. Pesch, *Apostelgeschichte* 2:114–15.

139. W. Elliger, *Paulus*, 56.

140. Thus also K. Wengst, *Pax Romana*, 119; to the contrary D. R. Schwartz, "Accusation," 357ff.

141. See, e.g., R. Pesch, *Apostelgeschichte* 2:114; E. Haenchen, *Acts*, 496; H. Conzelmann, *Acts*, 131–32; W. Elliger, *Paulus*, 56.

142. See pp. 117–25 and 237–39.

143. R. Pesch, *Apostelgeschichte* 2:109.

144. See the positions of the exegetes cited above in the review of research on pp. 168–70 and 173–74.

145. On the subject of educated and artistically gifted slaves who were more likely to receive their freedom or be able to purchase it, see N. Brockmeyer, *Antike Sklaverei*, esp. 158–66.

146. Thus, for example, E. Haenchen, *Acts*, 495, who in this represents a common exegetical opinion; his assertion in turn was repeated by other exegetes: see, e.g., G. Schille, *Apostelgeschichte*, 345, on this verse.

147. See pp. 87–90.

148. For evidence that synagogues and other sacred temples offered asylum, or the opportunity for asylum, to enslaved persons and other refugees, see N. Brockmeyer, *Antike Sklaverei*, 112ff. The point should be developed more fully, but that is not possible here.

149. For documentation and literature, see below.

150. This custom of "sacral release" is documented from the third century B.C.E. to the third century C.E., according to A. Deissmann, *Licht vom Osten*, 271ff. See the evidence and literature given there, as well as the further information in M. Hengel, "Proseuche," 157ff.; also S. Krauss, *Synagogale Altertümer*, 197, 240, and elsewhere.

151. See B. Latyschev, *Inscriptiones*, 2:52, appendix.

152. Ibid., 2:53.

153. For the interpretation of this demand (χωρὶς ἰς τ[ὴ]ν προ[σ]ευχὴν θωπείας τε καὶ προσκα[ρτερ]ήσεω[ς]) see M. Hengel, "Proseuche," 174, who—on the basis of other witnesses—changes the text to read χωρὶς τοῦ προσκαρτερεῖν τῇ προσευχῇ ἐπιτροπευούσης τῆς συναγωγῆς, to make it clearer and so that the similarity with the passages in Acts 1:14; 2:42; 6:4 is made evident. See also E. Schürer, "Die Juden," 201ff., and A. Deissmann, *Licht vom Osten*, 273–74.

154. B. Latyschev, *Inscriptiones* 2:400, appendix. This inscription and the next were discussed above (θεὸς ὕψιστος); see also the literature listed there.

155. N. Brockmeyer, *Antike Sklaverei* 122, n. 137.

156. E. Schürer, "Die Juden," 201.

157. M. Hengel, "Proseuche," 174, writes: "The προσευχή was thus, as were the Greek sanctuaries, the place of liberation, but the community undertook the 'guardianship' of the freed person." From a legal point of view, then,

he speaks here not of patronage, but of *tutela*. See also A. Deissmann, *Licht vom Osten*, 273ff., and E. Schürer, "Die Juden," 204–5, who regards the community not as a "supervisory authority" (against B. Latyschev), but sees the votive offerings as the "moral property" of the community.

158. Oxyrhynchus Papyri 1207.7. See A. Deissmann, *Licht vom Osten*, 273.

159. Thus also J. Comblin, *Filipenses*, 64–65; W. de Boor, *Philipper*, 153–54; E. Lohmeyer, *Philipper*, 190–91. See also P. Lampe, *Christen*, 156.

160. On this whole subject, see F. Bömer, *Untersuchungen*, esp. 68ff., 84ff., 95ff., with further material.

161. This is not to say that the exorcisms depicted in the Gospels did not have a liberating effect, inasmuch as those spirits brought sickness and torture to the people they possessed. But, according to my presentation above, that was not at all the case here. For the liberating experiences of people possessed by "evil" spirits, see O. Böcher, *Mächte*, esp. 60ff.

5

The Missionary Artisan Priscilla and the Universal Praise That Is Her Due (18:1-3, 18-19, 24-28)

Introductory Observations

Priscilla is one of the few women mentioned more than once in the New Testament. Her memory, together with that of her husband, Aquila, is preserved not only by Luke, but also by Paul and in one of the Pastoral letters: 1 Cor. 16:19; Rom. 16:3; 2 Tim. 4:19; Acts 18:2-3, 18, 26-27. The individual passages combine to form a larger picture. What is reported is not complete in itself, nor is it separable from its context. It is embedded in the sphere of Paul's work and in his circle. But it should be said that we owe the preservation of the memory of this woman, or rather of this artisan couple, to the recollections of Paul's work and of his overall activity. It is recognized that Luke had a special interest in the deeds of Peter and Paul; for that reason, the stories of people who worked within their spheres of influence have a better chance of being remembered than those of others who did not come into contact with their missionary work. On the other hand, the fact that Priscilla and Aquila are mentioned only in passing is typical of the kind of historical writing that concentrates on "great personalities and events." The fact that historical composition of this type mentions them at all, in spite of this focus, points to their significance and the great influence of their activity on other groups of people.[1]

Priscilla was very important in the work of mission. This is evident from the fact that on four separate occasions she is mentioned first: in 1 Cor. 16:19, Rom. 16:3, and 2 Tim. 4:19 she is named before Aquila, and even Luke uses this sequence, except in Acts 18:2. Priscilla is men-

195

tioned before Aquila in Acts 18:18, 26. This is not some kind of bourgeois "ladies first" rule, as has often been suggested.[2] The witness of
Acts, and of the Pauline texts cited, by no means justifies the way in
which theologians have treated Priscilla and Aquila. They often put
Priscilla in Aquila's shadow: for example, many scholarly treatments
mention "Prisc[ill]a" with a reference such as: "see Aquila."[3] This procedure is certainly "appropriate"[4] in terms of the patriarchal treatment
and understanding of women, then and now, but it is not appropriate to
the New Testament testimony about Priscilla.

Priscilla and Aquila are mentioned by Luke in the context of Paul's
second missionary journey. It is very interesting that the word "Rome"
appears for the first time in the Lukan account in the story of Priscilla
and Aquila: and we find it in a report of a most inauspicious situation
for Jews and people who lived as Jewish Christians. We learn of the
banishment of these people from Rome as a result of an imperial edict
that fell especially on people who, as Jewish Christians, confessed Jesus
Christ as Messiah. That confession created an uproar in Rome that was
not tolerated by the Roman authorities. (For more detail, and a listing
of sources, see pp. 212–16 and 224–25 below.) This first mention of
Rome corresponds to the reference to Roman officials in Acts 16:16-39,
where they intervene in a riotous situation in the Roman colony of
Philippi. The result at that time was that Paul was taken prisoner. In the
Lukan account of Paul's second missionary journey, not only are important women mentioned, but we find for the second time a reference to
political conflicts with Roman power. These represent Paul's first contacts and experiences with Roman officialdom.

These experiences were part of the life of Jewish-Christian communities, a life that included daily labor both in the workplace and in missionary activities. At this point I will inquire what the work life of
Priscilla and Aquila, and hence of Paul also, may have looked like. It
appears to me that the text associates the two realms of craft work and
missionary labor very closely; consequently, I will attempt to determine
as precisely as possible the meaning of the occupation of σκηνοποιός,
"tent maker" (Acts 18:3), and whether Priscilla could have practiced it
as well.[5] I will have to treat this matter at length. A text-critical study is
necessary because Acts 18:1-28 has been very extensively revised. A
review of research will show how scholars have treated the text in
different times and places. This review will also include references to
ancient church literature. Next follows a description of representative
pieces of Christian exegesis, especially from the last two centuries. In

dialogue with the dominant exegesis, I will sharpen the focus of my own interest and my thesis, all of which I will summarize in the final section.

Text-Critical Problems in Acts 18:1-28

The story of Priscilla and Aquila has provided a great many occasions for alterations in the order and interpretation of the text. Let me begin with some text-critical observations. In doing so, I will refer especially to the two recensions of Acts 18:1-27 distinguished by Adolf von Harnack in 1900.[6] One he designates as text α (= the majuscule text), and the second as text β (= the text of D, Itala, and the Syriac). According to Harnack, text α is the older, and a variety of alterations have been made in it, especially in the so-called "Western" text (β). Harnack points to fifteen or sixteen important differences,[7] of which I will cite those that are most important because of their immediate application to Priscilla and Aquila:

Verse 2. First alteration: Text β makes some important changes in the older text. While α asserts that Paul met Aquila *and* (καί) Priscilla in Corinth, β writes that Paul met Aquila *with* (σύν with the dative) Priscilla. At first glance that may seem no major difference, but in fact it already points toward a subordinate position for the woman in β.

Second alteration: β inserts, before the meeting of the three, ὁ δὲ Παῦλος ἐγνώσθη τῷ Ἀκύλᾳ, διὰ τὸ ὁμόφυλον καὶ ὁμότεχνον εἶναι, καὶ ἔμεινεν πρὸς αὐτοὺς καὶ ἠργάζετο ("Paul, however, knew Aquila, and since they were of the same race and practiced the same trade, he stayed with them, and he worked"). Codex D (sixth century), which is part of the text β group, offers a weighty nuance to this, writing: "Paul went to [stay with] *him* (προσῆλθεν αὐτῷ), that is, with Aquila alone. Here we have a concentration of important differences, especially with regard to the craft by which they earned their living. While the oldest text, α, asserts that "Paul stayed with them, because they were of the same trade, and they worked [together]," β alters this statement to the extent that, in it, only Paul "worked." Add to this that Codex D omits the whole phrase "by trade they were tentmakers."

Verse 7. β inserts the name of Aquila, so that the text reads: "Paul left Aquila and went to the house of Titius Justus."

Verse 22. β inserts the name of Aquila again, indicating that he remained in Ephesus when Paul went to Caesarea.

Verse 26. β reverses the sequence "Priscilla—Aquila," so that Aquila is placed before Priscilla. Since this scene refers to the synagogue and the work of teaching, this reversal is of central importance for the interpretation of the passage.

Verse 27. Here β has a completely different version: "Some Corinthians were staying in Ephesus, and when they heard him, they asked him to travel with them to their own country. When he agreed, the Ephesians wrote to the disciples in Corinth to receive this man."

In summary: Text β three times inserts the name of Aquila without mentioning Priscilla, and attempts to create a stronger relationship between Paul and Aquila. It not only thrusts Priscilla out of her craft position, but out of the missionary work as well. All this culminates in v. 27, where the ἀδελφοί, the "brothers and sisters," among whom Priscilla and Aquila could also be counted, are turned into "the Ephesians." Thus in the sixth century it was no longer thought possible that Priscilla could have written or co-written a commendatory letter. Adolf von Harnack concluded from all this: "It is therefore evident that the α-text is the older, while β contains a chain of interpolations that are not without an ecclesiastical disciplinary tendency (namely the repression of women)."[8]

Since v. 3 contains a particularly large number of textual variants, I will show how this verse read in the words of the older recension:

και δια το ὁμότεχνον εἶναι
and, because he was of the same trade,

ἔμενεν παρ' αὐτοῖς,
he stayed with them,

και; ἐργάζοντο·
and they worked[9] [together] —

ἦσαν γὰρ σκηνοποιοὶ τῇ τέχνῃ.
for by trade they were tentmakers.

According to the older text tradition, Paul went to Priscilla and Aquila, and being of the same trade, remained with them. To the observation that Paul was associated not only with Aquila, but with Priscilla *and* Aquila, we should add the further note that they were all tentmakers by trade. The construction, continuity, and grammatical structure of the text all make it clear that Priscilla is also included within this plural

THE MISSIONARY ARTISAN PRISCILLA

(σκηνοποιοί); that is, that she, too, carried on this trade. I will go into this more fully in the exegesis below.

Interpretation of the Text

In the following exegesis I will concentrate especially on Priscilla, Aquila, and Paul's craft work and activity as missionary teachers. First, a survey of research on crafts will indicate the representative trends in interpretation. Then a more precise picture of the trade will be sketched, although the sources are inadequate in this field. This will be followed by the question of the missionary activity of this artisan couple, and finally I will offer some considerations toward a feminist liberation theological exegesis of the text.

"By Trade They Were Tentmakers"

In light of these text-critical considerations, it is clear that all three of the persons named in the text practiced the trade of tentmaking. At this point we may ask what kind of work was included in this term. The tradition of interpretation is long and contentious. However, it should at least be sketched here insofar as it can contribute to a clarification of the question thus posed.

The word σκηνοποιοί, "tentmakers," is a New Testament hapax legomenon. Therefore no New Testament passage can be adduced to explain it; nor is it found in the LXX, although there we do find σκηνή, "tent"[10] (e.g., Gen. 4:20: "those who live in tents . . ."). As far as I can see, the word σκηνοποιός is attested only twice in literary sources,[11] and not at all in Greek inscriptions. It is a composite of the two words σκηνή and ποιέω, which in the active voice means "to make tents," not in the sense of "pitching tents," but in that of producing them. In describing some of the attempts at solution in the interpretive tradition, I will first adduce a few theologians of the ancient church who were closer to the text at least in time, in order to clarify their understanding of the word. Then some later exegetes who have something concrete to contribute to the discussion will be heard.

John Chrysostom places some emphasis on artisanal work. It is probably for that reason that he repeatedly comments on passages in which there is mention of Paul's work. Because Acts 18:3 contains the only mention of the apostle's trade, he treats it intensively, and cites it again whenever Priscilla and Aquila appear in the lists of greetings in the Pauline letters. He gives an extensive treatment of Rom. 16:3 in his writing *Salutate Priscillam et Aquilam,* and there he says quite clearly that "they were very poor, and they lived from the work of their hands, for by trade they were tentmakers (σκηνοποιοί)."[12] This Greek word appears in the Latin version, which has been transmitted together with the original Greek, as *scenofactoriae artis,* with the added clarification *tabernaculorum opifices.* It thus appears that some explanation of the term was needed. That the Greek word created difficulties even for the church fathers and/or their readers is indicated by the fact that John Chrysostom added other terms to explain it, including σκυτοτόμος, which can mean "saddler," "leather worker," "shoemaker."[13] He intends in this way to make it clear that the three of them worked in leather. Chrysostom further specifies this work, as he imagines it, by saying that Paul was not ashamed to cut leather and sew tanned hides together as well as to preach.[14] The idea is one of despised labor, as Chrysostom also emphasizes in other places.[15]

In Origen's interpretation also, the σκηνοποιοί worked in leather. This is clear in his translation of Acts 18:3: "et quia erat consimilis artificii, mansit apud eos, et operabantur simul. Erant enim artifices tabernaculorum, hoc est sutores."[16] He thus translates the Greek word with "tabernaculorum," and clarifies the Latin term with the addition of "sutores," i.e., "leather workers." Theodoret is part of this same tradition of interpretation;[17] there are even supposed to have been people who imitated Paul's way of life. That is the opinion, at least, of Mark the Deacon in his biography of Porphyry: Saint Porphyry (ca. 410) is supposed to have worked just as Paul did: "He devoted himself to the art of leather-working, washing hides and sewing them together."[18]

This interpretive tradition from the early church is unanimous in the opinion that Priscilla, Aquila, and Paul worked in *leather:* all agree that they sewed hides together. We may venture to ask whether words like σκυτοτόμος, "leather worker," σμίλη, "cutting knife," βύρσας πλύνων καὶ ῥάπτων, "washing hides and sewing them together," are also meant to hint that the craft of tentmaking overlapped with that of tanning.[19] In any case, for these interpreters it meant working with leather.[20]

According to Rafael Silva's review of research, in the Middle Ages almost all the theologians who said anything about this passage agreed that σκηνοποιοί were tentmakers; some attempted to make the idea more precise. For example, Erasmus believed that they made tents from leather.[21] According to Silva, almost all the medieval theologians agree on this point as well. It is striking that, in contrast to Calvin,[22] for whom Paul was a tentmaker by trade, Luther, in translating Acts 18:3, understood Paul as a carpet maker.[23] It is still more surprising in this connection that Luther did not treat the greetings list from Romans 16 in his lectures on Romans,[24] and therefore did not mention Priscilla and Aquila or speak of their and Paul's occupation.

In later Western interpretation of the text, exegetes have repeatedly expressed the opinion that the tents were made of woven material. According to Silva's survey of research, J. L. Hug[25] was the first to associate Paul's homeland with his trade. This gave a reason for connecting the material from which the tents were made with *cilicium* (a material made of goats' hair, woven in Cilicia). This suggestion started a discussion that is still ongoing.[26] It is true that Luther's translation makes it clear that he already presumed that Paul worked with woven material in the making of tents, especially since he understood Paul (and also Priscilla and Aquila) concretely as "carpet maker(s)." But he did not make a connection with *cilicium*. Wilhelm Weitling also interpreted Paul as a "carpet maker."[27] In this tradition, Adolf Deissmann[28] developed the Western portrait of Paul with still broader strokes: a tentmaker working with woven stuff, and therefore seated at the loom as well.

The earlier commentators from this century continue this trend of interpretation: thus Rudolf Knopf (1906) and Gustav Hoennicke (1913) presume that Paul was a weaver.[29] Billerbeck summarizes for Acts 18:3: "σκηνοποιός = maker of tent cloths or tent covers. The rough cloth that served as a covering for the tent was woven of goats' hair."[30]

Joachim Jeremias and Wilhelm Michaelis are opposed to this interpretation of the word σκηνοποιοί to mean those who make tents from woven cloth or from *cilicium*. Jeremias asserts: "It therefore appears to me [i. e., because the craft of weaving was regarded as indecent in Palestine, partly because it was a women's trade] utterly impossible to translate σκηνοποιός" [note the singular!] in Acts 18:3 as 'weaver of tent cloths,' for weaving . . . was something avoided by educated people."[31] It seems to me, however, that the starting point of his argument makes it inconclusive, because the trade of a tanner or leather worker was also despised and was, for that reason, avoided by educated people.[32] We should emphasize in this context that, in spite of this contempt, at least one rabbi, Joseph ben Halafta, is supposed to have been a tanner by trade.[33] Michaelis argues in the same vein: "It is ... more probable that Paul and Aquila were 'leather-workers' or 'saddlers' and that as such they manufactured tents, for which there was considerable use in antiquity."[34]

The background of the idea that this trade implied the making of cloth woven of goats' hair was that Paul came from Tarsus in Cilicia. It was known that so-called *cilicium* was made there,[35] a "rough-haired loden cloth ... used by, among others, the Bedouins called 'Skenites' for making their tents."[36] Thus Paul made this product, and he learned weaving in his home town.[37] The argument is not conclusive: first, because *cilicium* is not synonymous with σκηνή, and second, because it stems only from Paul's home country. Aquila and Priscilla, however, were not from Cilicia. Acts 18:2 asserts that Aquila's origins were in Pontus. It was not only Paul who carried on this trade, but the couple as well! Even Theodor Zahn rightly observed that Paul could have learned his trade during his stay in Jerusalem, while he was sitting at the feet of Gamaliel (Acts 22:3), and we may suppose that he could possibly have managed it alongside his studies in the Torah.[38]

The majority of newer commentaries connect the trade of tentmaking with leather work.[39] I. Howard Marshall emphasizes that, although tents were often made of woven materials, the word used in Acts 18:3 points rather to "leather-worker."[40]

This discussion is not closed. Peter Lampe,[41] the most recent to assume the use of linen for the manufacture of these tent *coverings*, also cites a passage from Tacitus and asserts that Nero had "sun sails spread in his wooden amphitheatre on the Campus Martius (cf. Tac. *Ann.* 13.31.1)." In another context, Tacitus says that tents made of hides were used for military purposes: in *Annales* 13.35.1–3, he writes that Corbulo had a great deal of difficulty with the conscripted Roman soldiers because they were "lethargic" and "reluctant." He therefore discharged all the aged and infirm. At 13.35.3 we read: "Levies were held in Galatia and Cappadocia, and a legion from Germany was added with its complement of auxiliary horse and foot. The entire army was kept under canvas [better: in tents of hides = *sub pellibus*], notwithstanding the winter was of such severity that the ice-covered ground had to be dug up before it would receive tents."

As we can tell from this passage in Tacitus, leather tents were used by soldiers in camp. Scholarly works also speak frequently of the use of leather tents, especially by the army, and assert that those who make them are part of the imperial household: that is, the tentmakers produce leather tents for the use of the Roman armies.[42] According to Lampe, however, Aquila was not part of the imperial household, but an independent artisan. Lampe does not consider the possibility that leather tents could have served other than military purposes. For him, Aquila and Paul produce "sun shades" or "tent coverings" or "linen market stalls" for the use of shopkeepers. That is possible, but not necessary. Ultimately, Lampe supports his arguments by a reference to Paul's home town: "In my opinion, Paul the tentmaker would have been less likely to make leather military tents than these linen tent-coverings; Paul came from Tarsus, where linen was produced! (Dio Chr. *Or.* 34.21ff.). If he sewed linen tent coverings, he belonged to that branch of the business of his home town that processed the product."[43]

Rafael Silva is probably correct in emphasizing that this trade was understood in the East as having to do with the working of leather. In the West, on the other hand, and especially in the minds of German theologians, there is a presumption that it involves working with textiles or goats' hair.[44] I myself adhere to the tradition of interpretation from the ancient church. The ancient authors cited above had no difficulty in associating this trade with working in leather. It is possible that they were even acquainted with it, and therefore did not need to give a more thorough description. To the question of the nature of the work in its individual details, the recent exegetes give practically no answer at all. The early theologians thought that it included the cutting and sewing of leather, an interpretation that probably stems from their knowledge of the craft. It was a hard, and also a despised type of work.

Hugo Blümner offers an extensive description of the art of leather working.[45] He explains all the words that were used in the ancient church literature to describe tentmaking. *Sutor*, or σκυτοτόμος, can refer generally to cutting or working with leather, or specifically to shoemaking. The most important actions in any kind of leather work are cutting and sewing. The cutting knife (σμίλη) had a straight edge, and its use demanded significant physical strength. A *tabernacularius* was a tentmaker who worked in leather. Blümner's descriptions depict exactly what the ancient church tradition has in mind: in the kind of tentmaking that is referred to with the concepts just described, the artisans work with leather.[46] This understanding also coincides with that of the ancient church literature cited above. Samuel Krauss[47] attempts to describe how a tent was made: It was supported by poles; the internal living space was adorned with carpets and curtains; a separate covering was spread over the exterior, and that covering could be made of woven goats' hair, but also of leather, linen, mats or palm branches.

Priscilla as Artisan

Even among those commentators who read "and they worked" in their translation of the text there is only one whose commentary is not satisfied merely with treating Paul and Aquila at length, but also mentions

Priscilla, writing that Paul dwelt "with the Jewish couple Aquila and Priscilla, who practiced the same trade as he."[48] All the other exegetes I know[49] speak of the artisanal activity only of Paul and Aquila. Wilhelm Michaelis is a good example of how the exegetical thought process works: "Though παρ᾽ αὐτοῖς refers to Aquila and Priscilla, only Paul and Aquila can be the subjects of ἠργάζοντο and especially ἦσαν. Hence one does not have to think in terms of a τέχνη in which the co-operation of the wife was possible or even customary. The context itself does not show us what the τέχνη was,"[50] although in this regard the author concludes that it most probably was work with leather. Nor does he explain why Priscilla cannot be one of the subjects of the clause in v. 3c. Presumably the assumption is that this work was too difficult for a woman and, besides, that it was not "typical woman's work."

While Michaelis argues against reckoning Priscilla among those who practiced the trade of tentmaking, Gottfried Schille thinks that we should make no attempt at all to determine anything about Priscilla's and Aquila's life on the basis of Acts 18:1-4: "Those who want to know anything about the couple, Aquila and Priscilla, should not begin with our text, since it is apparently an inaccurate reproduction of some received information."[51]

In my opinion, even "received information" can be highly communicative. For example, without the note in Acts 18:3 we would have no concrete information at all about the working lives of Priscilla, Aquila, or Paul! It is the only notice that, in conjunction with other passages, enables us to have a more complete idea of the life of those who were engaged in the work of mission. It was apparently a "Western" tendency, as we can see from a comparison with Codex D, to attempt to exclude working life, especially the hard work of artisans, from this context.

I am assuming, especially since the text points in that direction, that Priscilla practiced the art of tentmaking alongside Aquila and Paul. As I have already said, this work included the cutting and sewing of pieces of leather. No doubt that was hard work, and it was done, at least in part, by women. Although I have not found any inscriptions about *tabernacularii* that mention women,[52] I believe that we should always proceed on the assumption that women's and men's lives were not restricted to what has been written or reported. Moreover, we may suppose that by no means all the material that could tell us about this has thus far been discovered or published.[53] Let me mention just one example of the changes that have taken place in our view of women's working lives as a result of the research that has been devoted to women. Whereas Natalie Kampen, in her very good description of the kinds of work done by women, based on iconographic material,[54] asserted on the basis of her sources from Ostia that women were excluded from work with metal, leather, and ceramics, by 1988 Monika Eichenauer was in a position to present some inscriptional evidence that contains concrete reference to women in leather work.[55] These were *sutrices*, women who cut and sewed leather, perhaps as shoemakers. This kind of insight requires an intensive examination and evaluation of already existing sources, and a specific type of inquiry as a basis for the investigation of and search for new sources.[56]

In addition, as early as 1980 Luise Schottroff pointed out[57] that women frequently worked alongside men, but ordinarily were not mentioned. Thus Acts 18:3 can attest that Priscilla and Aquila were a married artisan couple who produced their wares in common. It is all the more astonishing to see the efforts of exegetes to remove a woman from the work scene the moment she appears alongside men. Paul himself attests, in 1 Cor. 4:12; 1 Thess. 2:9, that it was hard work: "You remember our labor and toil, brothers and sisters; we worked night and day, so that we might not burden any of you while we proclaimed to you the gospel of God." Apostles and missionaries slave away, working with their own hands. Women also—and here Priscilla serves as an example—struggled with their overwhelming missionary work, as is obvious from Rom. 16:6, 12.

The Question of Priscilla and Aquila's Income Level

We may observe a developing trend in recent New Testament research regarding the question of Priscilla and Aquila's socioeconomic position. More and more theologians are adopting the opinion that this artisan couple belonged to a superior social group. Adolf von Harnack[58] counted them among the "most prominent" Christians in Rome (whatever that may have meant for him). In his opinion, this prominence is evident from the fact that Paul places them at the head of the list of persons greeted in Romans 16. Ernst Haenchen gives a more direct comment on the pair's socioeconomic status: Priscilla and Aquila "are no common labourers, but a well-to-do couple. . . . Paul worked for some weeks in their workshop, presumably together with other journeymen, and lived with them."[59] Unfortunately, at this point the author gives no information about or support for his argument that would enable one to confront it directly. Gerd Theißen simply asserts that the couple could not have been insolvent, since "[l]ater on, in Ephesus, they [Priscilla and Aquila] gathered a 'house congregation' around themselves."[60] At this point he mentions the idea that "Paul possibly worked as an 'employee' of Aquila and Priscilla in one of the shops which have been excavated by the agora." Rudolf Pesch[61] supposes that they were well-to-do because they had their own workshop: "Presumably they were well off, since they were able to open a new workshop immediately in Corinth." Whereas these exegetes express such ideas with some caution, the opinion seems to be spreading more and more widely in the form of a thesis, namely, that this couple possessed a higher than average socioeconomic status. Let me sketch several such proposals.[62]

H.-J. Klauck[63] regards Aquila as an entrepreneur: "In Corinth, Aquila opened a business as tentmaker or leather worker." Aquila not only had a house in Corinth, but others in Rome and Ephesus, which is why he must have been very well-to-do.[64] It has even been asserted that, during his stay in Corinth, Aquila left a slave behind in Rome to carry on his business there.[65] The supposition that Aquila was an entrepreneur with a number of branch workshops, in one of which Paul was employed alongside others, tends in the same direction.[66]

In contrast to this tendency, John Chrysostom and Mark the Deacon presumed that Priscilla, Aquila, and Paul were poor, and this was the understanding of the entire ancient church tradition. These writers presumably speak out of their own knowledge of the social situation of tentmakers. Paul was not ashamed to practice this trade. Chrysostom connects their identity as artisans with their socioeconomic status: "They were poor and without means, and earned their living from the work of their hands, for, as it says, they were tentmakers."[67] Probably this author still saw the same kind of work being done in his own vicinity, so that he could speak of it quite naturally and objectively.

Not only these literary evidences from the ancient church, but inscriptional, archaeological, and finally Pauline material as well can be adduced to challenge the new exegetical "well-to-do entrepreneur" thesis. But first we should point out still another internal contradiction or insecurity in the thread of argumentation connected with the thesis: Ernst Haenchen, who asserted that this couple, for whom Paul and other companions worked, were people of means, further commented on Acts 18:7-8 that after Paul had received assistance from Macedonia he no longer needed to work with his hands and was able to give his entire energies to the mission. Haenchen writes: "The result was that he had to look around for a room for this purpose. The synagogue did not stand at his disposal, nor was Aquila's [note the singular!] workshop the right place for constant discussion with individual visitors or addresses to groups. So the report that Paul moved with his missionary preaching from there, namely from Aquila [!], into a suitable private house can be understood without more ado."[68] Even though this working hypothesis is very questionable, it manages to express the idea that Priscilla and Aquila were, after all, not wealthy enough to be able to put some space at Paul's disposal! Gerd Theißen says of this statement by Haenchen: ". . . nothing is said about this. . . . We have no information about the social status of Titius Justus. It can only be assumed that it was not inferior to that of Aquila and Priscilla, as Paul would hardly have made claims on anyone who would have found it a greater burden than they had. The opposite is more probable."[69] In other words: Those who are trying to support the thesis that the couple was wealthy or well-to-do are continually working in the realm of conjecture. In my opinion, their conjectures are invalid, for the following reasons:

First, as far as inscriptional material is concerned, we find that "in comparison to their actual percentage in the population . . . artisans of Aquila's stamp are *underrepresented* in the inscriptions,"[70] precisely because they were among the socially despised. Their trade and its activities enjoyed very little prestige. They scarcely belonged to the "advanced level of entrepreneurs," as Lampe correctly concludes.[71]

Second, we may also obtain information from archaeological, inscriptional, and iconographic sources that sheds light on the general conditions under which this kind of craft work was conducted. At least two pieces of iconographic evidence are found in Natalie Kampen's book to support the statement that the space within which this kind of work was done was very small.[72] Peter Lampe produces archaeological material on the measurements of the combination workroom/shops or workshop/houses of artisans: "In Corinth, *tabernae* in the form of long rows of shops have been excavated. The little row of stalls north of the southern *stoa* contains 14 *tabernae* with a total frontage of 44 meters, which would mean that the individual shops were each only a little over 3 meters wide; their length was a little less than 4 meters. The section . . . west of the forum contained a row of "large" shops: these were about 4.5 meters wide and 6 meters long."[73] From this he calculates the size of an assembled house church: "In a space of 27 square meters, the maximum number of believers in a house church would be 20."[74] In addition, several inscriptions translated by Herwig Maehler[75] give some evidence for the question of house ownership. A common laborer (ἐργάτης) says in his census information that, in addition to the house and yard (οἰκία καὶ αὐλή) where he lives, he owns other parts of houses in which his many sons and daughters live.[76] These parts of houses (perhaps only rooms) are expressly called "houses" (οἶκος / οἰκία). In official documents we also find information that women and men owned parts of houses, often including equipment for artisanal work.[77] The size of such rooms can again be illustrated by the archaeological excavations in Corinth, as given by Lampe.

Third, Paul himself says a good deal about the exertions of his work and the way it was regarded, all of which applies, of course, to that of Priscilla and Aquila as well. He says of himself and those who work as he does: ". . . we are hungry and thirsty, we are poorly clothed and beaten and homeless, and we grow weary from the work of our own hands. When reviled, we bless . . ." (1 Cor. 4:11-12); they had to work "night and day" in order not to be a burden to anyone (1 Thess. 2:9). But of Corinth in particular, where Priscilla, Aquila, and Paul worked together, Paul says that he was in need, to the point that help had to be supplied from elsewhere (2 Cor. 11:9).

On this basis, it is impossible to understand why Priscilla, Aquila, Paul, and those like them should be counted among the well-to-do entrepreneurs of the time. Certainly the wealth, or even the character of Priscilla and Aquila as an entrepreneurial couple[78] is not supported by Acts 18:1-3; Rom. 16:3; 1 Cor. 16:19; 2 Tim. 4:19, or the material presented above. Rather, they belong to that "very populous lower order of minor craftspeople"[79] in Corinth who earned their living with their own hands and thus were probably able to extend help to other people who were less well off than they (Acts 20:35).

Priscilla, the Distinguished Missionary

As in the case of her business activity, so also with regard to the work of preaching, attempts have been made to reduce and minimize Priscilla's importance.[80] However, it is most interesting to note that in exegetical treatments Priscilla is more likely to be recognized as active in preaching than as an artisan. This may be a sign that the exegetes are using the Pauline letters as a basis and occasionally adding the text of Acts 18:1-3, but not for the purpose of referring to her craft work; instead, the intention throughout is to emphasize her work of preaching and teaching, in light of vv. 24-27. This emphasis is found both in the biblical texts and in the interpretive tradition. However, I do not think it is necessary to separate the two; one activity need not be neglected for the sake of the other. The biblical text and a major portion of the ancient church tradition, in fact, avoids any such separation.

John Chrysostom had no problem in speaking of these three people's craft and the poverty connected with it, nor did he have any difficulty about recognizing Priscilla's outstanding activity as a missionary. In *Salutate Priscillam* 2.1 he praises both: her handiwork and her preaching. He also emphasizes that, despite their work as artisans, the couple lived in poverty, yet because of their missionary work they are praised more highly than any kings.

In contrast to Chrysostom, who was able to keep both fields of activity united, modern research has created a split, or at least has focused on the "spiritual and intellectual" activity. This process of separation is still going on, but it was perceptible as early as Adolf von Harnack, who had no difficulty in describing Priscilla as "the distinguished missionary."[81] Even in speaking of Priscilla and Aquila as a couple, he can say: "or rather, Prisca the missionary, with her husband Aquila."[82] But no matter how often he mentions the two of them, he does not refer even once to their shared work as tentmakers.

I think it is important to keep these two fields of Priscilla and Aquila's—and Paul's—activity together, for reasons founded in the work of mission itself. From Paul's own writings and from the information in Acts 18:1-3 we know that the couple was constantly on the move. Travelers were in regular contact with other people, both those living in a given place and other strangers who were on the road. Traveling was especially characteristic of the lives of small merchants and artisans. These people were very important for the spread of Christianity, so that we are not surprised to learn that Priscilla and Aquila were praised throughout the whole *oikumene* (the known world) because of their missionary work.[83] This missionary activity was not a burden on others because of the craft practiced by Priscilla and Aquila. The fact that they had to earn their own living also gives us some clues about the socio-economic composition of the Christian communities.

Priscilla and Her Husband Aquila as Teachers

Acts 18:24-27 attests that Priscilla and Aquila not only took part in synagogue worship, but also taught. This is first stated in the text after Paul has left them (vv. 22-23), when Priscilla and Aquila remain behind in Ephesus. Only at this point is anything said about the couple's work as preachers. According to Acts 18:24-27, they come into contact with an Alexandrian Jew named Apollos, who had been instructed in "the way of the Lord," and taught accurately "the things concerning Jesus," but knew only the baptism of John (see also Acts 19:1-6). Apollos spoke boldly in the synagogue about the "way of the Lord," and that is where Priscilla and Aquila heard him. After hearing him, they took him aside and "explained the Way of God to him more accurately."

The words used in Acts 18:24-27 clearly allow us to infer that teaching was involved: this is true both of Apollos and of Priscilla and Aquila. What is said of Apollos is similar to what is predicated of Philip in Acts 8:35, that is, that he was "well-versed in the scriptures." There follow, in v. 25, two central concepts from the field of instruction: κατηχέω, "to instruct," and διδάσκω, "to teach." Apollos is said to have been instructed in the way of the Lord, that is, in Christian teaching. This instruction was followed by a handing on of what he himself has learned: he taught accurately. Here Luke indicates that, at this time, Christian catechesis was not yet connected with baptism in the name of Jesus, inasmuch as Apollos is said not to know it.[84] What appears to me important at this point, as regards the missionary activity of the artisan couple, is that although Apollos did all this teaching so accurately (ἀκριβῶς), their teaching was still more accurate (ἀκριβέστερον, Acts 18:26)!

This teaching is being done in the context of the synagogue. That can be a reference to instruction in Scripture,[85] which would at the same time underscore the attempt to understand Christian belief on the basis of Jewish Old Testament faith in the fulfillment of messianic hopes. There are three important items in the text that, taken together, point to a single whole: knowledge of Scripture, instruction, and teaching. If these are asserted for Apollos, they can be taken for granted as applying to Priscilla and Aquila, since it says that they explained the way of God more accurately to Apollos. It is possible, but not necessarily true, that this represents a "more developed Pauline theology."[86] In any case, they teach a teacher!

Ἐκτιθέναι, "to expound," "to set forth," appears only in Acts, and there only four times: at 7:21; 11:4; 18:26; and 28:23. Of these, Acts 11:4 and 28:23 can be considered in connection with 18:26. The word in 11:4 means, in context, to give an explanatory exposition of the progress of events in the mission. In 28:23, Paul describes the reign of God to some Jewish people, in the form of a discussion and personal testimony. The form of discussion or exposition described with ἐκτιθέναι is not hostile, but edifying and explanatory. This interpretation is reinforced by the use of προσλαμβάνω, "to take aside," "to receive," in Acts 18:26. This may, in fact, include the idea that Priscilla and Aquila took Apollos into their own circle because they wanted to "assist" him, especially since the verb can also have that meaning. Moreover, it seems to me especially important that this form of discussion is attested in Acts, and in the New Testament as a whole (Acts 11:4; 18:26; 28:23) only for Peter, Paul, and Priscilla with her husband, Aquila.

From the text it would appear that there was very good cooperation between Priscilla, Aquila, and Apollos. It is not reported that the highly educated Jew (now Jewish Christian) Apollos took offense at being taught by a missionary artisan woman. Acts 18:27 follows smoothly and without any problem after the preceding statement about Apollos's teaching. Apollos intended to travel to Achaia, and the "brothers and sisters" encouraged him and wrote a letter to the disciples, asking them to welcome him. Here, following the Codex D version of v. 27, Rudolf Pesch assumes[87] that Priscilla and Aquila are not included in the "brothers and sisters." He argues that otherwise Luke would have said that the couple themselves had written the letter of recommendation. He prefers to assign this writing to people who had been converted by Apollos. The word ἀδελφοί, "brothers and sisters,"[88] appears for the first time in this context (Acts 18:1-27), and is found alongside μαθηταί, "disciples," referring to those in Achaia. The word ἀδελφοί is used in Acts especially to describe brothers and sisters in the faith. Moreover, it very frequently refers to *Jewish* (or Jewish Christian) sisters and brothers. Hence it is not remarkable if, after the process of instruction, the relationship of these people had developed in such a way that the intimate notion of brother- and sisterhood was applied to Priscilla and Aquila as well. The Codex D recension, in fact, avoids this word, substituting "Ephesians." It thus denies any possible participation of Priscilla and Aquila in the composition of the letter of recommendation, because they were not "Ephesians." I see no compelling evidence in α[89] that would speak against a participation of the couple in the composition of the letter. Here, instead, we might see a reference to Priscilla's actually doing so: Priscilla, whom Adolf von Harnack ultimately considered as a possible author of the letter to the Hebrews.[90] In addition, these letters of commendation also indicate missionary authority,[91] and in this case Priscilla and Aquila are more likely recommenders than "the Ephesians."

In the reference to the two missionary parties (Apollos on the one hand, Priscilla and Aquila on the other) I see no hint of a competition, as if Luke had attempted to "minimize" the effectiveness and importance of Apollos, as Pesch thinks.[92] Such an interpretation conceals a danger of appearing to defend Apollos against Priscilla in the Lukan account. It does not seem to me that such a thing is necessary, especially since we know of Apollos's missionary activity from the Pauline texts (1 Cor. 1:12; 3:1-6; 4:6; 16:12; Titus 3:13). It is not necessary to set the two in contrast or competition to one another. In my opinion, Apollos is by no means disparaged here. Such an interpretation is not intended by Luke. And even the statement in 1 Corinthians 3 that Apollos is very confident says nothing against the report in Acts 18:24-27.[93] Here, too, he appears as confident and highly effective. But (this is the important detail) Priscilla and Aquila were still somewhat better able to "explain" matters than Apollos. The problem of competition between Apollos and the couple has, in my opinion, been created by the dominant exegesis.

Finally, one critical note should be added regarding the Lukan account. Luke probably is unjust to Priscilla and Aquila in not expressly calling them missionaries, as he does Apollos. A critical reading of Luke is called for at this point in light of Pauline and other ancient church witnesses. As already emphasized, teaching and missionary activity can be discerned within the Lukan account, but Luke says nothing directly about them. Still, I do not think one should conclude from this that Luke imagines there were no missionaries in Asia and Achaia besides Paul and Apollos.[94] Why, then, did Priscilla and Aquila travel with Paul and remain behind in Ephesus, on their own? What does it mean when Paul himself describes them as his "fellow workers" (Rom. 16:3)? We should take note of the fact that Paul describes Apollos and Priscilla, with her husband, Aquila, in equal terms as "fellow workers." This direct description is lacking in Luke's account. In his case, we need to pay sharper attention to the context (as well as the expressions used) in order to reconstruct the missionary activity of Priscilla and her husband, Aquila.

The Itinerary of Priscilla the Missionary and Her Husband, Aquila

The whole civilized world gives thanks for Priscilla and Aquila and praises them for their work. This statement[95] means that both were known everywhere, or almost everywhere in the Christian world of the time, and that they had been sojourners for a while in a number of different places. The New Testament evidence indicates that the reasons for their itinerant life were political, missionary, and work-related in nature. Peter Lampe[96] has already produced enough arguments against the misconception that these journeys by Priscilla and Aquila were a sign of their supposed wealth; therefore I will not go into that matter in detail at this point.

Acts 18:2 asserts that Aquila[97] and Priscilla had been expelled from Rome, together with other Jewish women and men. If both of them had already become Christians in Rome, this favors the conviction that at that time there was, as yet, no strict distinction drawn between Jews and Christians (see also Acts 16:20). At the same time, we may conclude from this fact that women and men had been active in the mission at Rome long before the Pauline message arrived by letter. That also means that quite a few women and men who were active in small merchandising and craft work had come to believe in Christ, and were passing the message along, especially since people traveling on business were very strongly represented in the Roman population.[98] Priscilla and Aquila are two examples of this.

Aquila, at least, came from Pontus, and thus from the Roman point of view was a foreigner from the east who, like many other women and men, was trying to carry on his business in Rome. Of Priscilla we know at least that she had also been in Rome. Whether it was her native place, or whether she had come with Aquila from Pontus, we cannot determine. In either case, both of them were expelled from Rome by the edict of Claudius.

The assertion in Acts 18:2 that all the Jews had been expelled from Rome has led to an extensive scholarly discussion.[99] The edict of Claudius should be dated to the year 49. There are two texts outside the New Testament that record an imperial expulsion of Jews (and/or Jewish Christians) from Rome. Suetonius[100] reports that the Jews who were immediately associated with "Chrestus," and because of him were causing disturbances, were expelled from Rome. According to Orosius (fifth century)[101] the Claudius edict was issued in the year 49 C.E.: the author repeats the information derived from Suetonius. According to Peter Lampe,[102] however, there was a reason why not all the Jews could have been expelled from Rome, namely that there were at the time "Roman citizens among the Jews of the city." The general allusion in Acts 18:2 to "all the Jews" thus really applies only to some of the Jews of Rome, namely those who were involved in unrest on account of "Chrestus," or "Christus."[103] There are numerous, although tendentious reports in Acts itself to the effect that belief in Christ as the fulfillment of Jewish messianic hopes created an uproar in the Jewish community.[104] Since

Acts 18:1-4 says nothing about the conversion of Priscilla and Aquila, as it usually does, we may suppose that the two of them had already become Christians while they were still in Rome. We know Priscilla and her husband as outstanding missionaries. Probably it was for that very reason that they were expelled from Rome. Because of their missionary activity they were counted among those who stirred up other people. Their expulsion would indicate that they did not have Roman citizenship. Expulsion is a political act on the part of the government, which does not wish to see any kind of "disorder" within its fixed boundaries. The expulsion also had major socioeconomic consequences for those concerned, especially since they had to reestablish themselves somewhere else. They are strangers and foreigners again; they have to start over from the beginning.

It is at this initial stage that they encounter Paul, for Priscilla and Aquila had only recently (προσφάτως) come from Italy. He stayed with them, and they worked together. How can anyone imagine that, given the conditions of the time, a woman and a man who had just been expelled from a city for political reasons were major entrepreneurs? Is it so difficult for exegetes in the Western world at the present time to appreciate that missionary activity is something that was and is possible *alongside* the work of earning one's living? When it is said that the missionaries had exhausted themselves at their work, that means nothing less than that their "work" included both these kinds of activity. After all, Paul can bear witness to that.

According to Acts 18:11, Paul was in Corinth for a year and a half, and in the course of his work there he also obtained the house of Crispus, the head of the synagogue, as a locus for Jewish-Christian mission. Before the continuation of the story of his travels, there is an account of a Jewish-Christian conflict that took place in Corinth during the proconsular term of Gallio (51–52 C.E.).[105] This time is congruent with the reported time of the group's residence in Corinth: they arrived near the end of the year 49 and moved in the year 51, a year and a half later, to Ephesus.[106] Hence a number of stages in the travels of Priscilla and Aquila can be determined from the reports in Acts: (Pontus), Rome, Corinth, Ephesus—in other words, Italy, Greece, and Asia Minor.

This picture can be expanded and illustrated by the aid of some Pauline texts. In 1 Cor. 16:19, Paul sends greetings from Aquila and Priscilla to the community in Corinth. If the letter was written in Ephesus around 54 or 55,[107] this could mean that at that time Priscilla and Aquila were still, or again, in that place. Acts 20:31 says that Paul was in Ephesus for three years, with some interruptions, but Priscilla and Aquila "vanish" from the Lukan account at 18:26-27. It is difficult to determine whether they are to be thought of as being present during Paul's "farewell address" in Acts 20:17-35. What may be decisive here is Paul's statement that everyone knows that he was not a burden to anyone during that whole time, because he worked with his own hands (20:34). We cannot prove whether Priscilla and Aquila remained in Ephesus during the whole time after their departure from Corinth. In any case, at the time when he wrote 1 Corinthians, Paul attests that they had their own house church: "Aquila and Prisca, together with the church in their house, greet you warmly in the Lord" (1 Cor. 16:19). This notice again attests to a strong relationship between the community in Ephesus and Priscilla, Aquila, and the community in Corinth.

In the list of greetings in Rom. 16:3-4, Paul also greets Priscilla and Aquila. It is uncertain whether this greetings list belongs to a fragment of a letter of Paul written to Ephesus, or whether it was originally part of the letter to the Romans.[108] In the latter case, there is some evidence that at the time Romans was written, about the year 56,[109] Priscilla and Aquila were again in Rome and had gathered a community about them. But if the greetings list was part of a letter to Ephesus, this is still the same house church whose greetings Paul sends in 1 Cor. 16:19. In either case, the greetings in Rom. 16:3-16 enable us to elaborate the picture sketched in Acts 18:1-28. Here the missionary activity of these two people is accorded the highest honor. Priscilla and Aquila are Paul's "co-workers" in Christ Jesus, even when he himself is absent. Thus they do not always work alongside Paul, but also independently, as was already clear from Acts 18:26. Paul says of them in Rom. 16:4 that they had risked their own necks for his life. Exactly what Paul means by that, and in what kind of conflict Priscilla and Aquila took his part, cannot be determined. In any case, their cooperative work was life-threatening. For this reason, too—because they did not seek to avoid this danger—all the churches of the Gentiles give them thanks. The reference to the Gentiles in this context can indicate that the conflict in question was some kind of intra-Jewish dissonance, perhaps in connection with the discussion of the acceptance of "Gentiles" into the Christian community. That discussion was not always nonviolent, as Acts 17:5-9; 18:12-17; 20:17-35, and other passages show.

Priscilla's and Aquila's memory was kept alive even at a later date (2 Tim. 4:19). That reference presupposes that their work and their personalities were still remembered. This letter, one of the Pastorals, was written at a later time, which makes it understandable that there is no mention of a church in their house. If 2 Timothy can be understood to be a kind of "testament of Paul,"[110] it is a magnificent accolade to the missionary artisan couple, Priscilla and Aquila: in this testament, they are handed over to the community, and as a result their memory is bound up with the memory of Paul.

Feminist Exegetical Initiatives in Confrontation with the Dominant Exegesis. Retrospect and Summary

In light of what has been described here, it is repeatedly the task of a feminist theology of liberation to uncover the mechanisms that have been and are at work in the minimizing of Priscilla (and other women). In particular, women theologians of our own time[111] have drawn attention to the two recensions of the story of Priscilla and Aquila in Acts 18:1-28 as collated and partly analyzed by Adolf von Harnack in 1900. Only a careful reading of the differently transmitted versions allows a critical access to the dominant exegesis, which often (although without saying so) rests on the "Western" text. Interpolations and reversals of the sequence of the names are not only subtle, but utterly massive interventions not only in the text, but especially in the history of women. In my opinion there are no small and unimportant alterations of a text. All such changes contribute to the destruction of an image. That this process began very early, even before the written compilation of Codex D, can be verified by the following observations: While John Chrysostom took a positive attitude toward Priscilla, the artisan and missionary, prizing and praising her highly, there is also another tradition that was silent about her. This is found in the work of Tertullian,[112] who asserts that it was Aquila, not Priscilla, who earned Paul's praise. This may be a sign of the very early attempts that were made to demote Priscilla from her high station, and, with her, other active women who called upon Priscilla as their authority.

I emphasize the very early beginnings of this weakening of the tradition because the process of suppression has never ceased. In this context, feminist exegesis can rejoice in the efforts of Adolf von Harnack, who attempted to retrieve the importance of Priscilla in the face of church disciplinary tendencies.[113] The retrieval and accenting of the history of Priscilla as a story that attempts to preserve Priscilla as a fully rounded individual is important for women and men who can and will live their faith in their daily lives. Priscilla is owed "reparation"[114] in the sense "that she is to be recalled again and again to memory in the fullness of her womanhood: as wife, tentmaker, highly valued co-worker of Paul and acquaintance of Apollos." But this retrieval is not simply for her sake. It should and can give others courage. It can encourage people who, just like Priscilla and Aquila, are risking their necks for others who are taking a stand against the terrifying power of sin and, as a result, are suffering repressive treatment at the hands of the powerful. Thus, for me, the goal of a feminist liberation-theological exegesis of this story is that we should take the history of Priscilla into our hands again, to preserve it and in this way to draw inspiration from it, especially for the manifold activities of women today.

Annemarie Ohler[115] also emphasizes the totality of Priscilla's work. Although she initially asserts that Paul looked for a job as a tentmaker in Corinth "and found one with his colleague in the trade, Aquila," she also holds that Priscilla was a tentmaker. She concludes this from the fact that Acts 18:1-28 consistently emphasizes that the couple worked together. According to her study, Luke sees "no occasion to distinguish between the work of the woman and that of her husband."[116] This author, like Hanneliese Steichele,[117] sees Priscilla's cooperation in the preaching of the Good News against the background of a situation in which church offices were not yet hierarchical: "Lack of concern for offices and honors still offered women the chance to follow the way of Jesus in freedom: to teach, as Prisca did together with her husband; to struggle just as Paul did, and to work for the spread of the gospel and the building up of churches as did Evodia, Syntyche, Mary, Tryphaena, Tryphosa, and Persis."[118] That is to say that the establishment of a system of hierarchical offices in the institutional church was one of the mechanisms by which women not only were forced out of broader and more liberating spheres of work, but also continue to be pushed aside. At the same time, it expresses the pain of innumerable women who experience this kind of church-political and dogmatic marginalization. It is a unified statement of longing and experience.

Feminist social-historical exegesis goes hand in hand with an interpretative perspective based on experience. The retrieval of the wholistic story of Priscilla acquires a subversive character because it returns to women a part of their own history, which for the most part has been veiled by the dominant tradition of exegesis; from it, women can extract new strength for their efforts on behalf of liberation today. The retrieval of the story of Priscilla has a subversive character especially because it is an assertion that good missionary work does not necessarily require institutionalized structures in order to find recognition among those for whom that work is and has been liberating. This results not least from the fact that such a retrieval brings with it a unified understanding of work, when the hard labor done by women in various fields is accorded its true honor: in that labor, missionary work is not a burden to anyone, and material work is not devalued. Here one kind of work does not render the other invisible;[119] instead, both are expressed simultaneously because they are not mutually exclusive. And yet, in the case of Priscilla, the woman's work has almost universally been pushed aside: from reading the dominant exegesis, one gets the impression that Priscilla sits at home and (of course) does the housework while the men are at their trade.

Feminist liberation-theological exegesis names and values both Priscilla's missionary work and her artisanal labor. That in itself is one of its strengths. Elisabeth Schüssler Fiorenza[120] emphasizes that craft work serves to finance the missionary labor of the couple, in order that they, like Paul and other missionaries, should not be a burden to any community and can remain independent of them. In my opinion, material labor should not bring private wealth or comfort; it should be placed in the service of the building up and maintenance of communities of the saints. This, surely, is also one of the Jewish-Christian treasures brought to the church by Priscilla and Aquila, and for a very long time it was something highly esteemed.[121]

Elisabeth Schüssler Fiorenza is correct when she writes that in her missionary work Priscilla was no more subject to the authority of Paul than were Barnabas and Apollos. She concludes this from the fact that Priscilla and Aquila accomplished their missionary work both within the house churches and outside, using them as a basis. This work was also regarded by Paul as cooperative and collegial. Women were equal in these house churches, not least because "traditionally the house was considered women's proper sphere, and women were not excluded from activities in it."[122]

Luke presents the work of Priscilla and Aquila as teamwork, but not in such a way that the woman remains in the man's shadow; instead, she takes the initiative. Their being married was not a determining factor.[123] Together with their teamwork in a community of equals, carrying on missionary work at the local level, they also had, according to Elisabeth Schüssler Fiorenza,[124] some missionary methods and practices that were different, for example, from those of Paul: "Insofar as they— like the 'other apostles' (1 Cor. 9)—traveled as a pair and gathered converts in house churches, they did not divide the apostolic *diakonia* into the eucharistic table sharing that establishes community and the word that aims at conversion of individuals." In my opinion this method differs from that of Paul to the extent that he, when missionizing at the local level, did not head a house church, but preached the word starting from the existing house churches; for him, they were the centers of his mission. Unfortunately, we cannot determine precisely the extent to which Paul also integrated himself in these communities and their (eucharistic) table fellowship by the work of his hands. In my opinion he also participated equally on that level, especially since he describes Priscilla and Aquila as equal συνεργοί, "fellow workers" (Rom. 16:3). This understanding is congruent with the account in Acts 18:1-28: not only in Paul's writing, but also in Luke's, Priscilla can be recognized as a highly esteemed missionary who is understood as Paul's "co-worker" and who stands as an equal not only alongside Aquila, but also in the company of Paul and other missionaries.[125] Not least we should emphasize that, in Acts, Priscilla is the only married woman for whom marriage poses no obstacle to the totality of her work on behalf of justice.[126] According to the testimony of Rom. 16:15, however, the possibility and the actuality of such non-patriarchal marriages was not unique to Priscilla and Aquila.

Notes

1. Thus also Elisabeth Schüssler Fiorenza, *In Memory of Her,* 178.
2. See, e.g., Susanne Heine, *Frauen der frühen Christenheit,* 51.
3. On this, see Hanneliese Steichele, "Priska," 155–56.
4. Annemarie Ohler, *Frauengestalten,* 203, describes this action on the part of scholars as "appropriate," arguing in fact that "Acts and the Pauline letters always [speak] of the two in the same breath." However, in my opinion this argues directly against the procedure of the majority of scholars.
5. A positive answer to this last question has not been a matter of course for scholars. See, for example, the work of Peter Lampe, *Die stadtrömischen Christen,* 156ff., a book that from a social-historical point of view is very good overall. In examining the evidence regarding the occupation mentioned in Acts 18:3, however, the author always speaks only of Aquila and Paul, and although the subheading reads "Aquila and Prisca," Priscilla does not appear in the central part of the discussion. It appears that Aquila was the sole worker in this household, or, rather, that he alone practiced the craft. Gerd Lüdemann, *Paul,*

Apostle to the Gentiles: Studies in Chronology, 157, says of Acts 18:2-3 that Paul meets Aquila and Priscilla in Corinth, lives with them, and "works with the couple, since they [!] practiced the same trade, tentmaking." With this formulation, the author indicates his assumption that all three practiced the same trade, since the pronoun "they," in context, refers to the couple and to Paul.

6. A. von Harnack, "Recensionen."

7. Not all these variants have been retained in the critical apparatus of Nestle-Aland, *Novum Testamentum Graece*, 26th ed.

8. A. von Harnack, "Recensionen," 10. On this, see also Eldon J. Epp, *Tendency*.

9. Nestle-Aland, 26th ed., has in the text the singular ἠργάζετο, "he [Paul] worked."

10. See F. Rehkopf, *Septuaginta-Vokabular*, as well as W. Michaelis, "σκηνή, κτλ," *TDNT* 7:368–94.

11. See the references in W. Michaelis, "σκηνή," *TDNT* 7:393–94.

12. John Chrysostom, *Salutate Priscillam*, 1.2.

13. See, e.g., *Epistulam II ad Timotheus*, 2.5.

14. John Chrysostom, *Salutate Priscillam*, 1.5: Καὶ Παῦλος μὲν οὐκ ᾐσχύνετο ὁμοῦ καὶ σμίλην μεταχειρίζων, καὶ δέρματα ῥάπτων, καὶ τοῖς ἀξιώμασι διαλεγό- μενος. The Latin text translates the Greek as follows: Ac Paulum quidem non pudet simul et scalprum manu tractare, pelles consuere, et viros alloqui in dignitate constitutos.

15. John Chrysostom, *Ad Romanos* 2.5; *Epistulam II ad Timotheus* 2.4, where the word σκυτοτόμος appears once again, and it is asserted that Paul was poor (πένης) and without means.

16. Origen, *Ad Romanos* 10.18.

17. Theodoret, *Graecarum Affectionem Curatio* 5; *De Providentia* 10.

18. Marcus Diaconus, *Vita Porphyrii* p. 9: ἐπέδωκεν οὖν ἑαυτόν εἰς τὴν τοῦ σκυτοτόμου τέχνην, πλύνων βύρσας καὶ ῥάπτων. The Greek text is taken from R. Silva, "Fabricantes," 126 n. 16.

19. Thus S. Krauss, *Talmudische Archäologie*, 262.

20. On this, see also R. Silva, "Fabricantes," 123ff.; T. Zahn, *Apostelge- schichte*, 632–33.

21. Erasmus, *In Acta Apostolorum* (Basilea, 1541), 6: "artifices tabernacu- lorum, i. d. sutores"; "ob id opinor, quod tabernacula apud priscos pellibus conficiebatur." Citations from R. Silva, "Fabricantes," 128.

22. Citations in R. Silva, "Fabricantes," 128, who refers to Calvin, *Actes des Apôtres* (Corpus Reformatorum), 85.

23. For this translation by Luther, see T. Zahn, *Apostelgeschichte*, 633.

24. Luther, *Vorlesung über den Römerbrief* (1515/1516), ed. of 1927.

25. J. L. Hug, *Einleitung in die Schriften des Neuen Testaments* (1808).

26. Details, and a survey of research, are in R. Silva, "Fabricantes," 130ff.

27. W. Weitling, *Evangelium*, 108, says that the apostles lived by the work of their hands, and that Paul was a carpetmaker.

28. A. Deissmann, *Paulus*, 35–36.

29. R. Knopf, *Apostelgeschichte*, 78; G. Hoennicke, *Apostelgeschichte*, 95 n. 2.

30. Billerbeck 2:746, citing Exod. 26:7 as proof. However, even if the "tent over the tabernacle" in Exodus 26 (LXX) was to be made primarily of "carpets" or "curtains," it was to be covered with tanned skins (δέρματα, δέρρεις); cf. Exod. 26:7-14.

31. J. Jeremias, "Zöllner," 299.

32. On this, see Billerbeck 2:695; S. Krauss, *Talmudische Archäologie*, 253ff.

33. S. Krauss, *Talmudische Archäologie*, 254. At this point he names many other trades, including a number that were despised and still were practiced by rabbis.

34. W. Michaelis, "σκηνή," *TDNT* 7:394. Thus also T. Zahn, *Apostelgeschichte* 2:634.

35. See, e.g., Pliny, *Naturalis Historia* 6.28.143; 8.203.

36. T. Zahn, *Apostelgeschichte* 2:633.

37. Billerbeck 2:473–74 presents exactly this train of thought and concludes: "From this we can see why it was that the apostle, as a σκηνοποιός, sought his living from one of the principal industries of his homeland."

38. Jewish scholars have traditionally placed great emphasis on the learning of a trade by those who study Torah: For example, in *Midr. Qoh.* 9.9 (42a) we read: "Acquire a handicraft for yourself together with Torah . . . R[abbi] Jose b. Meshullam and R[abbi] Simeon b. Menasia [both ca. 180] . . . used to divide the day into three parts—a third for studying Torah, a third for prayer, and a third for work"; *Aboth* 2.2: "Rabban Gamaliel [3rd c., ca. 220] . . . said: 'Excellent is the study of the Torah together with a worldly occupation' [e.g., craft work or trade]." And Rabbi Hillel the elder [ca. 20 B.C.E.], in order to pay for his study of Torah, worked as a day laborer. Quotations are from Billerbeck 2:745.

39. E. Haenchen, *Acts*, 534; R. Pesch, *Apostelgeschichte* 2:147; J. Roloff, *Apostelgeschichte*, 270; G. Schille, *Apostelgeschichte*, 363.

40. I. H. Marshall, *Acts*, 293.

41. P. Lampe, *Christen*, 157.

42. See, e.g., P. Lampe, *Christen*, 157, who also mentions other literature in the context. For the imperial *tabernacularii*, see *CIL* 6.5183a, 5183b, 9053, 9053a. More detail will be given below.

43. P. Lampe, *Christen*, 157–58. So also W. Elliger, *Paulus*, 250.

44. R. Silva, "Fabricantes," 124. On the shift brought about by German interpretation (Wettstein, Hug, and Eichhorn), see p. 132.

45. H. Blümner, *Technologie*, 268ff., with numerous bibliographical notes.

46. It is true that Blümner (*Technologie*, 300) asserts that tents could also be made by weaving, e.g., of flax. But these were not the words that were used.

The same is true when Blümner (*Thätigkeit*, 4–5, 30–31) speaks of the weaving of goats' hair (i.e., *cilicium*). There, too, when he describes the types of business most practiced in Pontus (pp. 40ff.), tentmaking is not mentioned in connection with the weaving of linen. See also B. Büchsenschütz, *Hauptstätten*, 64, with the assertion that the weaving of linen screens only reached significant proportions in Cilicia in the second century C.E.

47. S. Krauss, *Talmudische Archäologie* 1:7–8.

48. G. Hoennicke, *Apostelgeschichte*, 95.

49. See, for example, J. Comblin, *Atos* 2:87–88; E. Haenchen, *Acts*, 534, 538; W. Michaelis, "σκηνή," *TDNT* 7:393; J. Roloff, *Apostelgeschichte*, 270; U. Smidt, *Apostelgeschichte*, 136–37; R. Silva, "Fabricantes," esp. 133; T. Zahn, *Apostelgeschichte*, 632, 634; P. Lampe, *Christen*, 156ff.; H. Conzelmann, *Acts*, 151.

50. W. Michaelis, "σκηνή," *TDNT* 7:393.

51. G. Schille, *Apostelgeschichte*, 363.

52. P. Lampe, *Christen*, 156–57, has made an effort to collect all the *tabernacularii* inscriptions for the city of Rome. Only a few people practicing this trade are inscriptionally attested. They were employed in the imperial workshops: *CIL* 6.5183a, 5183b, 9053, 9053a.

53. On this point, see, e.g., R. S. Kraemer, *Maenads*, 79.

54. N. Kampen, *Image*, 133; thus also R. Günther, *Frauenarbeit*, 136.

55. M. Eichenauer, *Untersuchungen*, 87–88. Natalie Kampen also reproduces an iconographic representation of a *sutrix* (fig. 90). Earlier, H. Blümner, *Technologie*, 271 n. 9, also mentions a *sutrix*.

56. M. Eichenauer's documentary work is directed against the assertion that the state of the sources does not permit us to locate women in fields of labor that constitute "men's work." For example, she shows that women not only owned an *officina plumbaria*, a workshop for producing materials out of lead, but were also active in the production of lead pipes and well pipes; on this, see also H. Gummerus, "Industrie und Handel," 1499–1500. Moreover, we can also see that women participated, just as men did, in the hard labor involved in other fields of work as well: thus, for example, H. Thierfelder, *Unbekannte antike Welt*, 147, presents a receipt, inscriptionally attested, for a woman who worked five days on a dam.

57. L. Schottroff, "Women as Disciples," 88–91.

58. A. von Harnack, *Mission and Expansion* 2:242 n. 4.

59. E. Haenchen, *Acts*, 538.

60. G. Theißen, "Social Stratification," 90. For the "boutiques" or small shops mentioned in the following citation, see below.

61. R. Pesch, *Apostelgeschichte* 2:147.

62. For more detail, and a critique, see P. Lampe, *Christen*, 159ff.

63. H.-J. Klauck, *Hausgemeinde*, 3.

64. U. Wilckens, *Römer* 6.3:134.

65. See W.-H. Ollrog, *Paulus*, 26–27, with n. 105.

66. E.g., M. Hengel, *Eigentum*, 46; see also his "Arbeit," 197 n. 81, where the author considers the possibility that Priscilla and Aquila "may have" owned "a large business with workshops in various localities." After this consideration, Hengel continues by saying that it was an "exhausting job," by which Paul and his companions "could scarcely earn the minimum necessary for their existence." The whole conception seems to be that Paul worked for Priscilla and Aquila as a wage-earner.

67. John Chrysostom, *Salutate Priscillam* 1.2: πτωχοὶ καὶ πένητες, καὶ ἐκ τῆς τῶν χειρῶν ἐργασίας ζῶντες. Ἦσαν, γὰρ, φησὶ σκηνοποιοὶ τῇ τέχνῃ (pauperes et egeni, quique opere manuum victum quaererent. Erant enim, einquit, scenofactoriae artis).

68. E. Haenchen, *Acts*, 539.

69. Theißen, "Social Stratification," 90–91.

70. P. Lampe, *Christen*, 158. See the list of inscriptions there. We should note here that Lampe counts only Aquila within this artisanal group. The inscriptions are mentioned in his n. 49.

71. Ibid., 159.

72. See N. Kampen, *Image*, e.g., figures 90 and 79, as well as 37, 38, 39, and 40, depicting the tiny stalls of the merchants.

73. P. Lampe, *Christen*, 161. In addition, he mentions literary material in which it is stated that this kind of craft work was also carried on in the dwelling spaces, e.g., Apuleius, *Metamorphoses* 9.24–25.

74. P. Lampe, *Christen*, 161.

75. H. Maehler, *Urkunden*, esp. 71–72, 163ff.

76. See ibid., 11–12.

77. See ibid., esp. 158, 163ff.; also J. Hengstl, *Papyri*, 307–8.

78. K. Thraede, "Frau," 230; idem, "Ärger," 97, where he also expressly calls Priscilla a god-fearer. Against this thesis of the "entrepreneurial couple," see also L. Schottroff, "Women as Disciples," 123–24 n. 50; and P. Lampe, *Christen*, 159ff. H. Steichele, "Priska," 158ff., apparently follows this same line of reasoning. She does not simply opt for words like "wealth" and the like, but rather asserts that Priscilla and Aquila were tentmakers, and therefore had active employment. She does not, however, pose the social-historical question.

79. W. Elliger, *Paulus*, 250; this is also the conclusion of L. Schottroff, "Women as Disciples," 90–91 and n. 50.

80. The trend was started by the "Western" text recension of Acts 18:1-3, which still finds echoes in exegesis at the present time: for example, when R. Pesch, *Apostelgeschichte* 2:162 makes direct reference to parts of that recension in order to shield Apollos from what is said to be Luke's preference for Priscilla and Aquila. Still more striking, however, is the treatment by H. Conzelmann (*Acts*, 157–58), since in his work Priscilla does not appear either as an artisan or as active in missionary teaching. In the commentary on vv. 24-27, for example, v. 26 is completely omitted, so that he speaks only of Aquila!

81. A. von Harnack, *Mission and Expansion*, 1:75.

82. Ibid., 1:79 and all other passages, in the second volume as well, in which he speaks of the couple in connection with Paul. See, similarly, his "Probabilia," 33ff.

83. In addition to Rom. 16:4, see also Chrysostom, *Salutate Priscillam* 2.1.

84. On this point R. Pesch, *Apostelgeschichte* 2:161, believes in agreement with other exegetes that this is "historically improbable, and can scarcely be otherwise understood than as an (unsuccessful) attempt on the part of Luke to minimize the impact of Apollos in Ephesus."

85. Thus also K. H. Rengstorf, "διδάσκω, κτλ," *TDNT* 2:135–65, at 146. I do not, however, interpret instruction in Scripture as a "weapon against the attacks of Jews" (ibid., 146).

86. Pesch, *Apostelgeschichte* 2:161–62.

87. Ibid., 2:162, with n. 11.

88. The understanding of this word as including "sisters" corresponds to the androcentric usage in New Testament Greek. On this, see L. Schottroff, "Mary Magdalene," 169–71, 195; E. Schüssler Fiorenza, *In Memory of Her*, 43–48.

89. On this, see above, pp. 197–99.

90. See A. von Harnack, "Probabilia," 32ff., esp. 37–38. Whatever the case is with regard to the authorship of the letter to the Hebrews, it is especially striking that the word σκηνή, "tent," is nowhere so frequently used in the New Testament as here. Of twenty instances in the entire New Testament, ten appear in this letter. It is repeatedly emphasized that the sacred tent/tabernacle (cf. Exodus 26) was not made by human hands (Hebr. 8:2; 9:11, 24). This could very well indicate that the author was familiar with the making of tents (see also Hebr. 11:9, "living in tents").

91. See, e.g., Rom. 16:2 (Paul urges the community to welcome Phoebe); Phil. 2:29 (Paul asks the community to receive Epaphroditus).

92. R. Pesch, *Apostelgeschichte* 2:161.

93. In comparing 1 Corinthians 3 with Acts 18:24-27, a number of exegetes cast doubt on the "historical reliability of the account of Aquila and Priscilla teaching Apollos" (H. Steichele, "Priska," 160). Steichele agrees with that opinion, writing that the ecclesially oriented Luke could very well have introduced the teaching "redactionally," so that Apollos's mission would take place and be understood as belonging within the church. But by that very fact Luke would be demonstrating that he had no difficulty at all in considering Priscilla a teacher.

94. Thus R. Pesch, *Apostelgeschichte* 2:162, although (p. 163) he describes Priscilla and Aquila as an "active missionary couple." But he makes a distinction only insofar as Apollos is described as an independent missionary, while Priscilla and Aquila are attached to Paul.

95. Rom. 16:4 and John Chrysostom, *Salutate Priscillam* 2.1.

96. P. Lampe, *Christen*, 162ff., with citations of evidence and literature.

97. According to Billerbeck 3:486ff., Aquila appears to have been a name very frequently given to proselytes, and typical of Pontus.

98. See the evidence in P. Lampe, *Christen*, 141ff., 159.

99. See, e.g., G. Lüdemann, *Paul*, 162–71; P. Lampe, *Christen*, 4ff., with many bibliographical references.

100. Suetonius, *Divus Claudius* 25.4: Iudaeos impulsore Chresto assidue tumultuantes Roma expulit.

101. Orosius, *Historiae adversum Paganos* 7.6.15–16: Anno eiusdem nono expulsos per Claudium urbe Iudaeos Iosephus refert, sed me magis Suetonius movet, qui ait hoc mode: Claudius Iudaeos impulsore Chresto assidue tumultuantes Roma expulit.

102. P. Lampe, *Christen*, 7.

103. See the documentation in P. Lampe, *Christen*, 6, showing that confusion or alternation between Chrestus and Christus was very common.

104. See, e.g., Acts 7:1ff.; 18:12ff.; 22:1ff.; for the (danger of) unrest among the population as a whole, see Acts 19:23ff.

105. A. Deissmann, *Paulus*, 159ff.; G. Lüdemann, *Paul*, 162–71.

106. Thus also H. Steichele, "Priska," 159; R. Pesch, *Apostelgeschichte* 2:152; differently G. Lüdemann, *Paul*, 162–71, who dates the edict of Claudius to the year 41, and the proconsulate of Gallio to 51/52. In my opinion that would indicate that Priscilla, Aquila, and Paul spent time in Corinth on two separate occasions, which is not historically impossible. But against Lüdemann's arguments, see P. Lampe, *Christen*, 8.

107. For the dating of the letter and the place of composition, see H. Conzelmann, *1 Corinthians*, 3–4, with n. 31 (written in the year 55); H. Koester, *Introduction to the New Testament 2: The History and Literature of Early Christianity*, 120–21, thinks that 1 Corinthians was written in Ephesus around 53/54; P. Vielhauer, *Geschichte*, 141, believes that Paul wrote the letter in Ephesus in the spring of 54, 55, or 56; according to W. Michaelis, *Einleitung*, 175, Paul wrote it in Ephesus around the time of Easter 55.

108. On this, see H. Steichele, "Priska," 157; H. Koester, *Introduction*, 2:138–39.

109. P. Vielhauer, *Geschichte*, 175 (in Corinth, in 56 at the earliest, 59 at the latest); H. Koester, *Introduction*, 2:138–39 (in Corinth in the winter of the year 55/56); so also W. Michaelis, *Einleitung*, 164.

110. H. Koester, *Introduction*, 2:300.

111. See, e.g., Luise Schottroff, "Women as Disciples," 107; E. Schüssler Fiorenza, *In Memory of Her*, 178–79; H. Steichele, "Priska," 160ff.; S. Heine, *Women and Early Christianity*, 43–44.

112. Tertullian, "De Fuga in Persecutione," 12.

113. A. von Harnack, "Recensionen," 10. Unfortunately, until quite recently this attempt found very little positive echo; at any rate, it did not shape research on Priscilla until the most recent feminist initiatives.

114. H. Steichele, "Priska," 162. The following quotation is also from her work.

115. A. Ohler, *Frauengestalten*, 203ff.

116. Ibid., 210.

117. H. Steichele, "Priska," 162.

118. Ibid., 214.

119. On the way in which women's work is made invisible by the dominant exegesis, see L. Schottroff, "Unsichtbare Arbeit," 39ff.

120. E. Schüssler Fiorenza, *In Memory of Her*, 178–79.

121. For this understanding, see A. Ohler, *Frauengestalten*, 226.

122. E. Schüssler Fiorenza, *In Memory of Her*, 176.

123. See, similarly, Ben Witherington, *Women*, 153–54.

124. E. Schüssler Fiorenza, *In Memory of Her*, 179.

125. On this, see E. Schüssler Fiorenza, *In Memory of Her*, 172–75; L. Schottroff, "Women as Disciples," 88–92 and esp. 123–24; eadem, "Critique," 36–38.

126. Acts mentions only two married women: Sapphira and Priscilla. In Sapphira's case, however, the story turned out differently: see ch. 1 above.

6

Women Mentioned Briefly, or Not at All

To conclude this investigation, I want to recall the women who are mentioned only briefly in Acts, or are not explicitly named. The form of this chapter will be twofold: In an initial step I will briefly introduce some women who, although they are not explicitly mentioned in Acts, may be presumed to be included in generic masculine terms applied to several persons or to groups of persons, in accordance with Luke's androcentric usage. In a second section, I will comment on the passages in which women are mentioned explicitly, but only briefly.[1] It is clear that only these two steps taken together can yield a more accurate and complete picture of women in Acts.

A Remembrance of Unnamed Women

Making the unnamed women in Acts visible is only possible because there are passages in which women are explicitly mentioned. We may call this a process of deduction from what is said to what is unspoken.[2] The resulting movement of reading is as follows: We read a long section within one part of Acts, and suddenly we come to a passage in which, without introduction, the text mentions women. We can cite Mark 15:40-41 as a typical example of this kind of writing: it is only at Jesus' crucifixion that women are expressly mentioned, but we learn that they had always—from the very beginning—been with him and followed him:

227

There were also women looking on from a distance; among them were Mary Magdalene, and Mary the mother of James the younger and of Joses, and Salome. These used to follow him and provided for him when he was in Galilee; and there were many other women who had come up with him to Jerusalem.[3]

Consequently, in order to reconstruct the history of women we have to read stories not only from front to back, but from back to front. What is true of Mark is also true, for the most part, of Luke:

> Mark makes clear that so far he had been using the androcentric linguistic use common in antiquity, where women are included in the terminology that talks about men. He also makes clear that he is not critically predisposed toward this linguistic use. He shares this uncritical androcentric linguistic use with all other evangelists of the New Testament.[4]

Therefore, when Acts describes Peter's or Paul's preaching and it appears that only men are addressed as their audience, we should also presume the presence of women. Androcentric language is inclusive language: it is a language referring to men, but nevertheless presuming that women are included in its meaning.

> Such androcentric inclusive language mentions women only when their presence has become in any way a problem or when they are "exceptional," but it does not mention women in so-called normal situations. . . . In other words, androcentric language is inclusive of women, but does not mention them explicitly. Such androcentric inclusive language functions in biblical texts the same way as it functions today—it mentions women only when women's behavior presents a problem or when women are exceptional individuals.[5]

The androcentrism of Luke's language is especially marked in the book of Acts. The introductions to the speeches (1:11, 16; 2:22, 29, 37; 3:12, 17; 5:35; 6:3; 7:2; 13:15-16, 26, 38; 14:15; 15:7, 13; 19:25, 35; 21:28; 22:1; 23:1; 28:17) apparently make it clear that there are no women within the groups that make up the respective audiences. But some of these passages show plainly that women are subsumed under certain masculine terms. For example, in 13:15-16, 26, the "god-fearers" who are addressed include women, especially since they constitute the majority of this group.[6] It is difficult to imagine that women are not addressed in Peter's first speech, since it is emphasized in 1:14 that women were always part of the group of the saints. It is striking that only Peter speaks *publicly:* immediately after the ascension of Jesus, all are gathered together (1:13-14), and although Peter addresses the group of 120 as "men, brothers" (1:15-16), we must suppose that after his speech and before the choice of the twelfth apostle both men *and* women were present, since 1:24 speaks of the prayer of *all.* Again, according to 2:1-4, they were *all* together on the day of Pentecost—that is, a tongue of fire rested on every woman and every man: "All of them were filled with the Holy Spirit and began to speak in other languages, as the Spirit gave them ability." But it appears that only Peter addresses the crowd who heard the Spirit-filled believers speaking (2:14-39). In Peter's Pentecost speech it is evident that women have also participated in the Pentecost miracle, for in Acts 2:17-21 Peter quotes Joel 3:1-5 and interprets the Pentecost event as a fulfillment of this prophecy. According to the text of Joel, God will pour out the divine Spirit upon all flesh: "and your sons and your daughters shall prophesy . . . even upon my slaves, both men and women, in those days I will pour out my Spirit; and they shall prophesy." This last assertion, "and they shall prophesy," is an addition to the LXX text. Had it been Peter's (or rather Luke's) intention to exclude women from the Pentecost event, would this Old Testament text have been chosen, when it clearly says that both women and men will equally receive the gifts of the Holy Spirit? Would this text have been chosen to describe Christians' understanding of what had been fulfilled among them, and with the addition of the statement that slaves, both men and women, would prophesy? The presence of women prophets in the Jerusalem community and elsewhere is attested by Acts 21:9, among other passages.[7]

It appears to me that there are two elements within Acts that stand in tension with one another: The text itself uses an androcentric language that allows us to conclude the existence of a patriarchal society. And yet, the text is unable to write out of existence the presence and importance of women. Nevertheless, because Acts is constructed on the stories of "great individuals," the text concentrates on them. In the construction of Acts, central importance is given to Peter, Stephen, and Paul. Other women and men are only mentioned when they come into contact with them in the course of the mission. Women are mentioned primarily for two reasons: when some particular point requires emphasis, or when these women were outstanding figures in the history of the Christian mission.[8]

Since Acts places special emphasis on the spread of Jewish-Christian belief through the work of Peter and Paul, it overlooks people, other than Peter and Paul, who were engaged in the work of preaching the word. In Acts, this applies especially to Mary Magdalene. Although she had a central role in the whole story of Jesus' life, she is not even mentioned in Acts. This is a dubious procedure, not only because Luke begins Acts 1:1 at the very point at which the Gospels conclude with her report of the resurrection, but also because Acts 1:21-22 and 13:30-31 make being an eyewitness a criterion for apostleship. The fact that Mary Magdalene is not mentioned by the author in this context means that he did not understand or accept her as an apostle.[9]

Women Mentioned Briefly and By Name

Acts leaves unmentioned some important, actively engaged women who worked alongside or independently of Peter and Paul for the gospel of Christ: Mary Magdalene, Thecla, the widow Lemma and her daughter Ammia.[10] On the other hand, Acts mentions a great many women who do not appear in other books. The reason cannot be that Luke only mentions women by name if they are subject to the authority of Peter or Paul, for Tabitha, Lydia, and Priscilla, to name several examples, worked and organized independently of those two circles, as we can see from the passages in which they appear. Thus Acts is not a complete chronicle of the women and men who appear in it. Those who are remembered in it, however, can contribute to our development of a picture of the church's beginnings. In the following section I want to look more closely at the passages in Acts in which women are briefly mentioned. My interest focuses on the discovery of their role within Acts as a whole. I will follow the traditional outline of Acts.[11]

The first major section of Acts describes the witness and events in Jerusalem (1:1—8:3) and beyond (8:4—12:25). Initially, the major center of the Jewish-Christian community is Jerusalem. Antioch becomes the second great center, where, in particular, those who are driven out of Jerusalem gather (11:19-21). These two centers are closely united (11:22-26). The second major section begins at 13:1 and extends to 28:32. The mission of Paul and Barnabas as witnesses to Jesus Christ begins in Antioch (13:2-4), but after the end of the first missionary journey they both remain connected with Jerusalem (15:1-35). Paul and Barnabas's second missionary journey begins at Jerusalem (15:36) and ends in Antioch (18:22); its purpose is to revisit the communities in which they had already preached the word. Beginning at 16:6, this journey of visitation becomes a missionary journey: The missionaries travel through Asia Minor and enter Macedonia and Greece. Through their preaching, many women and men are converted. Paul's third missionary journey begins in Antioch (18:23) and ends in Caesarea or Jerusalem (21:16-17). This journey is characterized by farewell visits. Nothing is said directly about conversions, although 19:18 may be a conversion story. Beginning with 21:17, the text concentrates on Paul's account, or defense, of his mission before the elders in Jerusalem, his imprisonment there and in Caesarea, the negotiations with the Roman authorities, and his journey as a prisoner to Rome.

The Witnesses to the Risen One in Jerusalem, Judea, and Samaria: 1:1—12:25

The Women First Named (1:14)

After the account of Jesus' ascension (1:12-13), the text reports the return of the eleven Galilean men from the nearby Mount of Olives to Jerusalem. "When they had entered the city, they went to the room upstairs where they were staying. . . . All these were constantly devoting themselves to prayer, together with the women, including Mary the mother of Jesus, as well as his brothers." Here in v. 14, then, for the first time we learn that there were also women who were constantly gathered in the upstairs room. The word ὑπερῷον, "upstairs room" is used by Luke only in the book of Acts (1:13; 9:37, 39; 20:8). According to Jürgen Roloff this word describes:

. . . an additional room built on the flat roof of the taller houses, accessible only by an outside stairway, whose function, unlike that of the large living room below, was not to serve the ordinary, daily functions of life (sleeping, cooking, eating, etc.). The upstairs room is a quiet place to which one can withdraw for prayer and study of Scripture (1 Kgs. 17:19ff. . . .). It is the preferred place for scribal discussions.[12]

According to Rudolf Pesch,[13] this was "the gathering place of the eleven," that is, the eleven apostles. But he himself shows that the text (see 1:6; Luke 24:9, 33) does not think of the apostles alone, and that women also belong "to the community awaiting Pentecost."[14] In our text, the upstairs room is the place where this community—and not only the eleven apostles—continually gathers. The word καταμένειν, "to stay," appears only here and in a variant in 1 Cor. 16:6 (𝔓[34] B etc.;

Nestle-Aland, 25th ed.), where Paul emphasizes that he wishes to stay a while in Corinth ("with you"); he wants to remain there. It has the same meaning as the alternative reading in 1 Cor. 16:6, παραμένειν (𝔓⁴⁶ ℵ A C D [F G] Ψ 075. 088 𝔐; Nestle-Aland, 26th ed.), "to stay," "to remain."[15] Thus it is possible that the Galileans were staying in the upstairs room in Jerusalem because they were in prayer while awaiting the Pentecost event. This was a room known to Jews as a place for prayer, study of Torah, and as living space.[16] Quentin Quesnell's investigation of the verbs and concepts in the texts that are important for the description of the disciples' stay in Jerusalem supports the thesis that in Jerusalem the upstairs room served as a constant dwelling place for the (Galilean) women and men.[17]

In v. 14, two "groups" of women are mentioned: those who are not named, and Mary the mother of Jesus, in whose company Luke also mentions Jesus' "brothers." It is difficult to determine what tradition Luke is following here,[18] since Matt. 13:55-56 also mentions the mother of Jesus (Mary) together with his brothers (James, Joses, Simon, Judas) and sisters (unnamed); John 7:3 also mentions his brothers. Is Luke including Jesus' "sisters" in speaking of his "brothers"? The other group of women would seem to include those, perhaps all, who followed Jesus from Galilee and afterward (Luke 8:2-3; cf. 23:55; 24:10). Another text tradition, that of Codex D, stands contrary to this interpretation: it adds "and children" after "women," transforming the women who are mentioned as independent persons into the wives and children of the apostles. In this way, the disciples of Jesus become the "holy family of the earliest community."[19] Although many commentators oppose the textual change in D and emphasize that the "women" should not be understood as the wives of the apostles, but as "the group of Jesus' female disciples,"[20] the contrary tradition in exegesis still exists and continues to follow Codex D.[21] As will appear in other cases (e.g., 17:4, 17; 18:1-2), Codex D often changes passages in the text in which women appear. It attempts to suppress women by subordinating them to men.

If the women mentioned in 1:14 are to be thought of as the same women who met Jesus in Galilee and followed him from there until his death, resurrection, and ascension, they have been done a great injustice both by the text and by the tradition of interpretation. This injustice consists, first of all, in their not being named, in contrast to the men in Acts 1:13, and differently from Luke 8:1-3; 24:10. With their names, the memory of their deeds is also extinguished. Moreover, these women were not considered when it came to the choice of the twelfth apostle.

The objection does not sound so absurd if we look more closely at the preconditions and requirements for "candidacy" for election as an apostle. Acts 1:21-22 reads: "So one of the men who have accompanied us during all the time that the Lord Jesus went in and out among us, beginning from the baptism of John until the day when he was taken up from us—one of these must become a witness with us to his resurrection." The Synoptic Gospels attest the discipleship of women as followers of Jesus (from Galilee): Luke 8:1-3; Mark 15:40-41; Matt. 27:55-56; Luke 23:55.[22] These women disciples accompanied Jesus on the way until his bitter death on the cross, and according to Mark 16:1-8 they were the first witnesses of Jesus' resurrection. According to Luke 24:1-10 they were given the task of proclaiming Jesus' resurrection to the others. If the other disciples did not believe them (24:11, 22-24), it was not because they were women, but rather because the event itself was incredible.[23] But they were witnesses from the beginning! As such, they fulfilled the conditions for *diakonia* and for the apostolate (Acts 1:25).[24] But at this point Luke considers men exclusively.

Men and Women Become Believers (5:14)

Acts 5:14 is part of the so-called third summary (5:12-16) and contains a brief notice about the spread of Jewish Christian faith in Jerusalem. This verse contains the third "notice of growth," and here, for the first time in Acts, women are explicitly mentioned: "Yet more than ever believers were added to the Lord, great numbers of both men and women, so that they even carried out the sick into the streets, and laid them on cots and mats, in order that Peter's shadow might fall on some of them as he came by" (5:14-15). In 2:41 it had been said that three thousand ψυχαί ("persons") were added; 4:4 says that the number of ἄνδρες ("men") had risen to about five thousand; finally, 5:14 mentions women and men who were added. This growth in numbers of disciples is associated with miracles. After the sad story of Sapphira and Ananias it is said that many miracles were done through the hands of the apostles; some people remained at a distance, but others "held them in high esteem." Then comes the notice of growth in v. 14. It is at first somewhat disturbing that v. 15 begins with a ὥστε, "so that," clause. Exegetes have asked whether v. 15 should follow v. 13b or v. 12a: that is, v. 14 is seen as a Lukan insertion into a pre-existing tradition.[25] But is that appropriate? Luke has made an effort, following the disruption in the community caused by the story of Sapphira and Ananias, to coordinate a variety of information: the miraculous deeds done through the hands of the apostles; the (other?) gathering place in Solomon's portico in the Temple; the various reactions to Jewish Christian faith, which include the conversions; the information about Peter's healing shadow. The fact that he begins v. 15 with ὥστε could be connected with the circumstance that he includes the notice of conversions in v. 14 among the various reactions of the people toward the Christians. The ὥστε clause can thus refer to all the reactions, or be understood as a consequence of them all.[26] The notice of growth can continue to stand at the center of the summary, without causing disturbance; nothing need be omitted in order to make the statement comprehensible.[27] It can also be understood as a reference to a kind of chain reaction: The women and men who are being added to the community constitute a connection backward (reactions to the effectiveness of the Christians) and forward (more and more sick people hear about the miracles and are brought to be healed). Thus it is possible that Luke had no problem about describing conversion in the context of service to the sick. All are to be healed as a sign of the inbreaking reign of God. There is no reason to suppose that those converted did not help to bring the sick people to be healed, or to lay them on cots and mats. Luke may have had that image in mind when he wrote the sentence. It is improbable that he inserted v. 14 at random; instead, it may be a direct reflection of his own experiences with early Christian communities.

The Neglected Hellenist Widows (6:1)

This is the first point in Acts at which we learn that Hellenist widows were part of the community of saints in Jerusalem. As early as 2:5-11 there was mention of people from the Greek-speaking diaspora,[28] but none of them (apparently) women. They appear here explicitly for the first time, but only in the form of widows: "Now during those days, when the disciples were increasing in number, the Hellenists complained against the Hebrews because their widows were being neglected in the daily distribution of food [*diakonia*]" (6:1).[29]

The words "during those days" connect Acts 6:1-6 with what has gone before. "During those days" refers to the days in which the apostles had asserted themselves, in spite of the order of the Sanhedrin to remain silent, and had not ceased "in the temple and at home . . . to teach and proclaim Jesus as the Messiah" (5:42). This is immediately followed by the information that the number of disciples was growing.[30] It seems to me that, by this, Luke is attempting to explain why it happened that the Hellenist widows[31] were neglected in the "daily distribution of food," and also why the number of organized workers had to be expanded. Whether the reason given in Luke's account for the neglect of the Hellenist widows corresponds to the reality must remain an open question, for "Luke spends no time in examining who was at fault."[32] The rest of the story, in 6:2—8:8, indicates that the source Luke is using may have been "focused on the conflict between the 'Hellenists' . . . and the 'Hebrews.'"[33] Luke attempts to explain this conflict as the consequence of a difficulty in the matter of *diakonia*. That is why the widows among the Hellenists are mentioned here. The expression "*daily* διακονία," which appears only here in the New Testament, has presented interpreters with significant difficulties, and continues to do so. This problem is more serious than a correct translation of the word; it seems to me that at this point the subject of the debate is the treatment of women in the primitive Christian communities.

Not only the expression διακονία καθημερινή, "daily *diakonia*," but also the verb παραθεωρεῖσθαι, "to be overlooked," "to be neglected," appear only once in the New Testament. The use of this verb in the imperfect suggests the conclusion that the text is not speaking of a single instance, but that the widows "were frequently neglected."[34] To understand more precisely what could be meant by this, exegetes have inquired into the praxis of *diakonia* in the environment in which the early Christian communities existed.

A consensus in research holds that the daily *diakonia* was an example of "poor-relief."[35] This praxis was known both among Jews and in non-Jewish contexts.[36] Joachim Jeremias and Paul Billerbeck collected enough sources to attest to a well-organized ancient Jewish system of care for the poor.[37] A daily *diakonia* in the sense of "table service," that is, feeding of the impoverished, existed in Judaism. The institution that organized it was called *tamḥūy*, "the poor bowl," from which "itinerant paupers could receive at least two meals daily."[38] It seems likely that Acts 6:1 refers to something similar, since the "Hellenists" were also regarded as foreigners (see 2:5, 9-11, οἱ κατοικοῦντες, "sojourners," "settlers"). There is a fundamental agreement among exegetes that the Hellenist widows were being neglected by the "Hebrews," that is, the Hebrew- or Aramaic-speaking Jews.[39] This understanding is based on the reading of Codex D, which adds "in the Hebrews' *diakonia*" at the end of 6:1, and on the expression in 6:3 according to which a group of Hellenist men is to be selected to "wait on tables." Seven men are chosen by the community, but in the rest of the book they are not mentioned in connection with table service; instead, they preach and act as missionaries. Even if 6:2 tries to distinguish between "table service" and "service of the word," the work of the Seven nevertheless shows that the two were not separate.

However, the assertion in v. 1 must not necessarily mean that the Hellenist widows were being overlooked or neglected by the "Hebrews" in the daily distribution. H. W. Beyer had already pointed out that the expression διακονεῖν τραπέζαις (6:2) refers "not merely to the provision of food but to the daily preparation and organisation."[40] This may lead us to think that the Hellenist widows were overlooked "in the organization of the community meals." We may interpret this to mean that the conflict was not restricted to bad treatment of the widows; their neglect is explained as "a difference of opinion about whether the Hellenist women were to be part of this community at table, and thus part of the community, or not."[41]

Elisabeth Schüssler Fiorenza presses the question farther in this direction.[42] She does not dispute that in that period the distress of widows and orphans was very great, and for that reason they depended on institutionalized care for the poor. But she does not see it as completely clear that Acts 6:1 is about service to the poor, since "nothing is said in Acts 6 to indicate that the widows of the Hellenists were *poor*."[43] She attempts to understand the table service in Acts 6:2 by reference to 1 Cor. 10:21. According to Schüssler Fiorenza, in 1 Cor. 10:21 the "'table of the Lord' was the eucharistic table. Table ministry, therefore, was most likely the eucharistic ministry, which included preparation of a meal, purchase and distribution of food, actual serving during the meal, and probably cleaning up afterward. Such eucharistic table sharing, according to the Lukan summary statement in 2:46, took place 'day by day.'"[44] From this she concludes that it is possible "that the conflict between the Hellenists and the Hebrews involved the role and participation of women at the eucharistic meal."[45]

The reference to Luke's summary notice in 2:46 is important and helpful. We could also cite 2:42 and 4:35 in this sense. Luke attempts to paint a picture of unity and solidarity in the Jerusalem community. If any of the signs of cohesion that characterize this community (see 2:42) were to be neglected or destroyed, the unity of the community of saints would be damaged. If widows are neglected in the daily *diakonia*, that is a sign that there are deep conflicts within this community that is of "one heart and soul" (4:32). Thus it seems to me that daily *diakonia* should not be restricted either to the daily distribution of food to those in need or to community meals: it refers to a much more comprehensive "service," as described also in Matt. 25:35-40. All took an active part in this service (Acts 2:42-47). The ignoring or neglect of the Hellenist widows could thus apply both to the daily distribution and to active participation in the "cultic" activities that were part of the daily life of this community. Their daily life was their religious life. However, the fact that this everyday living was not as free of tension as Luke's account makes it appear at first glance is evident from the stories of Sapphira and Ananias and that of the Hellenist widows. It is striking, in this connection, that women are explicitly named precisely when and where such conflicts appear in Luke's narrative and are explicitly named. The widows are mentioned in connection with a crisis in the community that directly affects those who are engaged in the distribution of community goods to those in need (4:35).

The Persecution of Women and Men (8:3)

Acts 8:3 says that "Saul was ravaging the church by entering house after house; dragging off both men and women, he committed them to prison." According to v. 4, this persecution of Christians was followed by a scattering of many throughout Samaria. Thus 8:3 creates a bridge between the Jerusalem community of saints and the spread of Jewish-Christian belief beyond Jerusalem. What is especially significant about Saul's persecution of Christians in Jerusalem, therefore, is that it brought about an important change. One result of persecution is exile, but the exiles reorganized themselves and preached the gospel of Jesus Christ.

Another important observation is that this is the next mention of women in Acts. No woman appears in the whole of the "Stephen story" (6:8—8:2), but this story of the first martyr is immediately followed by this notice about the many female and male victims (8:1-4). This shows that women were already there during the whole story of Stephen, but the interest of the author was to concentrate the portrayal of the theological self-concept of a number of Jerusalem sisters and brothers—many of them from the Jewish diaspora (6:9)—in the narrative and speech of Stephen. The martyrdom of Stephen can be dated to the years 32–34.[46] Thus we can derive from it a dating for the "great persecution" of the sisters and brothers in Jerusalem.

The conflicts surrounding the community of the saints in Jerusalem were increasing. The last previous mention of women was in the context of an intracommunity conflict (6:1) that was solved at the same level. But now the frame expands, and there is no longer a positive solution to be found at the local level. The sisters and brothers must flee, or rather, they are driven out of Jerusalem. Paul now appears for the first time in Acts, in the context of this persecution (8:1-3), accompanied by the first use of the word διωγμός, "persecution." It is supposed to have been very "severe," so that "all" (except the apostles) were scattered throughout Judea and Samaria. The adjective "severe" indicates the intensity of the persecution, as is then explained in v. 3: "But Saul was ravaging the church by entering house after house; dragging off both men and women, he committed them to prison."

Several groups of people are mentioned in 8:1-3: v. 1 emphasizes the scattering of all except the apostles; v. 2 asserts that "devout men" buried Stephen (in Jerusalem);[47] and v. 3 emphasizes the pursuit of people into their houses, with Paul dragging out both women and men and throwing them into prison. Scholars have pointed out that it appears from the wider context (6:1-7; 8:4-5; 11:19-20) that those who are scattered are the Hellenists, i.e., "the Greek-speaking part of the community that was critical of the Law."[48] This can be taken as a suggestion for interpretation. In any case, it is correct to say that not all the Jewish Christian sisters and brothers were driven out of the city, because there continued to be house churches there (8:3; 12:12-17).

Saul's violence is powerfully emphasized here. Women are not excepted from his vicious attacks.[49] Saul the persecutor forced his way into houses, that is, into the sphere that was central to the life of the community of the saints: this was the place where they broke bread (2:46), the place where, in addition to the Temple, they taught and preached (5:42), the place where the sisters and brothers gathered (12:12-17). According to Jürgen Roloff, Saul as the "principal agent of the persecution . . . searched houses and threw the Christians he found there into prison."[50] On the one hand, it is pleasant to observe that in interpreting this text exegetes admit to the existence of dictatorial political tactics such as "searching houses." On the other hand, it is deeply disappointing to see them omit any consideration of the women, especially in the reading of this passage in Acts 8:3. They speak of "Christians" and "Hellenists" (both terms in the masculine in German), even though the text is careful to mention both women and men.[51] It is another matter when Acts 9:13 characterizes the women and men persecuted by Paul in Jerusalem as "saints," for that enables us to read other passages that speak of the "saints," or use similar terms, as including both women and men. The persecuted women and men are saints.

Saul himself is the persecutor. Nothing is said of anyone else having carried out the persecution, so that Paul could be understood to be "only" the supervisor or commander of an attack group: "He *is* the persecution *in person*."[52] The result of Paul's conversion is that the early Christian communities enjoy a period of peace (9:31). Luke emphasizes this again in Acts 26:9-23, in Paul's speech before King Agrippa. It is crucial also, in the last analysis, that Paul himself does not deny this fact. He confirms it in 1 Cor. 15:9 and Phil. 3:6, where he describes those he persecuted as "the church of God." That in Acts 8:1-3 he had already received authority from the high priest to capture Christians and bind them (as in 9:1) is possible, but cannot be determined with certainty.

The purpose of the persecution was the destruction of the Jewish Christian community in Jerusalem, but the repressive tactics adopted and applied by Paul had exactly the opposite effect to what was intended. What was dispersed was not destroyed, but grew with renewed energy (8:4-8). The communities were scattered, but not extinguished. In this context the word διασπείρομαι, "to be scattered," can even be an expression of hope in persecution, because it awakens associations with the "scattering" or "sowing" of seed.[53]

Men and Women Are Baptized (8:12)

In the wake of the dispersion, the missionary work of those scattered spread Jewish Christian belief throughout the region of Samaria. There women and men were baptized by Philip because they believed in the reign of God that he preached, and in the name of Jesus Christ. It was not just "the Samaritans" who were baptized,[54] but (some) Samaritan women and men now confessed the Jewish Christian faith.

Men and Women Put in Danger by Saul (9:1-31)

In their flight from Saul's persecution, some of the believers reached Damascus. Although considerable numbers of disciples were in Damascus (vv. 1 and 19), the only one mentioned by name is Ananias (vv. 10-17). Saul traveled to Damascus to expand his persecution. He was following on the heels of those who had been scattered. At this point the notice that both women and men were affected by his actions is repeated. Every woman and every man he found belonging to "the way" would be bound and brought to Jerusalem. In v. 2 it is again clear that the μαθητὰς τοῦ κυρίου mentioned in vv. 1 and 19 include both women and men: they are all disciples of the Lord Jesus Christ. Paul did not travel alone to Damascus, but took some men with him (9:7-8). This makes the situation of the persecuted seem even more threatening. We should emphasize that "Saul himself, not the unnamed High Priest

. . . is the driving spirit of the persecution;"[55] Paul only receives "letters" from the High Priest to the synagogues, giving him authority to act. In the context of the journey to Damascus, vv. 4-5 acquire an unusual theological-ecclesiological relevance: The risen Jesus intervenes in the course of events on behalf of his community. The question he addresses to Saul shows how Jesus identifies with the community of the saints: "Saul, Saul, why do you persecute me?" (9:4; cf. v. 5). What is done to the disciples because of their confession of Christ is done to Jesus himself![56] "Persecuting me" is synonymous with persecuting Christians.

Mary, the Mother of John Mark, and Rhoda the Slave (12:12-17)

Acts 12 tells of conflicts between the Christians and the powerful ruler Herod Agrippa I. He behaved viciously toward them: James, the brother of John, was killed with the sword, an event that recalls the murder of John the Baptist by Herod Antipas (Matt. 14:6-12). Herod Agrippa I also has Peter arrested (Acts 12:3), but Peter is delivered from prison and goes to the house of Mary, the mother of John (Mark). It seems to me important for the context to observe that the death of King Herod Agrippa I is not directly connected with the liberation of Peter from prison. It happens later, during a speech the king is making without having given glory to God. Luke, however, joins vv. 1-23 within a compositional unit, thus apparently interpreting the king's death retrospectively in terms of his wicked deeds (vv. 1-3). The death of Herod and the periods of persecution could be separated in time. King Herod Agrippa I died in the year 44 C.E.; his actions against some members of the Jewish-Christian community can be dated as early as the year 41.[57] According to 12:3, the king's behavior is meant to appease the Jews. "After he saw that it pleased the Jews, he proceeded to arrest Peter also," intending to bring him before the people after the Passover feast (v. 4). The following verses list details of Peter's imprisonment. He was not alone in his prison cell: he was kept under guard, and the community continued in constant prayer for him (vv. 4-5); during the night before the day on which Herod intended to bring him out, he slept between two soldiers, and was bound with two chains, while other soldiers stationed before the door kept watch (v. 6); nevertheless an angel came to him. This last observation indicates that God has heard the prayer of the community. Peter is then delivered from the prison.

In the next scene, Peter comes to the house of Mary, the mother of John Mark.[58] It is striking that Mary is not described with reference to her husband, but to a son. This may indicate that there were a number of Marys in the community. Describing her as the mother of John Mark can, however, indicate as well that both of them were very important in the spread of the Jewish-Christian faith. We learn more of her son later (12:25; 13:5, 13; 15:37; cf. Col. 4:10; 2 Tim. 4:11; Phlm. 24; 1 Pet. 5:13).

There, in Mary's house, many people are gathered to pray (v. 12): this illustrates what was said in v. 5. They are not praying individually, but together. This, in turn, corresponds to the picture of the community in Acts 2:42-47. And all this takes place in Mary's house. When Peter arrives, it is still night; this, in turn, conveys the idea of the persistence of the community's continual prayer. Not only that: they are gathered in the Passover night, for worship (συναθροίζω, cf. Luke 24:33). These women and men certainly have many events and many people to call to memory. *Memory also incorporates present events in the prayer.* It may even be that they have gathered in the place where they assembled after the ascension of Jesus (1:14—2:4), and that this is the reason why Peter went to that house.[59]

According to v. 13, Peter comes there and knocks on the door in the outer gate (πυλῶνος, "gate house"). There is consensus that the πυλών is a "gateway which separated the courtyard from the street."[60] But Gottfried Schille, for example, denies that this requires us to interpret ὑπακούειν as a description of the action of the παιδίσκη ("slave woman," "maidservant") in "answering" the door as being "used technically for the task of the doorkeeper."[61] The statement of the text is clear: Mary has a house in which "many" can gather; nothing is said about its actual size.[62] The single reference to a πυλών seems to me too little to permit us to conclude that Mary had great wealth, especially since it is also said that the house of Simon the tanner had a πυλών (10:19). In the latter case, however, exegetes utter not a word about any supposed wealth of the despised tanner!

> The case of John 18:17 may be different: Here we read of a slave who is a doorkeeper (ἡ θυρωρός), but the text speaks not of a πυλών, but of a door. Still, as early as v. 15 it is clear that it is referring to the palace (!) of the high priest. This passage is, incidentally, the only one in the New Testament in which the feminine article is used with θυρωρός; otherwise it is men who do this work: Mark 13:34; John 10:3.

In Mary's house there is a παιδίσκη, a "slave woman." The text does not say that Mary is her owner. If she was Mary's slave, opening the door may have been one of her tasks, but it need not have been her sole occupation. Much more important than this discussion, it seems to me, is the observation that the master-slave relationship is not expressed in the story, in sharp contrast to Acts 16:16-19. The slave woman Rhoda behaves as if she were not a slave. According to v. 14 she recognized Peter's voice, which indicates that she knew him well. She may have heard him teaching. Thus the slave woman Rhoda was not someone separate from the group of those who were gathered together. Her membership in the community may also be reflected in her great joy at seeing Peter again. In her joy, she ran into the house, forgetting to open the door. Is that a likely reaction on the part of someone whose responsibility it was to guard and open the door? Verse 15 also reflects something other than the ordinary master-slave relationship: Although the people inside do not believe the slave woman's statement that Peter has come, it is not because she is a slave; it is because the news she brings them is incredible in itself.[63] To stare a miracle (Peter's liberation from prison) in the face: that is just unbelievable! The slave woman stuck to her assertion, even though the others called her "crazy" (v. 15). She is determined to succeed, for the sake of the truth; she holds out against all those who do not believe her. She fights for her right to see the truth before all the others. A slave woman asserts herself in Mary's house! This fact indicates that she had a "space" in which to do so. It says that in this community in Mary's house the barriers between masters and slaves were broken down; here there are neither slaves nor masters/ mistresses, but all are one in Christ Jesus (Gal. 3:28). The narrative shows that the slave woman was right: Peter was really there, and he finally entered, saw his sisters and brothers again, and then departed. Before he left, however, he asked that the story of his deliverance be told to James and the "brethren." According to Elisabeth Schüssler Fiorenza, this brief note in the text means that "they [i.e., James and the 'brethren'] were not present at the meeting."[64] She therefore concludes that only Hellenists were members of this house church. Even if that was not the case, it is clear from the text that a community gathered in Jerusalem at Mary's house, and we may certainly conclude from this that Mary was engaged in the daily work of organization and preaching.

A last, very important, but only briefly indicated idea is contained in 12:18-19. The whole community of the saints in Jerusalem must already have known about Peter's deliverance by the next morning. The soldiers were in commotion, because they were in great danger. They were responsible for the prisoners, and when Herod's people could not find

Peter the guards were tortured and finally, at the king's orders, put to death. In other words, they were personally responsible for their prisoners. When Herod learned that Peter had escaped from prison, he had the soldiers "led away," which in this case means being led away to execution, just as Jesus was "led away" (Luke 23:26). Failure to carry out their duty meant capital punishment for the guards.[65] In saying this, Luke is not simply emphasizing the great cruelty of Herod; rather, the account corresponds to reality. This explains the panic of the guards in Acts 16:23-24, 27. But in this account of the cruel law of the ruling order a tiny spark of solidarity emerges: after Peter's deliverance, Herod and his soldiers were not able to discover where he was hiding. In this point, the community held together: no one betrayed the fugitive Peter. There were no denunciations within this group; they remained steadfast (see Luke 16–18), and after the death of Herod, the word continued to spread.

The Witnesses to the Risen One
"to the Ends of the Earth" (1:8): 13:1—28:31

I indicated above, on pp. 230–31, the reasons why I am treating the passages that follow according to the commonly accepted outline of Acts. Paul is undoubtedly the principal figure in the second major portion of the book of Acts. During his missionary journeys, he encounters many disciples of the Lord who worked independently, before and after him. In his missionary activity, Paul always begins in the synagogue communities: As a Jew, he first goes to people living according to the Jewish way of life (for more detail on this topic, see chapter 3, on Lydia in Acts 16:13-15). In the course of his work he met women in various contexts outside Palestine. Now I want to say something more specific about these women, who are explicitly mentioned and sometimes even named.

Paul's First Missionary Journey (13:1—14:28)

The Devout Women of High Standing
in Antioch (13:50)

This is the first passage in which Luke explicitly mentions women in the Pauline mission: "But the Jews incited the devout women of high standing and the leading men of the city, and stirred up persecution against Paul and Barnabas, and drove them out of their region." Thus from 9:41 to 13:50 we have been immersed in a language, or style of historical writing, that refers to women and men together under androcentric terms. There were certainly also women present in Salamis (13:15-16) and here in Pisidian Antioch (13:14-16, 42-43, 44, 48) before they appear in 13:50, for this is not the first context in which "the devout," or "god-fearers," a group that always included many women,[66] have appeared. They have already been seen in 13:43, where they followed Paul: that is, they believed in Jesus Christ. But at 13:50 women are concretely mentioned, because the intention is to emphasize something special: this is the first reaction against Paul within the context of the synagogue.[67] Luke asserts that "the Jews incited" two groups of people in the city. Whatever the action in question may have been, *not all* the god-fearers were stirred up (cf. v. 43), but only the women of high standing among them; an aloof attitude is thus established toward these women. A particular group within the city's upper classes comes together to act against this spreading popular movement (vv. 44-45, 48). Therefore it is important to Luke to say that these were the devout women *of high standing* and the *leading men* of the city. He is using sociological categories here: The women of high standing belong to the upper social class of the city, probably the noble families,[68] while the "leading men of the city" were "those who were socially prominent by birth or office or a significant degree of wealth."[69] There is no reason to suppose that these women of high standing were the wives or mothers of the "leading men of the city," as recently asserted by Jürgen Roloff and José Comblin.[70] There were, as we have already demonstrated above, social groups who were able to make their influence felt at the city level. They do not confess faith in Jesus Christ, and they do not join his community. Instead, according to Luke's account, they combine against it and cause Paul and Barnabas to leave the place. The disciples, however, remain in the city (v. 52), filled with joy and the Holy Spirit. In spite of persecution by the important people in the city, a "flourishing community" remains behind.[71]

Paul's Second Missionary Journey (15:36—18:22)

During Paul's first missionary journey there was mention of a group of devout women of high standing who acted against Paul and Barnabas. Nothing was said about any woman during the "apostolic council" in Jerusalem, which undertook the "regulation of the Gentile mission"[72] (15:1-33). On the other hand, many individual women are mentioned during Paul's second missionary journey. This is probably connected with the fact that 15:36—18:22 describes the principal episodes in Paul's propagation of the gospel. Here we find the most conversion accounts, and here Paul very often comes into contact with people who practiced the Jewish religion although they were not Jews: the proselytes and, in particular, the god-fearers.

The Jewish Woman Who Was a Believer (16:1)

In Lystra lived a Jewish woman believer whose name has been lost to the book of Acts. She and her Greek husband are mentioned only because of their son, who had become widely known through his participation in the Pauline mission. The mother of Timothy is mentioned because Jewish mothers bring up their children in the Jewish faith and teach it to them. The dominant exegetical opinion is that the phrase "a Jewish woman who was a believer" means that this Jewish woman had become a Christian. The adjective "believing" is said to be synonymous with Christian belief.[73] But she could also have been a Jewish believer, that is, a woman who did not have to separate herself from her Jewish faith, not even when she, together with her son, confessed the risen Christ—otherwise, Luke would no longer call her a "Jewish woman." The mother of Timothy, whose name Luke does not know, is also mentioned in 2 Tim. 1:5, along with his grandmother: the mother's name is Eunice. Here it is also emphasized that she stands within a very strong tradition of faith, within which she raised Timothy, who has been of service to so many. Timothy's line of descent is very closely bound up with his upbringing, for which his mother was responsible.[74]

"Not a Few of the Leading Women" of Thessalonica (17:4)

The Pauline mission had already been at work for a long time. Many people had accepted the Jewish Christian faith. Several conflicts with rulers and leadership groups had taken place. Paul and Silas's "missionary method" was the same everywhere: They entered a city and made contact with the Jewish population, going repeatedly to the synagogue and preaching. At this point they are in Thessalonica, a city near the Roman colony in Philippi (16:11-40). As elsewhere, a conversion takes place in the context of the synagogue, but a special detail is the emphasis on a particular social group: not a few of the "leading women" join Paul and Silas. Luke and the tradition have found it necessary to accent this fact, which means in the first instance that the conversion of such groups was not a matter of course (see 13:50!).[75]

"Not a Few Greek Women . . . of High Standing"
in Beroea (17:12)
Here we find a conversion story similar to that in 17:4, again concerning a group of god-fearing women of high standing. This time, men are also mentioned. Thus in Thessalonica and Beroea we for the first time encounter the report that not a few of the leading women, persons of high standing, have accepted the Jewish-Christian faith. This fact, so deliberately stated, is restricted to these two cities. The passages at 13:50; 17:4, 12 show that Luke makes a clear emphasis when the "newly-converted" include high-ranking or well-to-do people. In addition, it is striking that in Acts, in contrast to the Gospel, Luke does not use the word πλούσιος, "rich," and its cognates even once. He substitutes the words εὐσχήμων, "of high standing" (13:50; 17:12), and πρῶτος, "first," "leading" (13:50; 17:4), which indicate social rank. These two groups—those of high standing and those described as "leading"—cannot be equated, as we saw above in the discussion of 13:50.[76] While in 13:50 this leadership class in the city arose against Paul and Barnabas, now some of them adopt belief in Jesus as the Messiah. Luise Schottroff[77] emphasizes that "it is not remarkable here that women are mentioned in the first place but that upper-class men are won over at all." Ernst Haenchen[78] correctly observes that, nevertheless, the women are unable to avert the reaction by some of the Jews of Thessalonica and Beroea who stirred up "the people."

Damaris on the Areopagus at Athens (17:34)
Acts 17:34 contains a report of conversions: "But some of [the people] joined him and became believers, including Dionysius the Areopagite and a woman named Damaris, and others with them." The "brethren" having managed to get Paul out of Beroea (vv. 14-15), some of them have accompanied him to Athens, where he argues both in the synagogue and in the marketplace (v. 17). He comes into contact with some of the Epicurean and Stoic philosophers who want to know more details about the "new teaching" (ἡ καινή . . . διδαχή, v. 19). Verse 21 asserts that the Athenians, as well as the foreigners living in Athens, were especially interested in telling or hearing new things. Paul then stands up before the Areopagus[79] and makes a long speech. Although he addresses the crowd as "men of Athens" (ἄνδρες Ἀθηναῖοι), there are also women present, as is clear especially from v. 34. It is therefore necessary to read the whole story in light of the last verse. The fact that Damaris is mentioned alongside Dionysius the Areopagite[80] attests also

to her own significance in that circle. As a result, alterations have been made in the text to deny the existence of Damaris. Codex D reads: ". . . including *an Areopagite of high standing* and others with them." It omits Damaris and makes the Areopagite a man of high standing. Codex E does not deny Damaris's existence, but adds that she was τίμια, "respected." Exegetes have also made Damaris the wife of Dionysius, beginning with John Chrysostom.[81] Even those who are mentioned after Damaris in v. 34 "may have been part of their families or circle of acquaintances."[82] This implicitly says that this woman, Damaris, would not have been able to come to the Areopagus on her own in order to participate in the discussions there.

However, there were women philosophers. When, for example, Euripides[83] says that a mother has instructed her children in philosophy and cosmology, this means that she herself must have been instructed in those subjects. Klaus Thraede concludes from his investigation of the educational opportunities of women that Greek women in particular were able to study and even to write books. He lists a great number of women who were philosophers. Important in our context is his statement that "it was known particularly of the Epicureans that they favored women as students [!] and even as teachers [!]. . . . The Stoa also considered the possibility of female membership, as demanded by its fundamental rule of equality."[84] However, the opposition to such women must have been very strong, especially from educated men. For example, Livy writes:

> What sort of practice is this, of running out into the streets and blocking the roads and speaking to other women's husbands? . . . Our ancestors permitted no woman to conduct even personal business without a guardian to intervene in her behalf; they wished them to be under the control of fathers, brothers, husbands; we (Heaven help us!) allow them now even to interfere in public affairs, yes, and to visit the Forum, and our informal and formal sessions.[85]

Monika Eichenauer[86] has collected material on women who engaged in philosophical study and even taught.

It is wonderful that at least this tiny bit of information is retained in Acts 17:34. It was possible for philosophically engaged women to join early Christianity, in whatever form, for, because of her independence and her association with the Areopagus, Damaris should be regarded as a philosopher. It is marvelous that we can conclude from this that such women were also able to devote themselves to the service of God's righteousness (17:31) in the Christian community of equals.

Paul's Third Missionary Journey (18:23—21:16)

Taking Leave of the Men, Women, and Children in Tyre (21:5-6)

It is striking that no woman is explicitly mentioned in the account of the third missionary journey, even though Paul traveled through regions where he had previously been and visited communities founded by his mission: not even when further conversions are mentioned, as in 19:18, and in Macedonia, of all places, where so many women had come to believe in Jesus Christ and were actively working for the gospel (e.g., 16:13-15; 17:4, 12). The account of the third missionary journey is silent about them (see esp. 20:1-5). But the content of 21:5-6 again demands that we consider women always present in the preceding accounts. Here they are mentioned because the text wants to make clear that the *whole* community, without exception, takes part in the great farewell to Paul. The text thus shows that it takes for granted the existence of women and children in the communities, and it only needs some special reason to mention them at any given point.

The Four Prophetic Women of Caesarea (21:9)

Although Acts has spoken several times about Philip (6:5; 8:5, 26-40), his daughters, the four virgin prophets, are now mentioned for the first time, at the end of Paul's missionary activity. The information about them is very sparse. According to the passages just cited, these four prophets must belong to those who were driven out of Jerusalem. They have therefore taken part in the proclamation of the gospel. Even though they are very briefly mentioned in 21:9, we find there some important information about them, for example that they were "virgins" who were active as prophets. It is possible that they were so well known that Luke could not avoid mentioning them.[87]

Philip's four daughters are described as παρθένοι, "virgins." It is difficult to determine whether this simply means "unmarried,"[88] or "girls of marriageable age,"[89] or whether it refers to a necessary condition for prophetic activity.[90] According to Eusebius[91] at least one of Philip's four daughters was married. They should be regarded as women in whom the Old Testament prophecy has been fulfilled by the working of the Holy Spirit (Acts 2:18).[92] Virginity is often connected with prophecy, not only outside Christianity, but within it as well.[93] Other women and men in later prophetic-ascetical movements drew inspiration from women like Anna (Luke 2:36-38) and the four daughters of Philip.[94] Origen opposed them, arguing (against biblical texts like Luke 2:36-38) that "these women prophets did not speak in public or in the assemblies, but only in private."[95] The struggle against prophetic women reached a climax in the third century, when "what was at stake was not a doctrinal issue but a competition between radically different church structures and Christian self-understandings."[96] This struggle had certainly begun as early as the end of the first century,[97] but there is no trace of it in Acts 21:8-9. Although in vv. 10-14 it is Agabus who prophesies, and not the women, I see the reason for this in the fact that he had come directly from Judea and could give prophetic interpretation to the situation in Jerusalem. It is not a case of competition between the two prophetic parties.

Women Mentioned During Paul's Captivity and Trial (21:17—28:31)

No other women from the Christian community are mentioned in this section, except for a few who are recalled by Paul at 22:4. There are no more accounts of conversion in this last major section; instead, it is entirely concentrated on Paul, his defense, and his activity in Rome. However, in 28:23, 30-31, for example, we may presume the presence of women, in harmony with Rom. 16:1-16.

Recollection of Persecuted Women and Men (22:4)

In Paul's defense speech before the Jewish people (21:40—22:21) he refers to his own past, including his persecution of men and women and taking them prisoner, as reported in 8:3 and 9:2, 14. The women appear here in Paul's memory, alongside the men, at the time when he persecuted them because of their faith. Now he finds himself in a similar situation and seeks to defend himself.

Paul's Sister (23:16)

Paul is imprisoned in a barracks (23:10). In this situation, we learn for the first time that he has a sister. In v. 16 it is said that "the son of Paul's sister" comes into the barracks to tell him that an ambush is being planned for him (see vv. 12-15). We learn nothing more of the sister; instead, it is the nephew who plays the important role here.[98]

Drusilla, the Wife of Felix the Governor (24:24)

Luke first mentions Drusilla in v. 24 in the overall context of Paul's hearing before the governor and his imprisonment in Caesarea

(24:1-27). She is described as Felix's wife, and as a Jew. She accompanies her husband into Herod's praetorium, where Paul is held prisoner (23:35; 24:23). We know more about her through Josephus:[99] She had been married to King Azizus of Emesa, but Felix arranged for her to be divorced and married to himself, though he was not a Jew. She was his third wife. Although Acts 24:24 is brief, it gives some of the same details. The fact that Luke depicts her as present here indicates that she will also listen to Paul's speech:[100] He discusses justice, self-control, and the coming judgment of God, but vv. 25b-26 report only the reaction of Felix. Drusilla, who was also a sister of Agrippa II and Bernice,[101] does not play any active role according to this account.[102]

Bernice, the Wife of King Agrippa II (25:13, 23; 26:30)

Two years have passed, and Paul is still a prisoner (24:27). Felix has been replaced by Festus as governor. Paul has appealed to the emperor (25:10-11); that is, according to Luke's account he wishes to be tried by the emperor's court in Rome. In the mean time, King Agrippa II and his wife, Bernice,[103] come to Caesarea to visit Festus. Only after they have been there several days do they learn about Paul. In 25:22, Agrippa expresses an interest in hearing Paul. The king and Bernice come on the next day and, accompanied by the military tribunes and the prominent men of the city, enter the audience hall (v. 23). During the following scene and Paul's defense speech, only King Agrippa and Festus, the governor, are addressed, but 26:30 shows that Bernice was present the whole time. Neither Drusilla nor Bernice says a single word, nor do they decide anything. They probably exercise no influence on the events. According to 26:31, Agrippa, Bernice, and all the others are aware that the prisoner, Paul, does not deserve to die because of his Jewish-Christian missionary activity, but the process is not stopped.[104] None of the powerful people in Caesarea is won over to accept the gospel of justice, self-control, and hope for the coming judgment of God (see 24:25; 26:20, 24-28) by Paul's final missionary attempt there (see vv. 26, 28-29).

Summary and Retrospect

Many women adopted the (Jewish) Christian faith: many working and traveling women, and other women who were learned, women who had high standing in their communities. According to Luke's account in Acts, there was one group of women (and men) who were not brought to faith in Christ and solidarity with the believers: the small, but powerful group of the ruling class. Paul had indeed preached the word before kings and queens (see 9:15 and chs. 24–26), but he had no "success" with them. They did not believe the word of justice and resurrection.

Acts does not give a unified picture of women, because these women did not constitute a unit. They lived in different regions and different cultures. They were interested in different ways of life and made their own decisions about whether they would accept them or not. We encounter them in different life-contexts, where they are mentioned as being in agreement with or at a distance from those who confessed Jesus Christ.

Acts must be read critically, from the point of view of a feminist theology of liberation, especially under the following aspect: like all the New Testament writings, it is couched in androcentric language, which causes women to disappear. This problem can be overcome, however, simply by reading the whole Lukan text from the perspective of those passages in which women are explicitly mentioned. Normally, women are brought to the fore in the context of conversions, but they are also mentioned frequently in connection with another significant topos in Acts: namely, in the persecutions that led to the expulsion of many from Jerusalem! These exiles settled in other places and preached the good news. Out of the attempt to destroy the power of the Spirit that was at work in everyday life emerged a new power, one that planted the seeds of a righteous life in many other places. Among the exiles who preached the word there were certainly women. This can be asserted in retrospect, in light of Acts 21:9. The four prophets, the daughters of Philip the evangelist, are the last women mentioned in the major section 13:1— 28:31. This makes it clear that the mention of them is of central importance. It makes concrete the fact that women were always present, in the work of proclamation as well. Acts 21:9 links with 8:3-4. When 8:4-8 tells of the beginning of Philip's missionary activity in the city of Samaria, and then in Caesarea (v. 40), this can also mean that his four daughters were equally active in prophesying. Their fame was very great, and is attested in writing. In addition, women belonged to the community of the saints from the very beginning, as attested in 1:14. We may conclude from Acts 2:17-21 that some of them were prophetic missionaries. All were filled with the Holy Spirit. The promise, or prophetic hope, in Joel 3:1-5 was fulfilled: daughters and sons prophesied! The beginning of the Jewish-Christian community of equals and the end of Paul's missionary activity are thus connected by the prophetic work of women.

Acts needs to be read critically. This is especially true with regard to women's work of preaching. Luke does not speak *expressis verbis* even once of women preaching or working as missionaries, with the exception of the passages cited above about women prophets. The silence about women like Mary Magdalene or Thecla is unequivocal proof that Luke's historical writing has suppressed them. Whether it was a question of power struggles or not, Luke's work is incomplete. It should not be called "the Acts of the Apostles," for it concentrates almost exclusively on Peter and Paul.

And yet the very mention of independent women, named apart from any connection with men, also shows that these women were heads of house churches. They, too, bore principal responsibility for "their" house church. Their houses were important centers of the mission, to the extent that they offered space, support, and leadership for missionary movements like Paul's. But that was not the only source of their importance. They worked, both for the word of God and to earn their living. They were active in their trades and professions and simultaneously in the mission. We know from Paul's letters that these and other women were equal in rank to Paul himself; they were his fellow-workers and fought equally hard for the gospel. Therefore we can adopt a critical stance toward Luke's account, and yet we need not abandon the important information to be found there, nor should we be silent about it or neglect it, even when we criticize Luke for playing down the role of women as missionaries and church leaders. There is a significant slice of women's history contained in the Acts of the Apostles, but it must be read in conjunction with, and augmented by, other accounts, both Pauline and apocryphal.

Notes

1. The other passages from which certain details about the life and activities of women can be gleaned have already been treated separately. These were the stories of Sapphira, Tabitha, Lydia, the prophetic slave girl, and Priscilla.

2. Elisabeth Schüssler Fiorenza expresses this as follows: "Rather than reject the argument from silence as a valid historical argument, we must learn to read the silences of androcentric texts in such a way that they can provide 'clues' to the egalitarian reality of the early Christian movement" (*In Memory of Her*, 41).

3. The translation follows that in Luise Schottroff, "Mary Magdalene," 173. Schottroff explains the translation as follows: "At least in Mark's view, four (not three) women are mentioned. Mary the wife (or daughter) of James the

[younger] . . . has to be distinguished from Mary (15:47) the mother of Joses (15:40) . . ." (pp. 173–74).

4. Ibid., 169.

5. E. Schüssler Fiorenza, *In Memory of Her*, 44–45.

6. On this, see ch. 3 on Lydia, pp. 93–98.

7. For the women prophets as "contentious, Spirit-filled fighters" in the Christian tradition, see L. and W. Schottroff, "Hanna," 44.

8. See E. Schüssler Fiorenza, *In Memory of Her*, 44–48.

9. For the importance of Mary Magdalene as a disciple and apostle, see the following note.

10. For Mary Magdalene, see the *Gospel of Peter* 12–13, and the *Gospel of Mary*; for Thecla, see the *Acts of Paul and Thecla*; for the widow Lemma and her daughter Ammia, who joined Paul on his journeys to proclaim the gospel, see W. Schneemelcher, *New Testament Apocrypha* 2:387–90, the translation of an unpublished Coptic papyrus by R. Kasser. It mentions Priscilla and Aquila, and also Procla, a woman in Ephesus who was baptized by Paul, together with her household. She also presided over a house church.

11. On this, see, e.g., P. Vielhauer, *Geschichte*, 380–81; slightly different is R. Pesch, *Apostelgeschichte* 1:36ff.

12. J. Roloff, *Apostelgeschichte*, 27–28.

13. R. Pesch, *Apostelgeschichte* 1:78.

14. Ibid., 81.

15. BAGD s.v. καταμένω; see also Hauck, "μένω, κτλ," *TDNT* 4:574–88.

16. See the examples in Billerbeck 2:594–95; also the discussion of Acts 9:37 on pp. 41–44 above.

17. Quentin Quesnell, "Supper," 59ff., shows that Luke imagines a large group of women and men, not merely the twelve, in the "upper room" (ἀνάγαιον, Luke 22:12; ὑπερῷον, Acts 1:13) beginning at Luke 22:12.

18. See R. Pesch, *Apostelgeschichte* 1:81; J. Roloff, *Apostelgeschichte*, 28.

19. This phrase is from G. Lüdemann, *Traditions*, 27.

20. Thus, e.g., J. Roloff, *Apostelgeschichte*, 28; see also E. Haenchen, *Acts*, 154; R. Pesch, *Apostelgeschichte* 1:81; J. Comblin, *Atos* 1:83–84.

21. E.g., G. Lüdemann, *Traditions*, 27, emphasizes the redactional addition of the women mentioned in v. 14 and sees a great deal of probability in Codex D's suggestion that they are to be thought of as the apostles' wives, especially since it must have been known to the community "that the apostles had wives."

22. On this, see especially L. Schottroff, "Women as Disciples," 91–105; idem, "Mary Magdalene," 178–79.

23. For an interpretation of the participation of women in the story of Jesus' passion and resurrection, see L. Schottroff, "Mary Magdalene," 168–94.

24. R. Pesch, *Apostelgeschichte* 1:88, 90 considers the concepts of *diakonia* and apostolate as synonymous. For a discussion of the "twelve apostles," see, e.g., ibid., pp. 92–97. Pesch correctly sees that the "Lukan" criterion for aposto-

licity means being "'eyewitness[es]' (Luke 1:1) to 'everything Jesus did and taught' (Acts 1:1)." But in this connection, Pesch does not refer to the group of women who were witnesses. As regards the concept of *diakonia*, L. Schottroff ("Mary Magdalene," 176–78) has pointed out that it is historically incorrect, in considering early Christian relationships, to make a distinction between "women's and men's offices" with regard to *diakonia*. Nevertheless, we need to investigate more thoroughly why the text of Acts 1:15-26 restricts itself to men precisely at the point where what is at issue is undertaking the task of proclamation. On this, see pp. 195–97 above.

25. Thus, e.g., R. Pesch, *Apostelgeschichte* 1:205. See the survey of research in E. Haenchen, *Acts*, 243–46.

26. Similarly E. Haenchen, *Acts*, 245. It appears that G. Schille, A*postelgeschichte*, 157, is also thinking along these lines. He believes that v. 15 further develops the thought of v. 14, in the sense that "the community . . . is [increasing] so much in size that, similarly to Mark 2:2, it is no longer possible to convey the sick people who have been brought to it into the available space."

27. On the various attempts to remove one or more whole verses in order to make sense of the text, see E. Haenchen, *Acts*, 243–46.

28. For the topic of "Hebrew and Hellenist Jews," see E. Haenchen, *Acts*, 260–61, n. 3; M. Hengel, *Jesus und Paulus*, 151ff.

29. These Hellenistic Jewish-Christians certainly included many women, because in 21:9 there is further mention of four prophets, the daughters of Philip, who fled from Jerusalem because of Saul's persecution of the Christians. We must suppose that Philip's daughters were also in Jerusalem with him.

30. This is the first time in Acts that the word μαθητής, "disciple," is used. For this word, see pp. 33–36 above (Tabitha as disciple), and Rengstorf, "μαθητής," *TDNT* 4:414–61, esp. 457–59.

31. For the subject of widows generally, see G. Stählin, "Das Bild der Witwe," 5ff., and the review of research in H.-W. Neudorfer, *Stephanuskreis*, esp. 86ff.

32. E. Haenchen, *Acts*, 260.

33. R. Pesch, *Apostelgeschichte* 1:227; see also E. Schüssler Fiorenza, *In Memory of Her*, 162–68; A. Strobel, "Armenpfleger," 271ff. The review of research in H.-W. Neudorfer, *Stephanuskreis*, esp. 86ff., shows that the majority of exegetes argue that it was the "Hebrews" who *deliberately* discriminated against the Hellenist widows. A chronological review shows that this opinion has been upheld for a long time, but was especially strong as a *communis opinio* in the 1940s and 1950s!

34. For this interpretation, see also R. Pesch, *Apostelgeschichte* 1:227.

35. See, e.g., A. Strobel, "Armenpfleger," 271ff.; E. Haenchen, *Acts*, 261; for discussion of this point, see G. Lüdemann, *Traditions*, 73–79.

36. For more detail, and literature, see M. Korenhof, "Witwen," 239–40.

37. See J. Jeremias, *Jerusalem*, Part Two, "Economic Status," 126–34; Billerbeck 2:643ff.

38. A. Strobel, "Armenpfleger," 274; see also J. Jeremias, *Jerusalem*, 131. In addition to this daily service, Judaism also had a weekly institution (*quppāh*) for care of the poor, which provided the local poor with food and clothing every Friday.

39. See, e.g., E. Haenchen, *Acts,* esp. 268; for more on the whole subject, see R. Pesch, *Apostelgeschichte* 1:225ff. For a critique of Luke's "separation" and "mixing" of sources, see G. Schille, *Apostelgeschichte,* 165ff.

40. H. W. Beyer, "διακονέω," *TDNT* 2:81-93, at 84. The next quotation is also from here.

41. Ibid., 84.

42. E. Schüssler Fiorenza, *In Memory of Her,* 165–66; see also her "Dienst," 306ff. For the interpretation of *diakonia,* see also L. Schottroff, "Women as Disciples," esp. 98–99; idem, "Mary Magdalene," 176–78.

43. E. Schüssler Fiorenza, *In Memory of Her,* 165.

44. Ibid.

45. Ibid., 166.

46. Thus J. Roloff, *Apostelgeschichte,* 126; R. Pesch, *Apostelgeschichte* 1:267.

47. G. Schille, *Apostelgeschichte,* 198–99, points out that in reality it would have been impossible for the Christians to carry out a public burial in Jerusalem without endangering themselves, because of the situation of persecution. He thus sees the "devout men" as neutral persons who played a role similar to that of Joseph of Arimathea in Mark 15:42-46. On the danger involved for friends and relatives in burying the victims of persecution, see L. Schottroff, "Mary Magdalene," esp. 172–74, with notes on sources.

48. R. Pesch, *Apostelgeschichte,* 265; J. Roloff, *Apostelgeschichte,* 129. E. Haenchen, *Acts,* 297, thinks that only the "leaders" of the Hellenist group were driven out of the "city of murderers." The argument that it was precisely the Hellenists who constituted the "part of the community that was critical of the Law" should be questioned in light of Acts 7:1-53. What is criticized is not the Law, but particular actions on the part of ruling circles within Judaism.

49. See L. Schottroff, "Mary Magdalene," 172–73. For Roman procedures against Christian women, see F. Augar, "Frau," 5ff.

50. J. Roloff, *Apostelgeschichte,* 130.

51. The same phenomenon may be observed in the works of J. Roloff, R. Pesch, and J. Comblin with regard to this verse.

52. Thus also E. Haenchen, *Acts,* 298.

53. G. Schille, *Apostelgeschichte,* 197.

54. Thus, e.g., R. Pesch, *Apostelgeschichte* 1:274.

55. E. Haenchen, *Acts,* 319–20; thus also R. Pesch, *Apostelgeschichte* 1: 302–3.

56. Cf. Matt. 5:10; 25:40b, 45; Luke 21:12.

57. On this, see R. Pesch, *Apostelgeschichte* 1:368 and 361.

58. Ἔρχομαι + ἐπί with the accusative of the place has, according to BAGD, ἔρχομαι Iαβ (p. 310), the sense of "come to" (Luke 19:5; Acts 12:10, 12).

59. See T. Zahn, *Apostelgeschichte*, 389.

60. H. Conzelmann, *Acts*, 95.

61. G. Schille, *Apostelgeschichte*, 272, asserts that this service was only performed by slave women in exceptional cases; E. Preuschen, *Apostelgeschichte*, 78, thinks we should not imagine that there is a "doorkeeper," because it is night. The assumption that this refers to a porter's service is represented, e.g., by H. Conzelmann, *Acts*, 94–95; R. Pesch, *Apostelgeschichte* 1:366; E. Haenchen, *Acts*, 385; J. Comblin, *Atos*, 213.

62. Exact numbers of persons are absent throughout Acts; ἱκανοί is an indeterminate large number of people (Acts 14:21; 19:19). For the meaning of οἰκία, οἶκος, see pp. 109–14 and 205–208.

63. The response is similar to that in Luke 24:11, 22-23; see L. Schottroff, "Mary Magdalene," esp. 193. That this reaction of disbelief is not restricted to women's words is demonstrated by Acts 26:24!

64. E. Schüssler Fiorenza, *In Memory of Her*, 166.

65. R. Pesch, *Apostelgeschichte* 1:367.

66. On the topic of the "god-fearers," see above, pp. 93–98.

67. For this topic, and for a discussion of the relationship and connection of the (Pauline) mission and the synagogue, see W. Stegemann, "Synagoge," esp. 63ff.

68. One strand of the Syrian tradition, the Sahidic, and Codex C (5th c.), according to T. Zahn, *Apostelgeschichte*, 455 n. 45, translate the word εὐσχήμο-νας as "rich;" the word is then applied to "higher rulers." See the references there.

69. T. Zahn, *Apostelgeschichte*, 455 n. 45; E. Haenchen, *Acts*, 414; R. Pesch, *Apostelgeschichte* 2:47 calls them "the leading officials of the city." These "leading men" are also mentioned in Luke 19:47; Acts 17:4; 25:2; 28:7, 17; *Acts of Paul and Thecla* 11:26–27.

70. J. Roloff, *Apostelgeschichte*, 210; J. Comblin, *Atos*, 36.

71. J. Roloff, *Apostelgeschichte*, 210.

72. I take this phrase from R. Pesch, *Apostelgeschichte* 2:68.

73. Thus R. Pesch, *Apostelgeschichte* 2:96; J. Comblin, *Atos*, 61; E. Haenchen, *Acts*, 478; I. H. Marshall, *Acts*, 259; differently T. Zahn, *Apostelgeschichte* 2:558, who speaks simply of a "believing Jewish woman" educated in the Jewish scriptures; so also H. Conzelmann, *Acts*, 125 only calls her "a Jewish mother."

74. However, the fact that Timothy is the son of a Jewish mother and a Greek father does not necessarily mean that he stems "from a Hellenistic Judaism of a lax type," as G. Schille writes (*Apostelgeschichte*, 332). The question of lineage is treated by Billerbeck 2:741, according to which the legal situation agrees with the present text: children of a marriage between a Jewish woman

and a non-Jew are Jewish; that is, they follow their mother. Hence the report of Timothy's circumcision would also correspond to Jewish law.

75. Codex D and *lat* make these "leading women," mentioned independently of men, into "the wives of the leading men," thus subordinating the women to rich men.

76. H. Conzelmann, *Acts*, 135, believes that the women mentioned in v. 4 are equivalent to those in v. 12; so also E. Haenchen, *Acts*, 507.

77. L. Schottroff, "'Leaders of the Faith,'" 68.

78. E. Haenchen, *Acts*, 507.

79. There has been an extended discussion among scholars about whether the term "Areopagus" refers to a place or an office. According to R. Pesch, *Apostelgeschichte* 2:135, the definitions are: (1) local: the "narrow hill of Ares, a rocky outcropping to the northwest of the Acropolis; (2) official: "the most important official body in imperial Athens." According to J. Roloff, *Apostelgeschichte*, 258, this office was responsible for "education and scientific knowledge." For the status of the discussion, see both these commentators. It is important to emphasize that this scene is not a trial or hearing before a judicial body: Paul is not being accused, but simply asked about the "new teaching." On this, see also W. Elliger, *Paulus*, 173ff.

80. According to J. Roloff, *Apostelgeschichte*, 267, the title "Areopagite" can be understood to mean that he was a "member of the council for education and scientific knowledge."

81. See the reference in R. Pesch, *Apostelgeschichte* 2:141; John Chrysostom, *Sacerdotus* 4.7.

82. R. Pesch, *Apostelgeschichte* 2:141. J. Comblin, however, differs: he thinks that Damaris was an influential woman in the city.

83. See K. Thraede, "Frau," 201.

84. Ibid., 203, with notes on literature and sources.

85. Livy 34.2.8–12. From *Livy with an English Translation in 14 Volumes*, translation by Evan T. Sage. LCL.

86. M. Eichenauer, *Untersuchungen*, esp. 135–36.

87. According to Eph. 4:11 the call of Philip's daughters to prophesy and thus the exercise of their "office" was even more important than that of their father, the evangelist—if Eph. 4:11 describes a hierarchy.

88. Delling, "παρθένος," *TDNT* 5:826–37, at 827.

89. R. Pesch, *Apostelgeschichte* 2:213.

90. This is also a possible interpretation in the New Testament environment, especially since in religious life this designation was known as an expression for a special divine power residing in a woman. See Delling, "παρθένος," 827–28.

91. Eusebius, *Historia Ecclesiastica* 3.30.1.

92. On this, see also L. and W. Schottroff, "Hanna," 44.

93. On this, see E. Schüssler Fiorenza, *In Memory of Her*, esp. 294–309, 160–204.

94. On this, see ibid., 301–2 and elsewhere, and K. Thraede, "Frau," 238, 260ff.

95. E. Schüssler Fiorenza, *In Memory of Her,* 301; see also K. Thraede, "Frau," 262, with reference to p. 238.

96. E. Schüssler Fiorenza, *In Memory of Her,* 302–3.

97. On this, see I. Maisch's essay, "Isebel," 163ff.

98. On this, see R. Pesch, *Apostelgeschichte* 2:48–49.

99. Josephus, *Ant.* 20.141ff.

100. This is clearly expressed in a Syriac translation by the addition of the words: "[Drusilla], who wished to see Paul and hear the word; he wanted to please her and. . . ." According to this, she took the initiative to go to Paul.

101. Thus R. Pesch, *Apostelgeschichte* 2:261; J. Roloff, *Apostelgeschichte,* 339; E. Haenchen, *Acts,* 660.

102. Here she has nothing at all to do with those women who accepted this message and way of life (v. 25), as reported, for example, in the *Acts of Paul and Thecla;* see also the *Acts of Peter* 33.

103. For Bernice, see Josephus, *Ant.* 20.145ff.

104. For the legal questions, see R. Pesch, *Apostelgeschichte* 2:263ff.

Conclusion

In this book I have investigated all the passages in Acts in which women
are explicitly mentioned. I have also examined those passages in which I
could suppose that women were also present behind Luke's androcentric language. My observations about the androcentric nature of Luke's
account are a fundamental component of my work. It has become
obvious that Luke mentions by name, or explicitly, only a few women
who came into contact or conflict with the principal figures in the
Petrine and Pauline mission, as described by Luke. Most of these women
are found in the accounts of the Jerusalem community and in the report
of Paul's second missionary journey. Luke only mentions women by
name when their personalities are outstanding and their stories paradig-
matic for the continuing life of the community of the saints.

The Lukan account is androcentric and concentrates on the principal
figures in the apostolic mission, yet it contains and hands on many
facets of women's lives in the first century C.E. There are details that
express both their experiences of faith and their ordinary work. Examining these details more closely in light of other sources gives us access
to some realities of their lives and histories that are hidden in the text.
In this way we can uncover the stories of other women and men who
may have been companions in faith, work, or in life of those whom
Luke mentions. Even if the historicity of some stories, persons, or events
cannot always be established, the information found in the text may be
regarded as historical insofar as it throws light on the reality of people's
lives or the social context of the Lukan communities.

Luke's androcentric account is not intended to present a homogeneous and unified picture of the experiences or world of women, because Luke's interest is focused on the male personalities of Peter and Paul, and women are mentioned only in passing. He is unable to write a unified history of women in the community of the saints, or to connect the stories of individual women. Feminist theologians of liberation have demonstrated the necessity of distinguishing between individual women and their experiences if we are to draw more precise conclusions about their life contexts. To this extent, the absence of a unified account in Luke's work can be regarded as an opportunity for observing women in very different contexts and worlds of work, and not simply to see them as women confined to the household.

In the following pages, I will summarize the results of the preceding investigation and connect the stories of the different women in the Acts of the Apostles.

On the one hand, Acts has left unmentioned many women who were important and actively engaged in spreading the good news; on the other hand, it has left us a literary tradition of other women. The information in the text must therefore be read together with, and augmented by, other canonical and extra-canonical texts. The women mentioned by Luke frequently worked independently and some of them lived independently of men. They did their work, in house churches and on the road, to earn their living and to advance the reign of God. Women belonged to the community of the saints from the beginning, and took part in the events that touched that community, both in Jerusalem and in house churches elsewhere. Often women appear in the text when conflicts arise: Sapphira, the Hellenist widows, the women persecuted by Saul together with the men, the prophetic slave girl in Philippi. There were women among the believers who headed house churches: Mary, the mother of John Mark, in Jerusalem; Tabitha, in Joppa; Lydia, in Philippi; Priscilla, in Corinth and Ephesus. The growing community of the saints included women who were active in trades and crafts, but also in the mission, in philosophy, in prophecy. Acts also mentions, in two places, women who were socially and politically influential in their cities, but nothing is said of a conversion of Drusilla, the wife of Felix the governor, or of Bernice, the wife of King Agrippa II. Within that circle, the liberating word of justice and resurrection was not believed. The women who converted to the Jewish-Christian faith were those who found themselves addressed by the liberating message of the Jewish

Messiah, Jesus Christ, and who served him in the upbuilding of solidarity and just ways of life.

The story of Sapphira (Acts 5:1-11) began very positively for the Jerusalem community. It was said of that church that it was a community of solidarity in which no one had to suffer want. They had everything in common; those with property placed it at the disposal of the community, and as needed they sold what they had: for example, a piece of land. The proceeds they gave to the community. Sapphira and Ananias had also joined this community and were prepared to sell their field. Sapphira agreed to her husband Ananias's sale of the field; in doing so, she relinquished her *kethuba,* which was a legal claim she had against her husband's property: normally this consisted of a sum of money for which the husband's entire estate was encumbered. By her agreement to the sale of the field, Sapphira integrated herself totally into the community whose self-understanding Luke describes with the phrase "one heart and one soul" (4:32). In her dealing with property she demonstrated, on the one hand, her freedom and solidarity, but in agreeing with her husband's corrupt decision, she demonstrated a different aspect of her character: her complicity. She cooperated with the terms of a patriarchal marriage by functioning as accomplice in the concealment of part of the proceeds, a deed planned and executed by her husband, Ananias. Her role was not passive: she did nothing to counter her husband's decision. On the contrary, she united with him in tempting the Holy Spirit, who dwells in the community of the saints, and in putting God to the test. This tempting, or lying to the Holy Spirit, is expressed in the concealment. Deceiving the community is equivalent to deceiving the Holy Spirit and God. This expresses a unified pneumatological-theological-ecclesiological concept. Sapphira's initially passive participation becomes quite active when she lies in order to cover her husband's action. Both of them, by their sin—the concealment, which in turn called for repeated lying—become liable to death, which means total exclusion from the community of the saints. It is difficult to determine whether the two of them actually died, as Acts 5:5, 10 reports. The purpose of the narrative is to reveal to every individual, and to the church as a whole (vv. 5b, 11) the death-dealing power of sin, and to encourage everyone to act differently from Sapphira and Ananias. The power of sin finds expression here when Ananias and Sapphira attack the fundamental bases of the existence of this community of solidarity.

We may observe in this story a substantial difference between the sinfulness of the two: Ananias's action is characterized by self-assertion, that of Sapphira by a lack of self-determination. This is very important to a feminist liberation theological reading of the story. The story can produce liberating impulses for women who often feel themselves "powerless" within patriarchal and hierarchical structures, calling them to resist corrupt and corrupting power. In light of the negation of sin—and of death—this narrative derives a power to evoke change: Women must oppose death-creating structures if they and others are not to be destroyed. They should be able to trust that their disobedience will bring them a place in the community of the saints, where they will be received. Their disobedience can open for them a way to a liberated life. On the other hand, their resigned complicity can be fatal.

The account of the disciple Tabitha (Dorcas) in Joppa (Acts 9:36-43), who was independently active at the local level, attests to her social, organizational, and missionary work. This comprehensive field of activity is indicated not only by her being called "disciple," but also by the further description of her in terms of her good works. Here, for the first time in Acts, we read of a Jewish-Christian house church outside Jerusalem. Tabitha is its head. As a fully committed disciple of Jesus Christ, she also proclaims his good news. Her good works, acts of love, are connected with the widows, but need not be restricted to that group or to the making of garments. Her works should not be understood as alms, but as a more comprehensive field of charitable activity in the service of justice. The text expresses an internal coherence between faith and works. Both together constitute Tabitha's identity. This identity is still more strongly revealed in the narrative of her death. Tabitha is remembered; the weeping, mourning widows and the garments she has made bear witness to her. The mourning scene reflects the commitment she made with her entire person to the whole sphere of her activity.

The commitment of those who belong to this house church and the witness of the widows are central components in the raising of Tabitha. The latter is the most obvious demonstration of a power in relationship that is evident here on a number of levels. It takes its course in seeking, going, weeping, in the witness of those belonging to the community, and comes to full expression in Peter's action. The power of God was revealed, in this case, through the power in relationship between human beings. This raising of the dead was preceded by a great deal of action, beginning with the life of Tabitha. The power here revealed is not only to be understood as a new opportunity for Tabitha's own engagement on behalf of life for others. The miraculous power in relationship extends beyond the event affecting Tabitha. The memory of the life, death, and raising of Tabitha can continue to effect something miraculous: a continually renewed conversion or turning toward God, who empowers all disciples to translate divine love into the concrete works of love.

The story of Lydia in the Roman colony at Philippi (Acts 16:13-15, 40) attests both to the business activity of a woman and to her active participation in Jewish and Christian communities of faith. Lydia was not alone in Philippi. She does not appear alongside a man, but in the company of other women. Lydia is one of the women who gathered on the Sabbath in the place of prayer, the synagogue. These were a group who practiced the Jewish religion independently of men, and drew identity and strength from it. Lydia came from Thyatira in Asia Minor. That city and the region were known and valued for their traditional production of textiles, including dyeing. Among the dyes produced was purple, most probably derived from plants and used in the dyeing of wool. The dyed products were sold, for the most part, by those who made them. This kind of work was despised by the upper class because the production of such goods and all retail trade was considered "dirty." Lydia, who was probably a freedwoman, did her work alongside other workers who probably made up her household. From her work, they together earned the basic subsistence of the house headed by Lydia.

Paul and Silas came into contact with Lydia and her household on a Sabbath and preached to them the message of the Jewish Messiah, Jesus Christ, and Lydia and her household were baptized. Because of Lydia's fidelity to Jesus Christ, this house became the base of the Jewish-Christian mission in Philippi. On a local level, Lydia had the function of a presider entrusted with the tasks of organization and preaching. Lydia also placed her house at the disposal of the missionaries, in which and from which they could live and work. But she was unable to shield the missionaries from anti-Jewish attacks, expressed in terms of political conflicts in Philippi. Her power was also limited at the higher ideological and political level because it was a counter-power. It was realized in the internal sphere. There, in the *cellula mater* of society, in the house, she constructed a new power not based on a *paterfamilias* and not required to create or legitimate any patriarchal hierarchical order of subordination. The house of a foreign worker in European Macedonia, in the Roman colony of Philippi, became the first center of a Jewish-

Christian community of equals, loyal to the crucified and resurrected Lord Jesus Christ, and attempting to shape its life according to his commandments. This story contains important religious- and social-historical information on a relevant part of the history of women within early Christianity, including especially Jewish Christianity, and at the same time it opens the door to an investigation of an aspect of the working world of women in the first Christian centuries.

The counter-image to Lydia and the community of equals in her house is presented by the story of the prophetic slave girl in the same Roman colony of Philippi (Acts 16:16-18). To obtain a more complete picture of women with whom the Jewish-Christian missionaries came into contact and the conditions of their lives, it is necessary to read these two stories in complementary fashion. Like Lydia, the slave is also religiously active. Like Lydia, she also has a speaking part in Luke's text. The former, Lydia, is probably a freedwoman; the other is a slave woman. A number of owners have claims on the slave girl and her abilities: according to the thinking of the time, she is "animate property." As such, she brings her owners considerable profit through her prophetic power.

The spirit that gives her that power is called "Python," which makes her a "Pythia," that is, a religious agent in the service of Apollo. The mantic spirit in her neither makes her ill nor tortures her in any way. Instead, it enables her to prophesy and thus provides her with a more respected position and better treatment from her owners, especially since it is in their interest to keep her "production-ready." Her prophetic words about Paul and Silas prove to be true: They are servants of the Jewish God, who was also called the "Most High." Thus on the one hand the slave girl functions as a precursor of the missionaries; on the other hand we may suppose that her public proclamation over the course of many days could endanger the missionaries, because they could be suspected of seeking proselytes among the Roman population, which was forbidden. Paul, becoming annoyed, drove the mantic spirit out of the slave girl. At this point, the narrative turns directly to the owners and the political charge they brought against Paul and Silas. As owners, they had received economic injury, and they charge the two men with dirturbing the city by propagating foreign customs. The Roman authorities undertook police measures against the missionaries.

We may conclude from the account that the slave girl was not liberated by the exorcism of the spirit in her. On the one hand, the mantic spirit was unable to free her from slavery, although it did guarantee her better treatment at the hands of her owners. On the other hand, Paul's exorcism did not bring her freedom from slavery either. Her concrete situation had, indeed, grown worse, inasmuch as she was now damaged goods, and had become worthless to her owners. With the expulsion of her prophetic power, they had lost the source of their profits. Now they had no further reason to take special care of her. Her future fate would probably consist in hard, physical labor as a slave. There could have been a concrete possibility of liberation for her if Paul or the community in Lydia's house bought her freedom by the payment of a compensatory sum and took her into their protection. The slave could have been received into the community of equals in Lydia's house; only then would she have had the opportunity for a qualitatively new and free life. But the text says nothing about it, and we can no longer know whether the slave was really welcomed there. This hypothesis remains a historical possibility, supported by other examples. Without at least considering it, I could not speak of any liberation for the slave girl in this exorcism story.

The story of the missionary artisan Priscilla (Acts 18:1-28) and her husband, Aquila, is a high point in Paul's missionary activity. This is attested not only through Pauline and deutero-Pauline witnesses, but by the Lukan account. Acts 18:1-28 offers us social-historical information not only about the life and work of Priscilla and Aquila, but also about Paul himself. Only here do we find mention of the craft of tentmaking, which all three of them practiced. This story can be used to augment and interpret Paul's own statements, when he says that he had to work hard to earn his living (1 Cor. 4:11-12; 1 Thess. 2:9; 2 Cor. 11:9). As craftspeople, they earned their living by tedious and tiring work. Because of their work and their mission, they traveled a great deal: from Pontus to Rome, from Rome (ejected for religio-political reasons) to Corinth, from Corinth to Ephesus. Part of their journeying was done as companions and fellow workers of Paul, but they worked on their own, and even independently of Paul. They were at work both before and after him. Their work in teaching the Jewish-Christian faith was highly important: according to Luke's account, they even taught Apollos, who was already famous as a brilliant and learned preacher and speaker. The kind of teaching they did, as reported by Luke, is attested in the New Testament only of Peter, Paul, Priscilla and Aquila: it is a form of challenge and dialogue that builds up and clarifies. It is done by those in possession of acknowledged authority. The high position held by Priscilla in the early Jewish Christian movement is also attested by the fact that, except for the four prophetic daughters of Philip, she is the only woman mentioned by Luke in connection with teaching.

Some changes were made in the texts concerning Priscilla at a very early date in order to weaken the power of the traditions handed on about Priscilla's importance. Such attempts represent interventions not merely in the text, but in the history of women. These interventions in the tradition have certainly not been, and are not, without harmful effect. On the contrary, they reflect a conflict between different spheres of authority. The attempt to reduce Priscilla's high status is at the same time an attempt to strike at other women and men who, in their daily missionary work and in the building up of their communities, referred to the authority of the outstanding missionary Priscilla. The strength and importance of a recovery and preservation of the history of Priscilla can be seen in the way in which this story can encourage women and men to engage in a liberating missionary praxis, for it also shows that good missionary work, even without a hierarchical institution, can be liberating in daily life and can achieve recognition. Sticking one's neck out for others, in opposition to the terrifying power of sin, is an ongoing challenge and at the same time an encouragement, both of which can be derived from the story of Priscilla and her husband, Aquila.

Some observations uniting a number of "women" passages in Acts can be summarized as follows.

Luke hands on some very different pictures of women and their experiences. The facets of women's history retained here thus reveal that women did not have a unified history. Many of them, however, had important characteristics in common, some of which I want to emphasize.

Women's membership in a Jewish Christian community of the saints and their active participation in the events within this community are characterized by the fact that they contributed to the creation of this community of solidarity through their artisan work and their missionary activity, and not only at the local level. They did not withdraw from the world, but within a world that was hostile toward them they attempted to shape a new life in a community of solidarity based on the liberating message of the crucified and risen Christ.

The passages in Acts in which women's experiences in Jewish Christian communities are depicted offer neither arguments nor legitimation for patriarchal and hierarchical attitudes and structures. The experiences reported do not serve the preservation of the patriarchal system of the time, because within these house churches there was no need of a *paterfamilias* to organize life. This life was not based on any of the patriarchal ruling structures of the society of that time: master/slave, man/woman, etc. Instead, these communities should be understood as communities of resistance, also in the sense that, on the one hand, women presided over their households independently of men, and on the other hand when, like Priscilla, they are mentioned together with the men of their families they nevertheless led lives of their own. Acts gives us an example of one attempt to live in the community of the saints and still to retreat into the patriarchal system. The result of that attempt was total exclusion from the community: this is the story of Sapphira and Ananias.

One story in Acts reveals a set of patriarchal relationships: that of the prophetic slave girl in Philippi. The society in which she lived was patriarchal; in her case it was characterized by subordination within the master/slave system. Luke's account is also patriarchal in the sense that it takes no interest in the fate of the slave before and after the "exorcism." The dominant tradition of interpretation is equally patriarchal, defining the slave's "difference" from the perspective of those in power insofar as it compares the slave girl's religion with Christianity and declares it to be of lesser value.

The Acts of the Apostles reflects no particular tendency to keep women at home and subject them to men, i.e., to their own husbands. Even though it is silent about important women like Mary Magdalene, it is still far from what was written, at about the same time as its composition, in the Pastoral letters and similar works (e.g., Titus 2:5; 1 Pet. 3:1; Col. 3:18) regarding the subordination of women and slaves. The example of Sapphira makes it clear that women should not simply function as cooperators and co-conspirators. The flip side of this story, in fact, shows that here women were given an example of how they might break with patriarchal and hierarchical structures and, together with others, attempt to build a life dedicated to the preservation of all life.

I hope that my attempt to reconstruct the stories of the women in the Acts of the Apostles has succeeded in reviving memories of the life, the work, and the struggles of women of the past. It is my desire that their stories may inspire and strengthen women and men in the present in their struggle against oppression and for liberation.

Abbreviations

AB	Anchor Bible
ANRW	*Aufstieg und Niedergang der römischen Welt*
Apoc. Elijah	*Apocalypse of Elijah*
ATD	Das Alte Testament Deutsch
Ath. Mitt.	*Mitteilungen des deutschen archäologischen Instituts, Athenische Abteilung*
BAGD	W. Bauer, W. F. Arndt, F. W. Gingrich, and F. W. Danker, *A Greek-English Lexicon of the New Testament*
2–3 Bar.	Syriac, Greek *Apocalypse of Baruch*
BDR	F. Blass, A. Debrunner, and F. Rehkopf, *Grammatik des neutestamentlichen Griechisch*
Ber.	*Berakot*
BGU	*Ägyptische Urkunden aus den Kgl. Museen zu Berlin*
BTZ	*Berliner theologische Zeitschrift*
Bull. Corr. hell.	*Bulletin de Correspondance Hellénique*
CBQ	*Catholic Biblical Quarterly*
Cicero, De off.	Cicero, *De officiis*
CIG	*Corpus inscriptionum graecarum*
CII	*Corpus inscriptionum iudaicarum*
CIL	*Corpus inscriptionum latinarum*

269

1 Clem.	*The First Epistle of Clement*
CPJ	*Corpus papyrorum Judaicorum*
EdF	Erträge der Forschung
EHS	Europäische Hochschulschriften
EKK	Evangelisch-katholischer Kommentar
EvK	Evangelische Kommentare
EvTh	*Evangelische Theologie*
FRLANT	Forschungen zur Religion und Literatur des Alten und Neuen Testaments
Hag.	*Hagiga*
HAT	Handbuch zum Alten Testament
HNT	Handbuch zum Neuen Testament
HThK	Herders theologischer Kommentar zum Neuen Testament
HTR	*Harvard Theological Review*
IG	*Inscriptiones graecae*
Inst. Iust.	*Institutiones Iustiniani*
JBL	*Journal of Biblical Literature*
JFSR	*Journal of Feminist Studies in Religion*
Josephus, *Ant.*	*Antiquities of the Jews*
Bell.	*Bellum Judaicum*
JSJ	*Journal for the Study of Judaism in the Persian, Hellenistic and Roman Period*
KEK	Kritisch-Exegetischer Kommentar über das Neue Testament
KNT	Kommentar zum Neuen Testament
LCL	Loeb Classical Library
LXX	Septuagint
Mart. Pol.	*Martyrdom of Polycarp*
Midr.	*Midrash*
Midr. Qoh.	*Midrash Qohelet*
Mur	Wadi Murabba ʾat texts
Nid.	*Niddah*
NRSV	New Revised Standard Version
NTD	Das Neue Testament Deutsch
OGIS	W. Dittenberger, ed., *Orientis Graeci Inscriptiones Selectae*
Or. Sib.	*Oracula Sibyllina*
ÖTB	Ökumenischer Taschenbuchkommentar
PAAJR	*Proceedings of the American Academy of Jewish Research*

Philo, *Deus imm.*	*Quod Deus sit immutabilis*
Flacc.	*In Flaccum*
Leg. Gaj.	*Legatio ad Gaium*
Plutarch, *De def. or.*	*De defectu oraculorum*
PRE	*Paulys Real-Encyclopädie der classischen Alterthumswissenschaft*
Ps. Sol.	*Psalms of Solomon*
QD	*Quaestiones disputatae*
Q*Rosc.*	Cicero, *Pro Roscio Comoedo*
1QS	*Serek hayyahad (Rule of the Community, Manual of Discipline)*
RAC	*Reallexikon für Antike und Christentum*
RE	*Realenzyklopädie für protestantische Theologie und Kirche*
RHE	*Revue d'histoire ecclésiastique*
RNT	Regensburger Neues Testament
SB	Sources bibliques
SBL	Society of Biblical Literature
SBLDS	SBL Dissertation Series
SBS	Stuttgarter Bibelstudien
SIG	Sylloge Inscriptionum Graecarum
SNTSMS	Society for New Testament Studies Monograph Series
StNT	Studien zum Neuen Testament
T. 12 Patr.	*Testaments of the Twelve Patriarchs*
T. Benj.	*Testament of Benjamin*
T. Jud.	*Testament of Judah*
TDNT	G. Kittel and G. Friedrich, eds., *Theological Dictionary of the New Testament*
THAT	*Theologisches Handbuch zum Alten Testament*
ThB	Theologische Bücherei
ThHK	Theologischer Handkommentar zum Neuen Testament
ThR	*Theologische Rundschau*
ThWAT	*Theologisches Wörterbuch zum Alten Testament*
ThZ	*Theologische Zeitschrift*
USQR	*Union Seminary Quarterly Review*
UTB	Uni Taschenbücher

Val. Flacc.	Valerius Flaccus, *Argonautica*
WdF	Wege der Forschung
WMANT	Wissenschaftliche Monographien zum Alten und Neuen Testament
WuD	*Wort und Dienst*
WUNT	Wissenschaftliche Untersuchungen zum Neuen Testament
y. Nid.	Jerusalem Talmud, *Niddah*
ZBK	Zürcher Bibelkommentar
ZNW	*Zeitschrift für die neutestamentliche Wissenschaft*
ZSRG RA	*Zeitschrift der Savigny-Stiftung für Rechtsgeschichte. Romanistische Abteilung.*
ZThK	*Zeitschrift für Theologie und Kirche*

Bibliography

Abrahamsen, Valerie A. "Women at Philippi and Paul's Philippian Correspondence," paper delivered at Society of Biblical Literature National Meeting, 2 May 1987.

_____. "Women at Philippi: The Pagan and Christian Evidence," *JFSR* 3 (1987): 17-30.

Albrecht, Ruth, and Franziska Müller-Rosenau. "Apostelgeschichte 16, 11-15. Lydia." In *Feministisch gelesen* 1, ed. Eva Renate Schmidt et al., 246-52. Stuttgart, 1988.

Alföldy, Géza. "Die Freilassung von Sklaven und die Struktur der Sklaverei in der römischen Kaiserzeit." In *Sozial- und Wirtschaftsgeschichte der römischen Kaiserzeit*, WdF 552, ed. Helmuth Schneider, 336-71. Darmstadt, 1981.

Almeida, Wanda Morales de. "Vidas que inspiram Dorcas—At 9,36-43," *Voz Missionária* 59, no. 1 (São Bernardo do Campo, Brazil, 1989): 27.

Applebaum, Shimon. *Judaea in Hellenistic and Roman Times; Historical and Archaeological Essays*. Leiden and New York, 1989.

_____. "The Legal Status of the Jewish Communities in the Diaspora," in S. Safrai and M. Stern, eds., *The Jewish People in the First Century*. Philadelphia, Fortress Press, 1974, 1:420-63.

_____. "The Social and Economic Status of the Jews in the Diaspora" in S. Safrai and M. Stern, eds., *The Jewish People in the First Century*. Philadelphia, Fortress Press, 1976, 2:701-27.

Aristides Marcianus of Athens. *Apologia*. In *Bibliothek der Kirchenväter* 12 (= *Frühchristliche Apologeten und Märtyrerakten* 1) trans. K. Julius. Munich, 1913.

Athenaeus of Naucratis. *The Deipnosophists*. English translation by Charles Burton Gulick. LCL. Cambridge, 1957-63.

Augar, Friedrich. *Die Frau im römischen Christenprozess. Ein Beitrag zur Verfolgungsgeschichte der christlichen Kirche im römischen Staat.* Texte und Untersuchungen zur Geschichte der altkirchlichen Literatur, n.s. 13. Leipzig, 1905.

Bächi-Nussbaumer, Erna. *So färbt man mit Pflanzen. Ein Werkbuch zum Färben von Schafwolle mit vielen praktischen Hinweisen, Rezepten, Abbildungen, einem Pflanzenatlas und einem Lehrgang zum Karden und Spinnen.* 2d ed. Berne and Stuttgart, 1978.

Baltensweiler, Heinrich. "Wunder und Glaube im Neuen Testament," *ThZ* 23 (1967): 241-56.

Bauernfeind, Otto. *Kommentar und Studien zur Apostelgeschichte.* WUNT 22. Tübingen, 1980.

Becher, Ilse. "Plutarchos." In *Lexicon der Antike,* 439-40. 7th ed. Leipzig, 1985.

Becker, Jürgen. "Paulus und seine Gemeinden." In *Die Anfänge des Christentums. Alte Welt und neue Hoffnung,* ed. Jürgen Becker et al, 102-59. Stuttgart, 1987. English translation by Annemarie S. Kidder and Reinhard Krauss: *Christian Beginnings. Word and Community from Jesus to Post-Apostolic Times,* ed. Jürgen Becker, 132-210. Louisville, 1993.

Bergmann, Judah. "Die Rachegebete von Rheneia," *Philologus* 70 (1911): 503-10.

Besnier, Maurice. "Purpura (Πορφύρα)." In *Dictionnaire des antiquités grecques et romaines* 4/1 (1877ff.), ed. Charles Daremberg and Edm. Saglio, 769-78.

Beydon, France. "Luc et 'ces dames de la haute société,'" *Etudes Théologiques et Religieuses* 61, no. 3 (1986): 331-41.

Beyer, Hermann W. *Die Apostelgeschichte.* NTD 5. Göttingen, 1921; 4th ed., 1947.

Biale, Rachel. *Women and Jewish Law. An Exploration of Women's Issues in Halakhic Sources.* New York, 1984.

Bieritz, Karl-Heinrich. "Rückkehr ins Haus? Sozialgeschichtliche und theologische Erwägungen zum Thema 'Hauskirche,'" *BTZ* 1 (1986): 111-26.

Billerbeck, Paul, and Hermann L. Strack. *Kommentar zum Neuen Testament aus Talmud und Midrasch.* 6 vols. 9th ed. Munich, 1986-1989.

Bingemer, María Clara. "Reflections on the Trinity." In *Through Her Eyes. Women's Theology from Latin America,* ed. Elsa Tamez, 56-80. Maryknoll, N.Y., 1989.

Blümner, Hugo. *Die gewerbliche Thätigkeit der Völker des klassischen Althertums.* Leipzig, 1869. Repr. in *Ancient Economic History,* ed. Moses I. Finley. New York, 1979.

_____. *Technologie und Terminologie der Gewerbe und Künste bei Griechen und Römern* 1. Leipzig, 1875.

Böcher, Otto. *Das Neue Testament und die dämonischen Mächte.* SBS 58. Stuttgart, 1972.

Boff, Clodovis. *Die Befreiung der Armen. Reflexionen zum Grundanliegen der lateinamerikanischen Befreiungstheologie.* Freiburg, 1986.

Bolkestein, Hendrik. *Wohltätigkeit und Armenpflege im vorchristlichen Altertum. Ein Beitrag zum Problem "Moral und Gesellschaft."* Utrecht, 1939; repr. Groningen, 1967.

Bömer, Franz. *Untersuchungen über die Religion der Sklaven in Griechenland und Rom.* 2d ed., revised by Peter Herz in consultation with the author. Forschungen zur antiken Sklaverei 14/1. Wiesbaden, 1981.

Boor, Werner de. *Die Apostelgeschichte.* Wuppertaler Studienbibel. Wuppertal, 1965.

———. *Die Briefe des Paulus an die Philipper und die Kolosser.* Wuppertaler Studienbibel. Wuppertal, 1967.

Brakemeier, Gottfried. *Der "Sozialismus" der Urchristenheit. Experiment und neue Herausforderung.* Kleine Vandenhoeck-Reihe 1535. Göttingen, 1988 (= São Leopoldo, 1985).

Brelich, Angelo. *Paides e Parthenoi* I. Incunabula Graeca 36. Rome, 1969.

Brockmeyer, Norbert. *Antike Sklaverei.* EdF 116. Darmstadt, 1979.

———. *Sozialgeschichte der Antike. Ein Abriß.* UTB 158. Stuttgart, 1972.

Brooten, Bernadette J. "Frühchristliche Frauen und ihr kultureller Kontext. Überlegungen zur Methode historischer Rekonstruktion," *Einwürfe* 2 (1985): 62-93. Cf. her "Early Christian Women and Their Cultural Context: Issues of Method in Historical Reconstruction," in *Feminist Perspectives on Biblical Scholarship,* ed. Adela Yarbro Collins, 65-91 (SBL Centennial Publications; Atlanta, 1985).

———. *Women Leaders in the Ancient Synagogue. Inscriptional Evidence and Background Issues.* Brown Judaic Studies 36. Chico, CA, 1982.

Büchsenschütz, Bernhard. *Die Hauptstätten des Gewerbefleisses im klassischen Alterthume.* Leipzig, 1869. Repr. in *Ancient Economic History,* ed. Moses I. Finley. New York, 1979.

Campenhausen, Hans Freiherr von. "Bearbeitungen und Interpolationen des Polykarpmartyriums." In *Sitzungen der Heidelberger Akademie der Wissenschaften.* Philosophisch-historische Klasse 1957. Heidelberg, 1957.

Cassidy, Richard J. *Jesus, Politics, and Society. A Study of Luke's Gospel.* 2d ed. Maryknoll, N.Y., 1979.

Cavalcanti, Tereza. "The Prophetic Ministry of Women in the Hebrew Bible." In *Through Her Eyes. Women's Theology from Latin America,* ed. Elsa Tamez, 118-39. Maryknoll, N.Y., 1989.

Cavallin, Hans C. "Leben nach dem Tode im Spätjudentum und im frühen Christentum. I. Spätjudentum," *ANRW* II (Principat) 19/1, ed. Wolfgang Haase (1979): 240-340.

Charlesworth, James H., ed. *The Old Testament Pseudepigrapha.* 2 vols. Garden City, N.Y., 1983-1985.

Chrysostom, John. *In Epistulam II ad Timotheus.* PG 62.

_____. *In Illud: Salutate Priscillam et Aquilam*. PG 51, 187-207.

_____. *In Romanos homilia*. PG 60.

Cicero, Marcus Tullius. "Rede für den Schauspieler Q. Roscius," In *Neue Sammlung auserlesener Reden des Marcus Tullius Cicero* I, trans. and ed. by F. C. Wolff. Altona, 1825.

Clerc, Michel. *De rebus Thyatirenorum. Commentario epigraphica*. Paris, 1893.

Clévenot, Michel. *Von Jerusalem nach Rom. Geschichte des Christentums im I. Jahrhundert*. Fribourg, 1987.

Cohen, Boaz. "Peculium in Jewish and Roman Law," *PAAJR* 20 (1951): 135-234.

Collart, P. "Philippes," *Dictionnaire d'Archéologie Chrétienne* 14:712-41. Paris, 1939.

Colpe, Carsten. "Die älteste judenchristliche Gemeinde." In *Die Anfänge des Christentums. Alte Welt und neue Hoffnung*, ed. Jürgen Becker, et al., 59-80. Stuttgart, 1989.

Comblin, José. *Atos dos Apóstolos*. Comentário Bíblico NT. 2 vols. Petrópolis, 1987.

_____. *Epístola aos Filipenses*. Comentário Bíblico NT. Petrópolis, 1985.

_____. "Os pobres como sujeito das história," *Ribla* 3 (Petrópolis, 1989): 36-48.

Conzelmann, Hans. *Acts = Die Apostelgeschichte*. HNT 7. Tübingen, 1963. English translation from the 2d ed. of 1972 by James Limburg, A. Thomas Kraabel, and Donald H. Juel, ed. by Eldon Jay Epp with Christopher R. Matthews: *Acts of the Apostles*. Philadelphia, 1987.

_____. *1 Corinthians = Der erste Brief an die Korinther*. KEK 5. Göttingen, 11th ed. 1969. English translation by James W. Leitch: *1 Corinthians: A Commentary on the First Epistle to the Corinthians*. Philadelphia, 1975.

Crüsemann, Frank. "Fremdenliebe und Identitätssicherung. Zum Verständnis der 'Fremden-' Gesetze im Alten Testament," *WuD* n. s. 19 (1987): 11-24.

Csillag, Pál. "Die Stellung der Arbeit im römischen Recht," *Klio* 53 (1971): 169-77.

Cumont, Franz V. M. "Παῖς" (Mysterien)," *RE* 18.2 (1942): 2428-35.

Deifelt, Wanda. " 'Justificação pela fé' fala para a experiência das mulheres?" *Informativo CEBI-Sul* 15 (São Leopoldo, 1986): 16-21.

Deissmann, Gustav Adolf. *Licht vom Osten. Das Neue Testament und die neuentdeckten Texte der hellenistisch-römischen Welt*. 4th rev. ed. Tübingen, 1923.

_____. *Paulus. Eine kultur- und religionsgeschichtliche Skizze*. Tübingen, 1911.

Drexhage, Hans-Joachim. "Die wirtschaftliche Stellung der Christen in den ersten drei Jahrhunderten unter besonderer Berücksichtigung ihrer Beteiligung am Handel," *Römische Quartalschrift für christliche Altertumskunde und Kirchengeschichte* 76, nos. 1-2 (1981).

Ehrhardt, Arnold. "Rechtsvergleichende Studien zum antiken Sklavenrecht I. Wehrgeld und Schadenersatz," *ZSRG RA* 68 (1951): 74-130.

Eichenauer, Monika. *Untersuchungen zur Arbeitswelt der Frau in der römischen Antike.* EHS 3, 360. Frankfurt am Main, 1988.

Elliger, Winfred. *Paulus in Griechenland. Philippi, Thessaloniki, Athen, Korinth.* SBS 92/93. Stuttgart, 1987.

Eusebius. *Ecclesiastical History. The History of the Church from Christ to Constantine.* Translated with an introduction by G. A. Williamson. New York, 1965.

Fauth, Wolfgang. "Pythia," *RE* 24 (1963): 515-47.

Felten, J. *Die Apostelgeschichte.* Freiburg, 1892.

Fieler, Gretel. *Farben aus der Natur. Eine Sammlung alter und neuer Farbrezepte für das Färben auf Wolle, Seide, Baumwolle und Leinen.* Hannover, 1978.

Figur Messer, Ruth Miriam. "A história de Tamar com Judá," *Informativo CEBI-Sul* 15 (São Leopoldo, 1986): 5-15.

Finley, Moses I. *Die Sklaverei in der Antike. Geschichte und Probleme.* Munich, 1981.

Fraenkel, Ernst. "Namenwesen," *RE²* 16:1611-70.

Frauenpolitik: Opfer/Täter/Diskussion, ed. by the Frauenredaktion. Berlin, 1983.

Fusco, Sandro-Angelo. "Rechtspolitik in der Spätantike: Unterschiede zwischen dem Westen und dem Osten und ihre Bedingungen," *Saeculum* 32, no. 3 (1981): 255-72.

Gayer, Roland. *Sklaven = Die Stellung des Sklaven in den paulinischen Gemeinden und bei Paulus. Zugleich ein sozialgeschichtlich vergleichender Beitrag zur Wertung des Sklaven in der Antike.* EHS 23/78. Frankfurt am Main, 1976.

Gebara, Ivone. "Women Doing Theology in Latin America." In *Through Her Eyes: Women's Theology from Latin America,* ed. Elsa Tamez, 37-48. Maryknoll, N.Y., 1989.

Georges, K. E. *Kleines Lateinisch-Deutsches Handwörterbuch.* Leipzig, 1885.

Gesenius, Wilhelm, and Buhl, Frants. *Hebräisches und aramäisches Handwörterbuch über das Alte Testament.* Berlin, 1915; 17th ed., 1962.

Goodwin, William W., ed. *Plutarch's Morals.* Boston, 1870.

Graeber, Andreas. *Untersuchungen zum spätrömischen Korporationswesen.* EHS 196. Frankfurt am Main, 1983.

Gräßer, Erich. "Acta-Forschung seit 1960," *ThR* 41 (1976): 141-94, 259-90.

_____. "Acta-Forschung seit 1960," *ThR* 42 (1977): 1-68.

_____. "Die Apostelgeschichte in der Forschung der Gegenwart," *ThR* 26 (1960): 93-167.

Gulak, Asher. *Das Urkundenwesen im Talmud im Lichte der griechisch-aegyptischen Papyri und des griechischen und roemischen Rechts.* Jerusalem, 1935.

Gummerus, H. "Industrie und Handel," *PRE* 18 (1969): 1454-1535.

Gunkel, Hermann. *Genesis.* HAT 1/1. Göttingen, 5th ed. 1922.

Günther, Rosemarie. *Frauenarbeit—Frauenbindung. Untersuchungen zu unfreien und freigelassenen Frauen in den stadtrömischen Inschriften.* Munich, 1987.

Gutiérrez, Gustavo. *A Theology of Liberation.* Trans. and ed. by Sister Caridad Inda and John Eagleson (= *Teología de la liberación*). Maryknoll, N.Y., 1973.

Haag, Herbert. "Die biblischen Wurzeln des Minjan." In *Abraham unser Vater. Juden und Christen im Gespräch über die Bibel,* ed. Otto Betz, Martin Hengel, and Peter Schmidt, 235-42. Festschrift for Otto Michel. Arbeiten zur Geschichte des Spätjudentums und Urchristentums 5. Leiden and Cologne, 1963.

Haenchen, Ernst. *Acts = Die Apostelgeschichte.* KEK 3. 13th ed. Göttingen, 1961. English translation from the 14th ed. of 1965 by Bernard Noble and Gerald Shinn, under the supervision of Hugh Anderson, revised by Robert McLean Wilson: *The Acts of the Apostles. A Commentary.* Philadelphia, 1971.

Hahn, István. "Freie Arbeit und Sklavenarbeit in der spätantiken Stadt." In *Sozial- und Wirtschaftsgeschichte der römischen Kaiserzeit,* ed. Helmuth Schneider, 128-54. WdF 552. Darmstadt, 1981.

Harnack, Adolf von. *Mission and Expansion = Die Mission und Ausbreitung des Christentums in den ersten drei Jahrhunderten.* 3d. rev. and enlarged ed., vols. 1 and 2. Leipzig, 1915. English translation and edition by James Moffatt: *The Mission and Expansion of Christianity in the First Three Centuries.* 2 vols. Theological Translation Library vols. 19-20. 2d rev. ed. New York and London, 1908.

————. "Probabilia über die Adresse und den Verfasser des Hebräerbriefs," ZNW 1 (1900): 16-41.

————. "Über die beiden Recensionen der Geschichte der Prisca und des Aquila in Act. Apost. 18, 1-27," *Sitzungsberichte der Preußischen Akademie der Wissenschaften* (1900): 2-13.

Haug, Frigga, ed., with Ursula Blankenburg, et al. *Frauen—Opfer oder Täter? Diskussion.* 2d ed. Berlin, 1982.

Heine, Susanne. *Women and Early Christianity = Frauen der frühen Christenheit. Zur historischen Kritik einer feministischen Theologie.* Göttingen, 1986. English translation by John Bowden: *Women and Early Christianity: A Reappraisal.* Minneapolis, 1988.

Heinrici, G. "Die Christengemeinde Korinths und die religiösen Genossenschaften der Griechen," *Zeitschrift für wissenschaftliche Theologie* 19 (1876): 465-526.

Hemer, Colin J. *The Book of Acts in the Setting of Hellenistic History,* ed. Conrad H. Gempf. WUNT 49. Tübingen, 1989.

Hengel, Martin. "Der Historiker Lukas und die Geographie Palästinas in der Apostelgeschichte," *Zeitschrift des Deutschen Palästina-Vereins* 99 (1983): 147-83.

_____. "Die Arbeit im frühen Christentum," *Theologische Beiträge* 17, no. 4 (1986): 174-212.

_____. "Die Synagogeninschrift von Stobi," *ZNW* 57 (1966): 145-83.

_____. *Eigentum und Reichtum in der frühen Kirche.* Stuttgart, 1973. English translation by John Bowden, "Property and Riches in the Early Church." In: *Earliest Christianity,* ed. Martin Hengel. London, 1986.

_____. "Proseuche und Synagoge. Jüdische Gemeinde, Gotteshaus und Gottesdienst in der Diaspora und in Palästina." In: *Tradition und Glaube. Das frühe Christentum in seiner Umwelt,* ed. Gerd Jeremias, Heinz-Wolfgang Kuhn and Hartmut Stegemann, 157-84. Festgabe für Karl Georg Kuhn zum 65. Geburtstag. Göttingen, 1971.

_____. "Zwischen Jesus und Paulus. Die 'Hellenisten,' die 'Sieben' und Stephanus (Apg 6,1-15; 7,54—8,3)," *ZThK* 72 (1975): 151-206.

Hengstl, Joachim, ed., with Günther Häge and H. Kühnert. *Griechische Papyri aus Ägypten als Zeugnisse des öffentlichen und privaten Lebens. Griechischdeutsch.* Munich, 1978.

Hertzberg, Hans Wilhelm. *Die Bücher Josua, Richter, Ruth.* ATD 9. Göttingen, 1953.

Heyward, Isabel Carter. *The Redemption of God: A Theology of Mutual Relation.* Washington, D.C., 1982.

Hock, Ronald F. "Paul's Tentmaking and the Problem of His Social Class," *JBL* 97, no. 4 (1978): 555-64.

_____. "The Workshop as a Social Setting for Paul's Missionary Preaching," *CBQ* 41 (1979): 438-50.

Hoefelmann, Verner. "A comunhão de bens da comunidade primitiva no contexto da proclamação de Jesus," *Palavra Partilhada* 7, no. 1: (São Leopoldo, 1988): 20-28.

Hoennicke, Gustav. *Die Apostelgeschichte.* Evangelisch-Theologische Bibliothek. Kommentar zum Neuen Testament. Leipzig, 1913.

Höfer, O. "Pythia, Pythios, Python." In *Ausführliches Lexikon der griechischen und römischen Mythologie* 3, 2, ed. Wilhelm Heinrich Roscher, 3370-3412. Leipzig, 1902-1909.

Hölder, Eduard. *Institutionen des Römischen Rechtes.* 2d expanded ed. Freiburg and Tübingen, 1883.

Holtzmann, Heinrich Julius. *Die Apostelgeschichte.* Hand-Commentar zum Neuen Testament 1. Tübingen, 1901.

Hug, August. "Παῖδες," *RE* supp. 8 (1956): 374-400.

Hug, J. L. *Einleitung in die Schriften des Neuen Testaments.* 1808.

Huttunen, Pertti. *The Social Strata in the Imperial City of Rome. A Quantitative Study of the Social Representation in the Epitaphs Published in the Corpus Inscriptionum Latinarum Volume VI.* Oulu, 1974.

Irvin, Dorothy. "The Ministry of Women in the Early Church: The Archaeological Evidence," *Duke Divinity School Review* 45 (1980): 76-86.

Jensen, Anne. "Isebel. Autoritätskonflikt—nicht nur in Thyatira." In: *Zwischen Ohnmacht und Befreiung. Biblische Frauengestalten*, ed. Karin Walter, 163-72. Freiburg, 1988.

Jeremias, Joachim. *Jerusalem zur Zeit Jesu. Kulturgeschichtliche Untersuchung zur neutestamentlichen Zeitgeschichte* 1/1 and 2. Göttingen, 1923. English translation by F. H. and C. H. Cave: *Jerusalem in the Time of Jesus; An Investigation into Economic and Social Conditions during the New Testament Period*. Philadelphia, 1969.

_____. "Untersuchungen zum Quellenproblem der Apostelgeschichte," *ZNW* 36 (1938): 205-21.

_____. "Zöllner und Sünder," *ZNW* 30 (1931): 293-300.

Johnson, Luke Timothy. *The Literary Function of Possessions in Luke-Acts*. SBLDS 39. Atlanta, 1977.

Jones, Arnold Hugh Martin. "Das Wirtschaftsleben in den Städten des römischen Kaiserreiches." In *Sozial- und Wirtschaftsgeschichte der römischen Kaiserzeit*, ed. Helmuth Schneider, 48-80. WdF 552. Darmstadt, 1981.

_____. "Der soziale Hintergund des Kampfes zwischen Heidentum und Christentum." In: *Das frühe Christentum im Römischen Staat*, ed. Richard Klein, 337-63. WdF 267. Darmstadt, 1971.

_____. "Die Bekleidungsindustrie in der Zeit des Römischen Imperiums." In: *Sozialökonomische Verhältnisse im Alten Orient und im klassischen Altertum*, ed. Hans Joachim Diesner et al, 156-67. Berlin, 1961.

Josephus, Flavius. *The Works of Josephus*. Trans. William Whiston. Peabody, Mass., 1987.

Kampen, Natalie. *Image and Status: Roman Working Women in Ostia*. Berlin, 1981.

Käsemann, Ernst. *Der Ruf der Freiheit*. 3d rev. ed. Tübingen, 1968. English translation by Frank Clarke: *Jesus Means Freedom*. London, 1969.

Kaser, Max. *Römisches Privatrecht. Ein Studienbuch*. 10th rev. ed. Munich, 1977.

Keil, Josef. "Thyateira," *PRE* 11 (1936): 657-59.

Klauck, Hans-Josef. *Hausgemeinde und Hauskirche im frühen Christentum*. SBS 103. Stuttgart, 1981.

Klees, Hans. *Herren und Sklaven. Die Sklaverei im oikonomischen und politischen Schrifttum der Griechen in klassischer Zeit*. Forschungen zur antiken Sklaverei 6. Wiesbaden, 1975.

Knopf, Rudolf. "Die Apostelgeschichte." In: *Die Schriften des Neuen Testaments* 1/2, ed. Johannes Weiß. Göttingen, 1906.

Koester, Helmut. *Introduction to the New Testament*. 2 vols. Philadelphia, Berlin, and New York, 1982.

Koffmahn, Elisabeth. *Die Doppelurkunden aus der Wüste Juda. Recht und Praxis der jüdischen Papyri des 1. und 2. Jahrhunderts n. Chr. samt Übersetzung der Texte und deutscher Übersetzung*. Studies on the Texts of the Desert of Judah 5. Leiden, 1968.

Korenhof, Mieke. "1. Timotheus 5,3-16. Witwen—Betschwester, Klatschbase, Ketzerin." In: *Feministisch gelesen* 2, ed. Eva Renate Schmidt, et al., 238-50. Zürich, 1989.

Kraabel, A. Thomas. "The Diaspora Synagogue: Archaeological and Epigraphic Evidence since Sukenik." In: *ANRW* II (Principat) 19/1, ed. Wolfgang Haase (1979): 477-510. Berlin and New York, 1979.

_____. "The Disappearance of the 'God-Fearers,' " *Numen* 28, no. 2 (1981): 113-26.

Kraemer, Ross S., ed. *Maenads, Martyrs, Matrons, and Monastics. A Sourcebook in Women's Religions in the Greco-Roman World.* Philadelphia, 1988.

Krauss, Samuel. *Synagogale Altertümer.* Berlin and Vienna, 1922.

_____. *Talmudische Archäologie.* 3 vols. Leipzig, 1910-1912; repr. Hildesheim, 1966.

Kreck, Bettina. *Untersuchungen zur politischen und sozialen Rolle der Frau in der späten römischen Republik.* Marburg, 1975.

Kremer, Jakob. "Auferstehung der Toten in bibeltheologischer Sicht." In: *Resurrectio mortuorum. Zum theologischen Verständnis der leiblichen Auferstehung,* ed. Gisbert Greshake and Jakob Kremer, 7-164. Darmstadt, 1986.

Kreyenbühl, Johannes. "Ursprung und Stammbaum eines biblischen Wunders," *ZNW* 10 (1909): 265-76.

Kuhn, Karl G., and Stegemann, Hartmut, "Proselyten," *RE* supp. 9 (1962): 1248-83.

Lake, Kirsopp. "Proselytes and God-fearers." In: *The Beginnings of Christianity* 1/5, ed. Kirsopp Lake and Henry Cadbury, 74-96. London, 1933.

Lampe, G. W. H. "Miracles in the Acts of the Apostles." In: *Miracles. Cambridge Studies in their Philosophy and History,* ed. C. F. D. Moule, 163-78. 2d ed. London, 1966.

Lampe, Peter. *Die stadtrömischen Christen in den ersten beiden Jahrhunderten.* WUNT 18. 2d ed. Tübingen, 1989.

Latyschev, Basilius, ed. *Inscriptiones Regni Bosporani Graecae et Latinae.* Inscriptiones Antiquae Rae Septentrionalis Ponti Euxini Graecae et Latinae II. Hildesheim, 1965.

Lee, Clarence L. "Soziale Unruhe und Christentum." In: *Zur Soziologie des Urchristentums,* ed. W. A. Meeks, 67-87. Theologische Bücherei 62. Munich, 1979.

Leonhard, Richard. "Hospitium," *PRE* 16 (1913): 2493-98.

_____. et al. "Ius," *PRE* 19 (1918): 1200-1254.

Levinson, Pnina N. *Einführung in die rabbinische Theologie.* Darmstadt, 1982.

Liebs, Detlef. *Römisches Recht. Ein Studienbuch.* UTB 465. Göttingen, 1975.

Lightfoot, Joseph B., and John R. Harmer. *The Apostolic Fathers: With an Introduction Comprising a History of the Christian Church in the First Century* by the late Dr. Burton. London, 1908.

Lindars, Barnabas. "Elijah, Elisha and the Gospel Miracles." In: *Miracles. Cambridge Studies in Their Philosophy and History,* ed. C. F. D. Moule, 63-79. 2d ed. London, 1966.

Lohmeyer, Ernst. *Das Evangelium des Markus.* KEK 2. Göttingen, 1959.

_____. *Das Evangelium des Matthäus.* KEK Extra Volume. 2d rev. ed. Göttingen, 1958.

_____. *Philipper = Die Briefe an die Philipper, an die Kolosser und an Philemon.* KEK 9. 11th ed. Göttingen, 1956.

Loisy, A. F. *Les Actes des Apôtres. Traduction nouvelle avec introduction et notes.* Paris, 1925.

Lüdemann, Gerd. *Paul, Apostle to the Gentiles = Paulus, der Heidenapostel. I: Studien zur Chronologie.* FRLANT 123. Göttingen, 1980. English translation by F. Stanley Jones: *Paul, Apostle to the Gentiles: Studies in Chronology.* Philadelphia, 1984.

_____. *Traditions = Das frühe Christentum nach den Traditionen der Apostelgeschichte. Ein Kommentar.* Göttingen, 1987. English translation by John Bowden: *Early Christianity According to the Traditions in Acts: A Commentary.* Minneapolis, 1989.

Luther, Martin. *Vorlesung über den Römerbrief* (1515/1516). Modernized by E. Ellwein. Munich, 1927.

Maehler, Herwig. *Urkunden römischer Zeit.* Ägyptische Urkunden aus den Staatlichen Museen Berlin. Griechische Urkunden 11/1. Berlin, 1966-1968.

Marcus Diaconus. *Das Leben des Heiligen Porphyrios, Bischofs von Gaza.* Berlin, 1927.

Marcus, Ralph. *Josephus with an English Translation by Ralph Marcus.* 7: *Jewish Antiquities, Books XII-XIV.* London and Cambridge, 1943; 1966.

_____. "The Sebomenoi in Josephus," *Jewish Social Studies* 14 (1952): 247-50.

Marshall, I. Howard. *The Acts of the Apostles. An Introduction and Commentary.* Tyndale New Testament Commentaries. 2d ed. Leicester, 1986.

McNamara, Jo Ann. *A New Song: Celibate Women in the First Three Christian Centuries.* New York, 1983.

Mesters, Carlos. *Flor sem defesa. Uma explicação da Bíblia a partir do povo.* 2d ed. Petrópolis, 1984. English translation by Francis McDonagh: *Defenseless Flower: A New Reading of the Bible.* Maryknoll, N.Y., 1989.

Meyer, Gérson, ed. "La acción del espiritu en la iglesia solidaria—At 2,42-47; 3,1-10." In *Cosecha de Esperanza—Iglesia: Hacia una Esperanza Solidaria* 2:325-30. Quito, 1988.

Michaelis, Wilhelm. *Einleitung in das Neue Testament. Die Entstehung, Sammlung und Überlieferung der Schriften des Neuen Testaments.* 3d ed. Berne, 1961.

Mies, Maria. "Patriarchat" = *Patriarchy and Accumulation on a World Scale: Women in the International Division of Labour.* London and Atlantic Highlands, N. J., 1986.

Mommsen, Theodor. "Die Geschichte der Todesstrafe im Römischen Staat." In idem, *Reden und Aufsätze*. Berlin, 1905.

_____. *Römische Forschungen* 1. Berlin, 1864.

_____. "Zur Lehre von den römischen Korporationen." In idem, *Juristische Schriften. Gesammelte Schriften* 3, 53-68. Berlin, 1907.

Mönning, B. H. *Die Darstellung des urchristlichen Kommunismus nach der Apostelgeschichte des Lukas*. Dissertation. Göttingen, 1978.

Muhlack, Gudrun. "Die Parallelen von Lukas-Evangelium und Apostelgeschichte." In *Theologie und Wirklichkeit* 8. Frankfurt am Main, 1979.

Munck, Johannes. *The Acts of the Apostles*. Revised by William F. Albright and C. S. Mann. AB 31. Garden City, N.Y., 1967.

Neirynck, Frans. "The Miracle Stories in the Acts of the Apostles. An Introduction." In: *Les Actes des Apôtres. Traditions, rédaction, théologie*, ed. Jacob Kremer. Bibliotheca Ephemeridum Theologicarum Lovaniensium 48. Leuven, 1979.

Neudorfer, Heinz-Werner. *Der Stephanuskreis in der Forschungsgeschichte seit F. C. Baur*. Gießen and Basel, 1983.

Nösgen, C. F. *Commentar über die Apostelgeschichte des Lukas*. Leipzig, 1882.

Noth, Martin. *Die Geschichte Israels*. 6th ed. Göttingen, 1966. English translation: *The History of Israel*. Translated by Stanley Godman. 2d ed., with revised English translation by P. R. Ackroyd, New York, 1960.

Ohler, Annemarie. *Frauengestalten der Bibel*. 2d ed. Würzburg, 1987.

Ollrog, Wolf-Henning. *Paulus und seine Mitarbeiter*. WMANT 50. Neukirchen, 1979.

Oro, Ivo Pedro. "O conflito econômico nas primeiras comunidades—At 5,1-11," *Coluna Bíblica* 31(São Leopoldo, 1989):1.

Pekary, Thomas. *Die Wirtschaft der griechisch-römischen Antike*. Wissenschaftliche Paperbacks Sozial- und Wirtschaftsgeschichte 9. Wiesbaden, 1979.

Pelekanidis, Stylianos. "Kultprobleme im Apostel-Paulus-Oktogon von Philippi im Zusammenhang mit einem aelteren Heroenkult." In *Atti del IX Congresso Internazionale di Archeologie Cristiana (= International Congress of Christian Archeology)*, 393-97. Rome, 1978.

Pesch, Rudolf. *Die Apostelgeschichte*. EKK 5/1, 2. Neukirchen, 1986.

Petuchowski, Jakob J. "Das Achtzehngebet." In *Jüdische Liturgie. Geschichte, Struktur, Wesen*, ed. Hans Hermann Henrix. QD 86. Freiburg, 1979.

Petzke, Gerd. "Apostelgeschichte 9,36-43. Diakonie als Mission." In *Feministisch gelesen I: 32 ausgewählte Bibeltexte für Gruppen, Gemeinden und Gottesdienste*, ed Eva Renate Schmidt et al., 238-45. Stuttgart, 1988.

Pfeffer, Friedrich. *Studien zur Mantik in der Philosophie der Antike*. Beiträge zur klassischen Philologie 64. Meisenheim am Glan, 1976.

Philo of Alexandria. *The Works of Philo*, trans. C. D. Yonge. Peabody, Mass., 1993.

Pliny the Elder. *Natural History,* English translation by H. Rackham. 10 vols. LCL. Cambridge, Mass., 1947-63.

Pomeroy, Sarah B. *Goddesses, Whores, Wives, and Slaves.* New York, 1976.

Prado, Consuelo del. "I Sense God in Another Way." In *Through Her Eyes: Women's Theology from Latin America,* ed. Elsa Tamez, 140-49. Maryknoll, N.Y., 1989.

Prantl, Karl. *Aristoteles. Über die Farbe (Erleuchtet durch eine Übersicht der Farbenlehre der Alten von K. Prantl).* Munich, 1849; repr. Aalen, 1978.

Preisendanz, Karl, ed. *Papyri Graecae Magicae. Die griechischen Zauberpapyri.* 2 vols. 2d rev. ed. Stuttgart, 1973.

Preuschen, Erwin. *Die Apostelgeschichte.* HNT 4,1. Tübingen, 1912.

Pydd, Leomar. "Somos parecidos com Ananias e Safira," *JOREV* 7 (São Leopoldo, 1989):3.

Quesnell, Quentin. "The Women at Luke's Supper." In *Political Issues in Luke-Acts,* ed. Richard J. Cassidy and Philip J. Scharper, 59-79. Maryknoll, N.Y., 1983.

Quintilianus, Marcus F. *Institutionis Oratoriae,* English translation by H. E. Butler. 4 vols. LCL. Cambridge, Mass., 1953.

Rad, Gerhard von. *Genesis = Das erste Buch Mose, Kapt. 12,10-25,18.* ATD 3. Göttingen, 1952. English translation by John H. Marks: *Genesis: A Commentary.* Rev. ed. Philadelphia, 1972.

Rauschen, Gerhard, trans. *Echte Märtyrerakten.* Bibliothek der Kirchenväter 14, 291ff. Munich, 1913.

Rehkopf, Friedrich. *Septuaginta-Vokabular.* Göttingen, 1989.

Richard, Pablo. "Leitura popular das Bíblia na América Latina (Hermenêutica da Libertação)," *Ribla* 1 (Petrópolis, 1988):8-25.

Richter Reimer, Ivoni. "Reconstruir história de mulheres. Reconsiderações sobre trabalho e status de Lídia em Atos 16," *Ribla* 4 (Petrópolis, 1989):36-48.

Riessler, Paul, ed. *Altjüdisches Schrifttum ausserhalb der Bibel, übersetzt und erläutert von Riessler, P.* Heidelberg, 1927, repr., 2d ed., 1966.

Ritchie, Nelly. "Women and Christology." In *Through Her Eyes: Women's Theology from Latin America,* ed. Elsa Tamez, 81-95. Maryknoll, N.Y., 1989.

Rocchietti, Aracely de. "Women and the People of God." In *Through Her Eyes: Women's Theology from Latin America,* ed. Elsa Tamez, 96-117. Maryknoll, N.Y., 1989.

Roloff, Jürgen. *Die Apostelgeschichte.* NTD 5. Göttingen, 1981.

Romaniuk, Kazimierz. "Die 'Gottesfürchtigen' im Neuen Testament," *Aegyptos* 44 (1964): 66-91.

Rothe, Rosa Marga. "Duas mulheres 'violentas': Débora e Jael," *Estudos Bíblicos* 6 (Petrópolis, 1985):21-30.

Safrai, Shemuel. "The Synagogue," In *The Jewish People in the First Century. Historical Geography, Political History, Social, Cultural and Religious Life and Institutions,* 2 vols., ed. S. Safrai and M. Stern, with D. Flusser and

W. C. van Unnik, 2:908-44. Compendia Rerum Iudaicarum ad Novum Testamentum, Section One. Assen and Amsterdam, 1974-1976. Vol. 2 published in association with Fortress Press, Philadelphia.

Schäfke, Werner. "Frühchristlicher Widerstand," *ANRW* II (Principat) 23/1 (1979): 460-723.

Schaumberger, Christine. "Das Verschleiern, Vertrösten, Vergessen unterbrechen. Zur Relevanz politischer Theologie für feministische Theologie." In *Der Gott der Männer und die Frauen,* ed. Marie-Theres Wacker, 126-61. Düsseldorf, 1987.

_____. " 'Ich nehme mir meine Freiheit, damit ich nicht sterbe.' Überlegungen zu einer Feministischen Theologie der Befreiung im Kontext des 'Ersten Welt.'" In *Handbuch Feministische Theologie,* ed. Christine Schaumberger and Monika Maaßen, 332-61. Münster, 1986.

Schille, Gottfried. *Die Apostelgeschichte des Lukas.* ThHK 5. Berlin, 1983.

Schlatter, Adolf. *Der Glaube im Neuen Testament.* 4th ed. Stuttgart; 6th ed., with an introduction by Peter Stuhlmacher, 1982.

Schmid, Josef. *Das Evangelium nach Lukas.* NTD 3. Göttingen, 1940.

Schmidt, Jens-Uwe. *Valenzorientierte Syntax des Griechischen.* 3d ed. Bethel and Bielefeld, 1983.

Schmidt, Johanna. "Philippoi (Φίλιπποι)," *RE* 38 (1938): 2206-44.

Schmithals, Walter. *Die Apostelgeschichte des Lukas.* ZBK 3,2. Zürich, 1982.

Schneemelcher, Wilhelm. *New Testament Apocrypha = Neutestamentliche Apokryphen in deutscher Übersetzung.* 2 vols. 5th ed. Tübingen, 1989. English translation: *New Testament Apocrypha,* ed. R. McL. Wilson. 2 vols. Rev. ed. Louisville, Ky., 1991-94.

Schneider, Gerhard. *Die Apostelgeschichte.* 2 vols. HThK 5/1, 2. Freiburg, 1982.

Schneider, K. "Purpura, πορφύρα," *PRE* 46 (1959): 2000-2020.

Schniewind, Julius. *Das Evangelium nach Matthäus.* NTD 2. Göttingen, 1950.

Schonfeld, Shelomoh. *The Standard Siddur-Prayer Book with an Orthodox English Translation.* London, 1976.

Schottroff, Luise. "Alles entscheidet sich an den Opfern—Jesaja 58,1-12." In eadem, *Sucht mich bei meinen Kindern. Bibelauslegungen im Alltag einer bedrohten Welt.* Kaiser Traktate 94. Munich, 1986.

_____. *Befreiungserfahrungen. Studien zur Sozialgeschichte des Neuen Testaments.* ThB 82. Munich, 1989. Selections from this book are translated by Annemarie S. Kidder under the title, *Let the Oppressed Go Free. Feminist Perspectives on the New Testament.* Louisville, 1993. Those cited in this work include:

_____. "Critique" = "Wie berechtigt ist die feministische Kritik an Paulus? Paulus und die Frauen in den ersten christlichen Gemeinden im Römischen Reich," 229ff.; also in *Einwürfe* 2 (1985): 94-111 (= "How Justified is the Feminist Critique of Paul?" *Let the Oppressed Go Free,* 35-59).

_____. "Leaders" = " 'Anführerinnen der Gläubigkeit' oder 'einige andächtige Weiber'? Frauengruppen als Trägerinnen jüdischer und christlicher Religion im ersten Jahrhundert n. Chr.," 281-304 (= "'Leaders of the Faith' or 'Just Some Pious Womenfolk'?" *Let the Oppressed Go Free*, 60-79).

_____. "Lydia" = "Lydia. Eine neue Qualität der Macht." In *Zwischen Ohnmacht und Befreiung. Biblische Frauengestalten*, ed. Karin Walter, 148-54. Series "Frauenforum." Freiburg, 1988 (= "Lydia: A New Quality of Power," *Let the Oppressed Go Free*, 131-37).

_____. "Mary Magdalene" = "Maria Magdalena und die Frauen am Grabe Jesu," 134-59; also in *EvTh* 42 (1982): 5-25 (= "Mary Magdalene and the Women at Jesus' Tomb," *Let the Oppressed Go Free*, 168-203).

_____. "Women as Disciples" = "Frauen in der Nachfolge Jesu in neutestamentlicher Zeit," 96-133 (= "Women as Disciples of Jesus in New Testament Times," in *Let the Oppressed Go Free*, 80-130). First published in *Traditionen der Befreiung 2. Frauen in der Bibel*, ed. W. Schottroff and W. Stegemann, 91-133. Munich, 1980.

_____. "'Gerechtigkeit'/Mt 20, 1-26," *Junge Kirche* 47 (1986): 322-29.

_____. "Die befreite Eva. Schuld und Macht der Mächtigen und Ohnmächtigen nach dem Neuen Testament." In *Schuld und Macht. Studien zu einer feministischen Befreiungstheologie*, ed. Christine Schaumberger and Luise Schottroff, 15-151. Munich, 1988.

_____. "Patriarchatsanalyse als Aufgabe feministischer Theologie—Neutestamentliche Aspekte." Unpublished paper from the Kassel Summer Session 1988.

_____. "Mächtige." *Befreiungserfahrungen*, 247-56.

_____. "Schreckensherrschaft" = "Die Schreckensherrschaft der Sünde und die Befreiung durch Christus nach dem Römerbrief des Paulus." In *Befreiungserfahrungen* (1989), 57-72.

_____. "Unsichtbare Arbeit." In *Die Macht der Auferstehung. Sozialgeschichtliche Bibelauslegungen*, ed. Luise Schottroff and Willy Schottroff, 39-44. Munich, 1988.

_____. "Vergessene und Unsichtbare. Feministische Theologie und sozialgeschichtliche Bibelauslegung," *Junge Kirche. Eine Zeitschrift europäischer Christen* 12 (1987): 685-89.

_____. "Volk" = "Das geschundene Volk und die Arbeit in der Ernte Gottes nach dem Matthäusevangelium." In *Mitarbeiter der Schöpfung. Bibel und Arbeitswelt*, by Luise and Willy Schottroff, 149-206. Munich, 1983.

_____, and Willy Schottroff. "Hanna und Maria." In *Gotteslehrerinnen*, ed. Luise Schottroff and Johannes Thiele, 23-46. Stuttgart, 1989.

_____, and Wolfgang Stegemann. *Jesus von Nazareth, Hoffnung der Armen*. 2d ed. Stuttgart, 1981. English translation by Matthew J. O'Connell: *Jesus and the Hope of the Poor*. Maryknoll, N.Y., 1986.

Schrage, Wolfgang. *Ethik des Neuen Testaments.* Grundrisse zum Neuen Testament 4. Göttingen, 1982. English translation by David E. Green: *The Ethics of the New Testament.* Philadelphia, 1987.

Schürer, Emil. *Geschichte des Jüdischen Volkes im Zeitalter Jesu Christi.* English translation by T. A. Burkill et al: *The History of the Jewish People in the Age of Jesus Christ (175 B.C.-A.D. 135),* rev. and ed. Geza Vermes & Fergus Millar. 3 vols. in 4. Edinburgh, 1973-1987.

_____. "Die Juden im bosporanischen Reiche und die Genossenschaften der σεβόμενοι θεὸν ὕψιστον ebendaselbst." In *Sitzungsberichte der preußischen Akademie der Wissenschaften,* 200-25. Berlin, 1987.

Schüssler Fiorenza, Elisabeth. "Biblische Grundlegung." In *Feministische Theologie. Perspektiven zur Orientierung,* ed. Maria Kassel, 13-44. Stuttgart, 1988.

_____. *Bread Not Stone. The Challenge of Feminist Biblical Interpretation.* Boston, 1984.

_____. " 'Der Dienst an den Tischen.' Eine kritische feministisch-theologische Überlegung zum Thema Diakonie," *Concilium* 24, no. 4 (1988): 306-13.

_____. "Emerging Issues in Feminist Biblical Interpretation." In *Christian Feminism: Visions of a New Humanity,* ed. Judith L. Weidman, 33-182. San Francisco, 1984.

_____. *In Memory of Her. A Feminist Theological Reconstruction of Christian Origins.* New York, 1983.

_____. "Women in the Pre-Pauline and Pauline Churches," *USQR* 33 (1978): 153-66.

Schwantes, Milton. *Teología do Antigo Testamento. Anotações.* 1º Caderno. São Leopoldo, 1982.

_____. "Von unten gesehen. Die Bibel als Buch der Befreiung." *EvK* 19 (1986): 383-89.

Schwartz, Daniel R. "The Accusation and the Accusers at Philippi (Acts 16,20-21)," *Biblica* 65 (1984): 357-63.

Sherwin-White, Adrian Nicholas. *Roman Society and Roman Law in the New Testament.* Oxford, 1963.

Siegert, Folker. "Gottesfürchtige und Sympathisanten," *JSJ* 4 (1973): 109-64.

Silva, Rafael. "'Eran, pues, de oficio, fabricantes de tiendas [σκηνοποιοί]' (Act. 18,3)," *Estudios Bíblicos* 24 (Madrid, 1965): 123-34.

Simon, Marcel. "Gottesfürchtige," *RAC* 11 (1981): 1060-70.

Smidt, Udo. *Die Apostelgeschichte.* Bibelhilfe für die Gemeinde, Ntl. Reihe 5. 12th ed. Kassel, 1951.

Sölle, Dorothee. *Gott denken. Einführung in die Theologie.* Stuttgart, 1990. English translation by John Bowden: *Thinking about God: An Introduction to Theology.* London and Philadelphia, 1990.

Sparks, H. F. D., ed. *The Apocryphal Old Testament.* Oxford, 1984.

Staermann, E. M. "Der Klassenkampf der Sklaven zur Zeit des Römischen Kaiserreiches." In *Sozial- und Wirtschaftsgeschichte der römischen Kaiserzeit,* ed. Helmuth Schneider, 307-35. WdF 552. Darmstadt, 1981.

Stählin, Gustav. "Das Bild der Witwe. Ein Beitrag zur Bildersprache der Bibel und zum Phänomen der Personifikation in der Antike," *Jahrbuch für Antike und Christentum* 17 (1974): 5-19.

_____. *Die Apostelgeschichte.* NTD 5. Göttingen, 1962.

Stegemann, Wolfgang. *Zwischen Synagoge und Obrigkeit. Ein Beitrag zur historischen Situation der lukanischen Christen.* FRLANT 152. Göttingen, 1991.

Steichele, Hanneliese. "Priska. Ein verdrängter Fall." In *Zwischen Ohnmacht und Befreiung. Biblische Frauengestalten,* ed. Karin Walter, 155-62. Freiburg, 1988.

Stemberger, Günter. *Der Leib der Auferstehung. Studien zur Anthropologie und Eschatologie des palästinischen Judentums im neutestamentlichen Zeitalter (ca. 170 v. Chr.—100 n. Chr.)* Analecta Biblica 56. Rome, 1972.

Stern, Menahem. "The Jewish Diaspora." In *The Jewish People in the First Century. Historical Geography, Political History, Social, Cultural and Religious Life and Institutions,* ed. S. Safrai and M. Stern. 2 vols., 1:117-83. Compendia Rerum Iudaicarum ad Novum Testamentum, Section One. Assen and Amsterdam, 1974-1976.

Strabo. *The Geography of Strabo.* English translation by Horace Leonard Jones. 8 vols. LCL. London and New York, 1924-1960.

Strack, Hermann L., and Paul Billerbeck. *Kommentar zum Neuen Testament aus Talmud und Midrasch.* 6 vols. 9th ed. Munich, 1986-1989.

Strobel, August. "Armenpfleger 'um des Friedens willen,'" *ZNW* 63 (1972): 271-76.

Stuhlmacher, Peter. *Der Brief an Philemon.* EKK. Neukirchen, 1975.

Tamez, Elsa, ed. "A mulher que complicou a história das salvação," *Estudos Bíblicos* 7 (1985): 56-72.

_____. ed. *El Rostro Feminino de la Teología.* San José, Costa Rica, 1986. English translation: *Through Her Eyes: Women's Theology from Latin America,* edited by Elsa Tamez. Papers presented at Reunion Latinoamericana de Teología de la Liberacion desde la Perspectiva de la Mujer, held in Buenos Aires, Argentina, Oct. 31-Nov. 4, 1985. Maryknoll, N.Y., 1989.

_____. "Introduction: The Power of the Naked." In *Through Her Eyes: Women's Theology from Latin America,* ed. Elsa Tamez, 1-14. Maryknoll, N.Y., 1989.

_____. "Mujer y Biblia," *Revista Iglesias* 39 (Mexico, 1987): 12-16.

_____. *Teólogos de la Liberación hablan sobre la Mujer.* Entrevistas. San José, 1986. English translation: *Against Machismo.* Yorktown Heights, N.Y., 1987.

Taubenschlag, Rafael. "Das Sklavenrecht im Lichte der Papyri," *ZSRG RA* 50 (1930): 140-69.

Tcherikover, Victor A., ed., in collaboration with Alexander Fuks. *Corpus papyrorum Judaicarum.* 3 vols. Vol. 2 ed. Victor A. Tcherikover and Alexander Fuks; vol. 3 ed. Victor A. Tcherikover, Alexander Fuks, and Menahem Stern. Cambridge, Mass., 1957-1964.

Theißen, Gerd. "Social Stratification" = "Soziale Schichtung in der korinthischen Gemeinde. Ein Beitrag zur Soziologie des hellenistischen Christentums." In *Studien zur Soziologie des Urchristentums*, ed. Gerd Theißen, 231-71. WUNT 19. Tübingen, 1983. English translation by John H. Schütz: "Social Stratification in the Corinthian Community: A Contribution to the Sociology of Early Hellenistic Christianity." In *The Social Setting of Pauline Christianity*, ed. Gerd Theißen, 69-119. Philadelphia, 1982.

_____. *Miracle Stories* = *Urchristliche Wundergeschichten. Ein Beitrag zur formgeschichtlichen Erforschung der synoptischen Evangelien.* StNT 8. Gütersloh, 1978. English translation by Francis McDonagh: *The Miracle Stories of the Early Christian Tradition*, ed. John Riches. Philadelphia, 1983.

Thierfelder, Helmut. *Unbekannte antike Welt. Eine Darstellung nach Papyrusurkunden.* Gütersloh, 1963.

Thoma, Clemens. "Auferstehung." In *Lexicon der jüdisch-christlichen Begegnung*, ed. Jakob J. Petuchowski and Clemens Thoma, 30-35. Freiburg, 1989.

Thraede, Klaus. "Ärger mit der Freiheit. Die Bedeutung von Frauen in Theorie und Praxis der alten Kirche." In *"Freunde in Christus werden..." Die Beziehung von Mann und Frau als Frage an Theologie und Kirche*, ed. Gerta Scharffenorth and Klaus Thraede, 31-182. Gelnhausen and Berlin, 1977.

_____. "Frau," *RAC* 6 (1970): 197-267.

Thürmer-Rohr, Christina. *Vagabundinnen: Feministische Essays.* Berlin, 1987.

Trible, Phyllis. *Texts of Terror. Literary-Feminist Readings of Biblical Narratives.* Overtures to Biblical Theology 13. Philadelphia, 1984.

Verhoeven, Alida. "The Concept of God: A Feminine Perspective." In *Through Her Eyes: Women's Theology from Latin America*, ed. Elsa Tamez, 49-55. Maryknoll, N.Y., 1989.

Vielhauer, Philipp. *Geschichte der urchristlichen Literatur. Einleitung in das Neue Testament, die Apokryphen und die Apostolischen Väter.* Berlin and New York, 1975.

Viteau, Joseph. "L'Institution des Diacres et des Veuves. Actes VI,1-10; VIII,4-40; XXI,8," *RHE* 22 (1926): 513-37.

Waltzing, Jean-Pierre. *Etude historique sur les corporations professionnelles chez les Romains. Depuis les origines jusqu'à la chute de l'Empire d'Occident.* 4 vols. Repr. of the edition published in Brussels (vol. 1, 1895; vol. 2, 1896) and Louvain (vols. 3 and 4, 1900). Hildesheim and New York, 1970.

Weber, Volker. "Zur Geschichte des römischen Vereinswesens." Review of F. M. de Robertis, *Storia delle corporazioni.* In *Klio—Beiträge zur alten Geschichte* 59 (1977): 247-56.

Weigle, Palmy. *Naturfarben für modernes Weben. 125 Rezepte zum Färben von Garnen und Geweben.* Bonn-Röttgen, 1976.

Weiser, Alfons. *Die Apostelgeschichte.* 2 vols. ÖTB 5/1, 2. Gütersloh, 1985.

_____. "Die Rolle der Frau in der urchristlichen Mission." In *Die Frau im Urchristentum*, ed. Gerhard Dautzenberg et al., 158-81. Freiburg, 1983.

Weitling, Wilhelm. *Das Evangelium des armen Sünders,* ed. W. Schäfer. 1843; Hamburg, 1971. English translation by Dinah Livingstone: *The Poor Sinner's Gospel.* London, 1969.

Wendt, Hans Hinrich. *Die Apostelgeschichte.* KEK 3. Göttingen, 1880.

Wengst, Klaus. "Barnabasbrief." In *Didache (Apostellehre), Barnabasbrief, zweiter Klemensbrief, Schrift an Diognet. Eingeleitet, herausgegeben, übertragen und erläutert von K. Wengst,* ed. Klaus Wengst. Schriften des Urchristentums. Munich, 1984.

_____. *Demut, Solidarität der Gedemütigten. Wandlung eines Begriffes und seines sozialen Bezugs in griechisch-römischer, alttestamentlich-jüdischer und urchristlicher Tradition.* Munich, 1987. English translation by John Bowden: *Humility: Solidarity of the Humiliated. The Transformation of an Attitude and Its Social Relevance in Graeco-Roman, Old Testament-Jewish, and Early Christian Tradition.* Philadelphia, 1988.

_____. *Pax Romana. Anspruch und Wirklichkeit.* Munich, 1986.

White, L. Michael. "The Delos Synagogue Revisited. Recent Fieldwork in the Graeco-Roman Diaspora," *HTR* 80, no. 2 (1987):133-60.

Wikenhauser, Alfred. *Die Apostelgeschichte.* RNT 5. Regensburg, 1961.

_____. *Die Apostelgeschichte und ihr Geschichtswert.* Neutestamentliche Abhandlungen 8, nos. 3-5. Münster, 1892.

Wilckens, Ulrich. *Der Brief an die Römer.* EKK 6/1-3. Zürich and Neukirchen, 1978-1982.

Wilsdorf, Helmut. "Purpur." In *Lexikon der Antike,* 562. 7th ed. Leipzig, 1985.

Witherington, Ben. *Women in the Earliest Churches.* SNTSMS 59. Cambridge, 1988.

Wolff, Günter A. "E todos tinham tudo em comum (At 4,32-35)," *Coluna Bíblica* 49 (São Leopoldo, 1988):1.

Xenophon. *Cyropaedia,* ed. L. Breitenbach. Leipzig, 1869.

Yonge, C. D., trans. *The Works of Philo.* Peabody, Mass., 1993.

Zahn, Theodor. *Die Apostelgeschichte des Lukas* (parts 1 and 2). KNT 5. Leipzig, 1919, 1921.

Zöckler, Otto. *Die Apostelgeschichte.* Kurzgefaßter Kommentar zu den heiligen Schriften Alten und Neuen Testaments sowie zu den Apokryphen. Nördlingen, 1886.

Subject and Name Index

Scripture Index